MUSLIM MAFIA

MUSLIM MAFIA

INSIDE THE SECRET UNDERWORLD
THAT'S CONSPIRING TO ISLAMIZE AMERICA

BY P. DAVID GAUBATZ AND PAUL SPERRY

WND Books

MUSLIM MAFIA

Copyright © 2009 by P. David Gaubatz and Paul Sperry

Published by WND Books, Washington, D.C. WND Books is a registered trademark of WorldNetDaily.com, Inc. ("WND")

Book designed by Linda Daly. Jacket designed by Mark Karis

WND Books are available at special discounts for bulk purchases. WND Books also publishes books in electronic formats. For more information call (541) 474-1776, e-mail orders@wndbooks.com or visit www.wndbooks.com.

Hardcover ISBN: 978-1-935071-10-5
Paperback ISBN: 978-1-944229-72-6
eBook ISBN: 978-1-935071-64-8

Library of Congress Control Number: 2009931566

Printed in the United States of America
17 18 19 20 21 22 LBM 9 8 7 6 5 4 3 2 1

I dedicate this book to the innocent children of all races, religions, and cultures who are the ultimate victims of the errors of adults from all races, religions, and cultures.

—P. David Gaubatz

Dedicated to the memory of H. Baldwin Sperry

—Paul Sperry

A NOTE OF CAUTION FROM THE AUTHORS

This is not a book about Islam or Muslims in general. It is about the threat from *Shariah* Islam and violent jihad propagated by a criminal class of Muslims known as the Muslim Brotherhood or the "*Ikhwan* mafia." This secretive organization dominates most established Muslim groups and mosques in America while exploiting, manipulating, and even victimizing law-abiding Muslim Americans. Only a small share of the world's 1.3 billion Muslims are part of this dangerous group. This book is about them.

TABLE OF CONTENTS

FOREWORD

THE BOOK YOU ARE ABOUT TO READ is compiled by one of the foremost investigative teams in America.

I have known investigative journalist and writer Paul Sperry for some time now, and have turned to him for advice and counsel on many of the issues covered in this important book. He goes beyond just asking the questions that need to be asked, he provides answers ... answers that may shock you. Former federal investigator and co-author P. David Gaubatz, meanwhile, is a great American who deserves all our gratitude for his heroic service to our country.

If you are reading this book, I commend you. I commend you for wanting to know what is going on in our country. If you don't know the problem, you can't help fix the problem.

America is asleep to the danger that confronts us. Since the 1960s, there has been a concerted effort on the part of radical Islamists to infiltrate our major institutions. Front groups of terror now operate openly in our country, comprising a network of support for jihadists.

Most Americans do not know about recently declassified documents detailing their secret plot to take over the United States from within—a plot launched by Islamist groups tied to the dangerous Muslim Brotherhood, which is based in Egypt and which is funded primarily by wealthy Saudis and Emirates. And these groups are already in this country, building an impressive infrastructure of support for the jihadist enemy.

Our elected officials, by and large, are ignorant concerning the threat, or are afraid to speak out.

The general public is not being told about the danger.

In many instances, our laws are being used against us.

Many of the seemingly disconnected actions of these groups are actually connected in what the authors aptly describe as a highly organized "religious crime syndicate."

Government officials need to stop hiding behind political correctness and keep the American people informed. Until then, the people will not know the truth.

The radical Islamists overseas have repeatedly told us how they intend to infiltrate all areas of our society, and use the freedoms that are guaranteed under our Constitution to eventually replace it with *Shariah* law.

They have telegraphed their intent. Now we have proof—from the secret documents that this investigative team has uncovered, coupled with the ones recently declassified by the FBI—that their agents living among us have a plan in place, and they are successfully carrying out that subversive plan.

It is very alarming that we actually have the enemy's playbook for their so-called "Grand Jihad" against North America, yet we refuse to seriously confront the threat to our sovereignty and our way of life.

We Americans must wake up before it is too late!

—Sue Myrick

Member of the United States Congress

Co-Founder, Congressional Anti-Terrorism Caucus

PREFACE

THIS BOOK AND ITS FINDINGS are supported by reams of exclusive documentary evidence, including several boxes of confidential files obtained legally, if clandestinely, from the national offices of the Council on American-Islamic Relations, the inner sanctum of the Muslim mafia in America.

CAIR, which calls itself an advocate for Muslim-Americans, has operated largely in secret since its inception fifteen years ago. As a nonprofit group, it is exempt from paying federal income taxes and is protected from disclosing the identities of its financial donors.

These sensitive files, which have been gleaned without CAIR's knowledge, contain more than twelve thousand pages of documents that collectively amount to a smoking gun linking the nation's preeminent Islamic lobby group to terrorism, fraud, and sedition.

Sheet to sheet, the pages of evidence would stretch more than two miles, or the length of about thirty-five football fields. Stacked on top of each other, the boxes of printed material would weigh nearly a quarter of a ton and require a forklift to move. They include:

- confidential internal memos;

- proprietary minutes of board meetings;

- budget reports;

- real estate records;

- strategy papers;

- agendas;

- long-term goals;

- employee evaluations;

- emails;

- wire transfers and other bank statements;

- proposals;

- handwritten notes;

- letters;

- brochures;

- spreadsheets;

- visitors logs; and

- a host of other raw materials not reported by the media or even by law enforcement.

In addition, this book is backed by more than three hundred hours of videotaped footage taken by professionally trained investigators and researchers working undercover inside CAIR's headquarters, located just three blocks from the U.S. Capitol building in Washington DC.

Together with recently declassified FBI evidence, the internal documents and video surveillance for the first time provide a clear road map to the criminal conspiracy by CAIR, the Islamic Society of North America, and other outwardly benign Muslim organizations to support violent jihad and undermine law enforcement—with the ultimate goal of "eliminating and destroying" American society "from within." This "grand jihad," as they refer to it in their secret Arabic writings, requires infiltrating our political system and using our religious and political freedoms against us.

Now the tables are turned on the bad guys. For the first time, their own system has been infiltrated.

CAIR was targeted because it helps control this religious crime syndicate from its power base in Washington, the capital of the same government it wishes to overthrow. And its access to power will only widen now that its allies and apologists command both ends of Pennsylvania Avenue.

The undercover operation extracting these documents is led by P. David Gaubatz, a veteran federal investigator and counterterrorism specialist, whose ethnically diverse team of covert operatives includes Muslims as well as Christians and Jews.

Gaubatz, 51, served more than a decade as a special agent in the U.S. Air Force's elite Office of Special Investigations, where he held the U.S. government's highest security clearances—including Top Secret/SCI (Sensitive Compartmented Information)—and was briefed into many so-called black projects.

The U.S. State Department-trained Arabic linguist has more than two decades of experience in the Middle East, including tours in Saudi Arabia, Kuwait, Jordan, and Iraq, where in 2003 he led a fifteen-man team in extracting the family members of the Iraqi lawyer credited with saving Army Private First Class Jessica Lynch. Back in the U.S., Gaubatz invited Mohammed Odeh al-Rehaief and his family to live with him and his family. They remain close today.

When Gaubatz subsequently started a consulting firm to train law enforcement in Arabic language and customs, he found himself working alongside CAIR officials. Like many, he assumed CAIR was a moderate group and invited its speakers to join his lecture series—and they did.[1]

But after federal prosecutors named CAIR an unindicted co-conspirator in a major terrorism-financing case, Gaubatz realized he'd been working with the enemy.

Last year he turned his sights on CAIR, launching a six-month counterintelligence operation at its headquarters. He placed spies deep behind enemy lines to gather intelligence and fully inform the public about the threat it poses. He also hoped to help law enforcement build enough evidence to break through the political correctness that has allowed CAIR and other militant Islamic fronts to continue to operate with impunity.

The intelligence contained in this book is the Muslim mafia's worst nightmare. The last thing it wants is for a trusting and tolerant American public to see it and discover it has been the victim of their grand deception. And rest assured it will go to great lengths to distract attention from the damning evidence exposing its lies and secret agenda.

CAIR reacts to critics by attacking and smearing them. For example, it launched a months-long smear campaign against conservative TV personality Glenn Beck to drum him out of his chair at CNN. Memos written by CAIR officials reveal they monitored his show every night for several months. They assigned an "oppositional research" team to prepare "hit sheets" on him, painting him as an "Islamophobic" bigot. They prepared a PowerPoint presentation to intimidate his bosses into firing him. They even dispatched representatives to Atlanta to complain to CNN executives about him.[2]

Several other prominent talk-radio and cable-TV news hosts—including Fox News's Bill O'Reilly—have been targeted and remain on CAIR's "right-wing" hit list.[3]

CAIR views any critic as a threat, however, even liberals. When Senator Barbara Boxer (D-CA) questioned the group and its ties to terrorism, CAIR debated whether to "go all out against her" as well.[4]

CAIR's smear-the-messenger attack machine is well known. Its M.O. is to change the subject from the facts it doesn't want the American public to hear.

But these internal documents speak for themselves—after all, they're from CAIR's own files. And they will speak louder than any desperate denials or name-calling that CAIR or its co-conspirators can conjure up and spew with typical venom.

PART I

BELLY OF THE BEAST:

THE COUNCIL ON AMERICAN-ISLAMIC RELATIONS

INTRODUCTION

"Be extremely careful in our affairs, procedures, documentation, and statements to protect the organization." [1]

—Minutes of post-9/11 CAIR board meeting

DAVID MARSHALL TAPPED HIS FINGERS nervously on the steering wheel. He had a long drive to Washington from the Shenendoah Valley and a lot of time to think about what he was about to do.

What was he worried about? He had done the necessary prep work to appear *Shariah*-observant and as orthodox as possible. He'd taken the *Shahada*—the Muslim profession of faith—at a mosque where the Council on American-Islamic Relations maintained a booth. He'd altered his appearance to follow the example of the Muslim prophet Muhammad by growing a fistful-sized beard—sans mustache—and removing his gold jewelry, including his watch. (And if he needed a digital watch, he'd wear it on his right wrist to show he did everything opposite the Jews and Christians.)

As Interstate 66 stretched on ahead of him, Marshall practiced his Arabic greetings and phrases, rehearsing in his mind how he would respond in the office to various situations. He didn't want to say the wrong thing.

If you're introduced to a female employee, don't try to shake her hand, he reminded himself. *Just say* "Assalamu alaikum, *sister,*" *and put your hand over your heart.*

If you say you plan to do something, no matter how minor the act, make sure you always preface it by saying "insha'Allah"—*if Allah wills it. It's never your will but Allah's.*

And if something good happens, be sure to praise Allah: "humdillah"—
all thanks go to him.

He had to make a good first impression, gain their trust. This
was his chance to secure an internship and penetrate the heart of the
Hamas terrorist front group known as the Council on American-Islamic
Relations. He was on his way to CAIR's "First Annual Leadership and
Empowerment Conference." Another field researcher, acting as his
scout while she volunteered at CAIR, had vouched for him, and he was
registered to attend. Some of CAIR's top executives would be there, and
he hoped to get in their good graces.

He'd say he was a college student enrolled at Ferrum College in
Virginia (though twenty-nine, he looked young enough to pass for one).
He picked Ferrum because it was relatively unknown and wouldn't draw
much attention, and he was familiar with the town of Ferrum, having
lived nearby—which made it easier to sound convincing. The first rule in
conducting undercover operations is to stick as close to what you know
in your cover story as possible. You don't want to stray too far from what
you're familiar with in case you forget details about your assumed identity.

He'd also pretend to be a new convert to Islam—or a "revert" as his
devout interlocutors would say, since they believe every human being is
born free of sin and with a belief in Allah until their parents teach them
otherwise.

But no sooner had he convinced himself he had a solid cover story
than his plans nearly went awry.

While sitting among some thirty-five CAIR employees at the
conference, the tiny button-cam he'd concealed in his shirt to spy on
them popped off.

"It was the first day, and I was wearing that camera, and I had taped
it up too much underneath my shirt. And when I stood up, the button
popped off," due to a lack of slack in the wires, Marshall recalls. "And

there was the camera dangling out."

He coughed, covered his chest, and calmly left the room as if to get some water. Instead, he made a beeline for the parking lot to remove the camera. He returned to his seat missing a button, but luckily no one noticed except for the other undercover field researcher.

There would be other close calls, but eventually, Marshall gained the trust of even CAIR's then-director of operations, Khalid Iqbal, a dedicated Islamist, and earned a spot as an intern at CAIR's office in Herndon, Virginia. He would even pray during the day with Iqbal at a radical Islamic think tank across the street from their office on Grove Street, site of a massive raid by federal agents after the 9/11 attacks.

Within two months of beginning work there, he got his big break—a transfer to CAIR's national headquarters—thanks to the good word Iqbal put in for him.

His first day at the national office was in June of 2008, the start of a full-blown summer internship. It was a relatively short commute from his Dupont Circle flat to CAIR's headquarters on New Jersey Avenue, almost in the shadow of the U.S. Capitol. And that was a precious good thing, because the less time he had to think about it, the better. He was anxious, and didn't want to lose his nerve, didn't want to blow it. CAIR is the locus of political power for the secret Muslim Brotherhood in America—the parent of Hamas, al-Qaida, and other terrorist groups—and he had a chance to expose its secrets from the inside.

He parked his 1993 Toyota Tercel, walked up to the security intercom at the entrance to CAIR's three-story brick building, and announced himself as "Dawud," the Arabic name for David. They were expecting him and buzzed him in, and he got right to work. So far, so good. He was officially inside the belly of the beast, inside the political command center for Hamas and the Muslim mafia in America.

Later that morning he found himself in the basement storage room tasked with organizing supplies. He looked around and found a treasure trove of boxes loaded with files. One was labeled "Nihad Awad," the name of the executive director of CAIR. It contained various files and meeting notes. There also were several letters addressed to Awad from Saudi Arabia. Marshall tried to thumb through the files but was interrupted several times by people coming into the storage room. So he decided to wait another day to study the material in the boxes and evaluate their significance.

THE SHREDDER

He could hardly believe his luck when one day the office manager asked interns to destroy whole boxes of documents in the basement with the commercial shredder. Other interns groaned, as it was a mundane task, and few elected to do it. That left Marshall virtually alone in the basement if he stepped up.

"Nobody wanted to shred—it was boring, you know, nobody liked to do it—so I was, like, 'Ahh, I'll do it,'" Marshall says. "And I would sometimes spend hours going through the boxes and putting together one box that was good stuff, and shredding the rest. And then at the end of the day I would just walk down there [to the basement], pick the good box up, and walk out of the building with it."

Before long, he was routinely loading the trunk of his car with boxes of sensitive documents and delivering them into the custody of investigative project leader P. David Gaubatz who in turn stockpiled them at his offices in Richmond, Virginia.

CAIR's leadership wasn't the wiser. "There were a couple of times when people saw me walking out there with the box," Marshall explains. "But they didn't think anything of it because I had to set up tables for

CAIR at the *masjids* (mosques) on Fridays," part of his outreach duties. This required loading up and transporting a box full of brochures and pamphlets for the tables.

The hirsute "Dawud" blended in well at CAIR and drew little suspicion. He observed the afternoon prayers, bowing prostrate on the rugs CAIR laid out toward Mecca in the designated prayer room. He even went into the restroom beforehand and pretended to perform *wudu*, the elaborate Islamic ritual for washing before prayer, which includes snuffing water up the nostrils. (Muhammad believed the devil spends the night in the interior of the nose, and must be washed out each day.)

He made sure to abide by Islamic diet restrictions and eat only *halal* foods. He swore off cheeseburgers for lunch and always ate with his right hand, never his left, which the sacred texts say Muhammad reserved for toilet duties.

He also tried to stay out of political discussions, in spite of the historic presidential election. Whenever he was drawn into them, however, he was sure to always take a pro-Palestinian stance, criticizing the Republican administration for not formally recognizing Hamas as a legitimate government. At the same time, he counseled caution against Barack Obama, despite Obama's overtures toward Muslims, noting Obama's plans to send more troops to Afghanistan. Playing the role of the *Salafi* purist—the true believer—shored up his *bona fides* with the CAIR leadership and engendered greater trust.

Marshall's nonthreatening persona also helped lower the guard of his counterintelligence targets. His countenance is kind, and he wears a calm, almost mellow demeanor that belies his imposing size. He is a thick-boned man with a fair complexion and large, round blue eyes framed by prominent zygomatic arches. His nature is so nonthreatening, in fact, that he appears at times guileless to those who don't know better. Always helpful and respectful, he is the perfect candidate for undercover work, a natural-born spy.

As the weeks turned into months, he gained greater and greater access to CAIR's inner circle. And some situations were so intimate they seemed surreal. For example, he found himself asked to share a hotel room with CAIR's legislative director, Corey Saylor, during the Islamic Society of North America's annual convention in Columbus, Ohio. He manned CAIR's booth there with CAIR's communications director, Ibrahim Hooper.

Hooper, in fact, grew so fond of Marshall that he volunteered to arrange a marriage for him.

"Ibrahim kept asking me about getting married. He said, 'You know, Brother, you're at that age. And when you're ready, you need to talk to me. You know, I know people through the mosque,'" Marshall says. "And he was going to be my representative in marriage, because I was the only Muslim in my family."

Marriage is a rigid affair in orthodox or *Shariah* Islam. There is no dating for the faithful and betrothals are decided for young couples and arranged through the mosque. Offering to help arrange a marriage for a brother or sister, as Hooper did, is among the highest compliments.

Back in Washington, Marshall posed for casual photographs with CAIR executives including Awad (see photo gallery). He was a security guard at CAIR's fundraising banquet. He even found himself praying elbow-to-elbow with U.S. Representative Keith Ellison—the nation's first Muslim member of Congress and a de facto member of CAIR—during one Friday prayer attended by CAIR inside the U.S. Capitol.

MOSQUE OUTREACH

CAIR sent Marshall out each Friday with another intern to conduct outreach at Washington-area mosques. They passed out literature to worshipers and answered questions about CAIR. Marshall remained steadfastly *Shariah*-compliant, even rolling up his pant legs above the ankle before entering the mosques he visited.

Interestingly, CAIR was not welcome at the Islamic Center of Washington, located on Embassy Row, which receives official delegations including the president. "They won't let CAIR do outreach there," Marshall says. "They won't let them set up a table."

While working at another DC mosque, Marshall was approached by a follower of a radical Muslim cleric who declares Islam will dominate the world including the United States by the year 2050. Imam Abdul Alim Musa, his truculent protégé said, doesn't whitewash over the call to violent jihad like other clerics, and considers it the "sixth pillar of Islam." Indeed, Musa, who runs the Masjid Al-Islam on A Street, has praised suicide bombers as heroes while calling for the overthrow of the U.S. government. His follower added, defiantly, that Musa "doesn't care if the FBI follows him."

Across the Potomac is another radical Muslim Brotherhood mosque under FBI surveillance. Dar al-Hijrah Islamic Center of Falls Church, Virginia, is where some of the 9/11 hijackers received aid and comfort, and where Marshall took his *Shahada*. One of the congregants who witnessed his profession of faith—Umar Lee—reminded Marshall that doing the kind of undercover work he does is never safe.

Lee roomed with Ismail Royer when Royer worked for CAIR as a civil rights coordinator and before he was sent to federal prison on terrorism-related charges in the investigation of the Virginia Jihad Network. Lee now writes a popular jihadist blog. One of his recent entries glorifies Muslim bloodlust: "The Prophet (SAS) was a warrior and many of the *Sahabah* that he loved were straight-up killers."[2] (SAS is an Arabic notation of respect which literally translates, "Allah prayed over him and gave him peace," while the *Sahabah* refers to the companions of Muhammad.)

Lee also brags that "Islam spread through jihad and was sustained by the sword of very masculine men," who took "young girls" as sex slaves from the ranks of the *kaffir*, or infidels.[3] Judging from the sympathetic pings his blog gets, there is no shortage of young Muslim men living in the nation's capital—near the White House, Congress, and the Pentagon—who sympathize with his belligerent and misogynistic rants. One fellow Islamic supremacist posted this lovely sentiment: "The *kaffir* are to live under us, and their filthy status is below ours. Period."

Such views made Marshall's blood run cold. But to stay in their confidence, he had to keep walking their walk, talking their talk, even praying their prayers in their hate-filled mosques, where he was known as "Dawud."

Only his name isn't really Dawud or even David Marshall. That was the *nom de guerre* he used. His real name is Chris Gaubatz—the son of counterterrorism investigator Paul David Gaubatz. Chris works as his chief field investigator, along with assistants Stefanie Creswell and Charety Zhe, both of whom had covered their heads with *hijabs* to appear *Shariah*-compliant during the operation. Like the proverbial canaries in the coal mine, they determined the coast was clear for the younger Gaubatz to infiltrate.

His true identity should come as an even bigger shock to CAIR's leadership.

"The funniest thing that happened was at the ISNA convention, when I was spending a lot of time with Hooper and he was talking to Saylor about this 'Dave Gaubatz guy,' who they'd heard did undercover work in the Muslim community," Gaubatz says. "Hooper said, 'He's dangerous and knows too much. I was reading somewhere that his son works with him sometimes. So we've got to look out for his son, too.'

"And I was like, 'Do you know what he looks like or anything, so I can help?'" Gaubatz recalls with a chuckle. "And Saylor said, 'Nah, nobody has any pictures of him.'"

That he was able to puncture through CAIR's defensive screen and sneak behind enemy lines without getting caught or breaking cover is remarkable. The insular CAIR is paranoid of outside threats and had increased security only a year before Gaubatz came aboard, adding a magnetic card reader and buzz-in system at its headquarters. CAIR is also paranoid about inside information leaking to the press. In fact, it thought former chairman Parvez Ahmed was the source of some recent leaks.

CAIR's legal counsel Nadhira al-Khalili didn't even trust Arab TV crews. When one came through headquarters to film CAIR's bustling operations, she remarked in the break room that she didn't like them in the office, because they could be "spies."

Gaubatz thought she was kidding and began to laugh. "No, I'm serious," al-Khalili corrected him. "I wouldn't put it past anybody to send people in here like that."

To her chagrin, the spy was right there in front of her the whole time. This hated *kaffir* penetrated CAIR's inner circle. In fact, no one aside from Gaubatz has ever worked side-by-side undercover with CAIR's top executives, including Hooper, Saylor, and Awad, whose office was guarded like a "bulldog" by his secretary. He got to know their mindset and operational and strategic methods. And he captured hours of candid conversations with them on his hidden recording devices.

Is such spying bad or unethical? Not when the target is the enemy, and particularly not when the enemy spies on us. It's counterspying, and it's perfectly legal, especially when, as in this instance, incriminating evidence is unearthed. (It should be noted that Gaubatz never took any money from CAIR and even refused to cash a $300 travel stipend for mileage.) And make no mistake, CAIR is the enemy and the enemy is CAIR, something recently declassified FBI documents make crystal clear. They reveal CAIR is part of the pro-jihad, anti-USA Muslim Brotherhood, which directs its terror-supporting fronts to infiltrate government agencies, collect intelligence for the enemy, and "sabotage" the government from within.

So gathering intelligence against CAIR is necessary to protect the nation. And this counterintelligence operation is unprecedented not only in its scope and size, but because it broke taboo and the spell of political correctness that has handcuffed street agents from doing similar operations.

These bad guys have been alarmingly successful at infiltrating our PC-addled system, but we have not been successful at infiltrating their system—until now.

Last September, Raabia Wazir presented "David Marshall" with a certificate of completion "in recognition of his valuable contribution to the Council on American-Islamic Relations." It's signed by CAIR chief Awad. (See photo gallery.) Gaubatz was hailed as a model intern and recommended for a full-time job doing chapter development. He turned it down only because it would have required a more stringent background check revealing his true identity.

MAJOR REVELATIONS

Gaubatz left, but not before uncovering not only the inner secrets of the dangerous Muslim mafia, but also the inner workings of the anti-Israel lobby and the entire left-wing anti-American conspiracy that includes the ACLU, Congressional Black Caucus, and others.

What follows is a bullet-by-bullet description of the major revelations unearthed from the boxes of CAIR files Gaubatz intercepted on their way to the shredder, including many documents marked "Not for Distribution—For Board Members Only."

Ironically, the voluminous paper trail created by this notoriously

litigious group may just be its undoing. Among the explosive revelatio..
detailed in the chapters that follow:

- CAIR is trying to spring from prison a former headquarters official who
trained for jihad with the same Pakistani terrorist group that last year massacred
more than 150 people in Mumbai, India.

- CAIR officials are secretly coaching terrorism suspects and witnesses to
withhold information from FBI investigators, and have successfully obstructed
at least one investigation in Maryland.

- CAIR is donating thousands of dollars to the legal defense fund of a Muslim
cop killer.

- CAIR's visitor logs show the father of an al-Qaida terrorist visited CAIR
director Awad several months before he was convicted of plotting to assassinate
President Bush.

- Curiously, the logs do not register any guests around September 11, 2001—
in fact, the entire month of September is blank.

- CAIR has cultivated Muslim moles inside a Washington-area law enforcement
agency, including one who illegally accessed classified FBI records to tip off a
terrorist under investigation and another with ties to Pakistani intelligence.

- A longtime CAIR advisory board member and top fundraiser has preached
violent insurrection, including calling on street gangs to lead an "Uzi" jihad in
America's cities.

- Another imam whom CAIR frequently books to speak at its events
has exhorted Muslims to hijack U.S. military aircraft, including C-130s
transporting the elite 82nd Airborne paratroopers out of Fort Bragg—which
happens to be part of the district represented by North Carolina state senator
Larry Shaw, who this year took over the reins of CAIR as its new chairman.

- CAIR is putting books into neighborhood libraries across the country advising
men to beat their wives—but only "lightly"—when they disobey them.

.ne time, CAIR is lobbying the Justice Department and local law
.ment to exempt Muslim wife-beaters from laws against domestic
.ence or at least look the other way and let Muslim clerics intervene when
Muslims are involved in spousal battery cases—not unlike the one involving a
prominent Muslim TV executive who ended up beheading his wife after serial
domestic abuse.

• CAIR's library package includes a guide to Islam edited by a radical Muslim
cleric who cheered the tragic space shuttle Columbia disaster as a "good omen"
for Islam and is now behind bars for inciting anti-U.S. warfare.

• CAIR is running an influence operation against members of key homeland
security committees on Capitol Hill and planting Islamist spies in congressional
offices.

• During the 2004 presidential campaign, CAIR organized a "task force" of
other radical Muslim Brotherhood fronts to hammer out a "Muslim platform"
that initially included a draft proposal "supporting Islamic groups including
Mr. Bin Laden and his associates."

• CAIR's leadership is coordinating political activities during monthly
breakfasts with Congressman Ellison, who boasted during a Juma prayer in the
Capitol building that they'll have fifteen Muslims like him in Congress by the
next election and then far more after that.

• CAIR is doing an inordinate amount of political lobbying and campaigning
possibly in violation of its 501(c)(3) tax-exempt status, which restricts such
activities.

• CAIR lists in a "strategy" document marked "Company Proprietary" a long-
term goal of "influencing congressmen responsible for policy that directly
impacts the American Muslim community," including "congressmen on the
judiciary, intelligence, and homeland security committees."

• CAIR last year teamed up with a terror-tied Islamic investment bank to
attack publicly traded American firms who refuse to comply with *Shariah* law
by using shareholder resolutions, divestitures, and boycotts against them.

• Stung by recent terrorism charges, CAIR is losing members and dues and operating in the red; in fact, it is struggling financially to the point where it has to rent out one of the three floors it operates at its Capitol Hill headquarters.

• CAIR is suffering from a whopping 50 percent employee turnover rate in the Washington area and having a difficult time recruiting new talent.

• Interns have refused to be formally photographed with CAIR officials for fear of being associated with terrorists and profiled at airports, and some have even removed their CAIR experience from their resumés.

• CAIR executives travel regularly to the Middle East to raise cash, and bank wire transfers show Saudi princes have donated hundreds of thousands of dollars to CAIR—even as it claims to receive no foreign support.

• While cash-poor, CAIR is asset-rich, and in recent years has partnered with Arab investors—including a UAE defense minister who once equipped Osama bin Laden's camps in Afghanistan—to finance its headquarters and buy up an alarming number of parcels of property in downtown DC while shielding them under a holding company.

• CAIR tried to muscle out other groups to represent the so-called Flying Imams against US Airways, promising them "large compensation," and in another revelation, CAIR had a previous history with the lead imam in the case, working with him on a similar stunt that occurred on board an America West flight.

• CAIR went to extraordinary lengths to shake down Bank of America in a frivolous claim of discrimination involving a Muslim employee, internal strategy documents reveal.

• In spite of claims it represents all Muslims, CAIR routinely discriminates against Shiites and other Muslims—including its own employees—in favor of Sunni Muslims.

• CAIR is actively training Homeland Security agents to respect Muslims and Islam, while brainwashing them to think jihad means "internal struggle against sin," and not holy war, as part of a dangerous disinformation campaign.

• CAIR quietly removed from its Web site an "Urban Legends" rebuttal it posted in response to growing criticism and terror charges after its falsehoods became transparently and embarrassingly obvious.

• Desperate for revenue, CAIR tasks its interns with researching and writing grant proposals while providing blatantly false information in grant applications.

• CAIR privately worries that "major roadblocks" to mainstreaming Islam in America include the religion's "treatment of women and violence," but instead of acknowledging misogyny and jihad as problems and disavowing them, CAIR coaches staff to use more effective methods to whitewash over them.

• CAIR and the ACLU have formed a strategic partnership to target the FBI with "ethnicity related" civil rights complaints.

• During the recent Lebanon crisis, which saw Israel defend itself from Hezbollah rockets, CAIR actually had the temerity to seriously consider suing the U.S. and Israel under RICO racketeering statutes for "conspiring to commit murder, kidnapping, property damage, and acts of terrorism."

But that's not all.

Early in the undercover operation, Gaubatz was given permission one day to work on a certain project in his boss's office at the Herndon chapter, which CAIR was abruptly closing. The atmosphere was tense.

"I just knew there was something going on," he says. "Nobody was saying anything about why the office was closing."

His boss at the time, Iqbal, was out and Gaubatz found himself alone in Iqbal's office. He spied on the desk in front of him a folder that looked suspicious.

"I just started looking at it," he recalls, "and then I saw some of the handwritten notes where they'd said this guy is threatening to sue, this guy is threatening to go to the media.

"And I knew we were on to something…"

CHAPTER ONE

MUSLIMS VICTIMIZING MUSLIMS

"CAIR is very concerned about its reputation in the community. Without the community (and Allah's help) CAIR would fail."

—From internal "status report" by CAIR's Civil Rights Department[1]

THE BOARD MEMBERS of the Washington-based Council on American-Islamic Relations were in full panic mode. Usually the group that calls itself the largest Muslim rights organization in America—the "Muslim NAACP"—threatens to sue non-Muslims. But this time, Muslims were threatening to sue CAIR.

And these angry constituents' timing could not have been worse. It was early 2008, and terrorism charges and bad press were taking their toll on CAIR's fundraising efforts. Just as the group was preparing to launch a major new money drive in the Muslim community, its operations director, Khalid Iqbal, informed the board that the organization was "inundated with phone calls" from angry Muslim clients complaining they'd been "scammed" by one of CAIR's attorneys.[2]

One brother, Issameldin Mohamed, "is verry [*sic*] upset and wants CAIR to return his money," according to an office log of complaints.[3] He thought CAIR had filed for his immigration papers but now felt that he "was scammed" and threatened to take CAIR to court. A Sister Taqwa called "extremely angry and threatened to sue CAIR" for the money she'd lost.[4] And, according to an interoffice memo, "Br. Ahmed Obaid called threatening to sue CAIR" to recover his $9,000.[5]

And on it went. Some thirty desperate victims and their families flooded CAIR with complaints and Iqbal struggled to field them all.

The situation had reached a "crisis," Iqbal warned CAIR executive director Nihad Awad and other board members, according to a series of internal email messages they'd hoped would never be disclosed.[6] And it was spinning out of his control.

What is the "board recommendation?" Iqbal pleaded. "This case has taken a lot of my time."[7]

Indeed it was a full-blown scandal. Dozens of Muslim immigrants seeking CAIR's help with citizenship delays, many of them indigents, had lost tens of thousands of dollars in legal and other fees and were demanding their money back. They'd been ripped off in a massive criminal fraud orchestrated by CAIR's "resident attorney" and "civil rights manager" for its Maryland and Virginia chapters. Jamil Morris Days wasn't even a licensed attorney; he was a con artist with a long rap sheet.[8] And not surprisingly, he didn't provide the services he'd promised. Yet CAIR knew about his malpractice and kept him on board anyway.

Some victims had to sell their cars, their furniture—even their refrigerators—to pay CAIR's bogus legal bills. The nonprofit group isn't supposed to accept money for any casework. Some lost their immigration status because their paperwork had been bungled or, in some cases, not even been filed with the proper government agencies.

Now a handful threatened to not only sue but go to the media with their stories, which would take the scandal outside any control of CAIR and into the court of public opinion.

"Three brothers came together," Iqbal noted in one CAIR document, "threatening to go to the media."[9]

With the scandal mushrooming out of control, CAIR's board decided to shift to "damage control" mode, emails reveal. It was imperative, they asserted, to "safeguard CAIR's name and reputation,"[10] and do whatever necessary to prevent news of the scandal from leaking out to the authorities or to the press.

Forget making whole the aggrieved Muslim clients it deigns to protect. Above all, protect the organization.

So CAIR's directors ordered actions that effectively swept the scandal under the rug, including:

- boxing up and sequestering the incriminating files;

- shredding documents;

- cleaning and erasing "all electronic data files from server and computers";

- shutting down email accounts; and

- even closing bank accounts.[11]

They quietly fired the attorney and closed down his office and the entire Maryland-Virginia chapter. They removed his name from the directory. They scripted a terse message to leave on the office answering machine to screen irate callers, trying to disown their dirty lawyer as only a "contractor" (which was news to his clients):

> If you are trying to reach Br. Jamil Morris Days, we wish to advise you that he no longer works as a contractor for CAIR Maryland and Virginia chapters. If you have a case that is time-sensitive, please leave us a message and we will try our best to assist you.[12]

Then they disconnected the phone lines. They even got rid of Iqbal, who took a job with a Muslim Brotherhood mosque affiliated with CAIR and not far from the CAIR chapter in Herndon, Virginia, where Days worked (and where Iqbal kept an office when he wasn't working out of

CAIR's headquarters on the other side of the Potomac). Just three years earlier, Iqbal had opened that chapter because, as CAIR said at the ribbon-cutting ceremony, "there is a dire need for CAIR's physical presence in this area."

Suddenly there was no need and the chapter was shuttered. Today there's hardly a trace the office ever existed. CAIR did everything to cover Days's and Iqbal's tracks short of removing their fingerprints.

They say in Washington that the cover-up is always worse than the crime. And this case is no exception, although both are bad.

Consider client-victim Kadiatu Korama, who paid CAIR "from mortgage money" and was in a "desperate situation." Or Chokri el-Kotel, who had to "sell [a] car to get the money" to pay CAIR's fake lawyer.[13]

HUSH MONEY

Yet there was little sympathy for the victims at CAIR's headquarters. For those victims who wouldn't go away quietly, CAIR's lawyers played the kind of hardball they usually reserve for *kaffirs*. They tried to frighten and intimidate them into silence by demanding they sign a secrecy agreement in violation of professional ethics.

The nondisclosure agreement also alleges to release CAIR from any legal claims in the fraud scheme in exchange for paying partial restitution to CAIR's victims—that is, hush money.

Adding insult to injury, CAIR threatened to turn around and sue *its victims* each for $25,000 if they talked about the settlement or the "incident" with "any third party," including the media or the police. According to the release form, the fee would cover "damages in the amount of $25,000 for the purpose of conducting meetings, workshops, press releases, flyers, and the like to reverse or minimize the damage to

CAIR's reputation caused by the recipient's breach" of the agreement to remain quiet about the "incident."[14]

CAIR calls the silence clause and the penalty for breaching it "standard legal practice."[15] But its victims say it feels more like a threat—a thuggish tactic, to be sure.

Legal analysts say the settlement agreement, which several victims signed, contains none of the exceptions typically found in such confidentiality provisions, such as an exception to permit disclosure to government authorities. They also doubt it is binding. Nor does it absolve CAIR of liability, since lawyers cannot escape disciplinary action in malpractice cases by simply reimbursing the client for any loss. And this certainly was a case of "malpractice," something even CAIR acknowledges in its internal memos.[16]

Though CAIR is not technically a law firm, its lawyers drafted the release form, and its lawyers covered up for Days's malpractice, thereby joining the malpractice—and the liability. And it was CAIR's national legal counsel Nadhira al-Khalili who agreed to drive to the Herndon office and bring the incriminating Days evidence back to CAIR's headquarters without ever turning it over to police.[17] What's more, CAIR's legal team at no point informed its client-victims that Days was terminated for fraud and was not, in fact, a lawyer.

When CAIR discovered the fraud, it joined the fraud by covering it up and deliberately set out to conceal the truth about Days, not just from the authorities and the media, but from the clients he defrauded. The only thing CAIR's headquarters told his defrauded clients when they called was that he no longer worked for CAIR. That's it.

Why? In a word, money. Immigration cases are big business for CAIR, a hook for bringing in fundraising revenue, which CAIR desperately needs. Immigrants account for a large segment of the Muslim community. If word got out that CAIR mishandles their cases, even steals from them, it would hurt donations from the community at large.

For that matter, CAIR amid the scandal had launched a $250,000 fundraising campaign touting its mission of helping Muslims who confront immigration and citizenship problems.

"Every day, CAIR works hard to defend the rights of American Muslims who encounter a delay in gaining citizenship," the group said in an advertisement promoting its fundraiser. "Let's help CAIR reach its goal of $250,000 so that CAIR can continue to defend our rights."

Its home page featured a button linking visitors to a donation page, along with photos of Muslims receiving certificates of U.S. citizenship. "CAIR helped me," one Muslim is quoted as saying. (He is identified as Chokri el-Kotel, the same client-victim who had previously complained about CAIR. He agreed to give a testimonial only after CAIR bought him off with partial restitution and stepped in, belatedly, to handle his case.)

Not featured, of course, were the other still angry twenty-nine clients that CAIR had ripped off with fraudulent fees for undelivered immigration and other legal services.

CAIR's fundraising pitch still centers on the boast that it helps Muslims with citizenship delays. It's one of the group's top selling points. Days had fit into that strategy.

Far from just a "contractor," the fifty-four-year-old Days was brought in as a rainmaker for CAIR, which promoted him with great fanfare. Not long after hiring him in 2006, CAIR put out a slick newsletter trumpeting his arrival and his accomplishments, which included allegedly processing "over one hundred civil rights cases" already at the Maryland/Virginia chapter. CAIR proudly touted him and his alleged legal qualifications in an article titled "Meet Our Resident Attorney!" which included a photo of Days along with a solicitation for donations.[18]

DRUMMING UP NEW BUSINESS

CAIR also encouraged Muslim immigrants to make appointments to see Days, a black convert to Islam, and avail themselves of his legal services. What's more, CAIR promoted Days in press releases and on its national Web site, drumming up new business for him—and new fundraising opportunities for CAIR.

In a July 2007 press release, CAIR sang Days's praises while calling on the Department of Homeland Security to expedite Muslim citizenship cases he was supposedly working on for Muslims in Maryland and Virginia. The press release led to a spate of sob stories in the media.

"Every citizen and permanent resident has a right to expect fundamental fairness," it quoted Days as saying. He called on immigration authorities to "do the right thing" and rubber stamp U.S. documentation for Muslim foreigners.

All the while, on his end, Days wasn't doing much of anything. Clients complained he'd routinely stand them and immigration officials up at scheduled meetings and sometimes wouldn't even show up for court dates. Some clients were strung along for several months after paying him a retainer.

In fact, some of the Muslims he garnered publicity for helping later proved to be the same victims he fraudulently shook down for fees. Consider the case of Issameldin Mohamed. CAIR posted on its main Web site an Associated Press story under the headline: "CAIR-MD/VA: Lawsuits End Citizenship Delays." It highlighted with boldface type the following section of the December 2007 article:

> Morris Days, an attorney with the Maryland-Virginia Chapter of the Council on American-Islamic Relations, has helped Mohamed and fifteen others file similar petitions at federal courthouses in the region in recent months.

If Mohamed was "helped," he wasn't helped very much. He's the same Issameldin Mohamed mentioned at the beginning of this chapter who was so "upset" with Days that he called CAIR demanding a refund of the fees he paid him.

Still, CAIR couldn't stop promoting their star pseudo-attorney. Days also was featured in an NBC News story that aired around the same time. CAIR promptly posted a link to the video under the headline, "CAIR-MD/VA: Muslims Granted Citizenship," along with a photo of Days.

The media publicity didn't end there. ABC News and the *Washington Post* also picked up on the angle of the "legal director for CAIR's Maryland and Virginia chapter" heroically rescuing Muslim immigrants from xenophobic government gatekeepers. Days was quoted in the *Post* story blaming citizenship and visa delays on post-9/11 discrimination. He demanded federal officials expedite the cases he was working on—or not working on, as it turned out.

No matter, what was important to CAIR was that the immigration cases attracted good publicity at the time. And the more media, the more donations. Seeing that Muslims actually get help was secondary.

And Days attracted a lot of media for CAIR. In fact, he got so much ink that he ranked as one of the most visible "lawyers" in the country, according to Martindale-Hubbell, which mistakenly listed Days in its directory of attorneys. In fact, he ranked number one of forty-one lawyers in the Herndon area. Little wonder CAIR looked the other way when it all went bad.

COUNSELING FOR THE CON ARTIST

Iqbal knew Days was fraudulently collecting legal fees from CAIR clients at least by November 2007. And he and the CAIR board took no action against him until February 2008—a delay of a minimum of three months.

And even then, they didn't fire him. They first gave him a warning and kept him on staff, even after learning of the malpractice he committed against so many CAIR clients while using CAIR offices, CAIR letterhead, and CAIR equipment. They finally sacked him after the complaints continued unabated. [19]

But even then, they didn't turn him over to the proper authorities or alert the relevant state bar associations about his con. Instead, emails reveal, they sought out a local Muslim cleric to "give him counseling," because he was "shaken and disturbed" by the news of his termination.[20]

They tolerated him ripping off clients until those clients threatened to blow the whistle in the media. Only then did they throw Days under the bus, because, as they explained to him in his termination notice, his continued association with CAIR endangered the reputation of "the organization as a whole." In other words, it was more what he was doing to CAIR than what he was doing to Muslims that was the firing offense. CAIR would look bad if it got out that an advocacy group victimizes the very people it is supposed to represent.

TIMELINE: ANATOMY OF A SCANDAL

December 2004	CAIR opens CAIR Maryland/Virginia Chapter.
June 2006	CAIR hires Jamil Morris L. Days as its "resident lawyer" and "civil-rights manager" for CAIR MD/VA.
November 2007	Days' immediate boss, Khalid Iqbal, operations director of CAIR National and executive director of CAIR MD/VA, learns (at the latest) that Days is charging CAIR's *pro bono* Muslim clients and falsely representing them.
February 6, 2008	CAIR warns Days in writing to end the "fraud" and "malpractice," which continued unabated.
February 10, 2008	CAIR finally terminates Days' employment after Days fails to end his fraudulent activities and after clients threaten to go to the media.
April 2008	CAIR closes CAIR MD/VA, hushes clients.

What really looks bad is that these weren't just any Muslims but poor immigrant Muslims who put their faith and trust in CAIR—and their hopes and dreams in the hands of its legal team. They also put their life savings in CAIR's hands. And CAIR returned the favor by never alerting them to Days's schemes or even letting them know he wasn't really a lawyer.

Sadly, it took an unpaid non-employee—a non-Muslim posing as a Muslim—to blow the whistle on senior CAIR managers victimizing fellow Muslims in their care.

After just a few months into his internship at CAIR, it became clear to undercover investigator Chris Gaubatz that CAIR doesn't really care about Muslim hardship cases.

"CAIR is interested only in things that get media attention or raise money," he says.

When he stumbled on the Days fraud, laid out in the files on Iqbal's desk, he took the files into the copier room and photocopied the evidence in them then returned the files to the desk.

"We knew we had an obligation [under whistleblowing statutes] to preserve evidence" of corruption or criminal activity, Gaubatz said. "So any time I was told to shred evidence, I would preserve it instead."

He also later came across evidence germane to the Days case in the storage room of the Herndon office.

All this evidence is now being used in a class-action lawsuit against CAIR naming Awad and other CAIR officials as defendants. (In fact, an unsuspecting Awad was served a court summons while conducting ceremonies at CAIR's fourteenth annual banquet in Arlington, Virginia's Marriott Crystal Gateway Hotel, the same banquet where Gaubatz worked security.) Some of CAIR's former clients claim they suffered "severe emotional stress" from the scheme and seek compensatory and punitive damages, which may be recoverable from CAIR's real estate and other assets valued at more than $6 million.

CAIR, which describes the Days fraud as an "unfortunate situation,"[21] has filed a motion to dismiss the federal case, which is being heard in the U.S. District Court for the District of Columbia.

CAIR maintains that it was just as much a victim of Days's fraud as his clients. It claims it did not know he was misrepresenting himself and the public as an attorney licensed to practice law.

However, Days's resumé was so transparently bogus any employer could have seen though it. Problem was, CAIR failed to conduct even the most basic background check prior to hiring him. If it had, it would have found glaring inaccuracies and inconsistencies in his story.

While CAIR was negligent in hiring him, it was reckless in promoting his qualifications to the local Muslim community. Here is CAIR's misleading profile of him in a 2007 newsletter offering his legal services to Muslims:

> Days, a graduate of Temple University Law School, joined the organization in June 2006. He specializes in Criminal Law and Civil Rights/Social Service Advocacy Law. He has been a member of the Philadelphia Bar Association and American Bar Association since 1997.
>
> His professional achievements include receiving the Rosa Parks Wall of Tolerance Award in 2005 given by the Southern Poverty Law Center.

Sounds impressive. Only none of the representations were true. Days, who died early in 2009, was not a lawyer. He never got a law degree nor was he licensed as an attorney to practice law in any jurisdiction in the United States.

Even the award is bogus.

JAILHOUSE LAWYER

CAIR knew or had reason to know that Days was not licensed to practice law in Virginia when it hired him. A simple search shows he was not admitted to the Virginia state bar. And his email address—morrisdays@ aba.net—which CAIR posted in its newsletter, is not even affiliated with the American Bar Association. (ABAnet.org is the domain for the American Bar Association. ABA.net is the domain for a diploma mill.)

CAIR even had Days lead monthly "legal literacy classes" for local Muslims at its Herndon office—"in order to empower our community to enact the legal protections afforded to us as American Muslims."

"Days himself kicked off the new project with a two-hour 'Introduction to American Law' class last month," CAIR gushed in a March 2007 newsletter promoting his so-called law classes. "The aim of this class is to provide community members with a solid background of civil rights and local and national law."

This is most amusing, as the only law that Days really knew is what he learned inside the correctional system—as an inmate. That's right; the con artist that CAIR hired was also an ex-con who served time in Philadelphia jails in the 1990s, according to the Investigative Project on Terrorism. He also was found guilty of several alcohol-related charges in Virginia in the early 2000s.

The Days affair serves as a cautionary tale for CAIR's remaining paid members (whose numbers have shrunk dramatically in recent years, as a forthcoming chapter will detail). CAIR hired an ex-con shakedown artist posing as a lawyer to misrepresent more than one hundred of its members, fired him only after his victims threatened to go to the press, and then covered up the criminal fraud by threatening the poor Muslim clients he ripped off to keep their mouths shut.

But that's par for the course for a criminal organization. CAIR even hires terrorists—then defends them after they're convicted and sentenced to prison.

CHAPTER TWO
TERRORIST TURNSTILE

"We've been actively working cases against CAIR for awhile, including key administration there."

—Senior investigator, FBI's Joint Terrorism Task Force in Washington[1]

T HE MUMBAI MASSACRE ranks as one of history's grisliest acts of retail terrorism. In the fall of 2008, a dozen young Muslim men armed with AK-47 assault rifles, grenades, and plastic explosives stormed a train station, the Taj Mahal Palace hotel, and a Jewish center in Mumbai, India, and slaughtered in cold blood about 160 people, including six Americans. They singled out Western tourists and Jews for attack. The barbaric terrorists sexually humiliated some of the hotel guests by first forcing them to strip, then shooting them. Police found the blood-drenched bodies of a *rabbi* and his wife completely nude, their genitalia mutilated.

These jihad-crazed troglodytes, who were ordered to "kill until the last breath" in the name of Islam, carried out their killing spree after training in neighboring Pakistan. Over five months they practiced their assault at a camp run by the terrorist group Lashkar-e-Taiba, an al-Qaida subcontractor.

Several years earlier, an American Muslim convert purchased the same weapon—an AK-47, the weapon of choice for jihadists—along with hundreds of rounds of ammunition, and practiced shooting it at a firing range near his home in the Washington DC area. Then he traveled to Pakistan to train for real at a Lashkar-e-Taiba camp similar to the one the Mumbai terrorists attended. He even fired live AK-47 rounds at Indian targets.

When this convert, Randall "Ismail" Royer, returned to Washington, he went back to work for his employer, the Council on American-Islamic Relations.

"I was the civil rights guy at CAIR, taking phone calls about women getting spit on, the FBI barging into houses where a woman was taking a shower and yanking her out of the shower," Royer said, his words dripping with contempt.

All the while he was training and plotting revenge against the U.S. government.

FBI agents eventually barged into his house in northern Virginia and locked him up before he could carry out his violent plans. If they hadn't arrested him, his path might have merged with Lashkar-e-Taiba's in Mumbai, as the terror group was recruiting English-speaking operatives for its cell there.

Or worse, Royer might have joined an attack against the homeland. Lashkar-e-Taiba had at one point solicited his own Virginia-based cell to case a chemical plant in Maryland, federal prosecutors say.[2] It's plain that America is a target of the terrorist group, whose offices in Lahore, Pakistan, are plastered with anti-American posters, according to U.S. government witnesses.

In fact, Royer was the ringleader of a group known as the Virginia Jihad Network that had been studying manuals on how to manufacture and use explosives and chemical weapons. Among other targets, it had been casing the FBI headquarters building.

One of their confederates, Ahmed Omar Abu Ali, even trained with al-Qaida to assassinate President George W. Bush.

Royer is now behind bars, serving a twenty-year federal sentence. But from 1997 to 2001, he worked for CAIR out of its Washington headquarters as a civil rights coordinator and communications specialist. He wrote news releases, spoke with journalists, conducted research, and monitored the media as an integral part of CAIR's national propaganda campaign.

During his employment there, Royer admits introducing some of his terrorist co-conspirators to Lashkar-e-Taiba leaders and helping them gain entry to terrorist training camps in Pakistan, prosecutors say. At least one traveled there with his help before the September 11, 2001, attacks, while another went right afterward, court records show. Royer told them if they wanted to fight U.S. troops in Afghanistan, they'd first need to participate in military training and that the camps in Pakistan were a good place to get that training. Royer still worked for CAIR through October 2001, when he resigned to rejoin the jihad overseas. He was arrested not long after returning home.[3]

The Justice Department charged the former high-level CAIR staffer with conspiring to wage war against the United States, aiding the Taliban and al-Qaida, and providing assistance to Lashkar-e-Taiba. Royer eventually pleaded guilty to lesser firearms- and explosives-related charges in exchange for his cooperation in the ongoing terrorism investigation.

Far from cooperating, however, Royer has worked tirelessly to appeal his conviction. Helping him in that effort is his old employer, CAIR.

FINDING A "LOOPHOLE" FOR ISMAIL

Despite overwhelming evidence of Royer's treacherous plans to help the Taliban and al-Qaida kill American men and women in uniform after 9/11, CAIR has been working behind the scenes with Royer's lawyer and wife to free him from prison. Confidential office memos show Royer's case is a top item on CAIR's executive agenda.[4] CAIR's legal department in Washington has been researching his appeal. Last summer, in fact, a CAIR legal intern from the University of Maryland law school, Fariha

Quasem, was tasked with helping to find a "loophole" in the law to gain his release.[5]

CAIR has also defended would-be al-Qaida assassin Abu Ali, who was in regular contact with Royer's group and participated in its paramilitary training. CAIR's logbook for visitors to its Washington headquarters shows that Abu Ali's father, who worked at the Saudi embassy, met with CAIR director Nihad Awad several months before his son's 2005 terrorism conviction.[6]

CAIR's continued interest in the Virginia Jihad case appears to go well beyond civil rights advocacy. Just what did CAIR know about its former employee's activities, and when did it know it?

Terrorism experts say Lashkar-e-Taiba's bold, coordinated attack on Westerners in Mumbai indicates the terror group is expanding its theater of operations, which may now include the U.S. They say the development is worrisome and begs for reinvestigation of CAIR's connection to the Lashkar-e-Taiba cell in Virginia.

"CAIR's civil rights coordinator in DC was the ringleader of that cell in Virginia," says Walid Phares, a Ph.D. Middle East scholar and counterterrorism consultant for the U.S. government. "Based on Royer's connection to L-e-T, it is important to now go back and question CAIR's role." [7]

CAIR's connections to terrorists and extremists hardly end with Royer, who's more the rule than the exception; and such ties are far more extensive than have been reported. These aren't garden variety extremists, either. Some like Royer are hardened members of terrorist groups who plotted against the U.S. while still on CAIR's payroll. They are sworn enemies in the war on terror, co-conspirators in the Islamic jihad against America.

And their resumés all have CAIR in common.

CAIR, which runs thirty-three offices and chapters nationwide, does not publicly disclose complete directories of its staff or advisors, current or historic. Nor does it make its federal tax filings, naming its officers and stakeholders, readily available to the public. All of which has left details about its associations sketchy.

But personnel records we've obtained, along with a review of federal tax and political donor records listing occupation, have helped fill in some of the gaps. Matching employee and volunteer worker names against legal databases reveals CAIR has been associated with an alarming number of convicted terrorists or felons in terrorism probes, as well as suspected terrorists and active targets of counterterrorism investigations. And our analysis is by no means exhaustive.

It's been widely reported that three CAIR officials have been linked to terrorism, with Royer topping the list. But there are at least twelve other CAIR officials who have been caught up in terror investigations, bringing the grand total to at least fifteen.

In fact, federal and local authorities say CAIR's offices have acted as a virtual turnstile for terrorists and their supporters.

"We've been actively working cases against CAIR for awhile, including key administration there," says a senior investigator assigned to the FBI's Joint Terrorism Task Force in Washington.[8]

And investigations, which continue apace, have resulted in convictions.

"CAIR has had a number of people in positions of power within the organization that have been directly connected to terrorism and have either been prosecuted or thrown out of the country," says former FBI agent Mike Rolf.[9]

Because of its growing terror ties and run-ins with the law, congressional leaders are warning lawmakers and other Washington officials to disassociate themselves from the group.

"Groups like CAIR have a proven record of senior officials being indicted and either imprisoned or deported from the United States," said U.S. Representative Sue Myrick (R-NC), co-founder of the Congressional

Anti-Terrorism/Jihad Caucus.

The organization itself recently was named as an unindicted co-conspirator in a scheme to funnel more than $12 million to the terrorist group Hamas. In the Holy Land Foundation case, federal prosecutors also listed CAIR as a member of the U.S. branch of the Muslim Brotherhood, a worldwide jihadist movement that gave rise to Hamas, al-Qaida, and other terrorist groups, and seeks to institutionalize Islamic law, or *Shariah*, in America.

CAIR's rap sheet is long and growing. In addition to Royer, whom we'll count as number one, it includes the following officials:

MUTHANNA AL-HANOOTI

Federal agents last year charged the former CAIR regional director with conspiring to work for a foreign government and with making false statements to the FBI.

Al-Hanooti's home was raided by FBI agents, who also searched the offices of his front group, Focus on Advocacy and Advancement of International Relations, which al-Hanooti operates out of Dearborn, Michigan, and Washington DC.

FAAIR claims to be a consulting firm raising awareness of Sunni Muslim grievances in Iraq, but investigators say it's a front that supported the Sunni-led insurgency.

Al-Hanooti, who immigrated to the U.S. from Iraq, formerly helped run a suspected Hamas terror front called LIFE for Relief and Development. Its Michigan offices also were raided in the investigation. In 2004, LIFE's Baghdad office was raided by U.S. troops, who seized files and computers.[10]

Al-Hanooti headed CAIR's Michigan office after working briefly for

CAIR National in Washington,[11] and he is related to Sheik Mohammed al-Hanooti, whom the Justice Department named an unindicted co-conspirator in the 1993 World Trade Center bombing. He currently leads prayers at a Washington-area mosque that aided some of the 9/11 hijackers and is closely affiliated with CAIR.

The FBI alleges al-Hanooti, an ethnic Palestinian who also emigrated from Iraq, raised money for Hamas. In fact, "al-Hanooti collected over $6 million for support of Hamas," according to a 2001 FBI report. He was also present with CAIR and Holy Land officials at a secret Hamas fundraising summit held last decade at a Philadelphia hotel.

Prosecutors recently added the sheik's name to the list of unindicted co-conspirators in the Holy Land case.[12]

LAURA JAGHLIT

A civil rights coordinator for CAIR,[13] her Washington-area home was raided by federal agents after 9/11 as part of an investigation into terrorist financing, money-laundering, and tax fraud. Her husband, Mohammed Jaghlit, a key leader in the Saudi-backed SAAR network, also known as the Safa group, has been a target of the still active probe. (The Safa group is a key financial hub in the Muslim Brotherhood crime syndicate, which is the focus of the second half of the book).

Mohammed Jaghlit, aka Mohammad El-Gajhleet, is a Brotherhood boss whom federal investigators describe as "an active supporter of Hamas." Last decade, he sent two letters accompanying donations—one for $10,000, the other for $5,000—from the SAAR Foundation to Sami al-Arian, now a convicted terrorist. In each letter, according to a federal affidavit, "Jaghlit instructed al-Arian not to disclose the contribution publicly or to the media."[14]

Investigators suspect the funds were intended for Palestinian terrorists via a U.S. terror front called WISE, which at the time employed an official who personally delivered a satellite phone battery to Osama bin Laden. The same official also worked for Jaghlit's group.

In addition, Jaghlit donated a total of $37,200 to the Holy Land Foundation, which prosecutors recently convicted as a Hamas front. Jaghlit subsequently was named an unindicted co-conspirator in the terror case.[15]

ABDURAHMAN ALAMOUDI

Another CAIR director,[16] he is serving twenty-three years in federal prison for plotting terrorism. Alamoudi, who was caught on tape complaining bin Laden hadn't killed enough Americans in the U.S. embassy bombings in Africa, was one of al-Qaida's top fundraisers in America, according to the U.S. Treasury Department.

NIHAD AWAD

For the first time, wiretap evidence from the Holy Land case puts CAIR's current national executive director at a Philadelphia meeting of Hamas leaders and activists that was secretly recorded by the FBI. Participants hatched a plot to disguise payments to Hamas terrorists as charity.

During the October 1993 meeting, according to FBI wire transcripts, Awad gave a report and was recorded discussing the pro-Hamas propaganda effort. He mentions Ghassan Dahduli, whom he worked with at the time at the Islamic Association for Palestine, another Hamas front controlled by the terror group. Both were IAP officers. Dahduli's name also was listed in the address book of bin Laden's personal secretary, Wadi al-Hage, serving a life sentence for his role in the U.S. embassy bombings. Dahduli, an ethnic Palestinian like Awad, was deported to Jordan after 9/11 for refusing to cooperate in the terror investigation. He recently was added to the government's blacklist of Hamas co-conspirators.[17]

Awad's and Dahduli's phone numbers are listed in a 1993 Muslim Brotherhood document seized by federal investigators revealing "important phone numbers" for the "Palestine Section" of the Brotherhood in America.[18] The court exhibit shows fugitive Hamas leader Mousa Abu Marzook listed on the same page with Awad, along with CAIR national board director Nabil Sadoun, who with Marzook co-founded another Hamas front detailed below. Not surprisingly, Marzook has enjoyed the undying public support of CAIR since the U.S. designated him a terrorist and deported him.

The 48-year-old Awad—who uses the alias Nehad Hammad—once publicly praised Hamas. "I am in support of the Hamas movement," he declared the year CAIR was founded. Known by law enforcement as "Jihad" Awad, he has turned down congressional invitations to answer questions under oath. He remains under FBI scrutiny.

"He's a bad guy—one of Hamas's senior [supporters] in the United States," says a veteran special agent with the FBI's Washington field office.[19]

OMAR M. AHMAD

U.S. prosecutors also named CAIR's founder and former chairman as an unindicted co-conspirator in the Holy Land case.[20] Ahmad too was placed at the 1993 Philly meeting, FBI special agent Lara Burns testified at the trial. In fact, wiretaps and other evidence show Ahmad arranged and led the secret Hamas meetings.[21] Federal prosecutors also designated him as a top leader of the Muslim Brotherhood's "Palestine Committee" in America, whose "designed purpose was to support Hamas," prosecutors say. He remains under active investigation.

Ahmad, like his CAIR partner Awad, is a Palestinian refugee who also uses an alias, Omar Yehia.

Though both Ahmad and Awad were senior leaders of IAP, the Hamas front, neither of their biographical sketches posted on CAIR's Web site mentions their IAP past.

CAIR's founder Ahmad, while claiming to be a moderate and patriotic American, has praised suicide bombers who "kill themselves for Islam."[22] He also hosted blind Sheik Omar Abdel Rahman at his home not long before he was arrested and convicted of terrorism, according to Ahmad's apartment manager at the time, who turned photographs and other evidence over to the FBI's San Jose, California, field office.

The Blind Sheik, as he's known, is serving a life sentence for his role in the early 1990s plot to blow up New York City tunnels, the United Nations, and other New York landmarks. He is a close ally of Osama bin Laden.

While the Blind Sheik was plotting terrorism in New York, he paid Ahmad a visit at his Villa Monroe apartment some three thousand miles away in Santa Clara, California, says then-apartment manager Andy Hyslop, who now works for the state of California. He says he witnessed a phalanx of bodyguards in green fatigue jackets escorting the Blind Sheik up the stairs to Ahmad's second-floor corner unit.

"Omar came out on the landing in traditional robe to receive him," Hyslop recalls, "and he gave him a big hug."[23]

A few years later, a Santa Clara mosque, which Ahmad helped found, hosted and raised thousands of dollars for bin Laden deputy Ayman al-Zawahiri, the second most wanted terrorist in the world. Al-Zawahiri was a follower of the Blind Sheik. The two met in Egypt, where they were both active in the militant Muslim Brotherhood.

What's more, Ahmad once told a group of local Muslims that they are in America to help assert Islam's rule over the country.

"Islam isn't in America to be equal to any other faith, but to become dominant," a local reporter quoted him as saying at the Muslim conference, adding, "The Quran should be the highest authority in America, and Islam the only accepted religion on Earth."[24]

Ahmad, 49, insists he was misquoted. However, an FBI wiretap transcript quotes Ahmad agreeing with terrorists gathered at a secret Philly meeting to "camouflage" their true intentions by employing "deception."

He compared it to the head fake in basketball. "This is like one who plays basketball: He makes a player believe that he is doing this, while he does something else," Ahmad said. "Like they say, politics is a completion of war."[25]

Ahmad has taken a low profile since 2003, when his seditious statements about replacing the Constitution with the Quran were widely circulated in the press. Though he stepped down as chairman of the CAIR board in 2004, he remained intimately involved in CAIR operations, working behind the scenes. (His replacement at the helm appeared to be a cardboard cutout with little actual power. Parvez Ahmed was an unpaid volunteer who never left his job as an associate professor in Jacksonville, Florida, and resigned last year due to conflicts with the board.)

NABIL SADOUN

A current CAIR National board member, Sadoun has served on the board of the United Association for Studies and Research, a known Hamas front in America. In fact, Sadoun co-founded UASR with Hamas leader Marzook. The Justice Department added Washington-based UASR to its list of unindicted co-conspirators in the Holy Land terror case.[26]

MOHAMED NIMER

CAIR's longtime research director also served as a researcher and board director for UASR, a strategic arm for Hamas in the U.S. Tellingly, CAIR neglects to mention Nimer's or Sadoun's roles at UASR in their bios.

RAFEEQ JABER

A founding board director and vice president of CAIR, Jaber was the long-time president of the Islamic Association for Palestine. In 2002, a federal judge found that "the Islamic Association for Palestine has acted in support of Hamas." [27] In his capacity as IAP chief, Jaber praised Hezbollah attacks on Israel. He also served on the board of a radical Muslim Brotherhood mosque in the Chicago area.

RABIH HADDAD

A CAIR speaker who helped raise funds for the group, he was one of the founders of the Global Relief Foundation, which after 9/11 was blacklisted by the Treasury Department for financing al-Qaida and other terror groups. Its assets were frozen in December 2001. Internal memos show CAIR has coordinated fundraising efforts with Global Relief. [28] Haddad, who raised money for CAIR's Ann Arbor, Michigan chapter, was arrested on terror-related charges and deported to Lebanon in 2003.

MOHAMMAD EL-MEZAIN

The former Holy Land chairman conducted fundraising for CAIR, soliciting more than $100,000 for the group at a 2004 CAIR event in New York, for example. He was convicted earlier this year of conspiring to provide material support to Hamas terrorists by a federal jury in Dallas, and is now behind bars. El-Mezain is related to Hamas leader Marzook and is close to the Muslim cleric who privately counseled some of the 9/11 hijackers.

SIRAJ WAHHAJ

A longtime member of CAIR's board of advisors, Wahhaj was named by the Justice Department as an unindicted co-conspirator in the 1993 World Trade Center bombing investigation. The radical Brooklyn imam was close to convicted terrorist Sheik Abdel Rahman and even defended him during his trial as a character witness.

Wahhaj, a black convert himself, is converting gang members to Islam and holding "jihad camps" for them.[29] With a combination of Islam and Uzis[30], he says, the street thugs will be a powerful force for Islam the day America "will crumble."[31]

His son also has had trouble with the law. Siraj Ibn Wahhaj in 2005 was detained by Homeland Security authorities at JFK International Airport after arriving on a Royal Air Morocco flight. Agents interrogated him for four hours on suspicion of jihadist activity.[32]

The elder Wahhaj remains heavily involved in CAIR business, internal documents show. In 2006, for example, CAIR National enlisted him to help raise $1 million for the organization, alongside Awad, Ahmad, and other board members.[33] In fact, Wahhaj conducted the fundraising at CAIR's annual banquet in 2008, raising $210,000 by the end of the night.[34]

BASSEM EL-KHAFAGI

Another CAIR official, Khafagi was arrested in 2003 while serving as CAIR's director of community affairs. He pleaded guilty to charges of bank and visa fraud stemming from a federal counterterror probe of his leadership role in the Islamic Assembly of North America, which has supported al-Qaida and advocated suicide attacks on America. He was sentenced to ten months in prison and deported to his native Egypt.

Since his arrest, CAIR has tried to distance itself from Khafagi, arguing he was a "contractor" and not a direct employee. Financial records, however, show CAIR National treated him like a high-level employee, even purchasing computer equipment for him in 2002 so he could work with CAIR's leadership out of its Washington headquarters.[35]

HAMZA YUSUF

After 9/11, the FBI investigated the *imam* and member of CAIR's board of advisors because just two days before the attacks, he made an ominous prediction to a Muslim audience in California.

"This country is facing a terrible fate and the reason for that is because this country stands condemned," Yusuf warned. "It stands condemned like Europe stood condemned because of what it did. And lest people forget, Europe suffered two world wars after conquering the Muslim lands."

Yusuf is also a regular keynote speaker at CAIR events. "Hamza Yusuf is a well-respected, well-known Muslim leader in this country," CAIR spokesman Ibrahim Hooper said in his defense.[36]

GHASSAN ELASHI

A founding director of CAIR's Texas chapter, he was convicted in 2004 of illegally shipping high-tech goods to terror state Syria, and is serving eighty months in prison. In addition to that conviction, a jury found him guilty in 2008 of providing material support to Hamas in the Holy Land Foundation trial. Elashi was chairman of the charitable front, which provided seed capital to CAIR. He also is related to Hamas leader Marzook.

CAIR has also tried to distance itself from Elashi by arguing that he did not work out of its national headquarters. "The fact that Elashi was once associated with one of our more than thirty regional chapters has no legal significance," CAIR asserted in a prepared statement.

However, CAIR's national office rushed to Elashi's defense when federal agents raided his Dallas office, blasting the government's actions as an "anti-Muslim witch hunt." The contacts listed on the press release issued by CAIR were Hooper, Awad, and Elashi himself.[37] What's more, Elashi attended the secret Hamas meeting in Philadelphia with Awad and co-founder Ahmad.

In its defense, CAIR protests that you can't incriminate an "entire" organization for a few bad apples (even if, in CAIR's case, they number more than a dozen and include its acting executive director and founders).

To try to demonstrate the point, CAIR's national legislative director last summer instructed interns to search public databases to find a Fox News employee who had been arrested and convicted of a felony. Corey Saylor wanted to show that every organization, including CAIR's critics, has criminals who have worked for it, and that management can't be held responsible for the activities of every employee.

"Corey wanted to use this in an interview [with the media] to show that you can't blame an entire organization for one person's missteps," undercover intern Chris Gaubatz says. However, the interns were "unable to find anything."

CHAPTER THREE

FRONTING FOR HAMAS

"From its founding by Muslim Brotherhood leaders, CAIR conspired with other affiliates of the Muslim Brotherhood to support terrorists."

—*U.S. Justice Department*[1]

DURING LAST YEAR'S Holy Land Foundation terror financing trial, FBI agent Lara Burns took the stand to go over wiretap transcripts from a secret 1993 Philadelphia meeting held by Hamas leaders in America. Federal prosecutors asked her about a passage from defendant Shukri Abu Baker, who was recorded talking about the need to form a new front organization to support their "movement," one seemingly detached from the Muslim Brotherhood and Hamas.

Existing fronts such as Holy Land were earning a reputation as extremist—they were "marked"—and he and others gathered at the meeting envisioned an "alternative" organization that would appear less "conspicuous" to the American public, according to FBI transcripts.

Prosecutor Barry Jonas—deputy chief of the Justice Department's terrorist financing unit—asked agent Burns whether any groups formed after the 1993 meeting fit their description. "CAIR," she replied.[2]

Indeed, CAIR was created less than one year after that Philadelphia meeting.

It has taken fifteen years for all of the extremist baggage to catch up to this self-proclaimed "moderate" Muslim group. But now there is no denying its terrorist roots.

How did this new, improved Hamas terror front evolve? It's instructive to go back to the beginning days of the Brotherhood movement in

America, when Brotherhood leaders created CAIR's parent. They called it the Islamic Association for Palestine, or IAP, and there's no doubt it was a U.S. "front" for Palestinian jihad against Israel, because that's the language they used to describe it in their secret manifestos.

Two well-educated, if radicalized, members of the Brotherhood's Palestine Committee took over the reins of IAP not long after Hamas launched its "blessed Intifada" against Israel in the late '80s. Omar Ahmad and Nihad Awad were born in the same Palestinian refugee camp and they burned with hatred toward Israel as well as their adopted country for supporting the Jewish nation economically and militarily.

In 1992, Hamas asked the committee for more American money to finance suicide bombing operations against Israel, complaining its "financial needs" were not being met. "Provide us with what helps us of funds and weapons," it pleaded in one letter from the Gaza Strip. "Weapons, weapons, our brothers."

"Jihad in Palestine is different from any jihad," the letter continued. "The meaning of killing a Jew for the liberation of Palestine cannot be compared to any jihad on earth."[3]

Ahmad dutifully stepped up support. Among other things, he brought in Hamas speakers to IAP conferences to help raise funds and joined them in exalting suicide bombers as martyrs for Islam.

Then in October 1993, Ahmad called to order a secret Hamas summit at a Courtyard by Marriott hotel in Philadelphia. There, IAP and Holy Land officials hatched a scheme to disguise payments to Hamas terrorists and their families as charity. Wiretaps also record them stating the need to deceive Americans about their true objectives while Hamas launched a campaign of terror attacks.

'A MEDIA TWINKLE'

The IAP and Holy Land officials worried, however, that the Hamas infrastructure in America was insufficiently equipped to launch a convincing propaganda campaign. Missing was a media office savvy enough to seduce both the American media and the government into looking the other way as they advanced their radical agenda of supporting violent jihad abroad while slowly institutionalizing a *Shariah* theocracy at home. They needed a new front group that, in Abu Baker's words, could give their subversive agenda "a media twinkle."

Enter the Washington-based Council on American-Islamic Relations.

CAIR is first mentioned by name in Brotherhood documents as part of the July 30, 1994, agenda of the Palestine Committee. This is the smoking gun linking CAIR directly to the Hamas network inside America. Minutes reveal the purpose of the meeting was to discuss "suggestions to develop [the] work of CAIR" and its "coordination" with the Hamas triumvirate of IAP, Holy Land (which shared its Dallas offices with IAP), and the Washington-based United Association for Studies and Research, or UASR.[4] Along with IAP, UASR was co-founded by the deputy chief of Hamas's political operations, Mousa Abu Marzook, who led the Brotherhood's Palestine Committee in America before being designated a terrorist by the U.S. He is now considered a fugitive living in Syria.

He and other participants at the July 1994 committee meeting also talked about satisfying the "need for trained resources in the media and political fields" to "exert more efforts in the advancement of the Palestine Cause from the Islamic aspect."

Fittingly, CAIR was incorporated less than two months later—on September 15, 1994.

The group's leadership was plucked directly from IAP and the Palestine

Committee. In fact, all three CAIR incorporators—Ahmad, Awad, and Rafeeq Jaber—have held senior positions at IAP. The *troika* simply shifted positions to CAIR, as you can see in this diagram. New name, same old management.

IAP (1993)	CAIR (1994)
Omar Ahmad	*Omar Ahmad*
President	President
Rafeeq Jaber	*Rafeeq Jaber**
IAP-Chicago Chapter President	Vice President
Nihad Awad	*Nihad Awad*
Public Relations Director	Secretary, Treasurer

*Jaber would later return to IAP as president.

Sources: Articles of incorporation, By-laws, CAIR, District of Columbia, 15 September 1994, 7; FBI documents.

Also, Ibrahim "Dougie" Hooper, a Muslim convert and TV producer who assisted Awad's media efforts at IAP,[5] became CAIR's communications director. And Mohamed Nimer, a protégé of Marzook at UASR, transferred to CAIR to head up its research department.

It's one big happy Islamofascist family at the new "alternative" front for Hamas in America.

CAIR continues to support Hamas and its wicked aims. The tax-exempt group stubbornly refuses to condemn Hamas by name, even in the wake of bus and pizza parlor bombings disemboweling innocent women and children. After one of its many suicide bombings killed teenagers at a Tel Aviv nightclub in 2001, Awad defended the atrocity and Hamas's murderous tactics. "Palestinians are using legitimate means of resistance," he said. "We should not be apologetic about it."[6]

Ever since Hamas was designated a foreign terrorist organization in 1995, it's been illegal to provide support to it within the U.S.

CAIR has strenuously denied such support, and has filed a request in a U.S. court to have its name stricken from the government's list of co-conspirators underwriting Palestinian terrorism.[7] The judge, however, has sided with the government and left the list intact.

As Assistant U.S. Attorney James T. Jacks argued, "Striking CAIR's name will not prevent its conspiratorial involvement with HLF [Holy Land Foundation] and others affiliated with Hamas from becoming a matter of public record."

And, he says, CAIR's involvement in the terror conspiracy is "ongoing": "CAIR has been identified by the government as a participant in an ongoing and ultimately unlawful conspiracy to support a designated terrorist organization—a conspiracy from which CAIR never withdrew."[8]

In federal court documents, prosecutors have explicitly stated that CAIR is part of the pro-jihad, anti-U.S. Muslim Brotherhood and its U.S. network to benefit Hamas and other terrorists. Their language has been plain and unambiguous, yet the mainstream media have still managed to ignore their alarming conclusions.

"From its founding by Muslim Brotherhood leaders," wrote Assistant U.S. Attorney Gordon D. Kromberg in a 2007 terrorism case involving CAIR, "CAIR conspired with other affiliates of the Muslim Brotherhood to support terrorists."[9]

This bears repeating: *The U.S. government says CAIR has conspired to support terrorists.* In other words, CAIR is the enemy in the war on terror. Its leaders are the bad guys.

Of course, you've probably heard CAIR insisting they're the good guys, standing "unequivocally against terrorism" with the rest of America.[10]

Don't be fooled, prosecutors say. CAIR and the other "conspirators agreed to use deception to conceal from the American public their connections to terrorists," Kromberg asserts.

FOLLOW THE MONEY

That deception takes many forms, and we'll explore them all in forthcoming chapters, but a key tactic is money laundering. Brotherhood leaders have conspired to conceal payments to terrorists as charity or business "investment." They play an elaborate shell game to hide illicit funds—using dozens, if not hundreds, of fronts, shell companies, and cutouts, investigators say.

The Holy Land Foundation, busted as the main fundraising arm for Hamas in America, commingled funds and assets with CAIR to a degree previously unreported, raising new alarms in the wake of Holy Land's recent conviction on terror money laundering charges.

As Steve Emerson's Investigative Project on Terrorism has already revealed, Holy Land provided at least $5,000 in revenues to CAIR as it was starting up operations.[11] CAIR, in turn, solicited funds for the Holy Land Foundation. After 9/11, as rescue workers were still pulling bodies from Ground Zero, CAIR tricked visitors to its Web site into contributing to the charitable front by telling them their donations would benefit World Trade Center victims—including New York firefighters— knowing full well their charity would help create new victims of terrorism. The link it posted actually took contibutors to the home page for the Holy Land Foundation—the main fundraising arm in America for Palestinian terrorists.[12]

All this is well known, however, at least among jihad watchers. What has not been reported is that CAIR in late 1995 contributed at least

$40,000 to a Holy Land subsidiary that also was raided and shut down after 9/11. This item is revealed on a balance sheet attached to the original corporation franchise tax return that CAIR filed the following year with the District of Columbia.[13] The subsidiary—InfoCom Corp.—fronted as a Web-hosting firm and shared officers and funds with Holy Land. In fact, InfoCom was located across the street from Holy Land's headquarters in Richardson, Texas.

The company was run by convicted terrorist and CAIR-Texas founding director, Ghassan Elashi. InfoCom itself was convicted on charges of terror money laundering in 2004. At least $250,000 in investment capital was funneled through InfoCom by senior Hamas leader Marzook, who was designated a terrorist in 1995 and had his accounts frozen. The FBI says he "financed terrorist activities."[14]

Most alarming, CAIR made its own $40,000 "investment" in InfoCom just months before InfoCom's parent, the Holy Land Foundation, wired an early 1996 payment of exactly $40,000 to the Islamic Relief Committee, a charitable front for Hamas in the Palestinian territories.[15]

Islamic Relief Committee had requested more money to finance "weapons to carry out the jihad operations," according to one handwritten missive.

"You do not know how happy people become when they watch those mujahideen," it added, referring to Hamas terrorists, "and how proud they feel when they parade in their uniforms and weapons—and the extent of their honor when they carry out their jihadist operations against the Jews and their tentacles."[16]

CAIR's "investment" in InfoCom (as the item is listed on its balance sheet) was a large sum for the young organization. In fact, it represented more than half its total assets at the time, tax records show.[17]

And it was made *after* the U.S. government officially designated Hamas a terrorist group. In January 1995, President Clinton banned transfer of money to Hamas through charitable donations from U.S. groups and citizens.

The financial transaction is yet another piece of evidence that can be added to the pile of evidence prosecutors presented at trial confirming CAIR conspired with Holy Land to raise money for Hamas.

"There is no question CAIR supports Hamas," says retired FBI special agent John Vincent, a twenty-seven-year veteran who worked Hamas terror funding cases in Chicago.

And not just Hamas, but terrorists operating here in our backyard, too.

CHAPTER FOUR
TERROR SUPPORT GROUP

"Washington must attempt to understand Islamic movements in the area, and start supporting Islamic groups including Mr. Bin Laden and his associates."

—Draft of 2004 talking points memo found in CAIR's executive files[1]

IT COMES AS LITTLE SURPRISE that a Palestinian terrorist front run by Palestinian refugees and created from a Palestinian terrorist group would support Palestinian terrorists. But CAIR also supports al-Qaida and Taliban terrorists, as well as homegrown terrorists who kill cops. It's a full-service terror support group.

Consider the following clients:

IMAM JAMIL AL-AMIN

The black convert to Islam was a founding member of the Islamic Shura Council of North America and a darling of the Muslim Brotherhood. Then he shot two sheriff's deputies and, instead of being shunned, became a martyr celebrated by CAIR and the rest of the Muslim mafia.

The Atlanta deputies were shot while trying to arrest al-Amin for failing to appear before a judge to answer auto theft charges. The Muslim preacher pulled out two guns and shot one deputy in both legs, the left arm, and the chest. He pumped another six bullets into the other deputy, killing him, before fleeing the scene. He was captured after a multistate manhunt.

The surviving officer identified al-Amin from mugshots. Formerly known as H. Rap Brown, al-Amin had done time in New York for robbery. Bullets removed from the officers and recovered from the scene of the shooting, which took place outside al-Amin's Atlanta home, matched al-Amin's weapons.

In 2002, a jury convicted al-Amin and sentenced him to life in prison without parole for the murder of Fulton County Deputy Ricky Kinchen. The Georgia Supreme Court upheld the verdict two years later.[2]

Despite overwhelming evidence of his guilt, CAIR has practically canonized this vicious cop killer. The group participated in a news conference in Atlanta decrying his guilty verdict, and CAIR's executive director even visited al-Amin in jail.

Worse, recent internal correspondence reveals that CAIR has been bankrolling the murderer's legal defense fund.

"We extend appreciation to you and CAIR for the additional contribution of $9,000 to be used for legal expenses relative to Imam Jamil al-Amin's case," attorney Karima al-Amin wrote CAIR director Awad in a 2007 letter. "The contribution particularly was needed to defray the cost of the recent habeas hearing held in Reidsville, Georgia."

"As always," al-Amin closed, "Imam Jamil sends his greetings and appreciation for the assistance."[3]

In other words, CAIR has been conspiring behind the scenes to release a cop killer from a maximum-security prison and put him back on the street.

AMERICAN TALIBAN

First CAIR defended John Walker Lindh, who's serving a twenty-year sentence for fighting alongside the Taliban against U.S. forces in Afghanistan. Then it tried to defend a second American Taliban before thinking better of it.

After the 2006 arrest of Kobie Williams, aka Abdul Kabeer, CAIR's legal department considered rallying to his defense until the Houston college student pleaded guilty to charges he conspired to aid the Taliban. Even his lawyer admitted he made a "grave mistake," creating a political dilemma for CAIR.

"It is a difficult case," concluded then-CAIR national legal director Arasalan Iftikhar in an email to Awad and Hooper. "We need to stay away from this case *publicly*, in my opinion" (emphasis added).[4]

CAIR ultimately decided to back off the case because of the PR problem it would generate. However, later that month CAIR sent a representative from Houston to support another homegrown terrorist who happened to be a confederate of Williams in the so-called Houston Taliban group. Unlike Williams, Shira Syed Qazi did not admit guilt. So CAIR's Houston chapter vice president showed up in court to cheer him on. A judge nonetheless found Qazi guilty.[5]

AHMED OMAR ABU ALI

CAIR's leaders have received in their executive suites the lawyers and relatives of not only convicts Randall "Ismail" Royer and Lindh, but also those of the al-Qaida operative convicted of plotting to assassinate President Bush.

On April 22, 2004, just before noon, Abu Ali's father left his office at the Saudi Embassy in Washington and met with CAIR director Awad, CAIR's visitor register for that year shows.[6] Then a few weeks later, Awad traveled to Saudi Arabia with the attorney for the Ali family. On May 14, Awad personally met with the U.S. consul in Saudi Arabia to challenge Abu Ali's ongoing detention in a prison there and to lobby for his release.[7]

Awad and Abu Ali's lawyer Ashraf Nubani met several times to coordinate efforts to free the al-Qaida-trained terrorist, even after he made a detailed confession.[8] After a federal jury convicted Abu Ali on all counts of aiding al-Qaida and plotting terrorist attacks, CAIR continued to support and defend him. The young terrorist, who was recently linked to the al-Qaida ringleader of the London suicide bombings, is serving a life sentence in a supermax facility.

Entries in CAIR's visitor register reveal its headquarters has an open door policy for such terrorists. CAIR is the only place in America (outside of criminal defense law firms) where terrorists are valued clients.

Curiously, there are no clients or visitors listed in CAIR's national register during the month of September 2001. By comparison, numerous visitors made entries during the months of August 2001 and October 2001.

SAMI AL-ARIAN

CAIR has long championed the case of this convicted Palestinian terrorist, including co-sponsoring the premiere of a documentary film lionizing him. CAIR in 2007 hosted the screening of *USA vs. Al-Arian* at a Washington theater just a year after al-Arian was sentenced to fifty-seven months in prison followed by deportation.[9]

In a plea deal, he copped to a reduced charge of "conspiracy to make or receive contributions of funds, goods, or services to, or for the benefit of, the Palestinian Islamic Jihad," a federally designated terror group.

After the former Florida professor was released from prison last year, CAIR issued a congratulatory statement. "We welcome Dr. al-Arian's release and hope that it is an indication that justice may ultimately be served in this disturbing case," said CAIR chief Awad.[10]

However, al-Arian remains under house arrest in northern Virginia on a federal contempt citation after refusing to testify in front of a Virginia grand jury investigating a network of Muslim Brotherhood fronts known as the Safa group, despite being granted immunity from prosecution. Al-Arian, a senior Muslim Brotherhood member, received funds from leaders of the Safa group.

TAHA AL-AWANI

Federal prosecutors listed al-Alwani as an unindicted co-conspirator in the al-Arian terror case. His International Institute of Islamic Thought, or IIIT, was the single biggest donor for al-Arian's Tampa-based terror front group.[11]

The Virginia think tank IIIT (pronounced "triple I-T") is at the center of a long-running terror financing probe vehemently protested by CAIR.

After federal agents raided IIIT and the other Brotherhood fronts in the Safa group network after 9/11, CAIR rushed to their defense, even lobbying members of Congress to pressure the Treasury Department and FBI to back off their investigations, internal CAIR documents detail.[12]

In one of its internal phone directories, CAIR lists another IIIT honcho among its "Recommended Community Leaders." Jamal Barzinji, a senior Muslim Brotherhood leader, remains the subject of a federal terror financing investigation. "Barzinji is not only closely associated with PIJ [Palestinian Islamic Jihad], but also with Hamas," said senior federal agent David Kane in a sworn court affidavit.[13]

CAIR has a lot at stake in the Safa investigation. The ties between it and the Saudi-backed group are incestuous. For starters, CAIR contracts with Barzinji's brother's printing company to publish the books and other propaganda materials it distributes. Amana Limited's offices were among those searched after 9/11.

Also, CAIR opened its Maryland/Virginia chapter right across the street from IIIT in Herndon, Virginia in an office owned by another Safa entity, Sterling Management Group.[14] CAIR's landlord, Sterling CEO Yaqub Mirza, a Safa ringleader also under terror suspicion, attended its ribbon-cutting ceremony in 2004.[15]

Of all the office space available in Fairfax County, CAIR chose to set up shop not just in Herndon, but on Grove Street, where many of the companies raided by federal agents are located. It was a natural fit, of course. CAIR intern Chris Gaubatz says he often walked across the street with CAIR employees—including his boss, Khalid Iqbal—to pray at the notorious IIIT, which has contributed thousands of dollars to CAIR's operations, internal donor records kept by CAIR show.

Lucky for CAIR it did not operate an office in Herndon back in 2002 when agents conducted their raids on IIIT and the other Grove Street fronts. If it had, investigators say CAIR more than likely would have been included in the search warrant.

ZAID SHAKIR

CAIR keeps inviting this radical Muslim cleric back to speak at its events even though the FBI questioned him about a copy of one of his incendiary pamphlets found in the apartment of a suspect in the first World Trade Center bombing. The pro-jihad pamphlet lauded the "armed struggle" that brought about the rule of the Taliban in Afghanistan.

In his lectures, Shakir preaches treachery against the United States. He once told a Muslim audience that hijacking U.S. military aircraft is fair game in jihad, as a forthcoming chapter will detail.

Shakir, who recently confided to the *New York Times* that he "would like to see America become a Muslim country" ruled by Islamic law,[16] is a regular speaker at CAIR and ISNA events. Recently, he helped host workshops or delivered the keynote speech at banquets held at CAIR chapters in Chicago, Orlando, and San Diego, among others.

"Imam Zaid's speeches are very practical and bring the best out of his listeners," claims former CAIR official Ibrahim Moiz, a close personal friend who invited Shakir to speak to Muslims in Maryland.[17]

Perhaps the cleric has tempered his jihadist views? Not a chance: "I don't regret anything I've done or said," Shakir says.[18]

JAMES "YOUSEF" YEE

CAIR has also championed the cause of this former Army Muslim chaplain charged with espionage while serving at the U.S. military detention camp in Guantanamo Bay, Cuba. Yee was caught returning to the U.S. with maps of Gitmo prison facilities and lists of U.S. interrogators and Taliban and al-Qaida detainees among other classified materials, and was arrested at a U.S. airport.

He was charged with espionage, mishandling classified documents, and lying to investigators; he served hard time in a South Carolina stockade. Two of his Muslim cronies at Gitmo, both Arabic interpreters, were convicted of stealing or mishandling classified documents.

Far from being exonerated, as he and CAIR contend, the military only dropped charges against him to protect national security. Guantanamo commander Major General Geoffrey Miller, who originally accused Yee of spying, explained that there were "national security concerns that would arise from the release of the evidence" if the case moved to trial.

There's no question that Yee, a captain who converted to Islam, was at the very least sympathetic to al-Qaida and Taliban captives at Gitmo.

Yet CAIR took up his case without reservation, calling his prosecution an "injustice" and his treatment "inhumane." During the 2006 congressional campaign, for instance, Awad flew to Minneapolis to appear alongside him as a featured guest at a Democratic fundraiser for U.S. Representative Keith Ellison. CAIR that same year hosted a "Shutting Gitmo Panel" featuring Yee at the U.S. Capitol building.[19]

And CAIR published a sympathetic portrait of the defrocked Gitmo chaplain—complete with a touching photo of him and his family—in the media guide it recently distributed to national journalists. Yee is featured as an example of the ideal Muslim, one who dutifully "counseled" fellow Muslims at Gitmo, as the photo caption reads.[20]

In fact, Yee acted more like a defense attorney for the hardened killers there, complaining that guards subjected them to cruel "abuse" and "psychological torture."

Waterboarding? Electric shock? No, they committed the sadistic act of mishandling copies of the Quran that Yee had made sure each inmate received. He also saw to it that each copy of the Quran came with a surgical mask to cradle the Muslim holy book above ground to keep it safe and clean.

In addition, Yee convinced his superiors to provide the Muslim terrorists with prayer beads, prayer oils, prayer caps, and up to half a dozen books on Islam from the library, which he stocked with some $26,000 worth of Arabic and English titles.

Thanks to him, the terrorists have been able to brush up on their jihad as they await repatriation to Saudi Arabia, Yemen, and Pakistan. No doubt some of the more than seventy-five former Gitmo detainees who have returned to the anti-American jihad were among those the former chaplain "counseled."

But not to worry, Yee says, he didn't see any terrorists there, not even the dozens confirmed to have resumed their terrorist activities. "It's safe to say there weren't any prisoners who could be definitely connected to hard-core terrorism," he recently maintained during a BBC Radio interview promoting his book.[21]

Yee's legacy lives on at Guantanamo. Today, even prayer rugs are standard issue for detainees there. Arrows point the way to Mecca in their cells. Speakers blare out the Arabic call to prayer five times a day. Hardbound, embossed copies of the Quran are wrapped in cloth and distributed by a sympathetic Muslim librarian, who now catalogs some ten thousand pieces of Arabic literature as well as Arabic movies. No infidel is permitted to touch the Quran, not even the post commander.

Worse, security officials at Gitmo have been investigating another possible spy ring involving several "dirty" Arabic linguists who are accused among other things of:

- omitting valuable intelligence from their translations of detainee interrogations;

- slipping notes to detainees inside copies of the Quran;

- coaching detainees to make allegations of abuse against interrogators; and

- meeting with suspects on the terrorist watchlist while traveling back in the states.

Gitmo security officials recently met with FBI agents in Philadelphia to aid their investigation into one of the Muslim linguists under contract at Gitmo, according to sources familiar with the investigation.[22] They also this summer briefed members of Congress about the prison camp's internal security breaches.

"Three years of investigations have revealed the presence of pro-jihad/anti-Western activities among the civilian contractor and military linguist population serving Joint Task Force Guantanamo," states a copy of a classified Gitmo briefing, which was prepared in May 2009 for the FBI and CIA, as well as the congressional intelligence committees.[23]

The report explains that dirty Arabic linguists have gathered classified data involving detainees, interrogations, and security operations in an effort to "disrupt" Gitmo operations and U.S. "intelligence-collection capabilities."[24]

It goes on to specifically finger the Muslim Brotherhood, which it calls a terrorist group, in the conspiracy.

"These actions are deliberate, carefully planned, global, and to the benefit of the detainees and multiple terrorist organizations, to include al-Qaida and Muslim Brotherhood," the briefing says.[25]

Shockingly, the enemy infiltration is not limited to Guantanamo. The report strongly suggests that its spies have penetrated nearly every sensitive U.S. security agency involved in the war on terror, potentially compromising intelligence government-wide. "Persons participating in this activity move regularly between multiple contracting companies, various intelligence agencies in the U.S. government [FBI, CIA, DIA, NSA, etc.], and every branch of the U.S. military."[26]

OSAMA BIN LADEN

Yes, CAIR has even come to the defense of the al-Qaida kingpin. In 1998, after he was fingered for blowing up the U.S. embassies, CAIR demanded that Los Angeles-area billboards with bin Laden's picture under the headline "Sworn Enemy" be taken down.

Then in 2001, when most of the civilized world condemned bin Laden for attacking New York and Washington, CAIR abstained for more than three months, while blaming instead "the Zionist network" and demanding a halt to U.S. bombing in Afghanistan, bin Laden's home base. In an interview with journalist Jake Tapper, now with ABC News, CAIR communications director Ibrahim Hooper refused to condemn bin Laden outright for 9/11, even after the government stated he was clearly responsible for the attacks.[27]

In fact, CAIR didn't assign guilt to the 9/11 mastermind, even under direct questions from the press, until bin Laden incriminated himself in a videotape aired in December 2001. (And even in CAIR's belated press release, the group does not expressly condemn bin Laden. It merely concedes the undeniably obvious fact that he is connected to "the events of September 11.")

On the other hand, CAIR has suggested Jews were behind 9/11. A month after the attacks, with Ground Zero still smoldering, CAIR made outrageous claims that Mohamed Atta and other hijackers were alive, that Atta's passport was stolen, that the attacks were not caused by Muslims, and that the media should investigate the Israelis.

"What about the world Zionist network?" demanded CAIR's New York executive director Ghazi Khankan. "Why are you in the media not looking at them?"[28]

CAIR has received funding from two of bin Laden's favorite charities. In 2000, for example, CAIR research director Mohamed Nimer solicited $18,000 from the Global Relief Foundation, an internal letter reveals.[29] The donation was made a year before the Bridgeview, Illinois-based foundation was shut down as a charitable front for al-Qaida. Global Relief, in fact, helped fund the bombings of the U.S. embassies, according to the Treasury Department.

And the U.S. offices of the Saudi-based International Islamic Relief Organization contributed at least $12,000 in financing to CAIR.[30] The Treasury Department has blacklisted IIRO's branches in the Philippines and Indonesia for fundraising for al-Qaida and affiliated terrorist groups.

CAIR also defended al-Qaida's spiritual leader in America, Sheikh Omar Abdel Rahman, after his conviction on charges he plotted to blow up bridges, tunnels, and buildings in New York. As noted earlier, CAIR's co-founder and former chairman hosted the Blind Sheik at his Silicon

Valley home last decade.

Cementing CAIR's support for bin Laden is a 2004 political "talking points" memo found in Awad's personal files dealing with the agenda of the so-called American Muslim Taskforce on Civil Rights and Elections, which CAIR and other Muslim Brotherhood fronts formed after 9/11 to help elect more sympathetic politicians, including the president. The memo is basically a wish list for pro-Islamist changes in Washington policy.

Under the heading "American-Islamic Relations," which are the last three words in CAIR's name, the memo recommends Washington abandon Israel and start currying favor with bin Laden and al-Qaida to avoid another 9/11. Here are the relevant demands listed (by talking point number) in the shocking memo:

1. Abolish the faulty Middle East policy of the past century.

2. Democrats and Republicans need to share the blame for the failure of our Middle East policy, and need to assume responsibility for the damage done to the country as a result of 9/11.

3. Recognize that the seeds for 9/11 were planted in 1948.

5. Do not make Fundamental Islam the enemy. It will not work long-term, and there is no need for it.

8. Attempt to understand Islamic movements in the area, and start supporting Islamic groups including Mr. bin Laden and his associates.[31]

ANWAR N. AULAQI

Born in New Mexico, Aulaqi is al-Qaida's go-to *imam* for preparing suicide cells in the West, including the 9/11 hijackers, for "martyrdom operations." He reminds them of the carnal "pleasures" and high "rewards" Allah has waiting for them in Paradise—foremost, a *harem* of *houris*, or virgins—in case they lose their nerve.

This rock star of the jihadi preaching circuit has cultivated some fans among CAIR. Heading his booster club within the organization is the civil rights coordinator for CAIR's Los Angeles chapter, Affad Shaikh, who has listened to Aulaqi's lectures and posted links to his Web site on his blog *Muslamics*. Shaikh, who in 2008 was questioned by Homeland Security agents near San Diego, appears to have a death wish. "In death there is something to celebrate," he recently wrote on his blog in a post titled "Celebrating Death."[32] The essay mirrors one Aulaqi previously posted on another Web site titled "Why Muslims Love Death."

"Our culture of martyrdom needs to be revived," the *imam* fumes, "because the enemy of Allah fears nothing more than our love of death." Global domination is the goal. "We will implement the rule of Allah on earth by the tip of the sword whether the masses like it or not," he has written.[33]

Who is Anwar Nasser Aulaqi? Investigators now suspect he was a key facilitator and advisor, and possibly even a surviving field commander, for the 9/11 cell that hit the Pentagon. He's also an American citizen. They suspect he knew details of the plot and girded the al-Qaida terrorists' resolve to carry it out. Evidence is strong that he was enlisted to, at a minimum, hold the hijackers' hands and take their temperature as they moved closer to Zero Hour. In short, he's (if as yet unofficially) an unindicted 9/11 co-conspirator, and he remains at large.

Three of the hijackers of that uniquely all-Saudi cell that torpedoed the Pentagon spent time at the Saudi-connected Aulaqi's mosques in both San Diego and Falls Church, Virginia, where he served as prayer leader. The phone number for the Falls Church mosque—Dar al-Hijrah Islamic Center, controlled by the Muslim Brotherhood and closely tied to CAIR—was found in the Hamburg, Germany, apartment of one of the planners of the 9/11 attacks, Ramzi Binalshibh.

The 9/11 Commission concluded Aulaqi, who aided and privately counseled the hijackers, was "suspicious" and should be brought in for questioning. The commission was not told, however, that he was taken into custody a year after 9/11 on a warrant, but then released after the warrant was mysteriously rescinded. Aulaqi was allowed to turn around and leave the country on a Saudi Arabian airline without any further investigation, even though he remained on the terrorist lookout as the subject of multiple investigations involving al-Qaida and Hamas financing.[34]

Law enforcement officials involved with the warrant are still steamed about the missed opportunity to wrap Aulaqi up and leverage him for information regarding the 9/11 operations and possible future plots and sleeper cells still secreted inside America.

According to a federal investigator with the Joint Terrorism Task Force in San Diego—where Aulaqi originally met with the Pentagon hijackers behind closed doors before they followed him to Washington—the warrant for his arrest was based on passport fraud charges. Aulaqi, who grew up in Yemen, also allegedly made false statements on an application for U.S. State Department grant money to attend engineering classes at Colorado State University (he received some $20,000 per year).

"Everyone was excited about the prospect of hooking this guy up," the federal investigator says. "The FBI was ecstatic that we were able to get the warrant and that we had a charge on him."

He added: "Everybody wanted to get this guy in a chair under a charge—under the cloud of potential prosecution—to motivate some conversation with him regarding his relationship with the hijackers."[35]

When investigators heard the warrant had been pulled back, they were stunned.

"We got the word that they wanted to rescind the warrant," the JTTF investigator recalled, "and everybody's, like, What the f*** do you want to do that for?"[36]

He says that for some reason federal prosecutors got cold feet. "It was odd," he says, offering that he wouldn't be surprised if it had something to do with Aulaqi's Saudi connections. The Saudi embassy booked him to lecture at its Islamic institute in Washington and sponsored him to take American Muslims on pilgrimages to Saudi's two great mosques.

Aulaqi ended up fleeing to Yemen, his family's ancestral home bordering Saudi Arabia. After the 9/11 Commission scolded the FBI for not investigating Aulaqi more thoroughly, he suddenly became a high-value U.S. target. And in 2006, U.S. authorities asked Yemen to detain Aulaqi, but the country released him before the FBI could build an airtight case against him.

Not that CAIR cares, but U.S. officials now believe that the thirty-nine-year-old Aulaqi has been involved in other serious terrorist activities since leaving the U.S., including plotting new attacks against America and its allies. For one, Aulaqi preached jihad and praised suicide bombers at London-area mosques before the 2005 attacks on the London subway.

And three of the New Jersey Muslims recently convicted of plotting to attack the Fort Dix Army base were inspired by one of Aulaqi's Internet sermons, as were some of the young Somali-American men who recently left Minneapolis to join al-Qaida's widening jihad in West Africa. Court testimony revealed the Fort Dix terrorists watched his "Constants of Jihad" lecture the day before they finalized their plot, convinced that the cleric had given a *fatwah*, or blessing, to strike military targets on American soil.

A senior Homeland Security official warns that Aulaqi—whom he describes as "an al-Qaida supporter"—is actively targeting "U.S. Muslims with radical online lectures encouraging terrorist attacks from his new home in Yemen."[37]

CAIR AND THE 9/11 IMAM

Aulaqi also was involved briefly with the Virginia Jihad Network, led by a CAIR official. Before fleeing the country, Aulaqi met with the spiritual advisor to the Virginia jihadists, whose ringleader, Royer, worked out of CAIR's national headquarters.

Federal court records show Aulaqi met with Royer's mentor, Ali al-Timimi, the *imam* of a small storefront mosque a few miles from Dar al-Hijrah. The two spiritual leaders discussed recruitment of young Muslim men for jihad. Members of Royer's cell drove Aulaqi to al-Timimi's home for the meeting, and at least one had Aulaqi's phone number stored on his cell phone. Al-Timimi was later convicted of soliciting jihad and treason against the U.S.[38]

There's more to the Aulaqi-CAIR connection.

Al-Timimi's storefront mosque was located in the same Falls Church office building as a Muslim-run travel agency that booked trips to Saudi Arabia for the *hajj*, or Muslim pilgrimage to Mecca. Copies of its travel itinerary show Aulaqi acted as a tour guide for the trips. Listed directly under him was a trip advisor named Mohammad el-Mezain, who happens to be the CAIR fundraiser recently convicted of providing material support to terrorists in the Holy Land Foundation trial. El-Mezain co-founded the Hamas charitable front with CAIR director Elashi.

El-Mezain and Aulaqi, both hardcore Muslim Brothers, knew each other from San Diego. Before his arrest, el-Mezain headed Holy Land's San Diego office and, like Aulaqi, served as a leader in local mosques there.

But that's not all. The pair once lived in the same small Colorado apartment complex together.

According to federal investigators, el-Mezain likely met Aulaqi in Fort Collins, Colorado, around 1990, when the two were neighbors and attended the same local mosque. Authorities have traced el-Mezain's address at the time to 500 West Prospect Road in Fort Collins. Aulaqi also listed an address then at 500 West Prospect Road. El-Mezain occupied Apartment 19C, while Aulaqi occupied Apartment 23L.[39]

Investigators say that although Aulaqi has not been known to carry out the acts of violence he encourages, he is many times more dangerous than the terrorists who do. By getting dozens, perhaps hundreds, of young Muslim men jacked up for jihad with his radical sermons, he's a force multiplier for the enemy.

If anybody knows the identity of al-Qaida terrorists here inside America, investigators say, it's the American Aulaqi. He may even know about terror plots in the pipeline. If ever there were a candidate for waterboarding, they say, it's him.

Yet CAIR looks up to this 9/11 *imam* as a guru.[40]

For its part, CAIR argues that just because it consorts with or defends terrorists and terrorist groups doesn't mean it necessarily agrees with their activities. Like a defense attorney, it is merely standing up for their right to fair representation.

"Do we defend unpopular issues? Yes," says Corey P. Saylor, CAIR's national legislative director.

If that makes CAIR unpopular with critics, he argues, so be it—the organization is in good company.

"Before he became president, John Adams acted as legal representation to British soldiers accused of perpetrating the Boston Massacre," Saylor points out. "This act did not make him popular with his peers."[41]

But Omar Ahmad is no John Adams. Nor is Nihad Awad. And neither of them are lawyers. They are co-conspirators who share the violent and subversive agenda of the massacrers they support.

And unlike a criminal defense attorney, whose job begins and ends with making sure the state proves its case, CAIR keeps on defending terrorists even when juries return unanimous and overwhelming verdicts of guilt, as one did in 2008's Holy Land case—guilty on all 108 counts.

Moreover, CAIR's internal documents betray Saylor's explanation. They make it plain that his attempt to compare CAIR's motives to those of a Founding Father is just more patriotic eyewash designed to conceal from the public CAIR's true seditious agenda.

Privately, CAIR believes that it doesn't matter if terrorist suspects are guilty as charged. If they are Muslims accused by non-Muslims they are automatically innocent—and must always be defended and supported.

Witness a talking points memo found among Awad's files, and written in 2004—as the cases of Ismail Royer and his terrorist co-conspirator Masaud Khan were going to trial. It discusses the duty of Muslim leaders to do all they can to release imprisoned fellow Muslims.

"Give this talk as if it were your last before meeting Allah," the document says. "Discuss verses from the Quran and *ahadith* regarding the degree previous Muslim leaders went through to release fellow Muslim prisoners."[42]

The memo, which cites the Royer and Khan cases by name, goes on to praise Muslims who don't plea bargain and refuse to rat out other Muslims.

"Relate the difference between the brothers that have turned on their brothers by pleading guilty," it says, "and why we should come to the aid of those who are standing firm because of their conviction and *iman*," or faith.[43]

The memo ends by noting that CAIR is "working to build a legal fund for the purpose of providing high quality legal representation for current and future litigation against our brothers and sisters."

"Our community is under direct attack," it warns, "and we must join hands to defend ourselves in this time of uncertainty."[44]

U.S. AND ISRAELI 'TERRORISM'

CAIR also believes the only real terrorism is committed by Israel and the United States—in response to Muslim terrorism, ironically enough.

In fact, one of CAIR's in-house lawyers fired off a memo to top CAIR executives proposing the organization file a lawsuit against the U.S. and Israel "for conspiring to commit murder, kidnapping, property damage, and acts of terrorism."[45]

The alleged crime? Israel's counteroffensive against Hezbollah terrorists in Lebanon who in 2006 launched unprovoked and relentless rocket attacks against Israel.

"Defendants would include the United States and certain officials in the Bush administration and Israel and certain officials in its administration," wrote CAIR's Omar T. Mohammedi in an August 2006 memo to Awad and then-CAIR Chairman Parvez Ahmed.[46] And the plaintiffs, he suggested, would include Muslims harmed by Israel's military counterstrikes against Hezbollah positions, ostensibly including the terrorists themselves.

More galling, Mohammedi proposed filing the claim under the same federal racketeering and corruption statute, known as RICO, that the FBI and U.S. attorneys have considered using to prosecute CAIR and other fronts in the Muslim mafia.

With the revelation of such a brash legal stroke on behalf of Hezbollah, it should come as little surprise that CAIR also refuses to condemn Hezbollah as a terrorist group. Hamas, al-Qaida, Hezbollah...to CAIR, they're all victims—martyrs for "justice"—and we're the terrorists.

The only thing worse than supporting all these bad guys is supporting bad cops who spy for them. CAIR's done that, too, as we document next.

CHAPTER FIVE
CAIR'S BAD COP

"The Muslim is the brother of the Muslim. He does not betray him, lie to him, or hang back from coming to his aid."

—Ahmad ibn Naqib al-Misri, Reliance of the Traveller: A Classic Manual of Islamic Sacred Law

"Employment by a non-Muslim government of a Muslim investigator to investigate other Muslims places the investigator in the position of violating the tenets of his beliefs and may force his recourse to deception, lying, and/or the giving of misleading impressions."

—Declassified Pentagon counterintelligence briefing[1]

FORMER POLICE SERGEANT Mohammad Weiss Rasool took an oath to protect this country several years ago when he joined the Fairfax County Police Department, which is the largest force in Virginia and a key partner with the FBI in investigating major terrorism cases in the Washington area, including the 9/11 attack on the Pentagon.

But Rasool, an Afghan immigrant, got wrapped up with CAIR and put his religion ahead of his adopted country. In fact, he betrayed it.

A devout Sunni Muslim, he worshipped at an area mosque with at least one fellow Muslim who found himself under surveillance in a major terrorism investigation and approached his pal Rasool with concerns about unmarked cars that had been following him. Rasool agreed to help him by searching a classified federal police database. After confirming that FBI agents were tailing him, the sergeant tipped his Muslim brother off in a phone call.

When agents one morning went to arrest the terrorist target in a predawn raid, they found him and his family already dressed and destroying evidence. They knew they had a mole and worked back through the system to find Rasool.

That's when agents discovered the Muslim police officer had breached their database at least fifteen times to look up names of other Muslim contacts, including relatives, to see if they showed up on the terrorist watch list. And he learned that indeed some were on it.[2] (Thanks to post-9/11 data sharing, local police now have access to classified FBI files on terror suspects maintained within the NCIC, or National Crime Information Center system.)

Prosecutors say Rasool's unauthorized searches "damaged the integrity of the NCIC system and jeopardized at least one federal investigation," according to papers filed in federal court.[3]

"The defendant's actions could have placed federal agents in danger," prosecutors argued. "The FBI has had to undo the harm caused by the defendant."

Rasool, 32, at first denied knowing the terrorist target. He confessed only after hearing an intercepted recording of his message for the suspect, a cleric in his local Taliban-sympathizing mosque. Rasool finally pleaded guilty to illegally searching a federal database.[4]

"He's a habitual liar and a traitor," a senior FCPD official says. "He disgraced the uniform."[5]

CAIR'S 'PLANT'

Despite confessing to a serious security breach, Rasool will do no jail time. He was sentenced instead to two years of probation.

And he continued to collect a paycheck from taxpayers several months after his conviction. Fairfax County left him on the force pending the outcome of an internal investigation. He wasn't forced to resign until the summer of 2008.[6]

"It took them a very long time to finally do the right thing, but it got done," says a veteran FCPD detective. "It was embarrassing."[7]

The leniency afforded Rasool was unprecedented, given how he copped to the crime—and not just any crime, but one that betrayed his fellow officers and country.

Rasool, however, had a powerful patron in Washington—the Council on American-Islamic Relations, which lobbied on his behalf during his prosecution.

"I have always found Sergeant Rasool eager to promote a substantive relationship between the Fairfax County Police Department and the local Muslim community," wrote CAIR Governmental Affairs Coordinator Corey Saylor in a letter to the federal judge, who ended up denying prosecutors the jail time they requested for Rasool.

"His efforts played a significant role in improving trust in a time when mutual misunderstanding could easily severe [sic] all positive ties between these two groups," Saylor added.[8]

But if there was a "substantive relationship," it was between Rasool and CAIR.

"He was deeply embedded with CAIR," the department official says. "He was the spokesman to the department for CAIR."[9]

As CAIR's representative on the police force, Rasool actually took direction from CAIR's headquarters, even traveling into the District of Columbia to meet with CAIR Executive Director Nihad Awad, according to copies of the visitors register CAIR kept at its front desk at the time. Rasool, in fact, had several meetings at CAIR's headquarters between 2005 and 2008.[10]

He also arranged meetings between CAIR and Fairfax County's police chief to complain about surveillance of mosques and demand Muslim sensitivity training of officers, reveal emails obtained from CAIR's executive files.

"Our topics of discussion will be: Educational programs for the officers on the department about Islam and Muslims; presence of officers at the holy Muslim holidays for recruitment into the police departments; inmate assistance program with their respective mosque *imam*; youth group tours of police facilities; and a few other ideas and focal points," Rasool wrote in a 2006 email to Awad and other CAIR officials outlining the agenda of a forthcoming meeting at police headquarters.[11]

He reminded them to appear "friendly" and to avoid creating too much tension, so they can come back with more demands later on. "This will not end here," he assured them.

Rasool also told CAIR that he would give the police chief a copy of a report advocating kid-glove treatment of Arabs and Muslims by law enforcement.

"He was their plant," the official says. "We were convinced he was recruited by the Muslim Brotherhood."[12]

RED FLAGS

Veterans of the police force are scandalized by the security breach. They call Rasool an Islamic "spy" who committed treason for the enemy in the middle of a war on Islamic terrorists.

"He's a spy. I don't know how he qualified to be hired in the first place," says retired FCPD officer Vernon Zick, a thirty-four-year veteran of the department. "The feds should revoke his citizenship for his treasonous activity, and send him and his family back to Afghanistan."[13]

The department official says there were red flags raised during Rasool's application process, but they were overlooked as the department sought to diversify its work force and better reflect the county's burgeoning Muslim population. He also had a friend – a Muslim brother in blue – inside the department, who vouched for his loyalty … an officer who's not only still on the force, but closely collaborating with CAIR (more on him later).

Rasool in his seven years on the force managed to do other damage besides spying for terrorists.

He and other Muslim officers also worked with CAIR to kill a successful counterterror-training program within the department—a program that was designed in part to help police ferret out moles like Rasool.

The action casts further doubt on claims by CAIR and other Muslim groups that they seek cooperation with law enforcement to help apprehend terrorists. As we'll see next, their claim of cooperation is actually one of the biggest frauds perpetrated on the American public since 9/11.

CHAPTER SIX

COOPERATION? WHAT COOPERATION?

"They were warned by CAIR that we were coming to do a search warrant. We were pissed. It was obvious to us they knew we were coming."

—Senior investigator, FBI's Joint Terrorism Task Force in Washington, recalling blown raid of a Saudi-controlled jihadi seminary[1]

THE WASHINGTON-BASED HIGGINS CENTER for Counter Terrorism Research has trained more than eight thousand law enforcement officers in counterterrorism methods. They include hundreds of detectives and patrol officers from the Fairfax County Police Department, which works with the National Counter Terrorism Center and has originated or aided many of the FBI's major terrorism cases in the Washington area. Its jurisdiction includes Falls Church, Virginia, an al-Qaida hotbed.

The large northern Virginia police force contracted with the Higgins Center for training for several years without a complaint. The courses were taught by respected instructors Brian P. Fairchild, a former CIA officer who operated against radical Islamic targets in Southeast Asia and Europe, and Peter M. Leitner, a former Pentagon official who has taught at George Mason University's National Center for Biodefense.

But in 2006, the Fairfax County PD suddenly canceled the courses and did not invite the instructors back.

"We were essentially blackballed," Leitner recalls.[2] He cites complaints from the Council on American-Islamic Relations—which like many

Muslim Brotherhood front groups, publicly appears eager to cooperate with law enforcement officials while sabotaging their efforts behind the scenes.

CAIR claimed that one of the courses taught by the Higgins Center portrayed Islam in a bad light, police sources say. In at least two phone conversations, CAIR officials complained directly to Fairfax County Police Chief David Rohrer, and the chief eventually canceled the training in 2006.[3]

That same year, Rohrer spoke at CAIR's annual fundraising dinner in Washington, crediting the group with "helping police departments to better understand the Muslim community."

But the chief was being used—by the Islamist enemy. While he was breaking bread with CAIR, one of his officers working with CAIR at the time was under federal investigation for aiding and abetting terrorists.

And so was CAIR—the group from whom Rohrer was accepting phone calls and on whom he was conferring legitimacy. In fact, U.S. prosecutors at the time were adding CAIR to a list of co-conspirators in a terror scheme to funnel more than $12 million to Hamas suicide bombers and their families.

Yet CAIR persuaded the politically correct Rohrer to nix the anti-terror training, which included counterintelligence measures to help police guard against the very infiltration from terror supporters and facilitators that has taken place on Rohrer's watch.

In fact, CAIR had help on the inside. "CAIR was successful through two Muslim officers in getting the Higgins group removed from our training curriculum," a high-ranking FCPD official says.[4]

One of them was Fairfax County police sergeant Mohammad Weiss Rasool, who in 2008 pleaded guilty to illegally accessing a classified federal database to tip off a Muslim friend under surveillance as part of a terrorism investigation.

"This is precisely why Fairfax PD needs our training," Leitner says.

"They need to learn about Fifth Column activities and penetrating agents."[5] Sadly, he says, the chief appears more concerned with protecting the force from charges of "Islamophobia" than Islamist penetration.

"Let us choose tolerance over intolerance, acceptance over prejudice, and understanding over ignorance," Rohrer intoned at CAIR's banquet, which raised more than $600,000 and only made the job of his detectives that much harder.

Such funds aren't used just to raise "cultural awareness," as CAIR would have the public believe. They're also used to raise the banner of jihad overseas, while blocking counterterrorism training and investigations at home. The chief unwittingly helped the bad guys stay in business while denying his squad valuable training.

And contrary to CAIR's bellyaching, the Higgins Center did not teach anti-Islamic propaganda, insists the high-ranking FCPD official, who wished to go unnamed. The instructors keyed in on the militant part of Islam that's promoting terrorism and never bashed the faith or Muslims in general.

"They came in and talked truth," he says, noting that the human resources office had approved the course content. "They didn't follow some PC check-off list."

CAIR simply had an ax to grind, he says. The police department has actively worked cases against CAIR, including the investigation of former CAIR official Randall Ismail Royer, now serving twenty years in prison on terrorism-related charges.

The official says the Higgins Center's instruction in counterterror methods, which began in 2003, was valuable to patrol officers and detectives.

"If the Fairfax County police can't hear this," he says, "we are diminishing our ability to be effective in this particular environment."

WASHINGTON AND NEW YORK WILL 'TREMBLE'

Leitner points out that one Muslim cop who complained about the training felt compelled to defend Islam's peaceful and tolerant nature. But in doing so, ironically, he quoted a notorious Islamic extremist. He says the unidentified officer praised Maulana Maududi, the late violent Pakistani radical who preached that Islam will destroy the West.

"The objective of Islamic jihad is to put an end to the dominance of the un-Islamic systems of government and replace them with Islamic rule," wrote Maududi, founder of Pakistan's religious party Jamaat e-Islami.

"A time will come when capitalistic democracy will tremble for its safety in Washington and New York," he ominously warned before the 9/11 attacks on those cities.

CAIR actually uses works by Maududi for internal training, and recommends his books as "sources of *dawah* training material," according to a document found at its headquarters.[6] *Dawah* is the Muslim mission to convert others to Islam (others such as Royer, unfortunately).

The other Muslim officer who worked with CAIR to kill the Higgins Center training course happens to be from Pakistan. His name is Sergeant Naveed I. Butt, and he was Rasool's partner on the inside. In fact, it was Butt who conducted the original employee background investigation of Rasool, who was easily hired on his recommendation.[7] Essentially, a Muslim spy for the enemy was vetted by another Muslim, who as it turns out is equally suspect.

While Rasool is gone, Butt remains on the force. The son of a Pakistani government diplomat, he's also deeply embedded with CAIR, the department official says, and openly brags about his contacts with the group.

CAIR's guest register shows Butt traveled with Rasool to CAIR's headquarters at least twice to meet with officials there, once in 2007 and again in 2008.[8]

Also, Butt arranged a critical meeting between CAIR and the director of FCPD's criminal justice academy. The powwow took place the year before the academy canceled the Higgins Center training courses.

CAIR memorialized the meeting in an "activity report" written under the heading, "FFPD [*sic*] Training of Employees on Bias-Related Incidents."

According to CAIR's summary of the meeting, CAIR and other members of the Muslim mafia gave Fairfax County police academy director Major Tyrone Morrow "input in the formulation of the PD's new bias policy regarding Muslims." They specifically warned against "racial profiling and police misconduct."[9]

They also asked to train patrol officers in the proper Islamic way to respond to domestic violence calls at Muslim residences. Instead of cuffing and stuffing batterers, they suggested police respect Islamic law and allow local Muslim clerics to sort out guilt, offering counseling where necessary. Under Islamic law, husbands have the authority to beat their wives for disobedience. Therefore, they argued, Muslim men who beat their wives should be treated different from the public at large by police.

CAIR's three-page report notes that a video on handling "domestic violence situations involving Muslims" was prepared for Fairfax County police by CAIR and a group called FAITH,[10] which runs a Muslim thrift shop located inside one of the Herndon, Virginia office buildings raided by federal agents after 9/11. FAITH is headed by a woman named Suad Barzinji, who is related to Jamal Barzinji. A senior Muslim Brotherhood leader, he was arrested in 2000 by Fairfax County police and charged with "domestic abuse and resisting arrest," according to court records.[11]

Watchdogs against so-called "*Shariah* creep" warn that such politically correct policing could give amnesty to wife-beaters and keep their victims trapped in a cycle of violence.

This year's brutal murder of Aasiya Hassan is an object lesson, they say, in why police cannot look the other way in Muslim domestic-violence cases solely to appease religious zealots like CAIR, who want to erect a parallel legal system for the Brothers.

For several years, the Buffalo, New York, woman was serially beaten by her husband, Muzzammil "Mo" Hassan, founder of Bridges TV, a Muslim cable network heavily endorsed by CAIR. She finally filed for divorce and asked police for a restraining order.

'THE WORST FORM OF DOMESTIC VIOLENCE POSSIBLE'

But a restraining order didn't stop Hassan's supposedly "moderate" Muslim husband from attacking her again. In a horrific final confrontation, he sawed off her head with a large hunting knife in a suspected Islamic "honor killing," leaving their young children motherless.

"Obviously," the local district attorney remarked after the beheading, "this is the worst form of domestic violence possible."

Bridges TV began broadcasting in 2004. Hassan, a Pakistani immigrant who called CAIR chief Awad a friend and advisor, said he launched the network hoping to portray Muslims in a more positive light. To say he failed in that endeavor would be a howling understatement.

More than 80 percent of women in his native Pakistan suffer from domestic violence, according to ABC News. While that may be the accepted norm in Pakistan—which also happens to be Sergeant Butt's family home—it's a serious felony in America and throughout the civilized Western world.

Nonetheless, Butt has been shaping official department policy on behalf of the theocrats at CAIR since at least 2004, when he celebrated CAIR's opening of its Herndon office and pledged to "lend us his support," according to the CAIR report cited earlier.[12]

One of his allies in that office was none other than CAIR's phony lawyer Jamil Morris Days, who was later accused of fraud and had to leave the organization under an ethical cloud.

Days lodged complaints against the Fairfax County police department, including one over a terror alert the department issued to local school bus drivers.

In 2007, federal law enforcement received a credible threat that Islamic extremists in the United States were planning to hijack school buses loaded with children. As a safety precaution, Fairfax County police dispatched a detective to brief local school officials and bus drivers. CAIR got wind of the meeting, which gathered together more than seventeen hundred county bus drivers, and fired off a letter to the department claiming the briefing discriminated against Muslims. It took particular exception to a Department of Homeland Security video showing Palestinian suicide bombers.

"It is my unfortunate duty to report a case of religious discrimination perpetrated by one of the officers of Fairfax County Police Department," Days wrote, claiming the detective made "derogatory statements concerning members of Islam."

In the future, Days demanded, CAIR will "expect officers assigned to the community not to be so biased and intolerant and insensitive" to Muslims.[13]

The police department's internal affairs bureau ruled his charges "unfounded," according to police records, and the detective, Kenneth Larson, was not disciplined. The police chief, meanwhile, received a letter signed by more than two hundred bus drivers thanking Larson for his "outstanding" presentation.[14]

It was yet another example of CAIR undercutting efforts by police to protect Americans—in this case schoolchildren—from Islamic terrorists.

Even more maddening to career law enforcement officials is that some of their own officers, including Sergeant Butt, are helping CAIR undermine their efforts to investigate suspicious activity in the Muslim community and keep the post-9/11 public informed about threats.

"The problem is, we're letting Muslim officers dictate policy and determine what we will and won't hear" about the threat from militant Islam and jihadists, says the high-ranking Fairfax County police official.

"These officers are advocates for CAIR," he adds, "and we're letting them win."

And Chief Rohrer is letting more of them into the department. He's promised the Fairfax County Board of Supervisors to continue diversifying the police force to reflect the county's changing demographics, which now include some of the heaviest concentrations of Muslims in the nation. This of course is music to the ears of the subversives at CAIR.

MUSLIM MOLES INSIDE THE NYPD?

CAIR may have also infiltrated law enforcement agencies in New York.

In August 2007, the president of the Brooklyn-based Islamic Officers Benevolent Association pledged his undying support to CAIR. "As Muslims and law enforcement officers, we are prepared to support your field operations in New York," wrote Michael G. Kilpatrick, aka Abdul Saboor, in a letter to CAIR research director Mohamed Nimer found among the files at CAIR's headquarters.[15]

That same month, CAIR mounted a PR offensive against a report from the intelligence branch of the New York Police Department. Entitled "Radicalization in the West: The Homegrown Threat," the report warned that seemingly law-abiding young Muslim men in America can be turned into terrorists through jihadi indoctrination.

CAIR quickly condemned the report as racist. And a confidential CAIR memo reveals its New York operatives feverishly lobbied NYPD officials to amend the report by softening its conclusion that young Muslim men pose a high security risk.

"There are not enough *caveats* in the report to prevent profiling" of such Muslims, worried Faiza N. Ali, community affairs director for CAIR's New York chapter.[16]

It's not the first time the militant Muslim pressure group has directly interfered in internal police anti-terror operations.

After CAIR complained that police in Anaheim, California were seeking information about terrorist suspects from Muslim owners of restaurants and bookstores clustered in a part of the city known as "Little Arabia," the Anaheim police chief reassigned part of his intelligence unit and agreed to put his entire force of seven hundred through Islamic sensitivity training taught by CAIR.

The group also torpedoed a program by Los Angeles police to map potential terror hotbeds in the Muslim community. CAIR cried "religious profiling" and joined the ACLU to kill the plan, which was announced as the FBI warned police that shopping malls in L.A. were possible al-Qaida targets.

The Los Angeles-based Muslim Public Affairs Council also joined the protest. "All Muslim organizations are united in purpose to defend the rights of Muslim Americans," said MPAC executive director Salam al-Marayati, if not necessarily united to defend the country from terrorism. (Until recently, MPAC's political operations were headed by a three-time felon and ex-con, who will be introduced in a later chapter.)

By mapping the local Muslim community, the LAPD would increase its chances of disrupting such plots. Its counterterrorism unit hoped to ID areas that might be more isolated and removed—and therefore riper targets for radicalization and even al-Qaida recruitment.

Shining a spotlight on these neighborhoods would take the terrorists and their facilitators out of the shadows where they prefer to operate.

"We just don't know enough about the communities," explained deputy LAPD chief Michael Downing, adding that the planned mapping project "has nothing to do with profiling."[17]

But predictably, CAIR claimed Muslims were not more likely to commit violent acts than people of other faiths, ignoring overwhelming statistical evidence to the contrary. Just since 9/11, more than nine thousand separate violent acts have been carried out in the name of Islam.[18]

As Islamic terror expert Robert Spencer points out, we don't "see Presbyterians blowing themselves up in crowded restaurants, Buddhists flying planes into buildings, and Amish waving placards crowing that they will soon dominate the world."[19]

It's in the moderates' best interest to help police expose the extremists. That way police can narrow their surveillance and gather more useful intelligence to protect not only society at large, but also moderate Muslims who eschew violence.

But of course, CAIR is not moderate, and it considers the police the enemy—despite its public rhetoric about helping the authorities.

In fact, there is growing evidence that CAIR is at war with police, along with the rest of the Muslim mafia.

MYTH OF MUSLIM COOPERATION

Dealing a major blow to CAIR, the FBI in 2008 cut off formal ties to the group due to its terrorist co-conspirator listing. When the disengagement policy was made public in early 2009, CAIR rallied other Muslim Brotherhood front groups to fire off a threatening letter to the FBI. The letter suggested that if the bureau didn't restore outreach relations with CAIR, they would band together and deny the FBI information about "acts of violence" and "threats" in the Muslim community (as if they had provided such information previously).[20]

Calling themselves "American Muslims in the American mainstream," this *cabal* of Muslim Brothers essentially threatened to boycott the FBI and its terrorism fighting efforts if it didn't reopen political access for a group that supports jihad and *Shariah* law, and has been named as an unindicted co-conspirator in the war on terror.

The list of signatories to their open letter to the FBI is a veritable who's who of Muslim Brotherhood front groups. And roughly half of the groups in its so-called American Muslim Taskforce either show up on the Justice Department's list of co-conspirators in the Holy Land Foundation terror case or in Muslim Brotherhood manifestos and other secret documents.

Regrettably, they represent the Muslim establishment in America. And outrageously, its leaders are now declaring war on law enforcement, threatening to withhold information about sleeper terrorists or homegrown jihadists secreted within the Muslim community.

But FBI agents in Washington suspect these groups are already withholding such information. And they say they could only chuckle when they read the taskforce's missive, entitled "U.S. Muslim Coalition Considers Suspending Relations With FBI." They were particularly amused by the claim that CAIR and the other Muslim groups have been instrumental in preventing terrorism.

"Muslim Americans continue to be a positive and stabilizing force in keeping our nation safe and secure from acts of violence and foreign threats," claims the letter demanding the FBI reinstate outreach with CAIR. "Despite fear-mongering by a vocal minority, Muslim Americans are natural allies of law enforcement agencies in ensuring the well-being of our nation."

In fact, agents assert, nothing could be further from the truth.

"That's pretty interesting, because I know the FBI can't point to one time—not even one time—when this [Muslim] outreach program has produced any information that's of investigative value," says a senior FBI special agent, who works counterterrorism cases out of the Washington field office.[21]

Fairfax County's return on its own politically correct outreach to CAIR and other Muslim groups isn't any better. "The number of leads we've received directly related to some major [counterterrorism] investigation is zero to none," says the high-ranking Fairfax County police official.

About the only information that CAIR has offered to law enforcement relates to civil rights infractions, they say, such as alleged hate crimes. And CAIR has wildly exaggerated anti-Muslim abuses, as we will document in a forthcoming chapter.

"They love to come to our outreach venues and bitch about their civil rights," the senior FBI agent says.

Indeed, the American Muslim Taskforce even called its 2008 election plan: "A civil rights plus agenda," with the "plus" focusing almost exclusively on issues of interest to Muslims. And according to its Web site, it solicits feedback from the Muslim community about civil rights more than about any other issue. Terrorism, in contrast, doesn't even rank as an issue.

The agent says cooperation is a one-way street with CAIR and other Muslim groups. The FBI listens and responds to their complaints, but they don't return the favor. The agency has to beg for their help in finding potential terrorists. Virtually the only kind of investigating they want the FBI doing involves hate crimes against Muslims—and CAIR lumps anti-terrorist crackdowns in with that category.

CAIR insists that it "sincerely values" the FBI and all that it does to protect the country. But more importantly, it values all that the bureau does to protect the Muslim community.

"When a hate crime is committed against Muslims or their institutions," CAIR's legislative director Corey Saylor says, "it is the FBI we turn to for help." Uh-huh, and if they value the FBI, it's mainly for that reason. And even then, they have little, if any, respect for it or other law enforcement.[22]

Listen to popular CAIR lecturer Zaid Shakir, for one example. He constantly belittles the agency in speeches to Muslims, even warning them that it frames Muslims for terrorism that it secretly commits. "The World Trade Center bombing of course was aided and abetted by our good friends at the FBI," the *imam* contends in just one of the many wild-eyed conspiracy theories he peddles.[23]

'RACIST, FASCIST, CRIMINAL FBI'

And a close ally of *imam* Siraj Wahhaj, a longtime CAIR advisory board member and major fundraiser, spews anti-FBI venom at Wahhaj's mosque in Brooklyn. Al-Hajj Idris Muhammad warns Muslims that the FBI is racist and "will fabricate a case against you." He advises followers to refuse cooperation:

> Never speak with the racist, fascist, criminal FBI. Never allow them in your home or office without a warrant. Have your attorney advise the racist, fascist, criminal FBI never to approach or harass you or any soldier in your Muslim community or political organization. If the racist, fascist, criminal FBI authorizes its criminal agents to harass the believers in your *masjid* (mosque), community or organization, you must alert all of the believers not to cooperate with the racist, fascist, criminal FBI.[24]

While CAIR says it encourages its members to cooperate with the FBI, it privately counsels them to clam up.

"They're trying to paint the picture that they're such a valuable tool to law enforcement," says the senior FBI officer in Washington. "Yet they tell their constituents: Don't speak to law enforcement."

In fact, CAIR distributes a "Muslim community safety kit" at mosques that advises Muslims to "Know your rights." Remember, it warns, if you are visited by agents:

> You do not have to talk to the FBI. You have no obligation to talk to the FBI, even if you are not a citizen. Never meet with them or answer any questions without an attorney present.

> You do not have to permit them to enter your home or office.... Even if they have a warrant, you are under no obligation to answer questions.

> ... It is better to refuse to answer any questions ... .[25]

Terrorist defense lawyer Ashraf Nubani, who works closely with CAIR, puts a finer point on it in a compact disc circulating in suburban Washington DC mosques:

> There is no reason that anyone should ever, ever, ever talk to law enforcement as Muslims in the United States. The FBI is just a tool of whoever is wielding it. And right now it is very bad, it is very bad, it is very bad.[26]

Remarkably, some of the *imams* who preach at these mosques, such as the ADAMS Center near Herndon, and who allow these CDs to be distributed, serve on the FBI advisory committee set up after 9/11 to alert the FBI to both terrorist threats and anti-Muslim crimes. Little wonder the only tips the FBI gets deal with the latter.

Dar al-Hijrah, the 9/11 mosque, has even "ex-communicated members who they suspected of cooperating with us," says an FBI case agent whose beat includes Dar al-Hijrah, which he describes as a "hotbed" of terrorist activity.[27]

During the last presidential election, GOP congressman Pete King of New York wondered why so many mosques around the country "don't cooperate with law enforcement."[28] The reason is now clear: CAIR and its allies are telling them not to.

But more than that, they're coaching them to mislead investigators and obstruct their terrorism investigations.

The smoking-gun evidence is contained in a six-page confidential report generated by a senior CAIR official, who on the third anniversary of 9/11 helped a prominent Muslim figure under FBI inquiry to obstruct a line of questioning by agents.

In September 2004, a pair of agents arranged an interview with the Muslim leader of a Maryland mosque that the FBI was investigating for suspicious activity. The mosque leader alerted CAIR, and CAIR sent Shama Farooq, then the civil rights director for its Maryland chapter, to coach him through the interview.

Farooq wrote a detailed plan covering what Dr. Sayeed Ahmed, president of the Islamic Society of Western Maryland, should and shouldn't say. The predominantly Pakistani mosque is controlled by ISNA and the Muslim Brotherhood.

"Oftentimes, these meetings are used to get information about other community members," she warned in the plan she devised. "It is important, first of all, *not to talk about anyone else at all*" (emphasis in the original).[29]

'DO NOT ADDRESS QUESTIONS RELATING TO TERRORISM'

Also, "If the agent wants contact information for anyone else, *you should not give any numbers or addresses out*—let him find the people the same [way] he found you," she advised (emphasis in original).

Farooq also insisted Ahmed turn his cell phone off, and keep it out of the sight and reach of the agents during the interview.

Finally, she advised, "You are not required to tell them which Islamic centers you attend, how many times a day you pray, who you give charity to, and which organizations you are associated with."

"Definitely," she stressed, "do not address any questions relating to terrorism or violence and their place in Islam."[30]

That was step number one. Then Farooq and Ahmed went to lunch the day of the scheduled interview with the FBI—September 1, 2004— to review her ground rules, the secret CAIR memo details. They agreed she would sit in on the meeting.

Following lunch, they went back to his office and continued to "discuss strategies," including introducing her to the agents only as "a sister in Islam," while not identifying her position with CAIR up front. And she again specifically advised Ahmed not to answer any questions regarding information he may know about terrorism or violence.

The agents arrived at Ahmed's office on time, and over the course of their interview, Farooq stepped in to stop Ahmed from answering several questions she felt could "incriminate" him, even though she was not his attorney.

As a result, Ahmed withheld critical information from the FBI. For example:

• Agents inquired about his recent travels abroad, and he mentioned only Canada, while neglecting to inform them that he'd also traveled to Saudi Arabia;

• Agents asked him about his charitable donations, and he withheld the fact that his wife had given cash to the Holy Land Foundation, which he knew at the time was designated a terrorist organization by the U.S.;

• Agents inquired what he knew about the Islamic Center of Morgantown, West Virginia, and he failed to tell them that one of his sons is a vice president there who's contributed more than $10,000 to its coffers.

The FBI agents, who were attached to the bureau's Pittsburgh field office and led by agent Terry Grzadzielewski, left the meeting unaware they were denied information relevant to their investigation—thanks to CAIR's operative running interference on behalf of the subject of their inquiry that day.

Farooq reported details of the FBI meeting, including Ahmed's omissions, to CAIR-Maryland/Virginia chapter executive director Rizwan Mowlana, who had assigned her to spy on the FBI. A copy of the confidential memo—which is marked DO NOT RELEASE OUTSIDE CAIR— was obtained from CAIR's internal files.[31]

At the end of her report, Farooq recommended CAIR gather local Muslims who worship at Ahmed's mosque in Hagerstown, Maryland, to formally train them in similar deception and obstruction tactics.

"Since the Hagerstown community seems to be a center of attention for several FBI agents," she wrote, "I recommend CAIR conduct a know-your-rights lecture at the location with some recommendations [on] how to respond to FBI agents when approached by them."[32]

At the same time, Farooq recommended mailing the FBI's Pittsburgh field office a copy of CAIR's "Law Enforcement Official's Guide to the Muslim Community," followed by "sensitivity training" for all its agents.

DON'T TOUCH MUSLIM SUSPECTS

We obtained a copy of CAIR's largely unhelpful law enforcement guide, which for the most part dictates terms to police—the dos and don'ts (and mostly don'ts) of investigating Muslims. Here is a summary:

• Don't demand eye contact from Muslim suspects.

• Don't frisk them.

• Never use dogs to search Muslim homes.

• Remove shoes before entering homes and mosques.

• Don't mishandle the Quran during searches.

• Don't step on prayer rugs.

• "Keep a physical space when dealing with members of the Muslim community," CAIR's police guide mandates. "Some Muslims may be uncomfortable with gestures that include any touching."[33]

The booklet spends nine pages lecturing cops about Islamic tenets and how to respect them, and none offering cops cultural clues to help them identify extremists and jihadists in the Muslim community.

Law enforcement officials say they are still waiting for the CAIR booklet entitled, "How Patriotic Muslims Can Help Law Enforcement Catch Terrorists."

Particularly galling, the expert whom CAIR tasked with lecturing cops has an extremist background himself. Mohamed Nimer, who wrote CAIR's police guide, previously worked for the United Association for Studies and Research, a known Hamas terrorist front.

The FBI would never actually respect any of CAIR's churlish wishes, would it? It would never give in to such demands at the expense of an investigation, right? Think again.

In 2004, for instance, the FBI raided an Islamic "cultural center" in a northern Virginia suburb on suspicions of terrorist activity. But before agents executed the search warrant, the FBI foolishly told CAIR that the raid was going to take place so that CAIR officials could be on site to monitor the conduct and sensitivity of agents.

By the time agents showed up at the Saudi-controlled Institute for Islamic and Arabic Sciences in America in Merrifield, Virginia, the building was practically an "empty box," as one investigator described it.

"By the time we went in, the place was sterile. They'd cleaned it out," adds the senior investigator, who works with the FBI's Joint Terrorism Task Force in Washington. "It was bad. It was really bad."

What happened? "They were warned by CAIR that we were coming to do a search warrant," explains the law enforcement official, who helped execute the search warrant. "We were pissed. It was obvious to us they knew we were coming."[34]

Who got the courtesy call from the FBI that morning? The same CAIR official cited earlier—CAIR-MD/VA executive director Rizwan Mowlana—who'd assigned the "sister in Islam" to coach the Maryland mosque president and help obstruct the FBI's questioning of him.[35]

"Being well-networked among the interfaith, law enforcement, and political leadership in your area allows you to be informed of many events before they happen," CAIR advises staff in training seminars.[36] The outreach strategy has paid off royally for CAIR and its terrorist constituents.

HUNT FOR EL-SHUKRIJUMAH

Consider also the case of al-Qaida operative Adnan el-Shukrijumah, the Saudi-born son of a Florida mosque leader who'd once served as a translator for the Blind Sheik, Omar Abdel Rahman. After the FBI added el-Shukrijumah, aka Jaffar the Pilot, to the most-wanted terrorist list as potentially "another Mohamed Atta," a national manhunt ensued.

Fairfax County police were heavily involved in the hunt because some of el-Shukrijumah's relatives—including a sister and a brother—lived in Herndon, Virginia, where CAIR and the Muslim Brotherhood have a strong presence. Even though police suspected el-Shukrijumah, a naturalized U.S. citizen, visited the area, they say the Muslim community there completely clammed up when they asked about his whereabouts.

"We went around to their employers around Herndon and showed pictures of their brother who's wanted, and miraculously, nobody ever saw him," says the high-ranking Fairfax County police official. Oddly, his family members claimed they had no phone number or address for him, and they couldn't explain why they kept no personal contact information for him.[37]

One time, Fairfax County police found el-Shukrijumah's father staying in Herndon. "We caught him back up here staying with the daughter when everybody was looking for his son," the official says. "Wouldn't you know he didn't know where he was either."[38] The father, an *imam* who received regular stipends from the Saudi embassy before passing away in 2004, strenuously denied his son has terrorism ties.

Desperate, authorities turned to CAIR in Washington and Florida to help get the word out to the Muslim community about the search. CAIR complied, while also issuing press statements holding up the el-Shukrijumah family as a pillar of the community and praising it for its cooperation—even as the suspected al-Qaida terrorist's mother and father made their own statements proclaiming their son's innocence and suggesting he should remain in hiding. El-Shukrijumah's parents even tipped him off that the FBI was asking questions about him when they spoke with him by phone.[39]

CAIR at the same time pooh-poohed el-Shukrijumah's connections to al-Qaida, suggesting the FBI had exaggerated the danger he poses.[40]

THE GUYANA BUNCH

In a related development, recently declassified U.S. Muslim Brotherhood documents reveal that the Brotherhood in America—which is led in part by CAIR's founders—has established operations in, of all places, the

South American country of Guyana.

El-Shukrijumah happens to have been raised in Guyana, and some suspect he may be hiding there, if not in Pakistan.

Brotherhood leaders over the past couple of decades have sent money to Guyana to support an unnamed *imam* and his mosque, and an unidentified "institute," according to one document.

They've also traveled to Guyana to visit the "Guyana brothers," but it's not immediately known if any of them had contacts with the el-Shukrijumahs while traveling there. Known among al-Qaida operatives as "the South American," el-Shukrijumah has a Guyanese passport, as well as possibly a Trinidadian passport. His late father, Sheik Gulshair, was born in Guyana and worked there as a Muslim missionary, helping to establish a mosque with Saudi funding. He also has aunts and uncles who still live in the country.

In that same, little-noticed Brotherhood document listing the 1991-1992 goals of its "South America Committee" (which includes the Caribbean), the final item on the list—goal No. 169—reads: "Organizing the Caribbean group in cooperation with Sh. New York."[41]

Sh. is a common abbreviation for sheik, and investigators believe the cryptic reference to "Sh. New York" may refer to the Blind Sheik, the convicted terrorist who at that time was in Brooklyn plotting to blow up the World Trade Center and other New York landmarks. Or possibly el-Shukrijumah's father himself, who was assigned to the Blind Sheik's mosque in Brooklyn to do translation work for him in the early '90s. He was commonly known among the Brothers as "Sheikh Gulshair."

Also recall that CAIR founder Omar Ahmad embraced and hosted the Blind Sheik at his home during this same period in which he and the Brotherhood wrote their South American plan. And during a 2001 staffwide CAIR meeting, internal notes reveal that Ahmad suggested stepping up CAIR's "Guyanese" outreach operations.[42]

These connections beg the question: How close are CAIR's leaders to the el-Shukrijumahs? And how much do they know about Adnan el-Shukrijumah's travels and contacts? Have they disclosed all they know to authorities?

These are critical questions because the U.S. government has fingered the street-smart el-Shukrijumah as the ultimate al-Qaida "sleeper agent," and a cell leader potentially more dangerous than even 9/11 ringleader Atta. In fact, he's said to have been handpicked by 9/11 mastermind Khalid Sheikh Mohammed to carry out an encore plot to detonate nuclear devices in several U.S. cities simultaneously.

El-Shukrijumah remains at large, however, thanks in part to a lack of cooperation from the Muslim community, investigators say.

'UMMAH FIRST'

The senior Fairfax County police official offers that while detectives have received help from Muslim leaders solving crimes such as bank robberies, terrorism is another story.

"We have gone to them and said, 'Hey, we want to know about the bad uncle from Baghdad. You know, tell us about that stuff,'" he says. "And they have cooperated with us."

"For instance," he says, "we had an Egyptian bank robber, and they helped us find the bank robber and bring him in."

But he says when it comes to ratting out jihadists in their midst, forget it. The Muslim Brotherhood-controlled mosques brainwash adherents to think spying on a Muslim for a non-Muslim is nothing less than *kufr*—or betrayal—and that Allah, in turn, will betray them on Judgment Day.

"Most of our [terrorism] leads are generated, or they're created. They're not walk-ins," the police official says. "They're not walking in and going,

'You know what? This isn't right. I'm an American first, and these people at my mosque are up to no good.'"

"No," he adds, "it doesn't happen."

He explains that Brotherhood leaders never let the faithful forget that their religion must trump any loyalty to country.

"It's the *ummah* first," he says, referring to the Arabic term for the global nation, or brotherhood, of Muslims.

Even when police get Muslim suspects in custody, it's hard to get them to talk. "We have flipped people," the official says, "but only after appealing to their darker angels" by threatening incarceration or deportation.

"They come around, but it's always kicking and screaming," he adds. "Or it's because they're not quite believing that there's seventy-two virgins waiting for them" in Paradise if they refuse to cooperate and rot as martyrs in prison.

While it's not impossible to develop sources in the Muslim community, the official cautions that "you have to make sure they're not doubled, and that they're not going to sell you out."

The high risk of Muslims double-crossing authorities makes recruiting good informants exceptionally difficult. And in lieu of trusted Muslim informants, they've had to resort to infiltrating mosques with undercover agents and non-Muslim informants posing as Muslims.

This practice, of course, has sent Muslim groups like CAIR and ISNA into high dudgeon. In fact, ISNA claims to have met this spring with FBI officials to formally complain about the FBI planting a spy in the Islamic Center of Irvine, California.

The spy helped the agency gather information about a brother-in-law of Osama bin Laden's chief bodyguard, Ahmadullah Niazi. According to the Associated Press, that spy "recorded Niazi on multiple occasions talking about blowing up buildings, acquiring weapons, and sending money to the Afghan *mujahideen*."

Never mind that, harrumphs ISNA. Mosques are sacred ground—inviolable. "The mosques are our communities' most valued assets," ISNA asserts, "and we will work to protect them."

CAIR also huffed about the FBI sending in an "agent provocateur" to the Irvine mosque and others in the area, claiming the move has rekindled American Muslims' "feelings of anger" and "mistrust" toward the FBI.

"Infiltrating mainstream mosques the way FBI informants infiltrate white supremacist groups illustrates the FBI's perception of American Muslims as a community that must be constantly monitored, instead of being treated as an equal partner in fighting crime and terrorism," it said in a prepared statement.

Once again, the Islamic supremacists at CAIR merely demonstrate they care more about protecting a mosque (that's hardly "mainstream") than helping the FBI prevent a massive attack on a shopping mall by a known al-Qaida operative using that mosque as a terror sanctuary and recruiting ground. The Islamic Center of Irvine is partnered with the Islamic Center of Orange County, a Muslim Brotherhood mosque that groomed Adam Gadahn, the "American al-Qaida" who's wanted by the FBI for treason.

CAIR spokesman Ibrahim Hooper warns that monitoring Muslims will only alienate "the very people whose help is necessary in the war on terrorism."

But such patriotic-sounding rhetoric has proved empty, and the FBI is no longer buying it.

CAIR'S PROTECTION RACKET

CAIR never fails to advertise how it's tried to partner with the FBI to help agents combat terrorism. But behind the scenes, they train Muslims not to talk to the FBI and not to inform on fellow Muslims who may be involved in violent activities against the U.S. They've put up a protective shield around the entire Muslim community in America to keep law enforcement out—and terrorists operating in the shadows.

"Why don't they tell us where they've provided all this information that's kept us safe, because it just hasn't happened," the senior FBI officer in Washington says. "It's a total fabrication."[43]

In fact, it's more likely CAIR has *withheld* information. CAIR's internal records show its executives have personally received correspondence from Muslim extremists threatening violence, and kept mum about it.

In 2007, for example, executive director Awad received a two-page fax marked "urgent" from an angry CAIR member threatening "to use force" against America and Israel to avenge what he called the "murder" of the Palestinian people by "those Zionist criminals." He begged Awad and CAIR to demand an end to Israeli "crimes" "before I respond with force."[44]

Equally wary of CAIR are the Fairfax County police, who are behind many of the big terrorism busts made along northern Virginia's so-called Wahhabi Corridor. Department officials say it's clear the group and its partners like ISNA are only pretending to cooperate with law enforcement to catch terrorists.

"I don't trust any of them," says the high-ranking Fairfax police official.

In fact, their efforts at outreach are more than likely part of a Muslim Brotherhood ploy to spy on law enforcement. "It says in their founding documents that they do outreach in order to keep tabs on the government," the FBI official says.

Indeed, according to one document found at a Muslim Brotherhood safehouse in Virginia, monitoring the FBI is a key function of the various front groups to secure the U.S. Brotherhood network against such "outside dangers."

In the document, Muslim Brotherhood leader Zeid al-Noman describes strategies they use to gather intelligence to thwart law enforcement investigations. "For instance," he says, "monitoring the government bodies—such as the CIA, FBI, etc.—so that we find out if they are monitoring us [and] how can we get rid of them."[45]

Since 9/11, the FBI has appeared to play right into the ploy. The bureau's political outreach to such front groups has been gratuitous to the point of embarrassment.

However, FBI headquarters recently has started to pull up the welcome mat to such groups in response to growing incriminating evidence against them and complaints from case agents demoralized by the repeated concessions.

CHAPTER SEVEN
PC OUTREACH RUN AMOK

"Political correctness has darn near beaten common-sense police work to death."

—Ben R. Furman, former FBI counterterrorism chief, Detroit[1]

L ESS THAN A WEEK after the 9/11 attacks, President Bush appeared at the Islamic Center of Washington alongside officials from CAIR and other outwardly benign Muslim groups that weren't properly vetted, as the White House basically surrendered the vetting process to the Saudi-funded Islamic Center.

"It is my honor to be meeting with leaders who feel just the same way I do," an unsuspecting Bush announced. "They're outraged, they're sad. They love America just as much as I do."[2]

Cameras captured the Muslim leaders rubbing shoulders with the president during the ill-advised photo opportunity, which unfortunately was just one of many that have provided CAIR and other Muslim mob bosses with valuable political insurance.

"CAIR Executive Director Nihad Awad stands to the president's left," CAIR notes below a treasured photo of Bush and Awad that the group has posted on its Web site. It offers it up as proof that "CAIR officials have met or regularly meet with U.S. presidents," and therefore can't possibly be in league with terrorists.[3]

The radical front group is even prouder of its engagement with federal law enforcement. It's a relationship based for the most part on threats and appeasement, however, with CAIR charging cultural insensitivity or outright discrimination, and federal authorities bending over backward to prove otherwise.

On its Web site, CAIR clucks about senior FBI officials attending its annual banquets, and senior CAIR officials huddling with FBI brass at the J. Edgar Hoover Building in Washington.

"CAIR has established a status of enviable prestige within [the] highest echelons of the 'Washington establishment,'" the group brags.[4]

While CAIR has been known to exaggerate, its boasts are all too true in this case. In fact, CAIR's hostile information campaign against the feds has been so successful that both the FBI and Homeland Security have invited it to conduct sensitivity training seminars for their agents, a dangerous disinformation campaign designed to desensitize police to the threat from Islamic terrorism.

How did this happen? After 9/11, the PC-addled FBI—the organization that's supposed to be on the front line in our domestic defense against terrorists and their supporters—made outreach to CAIR and other dubious Muslim groups a top priority, and even tied senior-level performance bonuses to outreach activity.

In perhaps the ultimate concession, headquarters recently proposed sending agents on field trips to area mosques allied with CAIR and its sister group ISNA for cultural awareness education. The FBI also offered to sponsor special summer camps for Muslim youth, internal bureau documents reveal.

"The FBI praises CAIR's dedication in representing the heart of the Muslim American community," the agency gushed in one congratulatory letter to CAIR.[5]

But then in the summer of 2008, the bureau suddenly stopped blowing kisses to CAIR. And the group's unfettered political access—and blanket immunity—came to an abrupt halt.

During a previous search of a terrorist suspect's home in the Washington suburbs, agents with the FBI's Washington field office discovered a trove of secret documents naming CAIR and other "mainstream" groups as part of a Muslim Brotherhood conspiracy to support terrorism and to infiltrate and destroy the American system from within. The documents were entered as evidence in the largest terror-financing case in American history, and prosecutors listed CAIR among the front groups participating in the conspiracy.

The listing reopened the debate over CAIR's terror ties, and made outreach to CAIR politically untenable for the bureau, as much as some politically correct higher-ups wanted it to continue. Fresh evidence also emerged triggering a closer look at CAIR's executives and their connections to Hamas – namely, CAIR's founding chairman Omar Ahmad and its active executive director Awad.[6] CAIR's legal defense team tried to flash the group's grip-and-grin photos with President Bush as proof it was not radical, but the federal judge hearing the case was not impressed. He left CAIR on the government blacklist.

"We were laughing about that one in the office," says a senior FBI agent in the Washington field office. "We said we wouldn't have to dig very deep and we can get you a picture of Alamoudi standing with Bush as well—and that guy is sitting in the pen."[7] Abdurahman Alamoudi, another Muslim Brotherhood leader and a former CAIR advisory board member, schmoozed Washington politicians while secretly raising millions for al-Qaida, and is now serving twenty-three years in federal prison for plotting terrorism.

FBI headquarters for years had put aside misgivings about CAIR, but faced with the new evidence, headquarters in August of 2008 finally decided to reverse its policy and sever formal outreach ties with CAIR and its national leadership.

"We have suspended any formal engagement with Council on American-Islamic Relations field offices around the country," FBI spokesman John Miller confirmed in a letter to Congress.[8] No longer will representatives of CAIR be a part of any organized committee or group sponsored by the FBI, including the FBI's Arab/Muslim, Sikh American Advisory Committee, which meets regularly in Washington.

"The adjustment in our contacts with CAIR comes in part as a result of evidence gathered through FBI investigations and presented in connection with the Holy Land Foundation trial," Miller explained. "CAIR was listed as an unindicted co-conspirator in that case."

A shaken CAIR responded by rallying other Muslim groups to threaten the FBI with a community-wide boycott. Calling itself the American Muslim Taskforce on Civil Rights and Elections, the coalition of predominantly Muslim Brotherhood fronts vowed it would never allow CAIR to be marginalized.

"If the FBI does not accord fair and equitable treatment to every American Muslim organization including CAIR, ISNA, and NAIT [the North American Islamic Trust, an ISNA subsidiary that underwrites U.S. mosques], then Muslim organizations, mosques, and individuals will have no choice but to consider suspending all outreach activities with FBI offices, agents, and other personnel," the coalition warned.[9]

It was a hollow threat, however, because the entire coalition brought little to the table and therefore had little to take away. The main reason the FBI created the Muslim outreach program was to generate counterterrorism leads, and these Muslim groups have not been helpful in that regard, FBI case agents agree.

CRACKS IN THE POLICY

Privately, CAIR says it regrets the recent FBI decision.[10] But it's counting on the more Muslim-friendly Obama administration reversing it.

"We're hoping that once [Attorney General] Eric Holder puts the department in order and places people in different positions, we can reestablish what were very positive relations [with the FBI] in our fifteen-year history," CAIR spokesman Hooper says.[11]

They may not have to wait very long. Cracks in the new disengagement policy have already formed.

Just seven days after it was put into effect, FBI spokesman and assistant director Miller created a questionnaire and promised CAIR officials he would let them back in the door if they could answer it satisfactorily and put certain doubts to rest. He invited them up to the executive suites located on the seventh floor of the Hoover building to discuss the policy.

Agents were floored when they found out.

"Miller decided to bring them up for tea," says veteran FBI agent John Guandolo, who has investigated CAIR and helped put the policy together. "We said, 'What the f***? No! These are the bad guys. This is Hamas. What are you doing?!'"[12]

They cracked that they wouldn't be surprised if Miller set up "a hookah bar for them on the seventh floor." The deal was scuttled after agents howled.

Miller, a former ABC News correspondent who once interviewed Osama bin Laden, is in charge of the bureau's outreach program, and has personally hosted "working lunches" with suspect Muslim leaders. Agents blame him for the FBI's constant capitulation to groups like CAIR and ISNA, and for allowing their leaders high-level access within headquarters, which they say only lends them the legitimacy they desperately seek.

"The bad guys have managed to achieve outrageous penetration at the senior level," Guandolo complains, and it's demoralizing rank-and-file agents and supervisors alike.

"The director [of the FBI] hasn't met or awarded anyone from the Muslim community yet who hasn't turned out to be wanted, unindicted, indicted, or someone with an open case or a likely Muslim Brotherhood background," he points out.

Agents don't expect things to change, though, when FBI Director Robert Mueller steps down in 2011. If anything, the bureau may become more accommodating to Muslim muscle groups. That's because retiring Los Angeles Police Chief Bill Bratton is said to be on the short list to replace Mueller—and the obsequious Miller previously worked as a top aide to Bratton.[13] Agents expect Miller to gain more power at headquarters under Bratton's leadership, expanding the Muslim outreach program beyond the liberal parameters he's already established.

It's been Miller's policy, for instance, to keep groups like CAIR in the loop about FBI plans to raid Islamic targets in counterterror investigations.

"When we execute a search warrant in a sensitive location—be it a charity, a mosque, a home of a member of the community—there's a lot of planning that goes into how to do it so that we don't deliberately offend sensitivities," Miller says.

"There's a lot of outreach," he adds, "where we reach out to the community and say...'Here's the information that we can give you'" about the counterterror raids.[14]

FBI CAMPS FOR MUSLIM YOUTH

In his role as assistant director of the FBI's Office of Public Affairs, Miller took appeasement to a new level in 1997, when he made an official offer to ISNA and other Muslim Brotherhood front groups to create a special "FBI camp for high-school-age Muslim youth," according to high-level FBI meeting notes obtained from sources within headquarters.[15] He proposed developing the camp in coordination with the Boys & Girls Clubs of America. The idea had the director's approval.

Miller also offered to send FBI agents on tours of local mosques "to learn about the mosque and Muslim culture" and receive a "block of instructions" from mosque leaders on respecting Islamic customs, according to the six-page memo marked "Meeting Notes for Robert S. Mueller III."[16] The February 1997 meeting included among its attendees Sayyid M. Syeed, who is a co-founder and director of ISNA, the unindicted terror co-conspirator, and a former director of IIIT, the Brotherhood's Islamic think tank raided after 9/11 on suspicion of funneling money to suicide bombers.[17]

In response to suggestions from ISNA and other Muslim groups, Miller proposed initiating "a program where new agent trainees visit a local mosque, similar to new agent trainees currently visiting the Holocaust Museum," the memo says.[18] Muslim leaders are angry over the attention the FBI pays to Jewish history and culture. Agents are sent to the Holocaust Museum to see for themselves what happens when law enforcement becomes a tool of oppression. More hate crimes are committed against Jews in America than any other people of faith, and dwarf those against Muslims.

Agents say Miller's outreach policies have created discord at all levels of the FBI—except the highest level where they say top brass continue to be clueless about the nature of the enemy.

Because of current infighting, agents say the disengagement policy with CAIR is already fragile and risks breaking down.

"The Washington field office keeps having to glue it together because headquarters is undermining them," says Guandolo, a twelve-year bureau veteran who after 9/11 worked in the Washington field office's counterterrorism division, where he developed the FBI's pilot Counterterrorism Training Program. And the special agents in charge of running the field offices across the country "don't want to offend local Muslims"—and risk their performance-related bonuses, which are tied in part to outreach and positive feedback from the Muslim community.

Guandolo, who also spent nine years as a member of the FBI's SWAT team, calls it "cowardice." Part of the problem, he says, is that senior executives think outreach will help inoculate them from discrimination lawsuits ginned up by notoriously litigious Muslim groups like CAIR.

"They scream racism and threaten to sue, and headquarters just rolls over," he says. "It's total appeasement."

But, "the other part of it is the bad guys are doing their job too well," he says. "They're good at spreading propaganda" to make themselves look good and law enforcement bad.

Even if the new policy holds, the damage from years of unbridled outreach may already be done.

SENSITIVITY TRAINING

Over the past several years, CAIR has formally trained the FBI and other law enforcement agencies across the country on Islam and how to treat Muslims. It lectures them to be sensitive to Muslims and respectful of Islamic customs, while misleading them about the meaning of jihad.

The "diversity workshops" are in fact a dangerous disinformation program, veteran counterterrorism agents say.

For starters, brainwashing police into believing jihad means "internal struggle against sin," and not holy war, desensitizes them to pro-jihad materials discovered in the possession of Muslims they've stopped on the road or during the inspections process at the international airports. Rather than ask probing questions, they may instead give them a pass.

CAIR crows on its Web site that it "has conducted diversity/sensitivity training on Islam and Muslims for the FBI [and] several local law enforcement agencies." And has it. Here is just a sample of the many police departments and law enforcement agencies CAIR has trained—at taxpayer expense—since 2001:

New York Police Department (115th Precinct)

FBI's St. Louis field office

Central Ohio law enforcement officials

Detroit Police Department

Elk Grove Police Department (California)

Sacramento Police Department

FBI agents in Lexington, Kentucky

FBI agents in Jacksonville, Florida

California Highway Patrol

Cleveland Police Department

Houston law enforcement officials

Chicago Ridge Police Department

Gwinnett County, Georgia, law enforcement office

Texas Police Association officers

Anaheim Police Department (California)

Florida Department of Law Enforcement officials

U.S. Citizenship and Immigration Services (USCIS)

Texas Municipal Police Association

FBI's New Haven, Connecticut, field office

U.S. Immigration and Customs Enforcement

U.S. Customs and Border Protection[19]

Most alarming, CAIR also has been training participants at the counterterrorism division of the Federal Law Enforcement Training Center in Glynco, Georgia. FLETC serves as the interagency law enforcement training organization for more than eighty federal agencies.[20]

If the feds knew CAIR were contributing heavily to the defense fund of a convicted Georgia cop killer, as detailed in a previous chapter, perhaps they'd rethink inviting the group to that state to train their officers.

And now that CAIR has been tied definitively to terrorism, the heads of all these police departments and agencies might consider deprogramming their officers following CAIR's brainwashing. Though the damage is done, it's not irreversible.

Experts warn that by whitewashing jihad, the sensitivity training misinforms agents and may prevent them from taking effective counterterror measures.

"The agents are going to be misinformed and they will be overly sensitive and they will not ask certain questions," asserts Zeyno Baran, senior fellow at the Hudson Institute, a Washington think tank.[21]

The Department of Homeland Security has invited CAIR to conduct sensitivity training for officers and supervisors with Immigration and Customs Enforcement, or ICE, which is charged with rounding up and deporting fugitive aliens. The course in Chicago, for example, was taught by local CAIR officials Christina Abraham and Mariyam Hussain. So far, more than thirty ICE staffers have gone through the CAIR program, which among other things, corrects "misconceptions about jihad" calling for holy war.[22]

The Chicago training led to Homeland Security taking CAIR on a VIP tour of security operations at the nation's busiest airport—at the same time British authorities were working to break up a major plot to blow up U.S.-bound airplanes.

In June 2006, a senior Homeland Security official from Washington personally guided officials from CAIR—and even one from the Holy Land Foundation—on a behind-the-scenes tour of customs screening operations at O'Hare International Airport in response to CAIR complaints that Muslim travelers were being unfairly delayed as they entered the U.S. from abroad.

The tour included secure areas normally off-limits to travelers. These Hamas operatives posing as moderate Muslim activists were squired around the entire facility, including a walk through the point-of-entry, customs stations, secondary screening, and interview rooms. In addition, customs agents were asked to describe for CAIR and its terror-supporting entourage various features of the high-risk passenger lookout system.[23]

So, unwittingly, the government explained to terrorist supporters how programs designed to catch terrorists work.

In a meeting that same day, Brian Humphrey, Customs and Border Protection's executive director of field operations, assured CAIR that customs agents do not single out Muslim passengers for special screening and that they all must undergo a mandatory course in Muslim sensitivity training.

That course includes watching a video featuring Margaret Nydell, director of graduate studies in the Arabic Department at Georgetown University, home to an Islamic studies center lavishly funded by the Saudis and closely allied with CAIR. A leading Islamic apologist, Nydell is the author of *Understanding Arabs: A Guide for Westerners*.

A Customs and Border Protection official describes her instruction as "politically correct drivel."

"It's all about how Islam means peace and tolerance," he says. "We're told how to deal with Arabs and Muslims, that they are loving people and not terrorists. And that jihad is struggle with sin, and has nothing to do with violence."

"*Mein Kampf* means my struggle," he adds, skeptically. "Jihad means something more than that, but they're not telling us."[24]

'THEY ADMIRE OUR VALUES'

A review of the government-produced video, which runs roughly thirty minutes, reveals several fallacies in consultant Nydell's presentation.

Referring to all Muslims, Nydell maintains that "certainly they don't approve of terrorist acts," adding that Islam "is a perfectly decent religion with good moral teachings or it wouldn't have survived."[25]

Her conclusion flies in the face of several major polls that show a sizable number of Muslims around the world support violent jihad, including Muslims in America. A 2007 Pew Research Center poll, in fact, found one in four younger Muslims in the U.S. believe suicide bombings are justified to defend Islam.

Nydell also claims that jihad does not mean holy war. She defines it as "a word that means effort" or "the daily struggle to keep yourself on the true path." If a Muslim attacks you, she says, "they're just trying to regain their honor" after suffering some form of indignity at the hands of infidels. Nydell completely glosses over the hardcore militancy codified and mandated in Islam's holy texts.

What of all the Muslim terrorists invoking Islam? She posits that these are primarily young, uneducated Arabs or South Asians who are "disenfranchised" by government oppression and poverty, and are lashing out for reasons other than religion. Never mind that most of the 9/11 hijackers, as well as the 7/7 bombers in London, were well-educated adults from affluent families.

Nydell also places a fig leaf over *Shariah* law and its call for Islamic domination, arguing it's no threat to Western institutions or the West's way of life.

There is no reason to question the motives of Muslim immigrants, Nydell lectures border agents in the training video. "They're not here to change us," she assures them. "Don't believe they're jealous, and they're going to try to come over here and make you and me go to the mosque and all this kind of stuff."

"They admire our values," Nydell continues, as orchestral music soars in the background of the video. "Don't let anyone tell you they hate freedom."

She asserts that it's incumbent upon agents to treat Muslim travelers with the utmost respect. For instance, if they come across a copy of the Quran in their belongings, "don't put something on top of it," because that could offend them. Nothing can sit on top of their sacred book.

And if they find a Muslim praying, she advises, "Don't walk in front of them," and be sure to "keep quiet."

Another Customs and Border Protection official says the video is virtually useless as a terror-fighting tool for border agents, who are the first line of defense against Islamic terrorists sneaking into the country.

"Just teaching Islam 101—you know, they pray five times a day, they face Mecca—without any inside analysis is like teaching a college graduate sex education," he says. "It's a waste of time."[26]

LOSING THE LEXICON WAR

After British authorities disrupted 2006's transatlantic skyterror plot, then-Homeland Security Secretary Michael Chertoff distributed a memo to department staff oddly bereft of any reference to the terrorists' religion.

"Over the last few hours," he wrote in the one-page "MESSAGE FROM SECRETARY CHERTOFF TO ALL DHS EMPLOYEES," "British authorities have arrested a significant number of extremists engaged in a substantial plot to destroy multiple passenger aircraft flying from the United Kingdom to the United States."[27]

The so-called "extremists" were known at the time to be British

Muslims of Pakistani descent, yet Chertoff neglected to identify them as such—or even address their motive for attacking America. Yet the plot was serious enough for him to raise the nation's threat level to severe, or red, for commercial flights.

It turns out that he and other homeland security officials have sanitized the language used in the war on Islamic terror following years of mau-mauing from CAIR, ISNA, MPAC, and other Muslim Brotherhood pressure groups about the language causing "offense" and "insult" to Muslims.

Both Homeland Security and the National Counterterrorism Center, or NCTC, have issued staffwide memos imposing Orwellian speech code. It is no longer advisable for staff to use terms such as "jihadist," "Islamist," or even "Islamic terrorist." Acceptable alternatives include "violent extremist" or just plain "terrorist."

The terms "jihad," "Islamofascism" and *caliphate* are also out. "Don't invoke Islam" in any way, says the new directive from NCTC, which was issued early in 2008.[28] Avoid "inflating the religious bases" for Islamic terrorism and make "no overt reference to Islam," lest you "cause offense," advises Homeland Security in its nine-page memo, also issued early in 2008 and marked "For Official Use Only."[29]

The FBI has followed a similar speech ban. And now, as a supposed gesture of goodwill to Muslims the world over, the Obama administration reportedly has dropped the already generic "war on terror" altogether from the Homeland Security vernacular.

The irony of allowing groups that want to censor debate over their own ties to terrorism to censor our language in the war on terror is not lost on FBI agents. They lament that the bad guys are winning the lexicon war.

"Political correctness has darn near beaten common sense police work to death," says Ben R. Furman, a retired FBI agent who led an international multiagency task force that investigated chemical and nuclear terrorism threats.[30]

How can we defeat the enemy if we can't even define it? Furman and others ask. This is a war on Islamic terrorists, yet it won't be won if agents have to stop every five minutes to make sure they're being PC. It won't be won if they're forced to put up blinders to the religious motivation of the enemy.

Such political correctness is the handmaiden of terrorism, agents say, because it appeases terrorism, and enables it to operate in the shadows.

RECRUITING ARABIC LINGUISTS AND AGENTS

To be fair, top FBI brass have to deal with things that are well above the pay grade and concern of agents. Besides the liberal press, they have to contend with the EEOC. Internal FBI records show the agency has been sued by no fewer than fourteen Arab and Muslim employees since 9/11, and the last thing headquarters wants is more accusations of discrimination, even if most of them are frivolous.[31] It's absolutely petrified of the bigot-branding machine deployed by CAIR and other Muslim- and Arab-rights groups—as well as the ACLU, which has asked CAIR for "FBI ethnicity related cases," according to a copy of notes obtained from a meeting between the ACLU and CAIR in Washington.[32]

But its solution could not be more wrongheaded: Hiring even more Arab and Muslim employees, while promoting the existing ones who are complaining.

FBI director Mueller has launched a national hiring blitz that includes setting up recruitment booths at ISNA conventions and placing full-page recruiting ads in ISNA's magazine *Islamic Horizons*. That's right, the FBI is recruiting among Muslim Brotherhood fronts that support jihad.

Republicans in Congress have rebuked the Justice Department for allowing such an unholy alliance. The evidence naming ISNA as a leading branch of the American Muslim Brotherhood is overwhelming, argue U.S. Representatives Sue Myrick (R-NC) and Pete Hoekstra (R-MI) and its links to U.S. fundraising efforts on behalf of Hamas are equally strong.

"Establishing a partnership with ISNA is exactly the wrong approach at this critical juncture in history, setting a precedent that radical jihadists should be the conduit between the U.S. government and the American Muslim population," the lawmakers wrote in a letter to the former attorney general.[33]

At the same time, the FBI is sending recruiters into Muslim Brotherhood mosques, including the CAIR-endorsed ADAMS Center, a Muslim Brotherhood hub singled out by the Freedom House as one of the top distributors of Saudi-sponsored anti-Semitic and anti-Christian dogma.[34]

"One of the things the FBI believes in is diversity. Diversity is important. We are critically seeking special agents and support staff who are Arabic speakers," an FBI recruiter last year told Muslims gathered at the Sterling, Virginia mosque. "We also need folks who candidly are familiar with Islam. We're learning, many of us."[35]

While the FBI actively solicits applications from Muslim Brother zealots, it has rejected scores of applications from Jewish Arabic speakers seeking to become translators and analysts.[36]

And it's expanding the role of Arabic linguists in the bureau to include intelligence reporting and analysis, while promoting these mostly Muslim translators and giving them even higher security access—even though some have been disciplined for "misconduct related to mistranslating wiretaps and/or documents, or omitting information or withholding information from agents" and other security breaches since 9/11, according to Kevin Favreau, assistant director of intelligence for the FBI's national security branch in Washington.[37] And it's doing this even after FBI translator

Nadia Prouty was busted for spying for Hezbollah.

One Arab agent who sued the bureau is a suspected Muslim Brotherhood "plant" who refused to tape-record Muslim suspects under terrorism investigation.[38] This same Muslim agent had no problem secretly tape-recording Fox News host Bill O'Reilly before suing him for libel, however.[39] O'Reilly won the case. What's become of the Muslim agent? The FBI now has him—get this—recruiting other Muslim agents and language specialists.

In fact, Gamal Abdel-Hafiz, an Egyptian-American and the first Muslim FBI agent, encouraged fellow Muslims at a recent American-Arab Anti-Discrimination Committee convention to join the FBI with the following pitch: "We will never change what we don't like unless we take part."[40]

ANOTHER 'DIRTY' MUSLIM AGENT

More recently, another Muslim FBI agent in Los Angeles allegedly compromised a multi-agency terrorism investigation by tipping off the ringleader of a Pakistani-based terror cell that the Joint Terrorism Task Force had under surveillance for more than two years.

According to a JTTF official, the agent is embedded with the bad guys through family businesses, and fed them critical information detailing the investigation. He allegedly not only tipped the cell leader off to a so-called "trash cover" investigators performed outside his home, but also identified surveillance vehicles for him.[41]

The cell leader has trained about a dozen young Muslim men in firearms use and hand-to-hand combat on the grounds of his mosque in Los Angeles, while arranging for more sophisticated training at camps inside Pakistan's northwest province that are run by the Taliban.

The allegedly "dirty" Muslim agent—an Egyptian-American married to an Afghan woman—allegedly compromised several investigations across the country, including ones in New York and Boston. The espionage was so extensive that FBI director Mueller has been briefed regarding the mushrooming scandal.

For this very reason, most career FBI agents are not thrilled about the bureau's post-9/11 policy of aggressively recruiting Arabs and Muslims. They say it's fraught with risk. In fact, a recent study conducted by the Vera Institute of Justice found that only one agent among hundreds of agents surveyed at sixteen FBI field offices across the country thinks it's a good idea to recruit more employees from the Muslim community.[42]

Headquarters does not learn from experience, even recent experience, however.

Agents complain the FBI still seems more worried about offending groups with proven ties to terror, such as ISNA, than infiltrating and investigating them. Time and time again, political correctness has overridden the better judgment of those on the ground and in the trenches. And PC red tape is handcuffing their efforts to dismantle the terror-support network in America (although, remarkably, they've still managed to disrupt more than thirty terrorism plots since 9/11, which is a testament to their dedication, professionalism, and skill).

"I am sad to note that the bureau remains awash in political correctness and risk aversion," says former FBI special agent George Sadler, who resigned in frustration from the Washington field office, where he worked counterterrorism cases in the wake of 9/11.[43]

While CAIR might want to savor its past tete-a-tetes at the Hoover building, its sister organization ISNA continues to enjoy *entree* there. The FBI's disengagement policy only applies to CAIR, even though ISNA was also named as a Muslim Brotherhood front and an unindicted co-conspirator with a charity convicted of funding terror.

Fresh on the heels of the Holy Land charity conviction, FBI General Counsel Valerie Caproni this March sat on a Yale University panel on civil rights with ISNA director Louay M. Safi.[44] That same month, ISNA says it met with the FBI to voice outrage over undercover agents in mosques and to badger headquarters into re-engaging with CAIR.[45]

In other words, the FBI is still engaged with the Wahhabi lobby, if not CAIR. And CAIR still has Congress. It continues its outreach and lobbying activities on the Hill with little shunning, an issue we'll explore in depth in a later chapter.

The late Egyptian Sayyid Qutb, one of the founding fathers of the international Muslim Brotherhood, argued that outreach and interfaith dialogue with the West should only be done to benefit the *ummah*. Outreach must not benefit non-Muslim states, he said, and certainly not *kaffir* police investigating the Muslim Brothers.

Build "a bridge" to the West, he said, but only so the infidels can cross over to Islam, bringing concessions with them.[46] The Brotherhood bridge, despite all the conciliatory rhetoric, is really a one-way street. The group's secret U.S. manifesto, which calls for eliminating America's Judeo-Christian society and making "Allah's religion victorious over all other religions," also calls for the creation of phony "Friendship Societies with other religions, and things like that."[47] Such olive branches are clearly a ruse.

The real outreach objective of CAIR and the other Brotherhood front groups in America, then, is to convert Americans to Islam, while registering grievances and extracting accommodations from the government. Another goal is gathering intelligence about law enforcement plans to investigate the Muslim community.

If confronted, the Brotherhood counsels the faithful to lie and deny— something CAIR does exceedingly well.

CHAPTER EIGHT

CAIR'S TEN BIGGEST WHOPPERS

"Believers should lie to People of the Book to protect their lives and religion."

—*Sunni Muslim scholar Ibn Taymiyah, referring to adherents of the Bible, the Jews and Christians*[1]

DOES CAIR LIE? A better question is, when doesn't it? At CAIR, lying is an instrument for communication. It's been caught trafficking in countless falsehoods, and as Beltway interest groups go, CAIR is arguably the least reliable and credible media source in Washington.

Its propaganda machine is run by Ibrahim Hooper, a belligerent Islamic convert who bullies and attacks journalists he considers a threat with a smashmouth style that resembles more a Chicago street tough than a professional spokesperson for a nonprofit organization.

Even Muslim members of CAIR don't trust or respect him. "I am alarmed at Brother Hooper's breezy unthinking attitude and loose talk," complains Jameila al-Hashimi in a letter to CAIR's board of directors.[2] She suggests Hooper should be sidelined for someone more professional.

"His language skills are grossly inadequate for undergraduate work, and [yet] somehow he is allowed to present himself as a spokesperson for the *ummah*? Please stop him. He does not possess adequate skills for a Muslim advocate," al-Hashimi wrote in a three-page letter obtained from files in CAIR's main office. "How did it happen that Brother Hooper, who clearly cannot express thoughts with depth, clarity, or compelling language, is our unilateral official spokesperson?"

The answer is cronyism. Hooper was a friend of CAIR co-founder

Nihad Awad. The two activists met in Minneapolis where they worked in support of Bosnian Muslims in their jihad against the Serbs. At the time, Osama bin Laden was actively recruiting and training jihadists to fight alongside the Bosnians.[3]

Hooper also worked closely with Awad when he was running propaganda operations for Hamas at the Islamic Association for Palestine, where he published a rag that celebrated Hamas suicide attacks on Israelis and publicized Hamas calls for the death of Israel.

"Ibrahim and I had worked together for years," Awad told a pro-Palestinian publication.[4]

In 1993, during their secret Hamas summit in Philadelphia, leaders of the Muslim Brotherhood discussed the need to form a new political front for public relations and media spin. Awad gave a report arguing for recruiting qualified English-speaking flacks to interface with the American press and gain their sympathies.

"We need to speak about the necessity of finding reporters to do media work," he said.

The participants agreed they needed someone who was good at manipulating public opinion and could "camouflage" their true activities and agenda with "a media twinkle." In short, they needed a slick spin-doctor—because as Awad noted, "media is stronger than politics."[5]

Not long after the meeting, Hooper was drafted to run the Brotherhood's new propaganda wing at CAIR.

"I contacted my friend Ibrahim Hooper, a professional journalist and communications genius," Awad recalls, "and tried to persuade him to move to Washington."[6]

Today, Hooper is a fierce advocate for Hamas and militant Islam, and they pay him well for it—more than $95,000 a year in total compensation (not including the thousands of dollars he has borrowed in personal loans from his nonprofit employer), tax records show. He also commands a six-figure annual budget for conducting opposition research against CAIR's enemies. [7]

A Canadian immigrant, Hooper was known as "Dougie" before he converted to Islam. His birth name is Cary Douglas Hooper, according to government records.

He became a member of the Cairo Foreign Press Association while working for computer periodicals in the Egyptian capital, which happens to be the global headquarters of the Muslim Brotherhood. He also worked for local TV stations in Minnesota. [8]

As CAIR's national communications director, Hooper a couple of years ago attempted to rebut the groundswell of charges against CAIR. He put out a ten-page document "de-mystifying 'urban legends' about CAIR" which only obfuscated the truth about CAIR. It's riddled with half-truths, deliberate omissions, and outright falsehoods about the size of the group's membership and the source of its donations, among other things.

CAIR and Hooper have had to climb down from many of the statements contained in the document—statements which are "no longer operative," as they say in Washington. In fact, it seems the entire document is no longer operative, because it's vanished from CAIR's Web site.

"We remain an open and transparent organization," CAIR says. Really? Then why did it take down the document after it was exposed as a tissue of lies?

Hooper authored another slurry of falsehoods called "A Journalist's Guide to Understanding Islam and Muslims" after recent polls showed a majority of Americans associating Islam with violence and intolerance. Sent to some forty thousand editors, reporters, and producers across the country, the publication is supposed to "educate" the media about Islam and disabuse journalists about "commonly held misconceptions" about the faith.

According to the fifty-five-page guide, common myths include:

- The notion that Islam does not respect women's rights;

- That it's not compatible with democracy or modern society;

- That the Quran teaches violence;

- That Muslims around the world hate the U.S.; and

- That all Muslims are Arab.

At least it got the last one right—Muslims are also predominantly Asian and African. Four of the other so-called myths are in fact truths (as examined in detail later). Which means CAIR is batting .200 in the accuracy department—in a publication advertised to, ironically enough, "help improve coverage of Islam in the American news media."

Once again, Hooper is the one spreading misinformation. But it's all part of the Brotherhood's strategy to guilt the media into writing glowingly about Islam and defer independent research and analysis that would expose the religion's dark underbelly and CAIR's own hidden agenda.

CAIR hopes to train a legion of young Hoopers to infiltrate the nation's newsrooms and reeducate the public about Islam.

"Whenever I speak to Muslim groups, I urge students to become majors in journalism, law, or political science," Awad says. "Journalism is especially important, and we urge Muslim adults to establish scholarships in that field. Muslims must become active in the nation's offices where news reports and headlines are written."[9]

Hooper isn't the only one at CAIR who stretches the truth. It's the habit of CAIR's entire leadership. They've been caught telling countless whoppers, but we've narrowed them down to the top ten. Consider the following tall tales they've told, counting down to the most pernicious:

WHOPPER NUMBER 10: In a prepared statement to Congress, Awad in 2003 asserted that it was "an outright lie" to say that CAIR had received any seed money from the Holy Land Foundation, the Islamic charity recently convicted of funding terrorism.

He also insisted there was not "a shred of evidence" to support what he called the "ridiculous" charge originally made by terror expert Steve Emerson that CAIR had received thousands of dollars in such funding.[10]

That same year then-CAIR Chairman Omar Ahmad also denied receiving such funds from the Hamas charitable front.[11]

Subsequent smoking-gun evidence puts the lie to their denials, however. Less than three weeks after CAIR was incorporated, bank records produced by Emerson reveal it had received a check for $5,000 from the "Holy Land Foundation for Relief and Development." A copy of the check—No. 1881—shows it was paid to the order of the "Council on American-Islamic Relations" of Washington, and debited from Holy Land's expense account with Bank One Texas. It's signed by Holy Land president Shukri Abu Baker, who's now a convicted terrorist. It was Abu Baker who coordinated the Philly meeting with Ahmad. He also met with CAIR executives in Washington before 9/11, the group's visitors logs reveal (see Appendix).

No wonder Awad skipped the hearing that senators held in part to afford him the opportunity to answer these and other charges against CAIR. Apparently he felt it was safer to courier over his demonstrably false denial than testify under oath and risk perjuring himself.

WHOPPER NUMBER 9: Dismissing the idea that CAIR or its leaders have had anything to do with Hamas, former CAIR chairman Parvez Ahmed claimed: "That's one of those urban legends about CAIR. It's fed by the right-wing, pro-Israeli blogosphere."[12]

Recent court documents, of course, validate the bloggers—while making a liar of Ahmed and CAIR.

In the Holy Land Foundation case, federal papers officially list CAIR and its founder as important figures in the conspiracy to fund Hamas terrorism.

And declassified transcripts of FBI wiretaps place CAIR executive director Awad, as well as co-founder and former chairman Ahmad, at the notorious Philly meeting with Hamas leaders, where a scheme was hatched to hide payments to Hamas suicide bombers and their families as charity. Both Awad and Ahmad have suffered a convenient bout of amnesia in claiming they cannot remember whether they attended the Hamas summit—even though it lasted three days, and even though Ahmad signed a reservation voucher for a room at the hotel where they met.[13]

They don't deny attending though. And both their names appear in a secret phone book alongside key Hamas leader Mousa Abu Marzouk, whom the government says directed and coordinated Hamas terrorist attacks on civilians in Israel.[14]

Moreover, Awad and Ahmad spun off CAIR from a known Hamas front they previously headed. As president of IAP, Ahmad paid to bring Hamas leaders to speak at annual conferences.[15] One IAP confab even featured a veiled Hamas terrorist.[16] Awad, for his part, proclaimed his support for Hamas in a speech, while churning out pro-Hamas and anti-Israel propaganda as IAP's public-relations director.

U.S. prosecutor Jim Jacks reiterated in a separate court filing that CAIR had "conspiratorial involvement with HLF [Holy Land Foundation] and others affiliated with Hamas," and that its involvement in the conspiracy to support Hamas is "ongoing" and did not end with the Holy Land trial and convictions.

Fearing CAIR remains actively involved with Hamas, the FBI has suspended all formal contacts with it. And the agency suggests CAIR and its leaders—namely "its current president emeritus [Ahmad] and its executive director [Awad]"—are the subject of an ongoing criminal investigation stemming from the Holy Land case. "Until we can resolve whether there continues to be a connection between CAIR or its executives and Hamas, the FBI does not view CAIR as an appropriate liaison partner," assistant FBI director Richard C. Powers recently informed the Senate Judiciary Committee.[17]

CAIR's insistence that it has no ties to Hamas rings absolutely hollow against these facts.

WHOPPER NUMBER 8: "CAIR has some fifty thousand members," Hooper contends.[18]

In fact, the actual figure is one-tenth that size—5,133—according to internal CAIR records.[19]

After the *Washington Times* reported in 2007 that CAIR's membership was rapidly shrinking due to negative publicity over its terror ties, CAIR accused the "right-wing" newspaper of "falsely suggesting there has been a drop."

"Our membership is increasing steadily," Awad insisted.

"Support for CAIR has grown," Hooper added.[20]

Two months later, CAIR filed a court brief in which it acknowledged membership indeed was down, blaming it on bad publicity from the Holy Land terror trial. It pleaded with the judge hearing the case to strike its name from the list of co-conspirators.

"This negative reaction by the American public can be seen in the decline of membership rates and donations resulting from the government's publicizing of CAIR as an unindicted co-conspirator," CAIR attorney William Moffitt wrote in the brief.[21]

Among the proof he submitted to the court was the same *Washington Times* article Hooper just two months earlier had trashed as false and biased. Apparently even CAIR's lawyers can't keep up with CAIR's lies.

WHOPPER NUMBER 7: CAIR calls allegations it receives money from foreign governments "disinformation." "This is yet another attempt to invent a controversy," Hooper says.[22]

There's no invention. CAIR, for example, has received at least half a million dollars from Saudi prince Al-Waleed bin Talal, who is a member of the ruling family of Saudi Arabia. Hooper argues he's technically not "an official of any foreign government."

But such hair-splitting doesn't hold up to scrutiny. Hooper himself admits that officials running the government of the United Arab Emirates have set up an endowment to help CAIR finance a massive $50 million public-relations campaign. And though he claims CAIR has not yet received "a penny" of those funds, CAIR did receive a nearly $1 million investment from the ruler of Dubai through his charitable foundation.[23]

In fact, Sheikh Mohammed Bin Rashid Al-Maktoum in the early 2000s owned a controlling stake in CAIR's three-story headquarters in Washington. Local land records show he held the deed to the building.[24]

A State Department cable, moreover, directly contradicts CAIR's denials about foreign governmental support.

The sensitive but unclassified *communiqué* was written by U.S. Embassy staff in Saudi Arabia, who in June 2006 reported the following after meeting with a CAIR delegation: "One admitted reason for the group's current visit to the KSA [Kingdom of Saudi Arabia] was to solicit $50 million in governmental and non-governmental contributions." The core delegation, according to the cable, consisted of then-CAIR Chairman Parvez Ahmed, Awad, and Hooper.[25]

Just three months after the trip, Hooper denied soliciting Saudi government funds. "To my knowledge, we don't take money from the government of Saudi Arabia," he said in a September 2006 appearance on MSNBC's Tucker Carlson show.[26]

What's more, some of CAIR's biggest private donors are members of the Saudi royal family, according to copies of wire transfers obtained from CAIR's executive files (see Appendix). The group's shady financing will be explored in detail in a separate chapter.

WHOPPER NUMBER 6: "Islam and democracy are compatible," and Islam values Western principles, CAIR maintains in its "Journalist's Guide to

Understanding Islam."[27]

Funny, because that's not what CAIR's longtime board member Ihsan Bagby thinks.

"Ultimately we can never be full citizens of this country," Bagby has lectured, "because there is no way we can be fully committed to the institutions and ideologies of this country."[28]

As the late Muslim Brotherhood leader Sayyid Qutb preached, Western-style democracy, as exemplified by the United States of America, is a man-made system of government, and therefore *haram*, or un-Islamic.

Sheik Yusuf al-Qaradawi, perhaps the most revered Brotherhood leader in the world today, agrees. Repeatedly championed by CAIR, al-Qaradawi also rejects the call for secularism.

"Acceptance of secularism means abandonment of *Shariah*," he argues. "The call for secularism among Muslims is atheism and a rejection of Islam. Its acceptance as a basis for rule in place of *Shariah* is downright apostasy."[29]

The Brotherhood views American democracy—with secularism and individualism as its hallmarks—as incompatible with Islam, because Islam does not believe in separation of mosque and state. It also considers Islam a complete system of religion and government, ethics and law, military and jihad, as well as worship. The Quran is the law for state and society, and supersedes even the authority of the U.S. Constitution.

No less than CAIR's co-founder and former chairman of the board has said as much. "Islam isn't in America to be equal to any other faith, but to become dominant," Ahmad has said. "The Quran should be the highest authority in America."

U.S. Brotherhood leaders advising CAIR—such as ISNA's Muzammil Siddiqi—constantly remind Muslims in America that "Allah's rules have to be established in all lands," including one day the U.S. Then there's senior Brotherhood leader Ahmad Totonji, who has stated: "We do not have any separation between religion and state." [30]

By pretending otherwise, however, CAIR makes *Shariah*-based Islam appear more palatable and acceptable. And by lowering the guard of skeptics, the Brotherhood gains bigger footholds in American politics and society.

To understand the cynical depths of CAIR's subterfuge regarding this issue, it's instructive to review its unusual interference in Egyptian politics in 2007, when the relatively secular Mubarak government amended that country's constitution to ban religious-based parties. CAIR ostensibly was angry that Egypt was further suppressing the Muslim Brotherhood, which is based there, and lodged a formal protest.

Egypt's constitutional amendments further restrict the outlawed Muslim Brotherhood movement, which is trying to turn Egypt away from secularism and toward an Islamic government based on *Shariah* law— something CAIR's own leaders say they'd like to see happen in this country.

In 2007, the Brotherhood drafted a party platform, under the banner "Islam is the solution," which called for establishing an undemocratically selected board of religious scholars with the power to veto any legislation passed by the Egyptian parliament and approved by the president that's not compatible with Islamic law. It also called for banning women and Christians from high office.

When the anti-theocracy amendments were passed by a majority of Egyptian voters, CAIR went ballistic, firing off a complaint to the U.S. State Department charging the referendum was rigged and "would essentially lock out any meaningful political opposition"—i.e., the Muslim Brotherhood—to challenge the more secular Mubarak regime. In a critical letter to Secretary of State Condoleezza Rice, then-CAIR chairman Ahmed chided the U.S. for its "tepid" response to what he characterized as the Egyptian government's "backsliding on promised democratic reforms."

CAIR is a domestic-based nonprofit organization, not a registered foreign agent. For its chairman to go out of his way to write the secretary of state about a foreign election speaks volumes about CAIR's vested interest in the Brotherhood.

But here's the ironic part: the Egyptian embassy got wind of the complaint and rebuked CAIR for its interference, reminding it that democracies are supposed to separate religion and state.

"I find this interference rather hypocritical," Egyptian Ambassador Nabil Fahmy blasted Ahmed in a letter obtained from CAIR's files, "since I assume you are aware of the notion of separation of church and state as enshrined in the First Amendment to the U.S. Constitution which governs your own country."

He closed by advising CAIR "to focus on its core mission" in America, and butt out of foreign affairs.[31]

It's a sad commentary when an Arab nation has to lecture an American "civil rights group" about Western jurisprudence and liberties.

'MOST MUSLIMS HAVE VERY POSITIVE ATTITUDES TOWARD AMERICA'

A companion lie CAIR peddles is that Muslims around the world love America and its values.

After 9/11, "some politicians and media commentators argued that there exists a clash of civilizations and values between the Muslim world and the West, claiming that the Muslim world hates 'Western freedoms' and the 'American way of life,'" CAIR intones in its media guide.

"The reality is that the relationship between the Middle East and the West—particularly the United States—is complex and multi-faceted," CAIR goes on. "In simple terms, Muslim attitudes toward the West are not shaped by American culture or values, but rather by U.S. foreign policy."

Beyond that sticking point, "most Muslims worldwide have very positive attitudes toward" America, CAIR insists.[32]

Now for a reality check: a Gallup poll conducted in nine Muslim nations after 9/11 found widespread hatred toward the U.S. Subsequent polls confirmed raging anti-Americanism throughout the Middle East and Pakistan.

There is a "violently deep hatred of America in the Islamic world," major international Muslim Brotherhood figures, including CAIR guru Sheik Qaradawi, warned President Obama in an open letter they signed after his inauguration.

And it's not just U.S. foreign policy (which they complain is tipped too heavily toward Israel) that they have a problem with. It's American values.

And it's not just foreign Muslims who hate America. It's American Muslims—including members of CAIR's own advisory board.

Take longtime CAIR advisor and fundraiser Siraj Wahhaj. He likens America to a dumpster.

"You know what this country is? It's a garbage can," he snarls. "It's filthy." He prays it "crumbles" and is replaced by Islam.[33]

Wahhaj, who also serves on ISNA's board, echoes Obama's longtime preacher Reverend Jeremiah Wright in calling America a "racist" nation.

"Deep down to its core this nation is racist!" the New York *imam* seethed in one sermon. "Racism is at the very root of this nation."

He also demonizes the U.S. government. "The government of America is so steeped in evil that most people are blinded by it," Wahhaj tells his flock. "America is the most wicked government on the face of the planet Earth."[34]

Wahhaj, known affectionately among the Muslim Brothers as "America's *Imam*," has been actively involved in CAIR's operations. Recent internal fundraising documents show CAIR has enlisted him to help raise large sums.

WHOPPER NUMBER 5: "Islam granted women the right to equality before the law," Hooper claims in CAIR's journalist's guide, "and to be free from spousal abuse."

This also deserts the truth. Under Islamic law, a man is allowed up to four wives, but women can have just one husband. A man can divorce his wife easily, but a woman has to ask her husband for permission to leave the marriage. And the witness of a woman in court is worth just half that of a man.[35]

Muslim women also lack equal rights in their houses of worship—even in America. At fully two-thirds of U.S. mosques, they're required to worship behind a curtain or partition—separated from the men—a recent national survey shows.[36] And many of them require women to enter the mosque from the back of the building, often near the dumpster, such as the 9/11 mosque in Falls Church, Virginia.

What's more, the Muslim declaration of faith, or *Shahada*, must be performed in front of two male witnesses. And women cannot make the pilgrimage to Mecca, or *hajj*—the fifth pillar of Islam—by themselves. They must be accompanied by a *mahram*—a first-degree male relative such as a father, husband, son, or brother—and marriage or birth certificates must be submitted as proof of their relationship. And if a married woman elects to go with her brother, she must still obtain a notarized "no-objection" letter from her husband. Even if a widow wishes to go to *hajj*, she cannot go without first obtaining a notarized letter from her son or brother addressed to the Saudi embassy stating that *he* has no objection with her traveling to *hajj*.

Surely CAIR—the supposed guardian of civil rights for all Muslims—does not condone such blatant sexism. Think again. No less than the female former civil rights director of CAIR's Maryland-Virginia chapter frowns on reforms proposed by feminist Muslim activists, such as Asra Nomani, who have pushed for equal treatment of women in U.S. mosques.

"The Asra Nomani position that men and women should be able to pray shoulder to shoulder is not the majority one," Farooq argues, "nor are her tactics really respected among the Muslim community."[37]

Also under Islamic law, men have permission to beat their wives, a "privilege" that is rooted in the Quran.

Astoundingly, CAIR gives its blessing to such domestic violence through the Quran it endorses and distributes, although in CAIR's watered-down English version, men are advised to merely "spank" their wives, and then only "lightly"—an adverb not even found in the original Arabic text.[38]

The CAIR-approved Quran—"The Meaning of the Holy Quran," as translated by Abdullah Yusuf Ali—also authorizes men to have sex with their wives "in any manner, time, or place." It compares them to a field to be plowed. "Your wives are as a tilth unto you, so approach your tilth when or how you will."[39]

Muslim Brotherhood leaders associated with CAIR have even issued *fatwahs* authorizing wife beating.

Sheik al-Qaradawi, for one, says its okay for men to slap around their disobedient wives, though only as a last resort. If other approaches to correcting their behavior fail, such as denying them sex, "it is permissible for him to beat her lightly with his hands, avoiding her face and other sensitive parts."[40]

Al-Qaradawi is part of the IIIT leadership, and is perhaps the most important leader of the global Muslim Brotherhood movement. IIIT, the Herndon, Virginia-based Islamic think tank raided by federal agents after 9/11, gave at least $20,500 in donations to CAIR between 2000 and 2007. Recall, too, that CAIR's former operations director often visited IIIT's office to pray during afternoon prayers. The radical IIIT, which remains under federal investigation for terror-financing, also recently pumped more than a million dollars into Islamic studies programs at Washington-based George Mason University and other colleges.

Then there's Jamal Badawi, a leader of ISNA's Fiqh Council of North America, a Muslim Brotherhood dispenser of Islamic jurisprudence. He has issued a *fatwah* authorizing American Muslim husbands to physically punish their wives.

"There are cases in which a wife persists in bad habits and showing contempt of her husband and disregard for her marital obligations," Badawi advises. "Instead of divorce, the husband may resort to another measure more accurately described as a gentle tap on the body."[41]

So much for CAIR's claim of Muslim women being "free from spousal abuse."

But perhaps Badawi, a key Brotherhood figure, has misinterpreted the Quran. Maybe he's been overruled by the chairman of the Fiqh Council, who happens to be former ISNA president and CAIR advisor Siddiqi. No such luck. Siddiqi actually confirmed Badawi's ruling in a 2004 *fatwah* of his own, which decrees:

> It is important that a wife recognizes the authority of her husband in the house. He is the head of the household, and she is supposed to listen to him.... In some cases, a husband may use some light disciplinary action in order to correct the moral infraction of his wife.[42]

Siddiqi goes on to define this disciplinary action as a "light strike." He also explains that a Muslim woman commits a moral infraction when she does not "obey" her husband.

No wonder Muslim Brotherhood leaders have been arrested for domestic violence. And no wonder many of them require their women to be fully covered in head-to-toe *abayas* and head scarves. The clothes can literally cover the evidence of male brutality inflicted on a wife's or daughter's body.

WHOPPER NUMBER 4: "'*Jihad*' does not mean 'holy war,'" CAIR maintains in its media guide. It means "striving in the cause of God, the struggle to better oneself or society."[43]

Really? That's not what Yusuf Ali says in his English translation of the Quran that CAIR has approved and is stocking in neighborhood libraries across the country.

"Here is a good description of jihad," Yusuf Ali says on page 442, referring to one of hundreds of violent passages in the Muslim holy book. "It may require fighting in Allah's cause, as a form of self-sacrifice," or martyrdom.

On page 1,315, Ali confirms that jihad means battling the enemy in the physical, not symbolic, sense. "When once the fight [Jihad] is entered upon, carry it out with the utmost vigor, and strike home your blows at the most vital points [*smite at their necks*]," he advises Muslims, quoting from the Quran. "You cannot wage war with kid gloves."

On page 438 of CAIR's recommended translation, Ali interprets the Quran's so-called "verse of the sword" as a battle cry against the "People of the Book," or the Jews and Christians. "The fighting," he says, "may take the form of slaughter, or capture, or siege, or ambush and other stratagems."

If this is Ali's interpretation, it must also be CAIR's interpretation, because CAIR has wholeheartedly endorsed Ali's translation of the Quran. In fact, it is being published by a Muslim Brotherhood printer in Maryland. (The uniquely militant nature of Islam bleeds through even in this English version of the Quran, which has been demilitarized and rendered more pacifistic for non-Muslim or Western consumption, compared with the more nakedly hateful Saudi versions.)

But then CAIR does not count on Americans actually reading Ali's commentary, which is published in tiny agate type throughout 6,311 footnotes in a tome that spans 1,760 pages.

CAIR-endorsed *imam* Zaid Shakir also contradicts what CAIR is saying publicly. Shakir, a frequent guest speaker at CAIR events, tells his Muslim audiences: "Jihad is physically fighting the enemies of Islam to protect and advance the religion of Islam. This is jihad."

Acceptable targets of jihad, he says, include U.S. military aircraft.

"Islam doesn't permit us to hijack airplanes filled with civilian people," Shakir says. However, "If you hijack an airplane filled with the 82nd Airborne, that's something else."[44] The 82nd Airborne Division's elite paratroopers fly out of Fort Bragg, North Carolina, which is part of North Carolina state senator Larry Shaw's district. Shaw happens to be CAIR's new chairman.

Shakir also gives his blessing to the use of bombs as a weapon of jihad, as long as the explosives hit "select" targets and are not indiscriminate in their destruction. Civilians can be legitimate targets, he says, if "there's a benefit in that."

Even "old elderly men" and "women who are conscripted"—including Israeli and American women in uniform—are eligible enemy combatants in jihad. "This is *Shariah*," Shakir asserts in a CD recording of one of his lectures, which the authors obtained from a mosque bookstore in Brooklyn.[45]

Shakir, a black convert, has been portrayed as a moderate in the mainstream media, including the *New York Times*, which recently ran a positive profile of him. His pro-jihad statements revealed here have not been previously reported.

Then there's CAIR advisor and fundraiser Wahhaj, who also completely contradicts what CAIR is telling the media about the meaning of jihad.

"If we go to war, brothers and sisters—and one day we will, believe me—that's why you're commanded [to fight in] jihad," the *imam* has told his flock in New York. "When Allah demands us to fight, we're not stopping and nobody's stopping us."[46]

Sheik Qaradawi has ruled that jihad can be an offensive means of expanding the Muslim state as well as a defensive response to attack:

> In the jihad which you are seeking, you look for the enemy and invade him. This type of jihad takes place only when the Islamic state is invading other [countries] in order to spread the word of Islam and to remove obstacles standing in its way. The repulsing jihad takes place when your land is being invaded and conquered.... [In that case you must] repulse [the invader] to the best of your ability. If you kill him he will end up in Hell, and if he kills you, you become a martyr.[47]

So not only does CAIR's guru believe that jihad is warfare, but he refutes those who believe that only defensive jihad is permissible in Islam.

This makes a mockery of CAIR's additional claim that "the Quran teaches peace" and not violence.

In fact, the only real peace the Quran teaches is peace for Muslims—which it says will come when all non-Muslims are converted or "subdued." When no fewer than twenty-six chapters of the Quran deal with military fighting and violence, and when it repeatedly states that fighting is "prescribed" upon believers, it's risibly false to claim it promotes no violence.

But don't take our word for it. Listen to Wahhaj, who preaches that Islam sanctions violent insurrection in infidel lands—including America.

"I will never tell people, 'Don't be violent,'" he says. "That's not the Islamic way."

But he cautions Muslims that their violence has to be "selective." Wait, train, be patient; then strike when the time is right.

"Believe me, brothers and sisters, Muslims in America are the most strategic Muslims on Earth," Wahhaj says, because the government cannot drop bombs on warring Muslims in America without causing collateral damage to U.S. cities and Americans who aren't Muslim.

Muslims in America also have an army of potential recruits in the inner city, he says, especially among minority gangs. Once they are converted to Islam, he says, they will be fearless in the jihad.

The U.S. government's "worst nightmare is that one day the Muslims wake these people up" in South Central Los Angeles and other inner-city areas, Wahhaj fumes in a videotape of a sermon obtained by the authors.

He exhorts the faithful to go into the 'hood and the prisons and convert disenfranchised minorities, and then arm and train them to carry out an Uzi jihad in the inner cities.

"We don't need to arm the people with 9mms and Uzis," he says. "You need to arm them with righteousness first. And once you arm them with righteousness first, then you can arm them [with Uzis and other weapons]."[48]

He says inner-city gang members will make formidable fighters because they are not afraid of death. All they lack is discipline, Wahhaj says, and Islam can provide that.

"They need to get out of the street and get into the *masjid* [mosque], learn Islam and then get [back] in the street," he preaches, "because these people have guts and courage that a lot of Muslims don't have. Some of these people are ready to stand in front of anyone and fight."

In contrast, "some Muslims have lost the desire to fight," Wahhaj adds. "Muslims have become soft. And they love the soft life. And they hate death. And this is why all over the world Muslims are getting their butts kicked—except those Muslims who fight back like in Afghanistan."[49]

CAIR of course hopes the trusting public never hears such violent rants from Muslim leaders. Worried about polls showing a majority of Americans associating Islam with violence, CAIR is desperate to sugarcoat such ugly truths.

"There is a common misconception among Westerners that the Quran teaches violence," CAIR maintains in its media guide.

Apparently CAIR's own guest speaker Shakir didn't get the memo. Speaking before private Muslim audiences, the *imam* readily confesses that Islam is a uniquely militant religion that believes in taking an eye for an eye.

"We don't have a turn-the-other-cheek philosophy" like the Christians, he says. "Allah has given us permission to fight them" so that the "word of Allah can be uppermost."[50] Brotherhood leader Totonji agrees: "In Islam, we do not believe in the formula, 'If someone smacks you on the right cheek, turn to him the left.' We believe that if someone smacks you on the right cheek, smack him on the right cheek."[51]

WHOPPER NUMBER 3: CAIR also claims "Allah is the same God worshipped by Christians and Jews." In fact, the group says, "Muslims love and revere Jesus."[52]

Many Americans have fallen for this Allah-God fallacy, including former President Bush, who not long after 9/11 said of Muslims, "I believe we worship the same God."

Some national polls show that as many as four out of five Americans agree that Muslims worship the same Almighty as Christians and Jews. It's a popular myth cultivated by years of propaganda by CAIR and liberal interfaith groups promoting shared religious values and themes. And it's nonsense on stilts.

Neither Christians nor Jews worship the same deity as Muslims, nor do Muslims worship the same God as the "People of the Book," and this is apparent from even a cursory reading of their sacred texts. If Muslims honestly believed CAIR's palaver about a common divinity, the first Muslim member of Congress would not have had reservations about taking his oath of office on the Bible. But Democratic Representative Keith Ellison, a close ally of CAIR, insisted on using the Quran instead.

A critical part of the Muslim Brotherhood's strategy to conquer America is establishing common ground between Islam and Christianity. As Sheik Qaradawi has said: "We will conquer America not by the sword but by *dawah*"—the mission to convert others to Islam.[53]

One of the tools the Brotherhood and CAIR use to blind Christian skeptics and convert easy marks—such as Hispanic immigrants—is to talk up Jesus and his mother Mary.

In fact, the book, *Jesus: Prophet of Islam* by Mohammed Ata-ur-Rehman and Muslim convert Ahmad Thomson, can be found among CAIR's *dawah* training materials. CAIR also recently launched a $60,000 advertising campaign that claims on Florida buses that Jesus was a Muslim. The signs read: "ISLAM: The Way of Life of Abraham, Moses, Jesus, and Muhammad."

"Hispanics are increasingly interested in Islam," CAIR boasts in its media guide, and they are "converting to Islam." That's because CAIR and groups like the Latino American Dawah Organization are targeting them for conversion. Knowing how much Latino Catholics revere Mary, they point out that Mary is mentioned more often in the Quran than the New Testament.

While true, the only reason the Muslim holy book cites Mary so many times is to brand Jesus a mere mortal in the Muslim mind. Christ is referred to exclusively in the text of the Quran as "Jesus, son of Mary," and never "Jesus, son of God," which would be blasphemous to Allah. If anything, the literary distinction points up how different the two faiths are, since Muslims don't believe that Jesus is God. In fact, they believe professing such a thing is *shirk*—the worst of all sins.

Still, Latino Catholics in particular are impressed with the attention Mary seems to get in the Quran. The "phenomenon" of their rapid conversion to Islam, as CAIR calls it, is predicated on this artifice.

And it's the same *dawah* trick used by bin Laden, who in a recently recorded message to America tried to draw Christians' attention to the allegedly similar beliefs that they and Muslims share regarding Jesus and Mary.

But don't be misled. Here are the facts:

• Islam rejects the central tenet of Christianity—that Jesus is divine and part of the Trinity.

• The Quran calls those who assign "partners" to Allah "blasphemers" who will roast in Hell.

• According to the Quran, Jesus was just a "messenger" and mortal like Muhammad.

• Muslims don't believe Jesus died on the cross, and the Quran clearly denies he was crucified.

• Muslims do believe Jesus will return at the end of time. But here's the part CAIR and other missionaries leave out of their proselytizing pitch:

On the Judgment Day, the Muslim Jesus will descend from Heaven and slaughter the Christian Jesus with a spear, along with all the Jewish "pigs." He'll also "break all crosses," confirming Islam as the only true religion.

But then CAIR knows this. It's spelled out in a pamphlet titled, "Khilafa" (*Caliphate*) found tucked in files stored in CAIR's executive offices. Under the heading, "World Wide Islamic Domination," it says that "Islam will prevail over every religion" when "Jesus, son of Mary," returns to slay the "false messiah" worshipped by the non-Muslims.[54]

Islamist doctrine also holds that all people were born Muslim, but due to the fault of their parents, most are not taught Islam. When they finally see the "truth," they "revert" back to Islam.

In public, CAIR and Islamic leaders refer to new Muslims as converts—as opposed to "reverts," which is the term they use in their private communications—because it would be a PR nightmare if they told Christians and Jews they were actually born Muslim. But make no mistake, this is what these Islamic supremacists believe.

Besides the Jesus-Mary stratagem, CAIR also uses the "Abrahamic faiths" pitch to entice non-Muslims to cross over to Islam. But it beards the truth as well.

CAIR argues that we are all children of Abraham; and since we share a common ancestry, we share a common God.

But CAIR knows full well that Arab Muslims believe they are descendants of Abraham's son Ishmael, while Jews and Christians believe they descended from Isaac—Abraham's other son, who was favored by God in the story of the Bible.

Muslims also believe their deity told Abraham to sacrifice Ishmael, not Isaac, as a test of his faith. They even celebrate Abraham's obedience—and Ishmael's willingness to be sacrificed for the sake of Allah—each year by sacrificing livestock on Eid al-Adha. (In fact, the throats of hundreds of goats are slit in Muslim enclaves across America during their annual festival.)

This is no minor theological point. The Bible says God chose to establish his covenant with Abraham and Sarah's son Isaac, instead of Ishmael, the son of the slave girl Hagar. In fact, God banished Ishmael—described in the Bible as "a wild donkey of a man" whose "hand will be against everyone"—to the desert.

Here's another fundamental difference: Unlike the God of the Bible, Allah does not recognize Jews as his chosen people.

WHOPPER NUMBER 2: After 9/11, CAIR cited an explosion in anti-Islamic hate crimes in demanding more outreach with the FBI and special rights and protections for Muslims. "Unlike any other past crisis," CAIR claimed, "the post-September 11 anti-Muslim backlash has been the most violent."

But the latest Justice Department data on hate crimes reveal CAIR has been crying wolf. Not only are anti-Islamic hate crimes way down, but they're a fraction of overall religious hate crimes. The overwhelming majority of such crimes target Jews, something CAIR and other Muslim groups don't seem all that concerned about.

In 2007, a whopping 69 percent of religiously motivated attacks were on Jews, while just 8 percent targeted Muslims—even though the Jewish and Muslim populations are comparable in size. Catholics and Protestants, who together account for almost 9 percent of victims, are subject to as much abuse as Muslims in this country.

In the most recent year, anti-Islamic hate crimes totaled 115. While just one hate crime is one too many, that's a 26 percent drop from 2006 and a 76 percent plunge from 2001. And the number is minuscule compared with the 969 offenses against Jews. For every attack on a Muslim in this country, there are nine against a Jew.[55]

The government data give lie to CAIR's alarmist narrative of "Islamophobic" lynch mobs marching on mosques across America. In reality, Americans have been remarkably tolerant and respectful of Muslims and their institutions since 9/11.

It's plain that CAIR, true to form, has been exaggerating the numbers and hyping tensions to advance its political agenda. Every year the pressure group releases a report citing thousands of alleged civil rights and physical abuses against Muslims, which largely are based on anecdotal reporting from members. Despite CAIR's obvious bias (and proven record of dissembling), the PC-drunk media report its numbers unfiltered and without question.

But if you peel them back, you find that many of them are victimless crimes. For instance:

In its 2008 report (covering 2007 cases of alleged abuses), CAIR included as a "hate crime" remarks made by Cincinnati talk-radio host Bill "Willie" Cunningham. "The great war of this generation's time is the war against Islamic fascists," he said on air. And referring to suicide bombers, he remarked, "They do not live for life, they live for death." Apparently CAIR thinks Cunningham should be arrested for exercising his First Amendment rights.

In its 2007 report, CAIR listed as a "hate crime" the following example: "A copy of the Quran was found in a toilet at the library of Pace University in

New York." There were other atrocities, too, such as someone trampling on a "flower bed" at a mosque in Texas.[56]

These are all inconvenient facts for CAIR and its antiwar agenda. It can't roll back the USA Patriot Act and key counterterror measures—such as mosque surveillance and passenger profiling—without ginning up sympathy in Washington for Muslims as a persecuted minority. Each time CAIR releases another over-hyped hate crimes report, it argues that violence and harassment against Muslims have multiplied because of the U.S. war on terror.

"Government acts"—including airport searches, detentions, and interrogations—"send a green light to mistreat Muslims," claims CAIR chief Awad.

With its 2008 report, CAIR recommends the enactment of "legislation banning racial, religious, or ethnic profiling."

But by crying wolf, CAIR shows it cares more about furthering its own political agenda than protecting ordinary Muslims. When real abuses occur, few Americans may pay attention. So CAIR is actually doing the Muslim community it claims to represent a disservice by exaggerating such crimes.

WHOPPER NUMBER 1: No official numbers exist for the size of the Muslim population in America, yet CAIR advises journalists that "six to seven million is the most commonly cited figure" and a safe number to use in stories.

What it doesn't say is that figure was made up by CAIR, and that it's been the one "commonly" citing it for years in press releases, alongside the claim that "Islam is one of the fastest-growing religions in America."

Obama parroted the bogus number in his speech to world Muslims in Cairo when he said there are "nearly seven million American Muslims in our country today."

This is CAIR's biggest, most pernicious fabrication of all, because it uses its mythical seven-million Muslim voting bloc to sway credulous politicians. They believe the figure, and CAIR uses it as a cudgel to help advance its subversive Islamist agenda.

The Pew Research Center recently put the lie to CAIR's claim, however. In an exhaustive scientific study of the size of the U.S. Muslim population, it was able to identify only 2.35 million Muslims—less than half the number commonly cited by CAIR, and less than 1 percent of the U.S. population of 305 million.

Pew, a liberal group with certainly no interest in marginalizing Islam, described its study as "perhaps the most rigorous effort to date to scientifically estimate the size of the Muslim American population."

Yet it practically apologized for its more accurate reading, being that it came in "significantly below some commonly reported estimates frequently cited by Muslim groups" like CAIR.

The report received little attention, however. And most media outlets— as well as Congress, the White House, and the State Department— continue to parrot CAIR's original figure to describe the size of the nation's Muslim population.

Only it's a wildly inflated estimate manufactured by CAIR, something that the media could easily refute if they dared—simply by deconstructing CAIR's unscientific methodology.

While the number of Muslims is growing thanks to higher birth rates and immigration, it's nowhere near CAIR's claim. Even the most generous independent estimate puts it at nearly half that size, or four million.

Finding reliable data for Muslims in America is hard because the Census Bureau does not survey creed. So CAIR, which has an agenda to Islamize America, gladly filled the vacuum.

To come up with its own figure, it hired a "respected scholar" by the name of Ihsan Bagby to lead its "study." But Bagby's not a trained demographer;

and as a longtime CAIR board member, he's not even independent.

Worse, he admits the number he arrived at is a "guesstimation." Here's how he came up with it:

1. With help from CAIR researchers, Bagby called the nation's 1,209 mosques and interviewed 416 of them, asking them how many people were involved in their mosque in any way. The average response was 1,625, which is probably high, given that two *imams* claimed fifty thousand when the nation's largest mosque—Dar al-Hijrah in the DC suburbs—has only about three thousand.

2. Bagby then multiplied that fuzzy participation figure by the 1,209 mosques and came up with two million "mosqued Muslims."

3. Next, he multiplied that sum by a magical factor of three to capture Muslims who might not participate in mosque activities, and arrived at the original six million guesstimate for the size of the Muslim population in America.[57]

4. He says his factor of three was an educated guess. More like a wild exaggeration. Or perhaps a political calculation, as it produced a number that conveniently matched the size—and potential political clout—of the Jewish population in the country, also estimated at six million.

5. CAIR then took the liberty of bumping up the Muslim count to seven million. Now—presto—it's at seven million, and climbing, according to new figures bandied about by Muslim activists.

6. But it's the Wahhabi lobby's big lie. CAIR and other militant Muslim groups use it to intimidate politicians, corporations, and media to change policy.

Eight-million-strong Muslims make the threat of bloc voting and boycotts a lot scarier. And the bigger the number, the bigger the foothold Islamists gain in American society.

But don't buy it. It's a total exaggeration—like most of the claims churned out by CAIR's propaganda machine.

THE GOEBBELS OF THE ISLAMIST MOVEMENT

All this false propaganda is peddled by CAIR's chief spokesman through press releases and email "action alerts." Hooper issued misleading press releases regarding the Days fraud scandal, as well, which led Muslim plaintiffs to add his name to the list of defendants in the case.

Known as "the Goebbels of the Islamist movement," Hooper has held workshops to help fellow propagandists "manipulate" (his word) the media into writing favorably of Islam, glossing over all its warts.

He teaches his pack of attack dogs to smear critics and shift the debate away from the truth of their message. "The credibility of the message depends on the credibility of the messenger," he is fond of saying. So kill the messenger, kill the message.

Hooper thinks journalists are lazy and last year gave a PowerPoint presentation to CAIR staffers on how to spoonfeed them information.[58] He monitors the media "gatekeepers" during luncheons and breakfasts and other outreach events, and brags that he seduces them into contacting his office for quotes through his incendiary "action alerts."

While MSNBC, NPR, CBS, and CNN serve as CAIR's useful idiots, Hooper warns the faithful to avoid doing interviews with:

• The Washington Times, New York Post, New York Sun and other "propaganda papers;"

• "Right-Wing Internet" news sites;

• Fox News' *O'Reilly Factor* and Glenn Beck and other "conservative cable" TV shows; and

• Rush Limbaugh and Michael Savage and other "conservative radio" hosts.[59]

That's because they, unlike his useful idiots, don't respect his wishes to sanitize reports about Palestinian and other Islamic terrorists by calling them "militants" or "rebels," or even "victims" of Israeli "occupation."

Hooper praises MSNBC, for one, for not using "the word 'terrorist' to describe every Palestinian who opposes the Israeli occupation of the West Bank and Gaza Strip." Reuters, he notes, also adopts more "neutral" terminology. He commends the wire service for not using the terms "Islamic terrorist" or "Muslim extremist"—or even "Islamist," which he also considers "pejorative." Stories by these friendly media outlets also carry his and other CAIR officials' quotes unquestioned, with no qualifiers regarding the source, shamelessly serving as megaphones for CAIR.

In addition to insisting journalists censor their stories and sacrifice accuracy for tolerance, Hooper recommends female reporters cover themselves before conducting interviews in mosques out of respect for the men there. He advises they show only their hands and face.[60]

CAIR acknowledges privately that Islam suffers from a negative image due to its treatment of women, as well as its promotion of violence. They are the "two major roadblocks" to mainstreaming Islam in America, CAIR confides in its internal training materials. Instead of disavowing them, however, CAIR advises its foot soldiers to find better ways to whitewash over them, while targeting their message at younger audiences, as they "are easier to sway."[61]

Some interns nonetheless expressed doubts last year about CAIR and its real agenda after they were exposed to critical Web sites like Anti-CAIR.com, which CAIR tried to shut down in a failed lawsuit. But Hooper would just tell them it was all Islamophobic "crap," whisteblower intern Chris Gaubatz says.

Image is everything to CAIR. Hooper never fails to trumpet the press it gets. "CAIR officials are regularly interviewed by national, local, and international media," he says triumphantly. "CAIR officials have been cited over eleven thousand times in major national and local media."

He also boasts that CAIR's work is now the subject of several "positive documentaries around the world."

Hooper is particularly proud of his personal appearances on CNN and C-Span and other networks. He's adorned the walls of CAIR's second-floor marble lobby in Washington with giant framed video stills of him and Awad during their major TV interviews. They are the media stars of CAIR, and the main entrance to its headquarters is their Hall of Fame.

"NOTE TO BROTHERS: Do not be afraid of makeup," media expert Hooper coaches amateur Muslim propagandists. "It is a part of the technical aspects of television."[62]

The more press CAIR attracts, the more powerful it looks. And the more power it projects, the more the money pours in from big Mideast donors.

"CAIR is receiving support by some big donors not because of perceived effectiveness but because of its image in [the] media," CAIR's research director Mohamed Nimer observed in handwritten notes he made during one meeting. "Now people think we are this big group moving and shaking in DC."[63]

CAIR's bark is clearly bigger than its bite, as the next chapter makes abundantly clear. But subterfuge and propaganda have made up for shortfalls so far, and Hooper has been instrumental in that department.

SOFTER FACE OF CAIR

These days, however, CAIR's high-profile spokesman is taking a lower profile. The pugnacious, six-foot, two hundred-pound Hooper has been nudged aside as the board tries to put a kinder, gentler face on its spin machine.

Besieged by negative publicity and plunging membership, directors have moved to soften CAIR's image by putting more women out front—

albeit in head scarves—as the public face of CAIR. Rabiah Ahmed and Amina Rubin are among the female Muslim flacks at CAIR who have gotten more face time in the media.

Hooper, 53, also became a lightening rod for controversy when un-American comments he made years ago resurfaced in the national press. He let it slip to a Minnesota reporter last decade that he wants Islam to rule America. Hooper failed to adequately disavow his subversive dream in recent radio interviews, which only reignited the debate over his loyalties.

Then he gave a particularly embarrassing performance on MSNBC during the so-called Flying Imams controversy. Host Tucker Carlson got the best of Hooper during an interview about the case, and Hooper imploded, and he's still stewing about it, insiders say.

Carlson, who's now high on CAIR's media enemies "hit" list, asked Hooper why CAIR was suing John Doe passengers for reporting suspicious behavior aboard a US Airways flight, when such legal action could scare other Americans into silence in the face of a terrorist threat.

CARLSON: Why are you supporting a lawsuit that would punish people for doing just that?

HOOPER: Because we're not in support of malicious reporting.

CARLSON: How do you know it was malicious?

HOOPER: Well, that's to be determined.

CARLSON: But you are supporting these people being sued. Their lives are disrupted.

HOOPER: That's how you…

CARLSON: You are punishing them, and yet you don't know it was malicious what they did?[64]

Flustered and visibly agitated, Hooper could only raise his voice and talk over the host, which he did for the rest of the interview before closing with a snarky remark suggesting Carlson was an anti-Muslim bigot.

Even ISNA considers Hooper radioactive. He was not invited to speak at the front group's convention last year, and he openly complained about it to colleagues during the event, recorded conversations reveal. (He was also caught on tape at the time calling decorated war hero Senator John McCain "an old geezer with cancer.")[65]

Behind the scenes, though, Hooper is busy launching an aggressive new propaganda campaign to depict CAIR as a civil-rights champion in league with the NAACP. CAIR is strengthening its alliance with the Congressional Black Caucus and has elected a black Muslim convert as its chairman in an effort to conflate the African-American struggle with the Muslim experience in America.

Newly elected CAIR chairman Shaw, a longtime North Carolina state senator and vice chairman of that state's legislative black caucus, has likened the U.S. government's co-conspirator charge against CAIR to the FBI's surveillance of civil rights leaders in the 1960s.

"We look forward to partnering with the Obama administration to help defend civil liberties," he says.[66]

Career FBI case agents say CAIR is doubling down on what has worked in the past. For over a decade, it's managed to hide its true agenda of supporting violent jihad and militant Islam under the cover of civil-rights advocacy.

"I don't care how many times they tell you they're a civil rights organization, they're not," says a senior FBI agent in Washington. "They're a front group for Hamas and the Muslim Brotherhood."[67]

Of course, if CAIR openly confessed its true mission, it wouldn't get a toe in the door of official Washington.

The nature of CAIR's very existence is a lie. And it doesn't just wildly exaggerate the size and influence of the American Muslim population it claims to represent. It also wildly exaggerates its own size and influence, as we reveal in the next chapter with data from its own records.

CHAPTER NINE

PULLING BACK THE CURTAIN ON CAIR

"CAIR is very concerned about its reputation in the community. Without the community (and Allah's help) CAIR would fail."

—**Former CAIR Civil-Rights Manager Joshua Salaam**[1]

CAIR PROMOTES ITSELF as "the most influential Muslim organization in America, with more than thirty chapters and offices nationwide and in Canada." It claims to be the official representative of all Muslim Americans. And it has carefully crafted an image of itself as professional, authoritative, credible, and most of all, powerful.

So powerful, in fact, that it can, at a moment's notice, marshal millions of angry Muslim voters or boycotters against Washington politicians or Fortune 500 companies who balk at its demands.

At least that's the image that CAIR projects.

But it's all bluff. Pull back the curtain on its internal operations and one discovers a largely hollow organization running a skeletal staff with high turnover and poor worker morale.

Internal communications and financial statements also reveal an organization struggling to stay afloat. CAIR is suffering from steadily shrinking membership dues and fundraising revenues, and has been operating at a loss for years.

Like the Wizard of Oz who used smoke and mirrors to transform his modest stature into something larger than life, CAIR furiously works its own levers and buttons to create an illusion of size and power. From behind the curtain, it thunders warnings not to arouse the wrath of the great and powerful CAIR; but without the veil, it stands exposed as a fraud.

Only through sheer *chutzpah* has CAIR been able to convince the Washington punditry it's a force to be reckoned with. Only through threats and intimidation has it been able to extract the concessions it has from corporate America, which often cowers before it, oblivious to its wile and deception.

From behind its loud speakers and smoke machine in Washington, CAIR has created a mythical status that's allowed it to impose itself on the national scene. But data from CAIR's own files expose the baling wire and duct tape holding the myth together.

MYTH: CAIR has a large, loyal, and dedicated work force.

FACT: The organization suffers from high employee turnover, with churn rates running as high as 50 percent, and operates with barebones staff and field offices that in some cases are nothing more than mail drops.

Witness this 2004 warning to CAIR's board from then-CAIR Director of Operations Khalid Iqbal: "I am very concerned about the employee turnover at CAIR National. Last year alone fourteen people left CAIR. That is more than 50 percent of our workforce."

In the memo, Iqbal added that he was worried about "low employee moral [*sic*]" and "loss of thousands of dollars to CAIR."[2]

Negative comments made by exiting staffers included too much "micromanagement" by CAIR executives, he noted.

Iqbal himself left CAIR last year. And several other high-ups over the past two years have joined him, including:

• Parvez Ahmed, CAIR's national board chairman;

• Ahmed Bedier, communications director for CAIR's Florida operations and executive director of its Tampa chapter;

• Arsalan Iftikhar, CAIR's national legal director;

• Omer Subhani, communications director for CAIR's Miami chapter; and

• Omar Ahmad, CAIR's co-founder and chairman emeritus, who retired from CAIR's board earlier this year after serving almost fifteen years as a director.

In a separate report to the board, the former head of CAIR's civil rights office complained that his department had "recently lost several experienced staff members." In his two-page memo, civil rights manager Joshua Salaam added that "we began to take steps backwards."[3]

CAIR is also having a tough time recruiting new talent after prosecutors linked it to a conspiracy to raise funds for the terrorist group Hamas.

Not a few young activists have left CAIR fearing they'd be blackballed by government or corporate America for working for a terrorist-supporting group.

The negative publicity is taking its toll on CAIR's internship program as well. Some interns last summer refused to have their photographs taken with CAIR, because they were afraid the images would come back to haunt them.

In fact, last year's Washington interns are conspicuously absent from CAIR's Web site. Despite coaxing from CAIR officials, interns broke with tradition and declined to be individually profiled on the group's Web site.

CAIR's national outreach coordinator, Raabia Wazir, expressed her disappointment last July in an email to the class of interns. She blamed "right-wing" detractors for the revolt.

Here is her message, written under the subject line: "Regarding the Online Intern Profiles," which she copied to CAIR executive director Awad and other headquarters officials:

We will not be posting intern profiles on the Web site as we had previously planned. A number of individuals voiced concerns regarding being publically [sic] associated with CAIR. While we certainly respect your right to privacy, we are disappointed that any intern would act out of fear of prejudice from a few right-wing fringe groups. Activism is rarely popular and never easy. It is an uphill struggle that we must face every day with passion and dedication. I thank all of you for your commitment to CAIR's mission of advocating for justice and mutual understanding. I pray that you will always have the courage to openly defend and support our mission and goals.[4]

Whistleblower intern Chris Gaubatz says CAIR had planned to use the profiles as part of a campaign to create a younger, edgier image to help in recruiting.

"This is why [Yaser] Tabbara [executive director of CAIR's chapter in President Obama's hometown of Chicago] and Raabia were so upset when the interns didn't want their pictures on the Web site," he says. "They were very stereotypical college students who looked and dressed the part of America's youth, and CAIR wanted them to be front and center on the Web site."

Several interns told Gaubatz they did not plan to list their CAIR experience on their resumés.

They are not alone. Even some former high-level CAIR officials have scrubbed their association with the group.

Subhani, for one, recently removed references to CAIR from his blog. And Iftikhar, despite working for several years at CAIR's headquarters, chose not to list his position there in his extensive bio posted on his personal Web site. There is not even an allusion to his work at CAIR in a *curriculum vitae* that runs almost five hundred words.[5]

CAIR'S 'CIVIL WAR'

What's more, tension has been growing between CAIR's board and

Awad and spokesman Hooper, who have become mired in controversy and bad press.

In fact, some members of the board recently wanted to push out the two founding executives, but reconsidered out of fear the organization would flounder absent their experience and institutional knowledge.

Insiders say former chairman Parvez Ahmed, who chafed at CAIR's "old guard mentality," resigned after directors voted to keep Awad and Hooper on board. Ahmed argued for "new blood at the executive levels" and greater transparency at the organization.[6]

The high-level dissension has become so intense that insiders refer to it as CAIR's "civil war." Bad blood even developed between old friends Awad and co-founder and former chairman Omar Ahmad, who retired from CAIR's board earlier this year.

Things got so rough for Hooper that at one point he was told by a director to stop talking to the media and consider working from his home. There was a time when he thought the board was monitoring his emails.[7]

Hooper couldn't understand why the board turned against him and Awad, and openly speculated that someone on the board had been "blackmailed," according to a transcription of a conversation with Hooper that Gaubatz videotaped at last year's ISNA convention. CAIR's spokesman is convinced of an outside "conspiracy" to divide CAIR.[8]

MYTH: CAIR represents all Muslims.

FACT: CAIR discriminates against Shiite Muslims—including its own employees who identify with that minority sect of Islam—and doesn't really represent all Muslims, even as it sues other employers for discriminating against Muslims.

"CAIR's constituency represents an even broader base" than Arab, South Asian, or African-American Muslims, Awad claims. "Many Muslims turn to it for help when facing job or religious discrimination."

But where do CAIR employees turn when they've been discriminated against by CAIR? Tannaz Haddadi found out the hard way.

A Shiite Muslim, Haddadi says she was "completely dishonored and mistreated" by senior CAIR managers because of her religious background while working in the membership department at CAIR's national office in Washington.

"I have been a victim of both gender and religious discrimination," she wrote in a blistering four-page letter to Awad and then-CAIR chairman Ahmad.[9]

"At first glance," she added, "it may appear unusual to claim discrimination while working for a civil rights organization. It may seem even more unusual that I am a Muslim claiming religious discrimination while working for a Muslim organization."

But, Haddadi continued, "I have struggled for two years—along with others—with frustration and acts of discrimination."

She says the discrimination against her started several years ago when CAIR operations director Iqbal tasked her to update CAIR's internship application form by adding a section asking applicants to identify which sect of Islam they belong to. Haddadi told Iqbal, a Sunni Muslim, that she felt uncomfortable making such a change. That upset him, she says, and led him to quiz her about her own beliefs.

"This is where he discovered that my background is Shia," she said, "and from that point his attitude changed towards me."

The leadership of CAIR is dominated by Sunni Muslims, who account for about 90 percent of the world Muslim population.

Soon, Haddadi says she was demoted to part-time receptionist. She spent the next couple of years answering phones. "I have been frustrated with discrimination at CAIR for two years," she complained to CAIR's front office.

"SECRET HISTORY OF DISCRIMINATION"

Tannaz Haddadi says hers was not an isolated case. CAIR has engaged in a pattern of gender and religious bias against employees.

"CAIR has it's [*sic*] own secret history of discrimination before Mr. Iqbal came, that has caused many employees to quit and very few to come back," Haddadi wrote.[10]

When she threatened to file a formal complaint of discrimination with the EEOC, she says she was told not to complain, because her mistreatment was "for the sake of Allah."

With that, Haddadi decided to resign.

CAIR declined comment. But at least three other office workers allegedly witnessed acts of discrimination against Haddadi, including CAIR's office manager, a civil rights coordinator, and an executive assistant.

CAIR has also discriminated against non-Muslim employees and volunteers.

CAIR intern Corina Chang, for one, confided to Gaubatz that she and two other non-Muslim interns—both of whom also happen to be women—had been discriminated against because they were not Muslim. She said CAIR excluded them from participation in its nationwide Mosque Census Project, a comprehensive survey of Islamic centers in America.

Indeed, CAIR invited only Muslims to meetings on the project and notified only Muslims about the conference calls to discuss project details. Upset, Chang complained to her boss and was allowed to sit in on a call.

Civil rights activists often volunteer at CAIR even though they are not Muslim.

MYTH: CAIR's membership is steadily increasing with the size of the Muslim population in America.

FACT: CAIR's growth is moving in the opposite direction. The Muslim group is rapidly losing members, even as the overall Muslim population rises from immigration, high birth rates, and religious conversions.

CAIR publicly claims to have fifty thousand members, but according to internal memos, its real number of paid members is a paltry 5,133— far short of CAIR's post-9/11 target of one hundred thousand.[11]

At a 2002 board meeting, CAIR set a goal to "increase CAIR membership" to one hundred thousand by the end of the year, in part by expanding the definition of "member" to include foreign Muslim donors living overseas and anyone whom CAIR registered to vote in the U.S., including non-Muslims.

"New definition is: Anyone who fill [sic] out a membership form ($10 fee) or donate to CAIR both on an annual basis or register to vote will be considered as a CAIR member, unless someone specifically decline [sic] to be a CAIR member," minutes of the high-level meeting state.[12]

"Membership will be open to all either American or international donor [sic], Muslim or non-Muslim," the meeting notes add.

CAIR also converted family and organization memberships to individual memberships to increase its totals.

The board advised staff involved in the new membership drive to use the slogan: "We need you to become a CAIR member."

Despite the ambitious campaign and sympathetic post-9/11 media coverage, CAIR didn't come close to meeting its goal. Lowering its expectations, it subsequently came up with a long-term goal of sixty thousand members by 2011.[13]

But if current trends continue, it will miss that mark as well.

In a court brief, CAIR's attorneys blamed slumping membership and donations on bad publicity from the Holy Land Foundation trial.[14]

While certainly a factor, membership began falling long before the trial began in 2007. Internal notes from CAIR's meetings predating the trial complain of "weak membership drives." In fact, internal records show that CAIR's membership hit a high of only 9,211 after its big post-9/11 push for new members.[15]

Using Pew Research's survey estimate of 2.5 million American Muslims, CAIR's current five thousand members represent just two-tenths of one percent of the U.S. Muslim population. Using CAIR's inflated guesstimate of seven million American Muslims, CAIR represents an even smaller fraction of the Muslim community.

CAIR's total membership in the nation's largest Muslim state of California is just 903—barely enough to fill one city mosque.[16]

Bottom line is, CAIR is unsupported by the broader Muslim population, which finds it more a liability than an asset.

And given the anemic size of its member database, CAIR cannot possibly deliver on its threats to bring the weight of the Muslim community to bear against national politicians, CEOs, or advertisers for media personalities it doesn't like.

The actual size of CAIR's political clout and boycotting potential is quite puny, which might come as a shock to weak-kneed advertisers who have caved in to CAIR's demands in the past. It turns out that the handful of vociferous Muslims whom CAIR activated into emailing or calling to protest ad sponsors never represented the millions of consumers CAIR suggested. They're merely CAIR's loyal henchmen who receive their marching orders through the group's "action alert" email list, which also is relatively anemic in size.

ALL BARK, NO BITE

So fear not, corporate America: CAIR has no real boycotting power in your state. And fear not, Washington: CAIR has no real voter leverage in your district. The only thing it has is a few loud mouths.

"This is the untold story in the myth that CAIR represents the American Muslim population," says Zuhdi Jasser, director of the Phoenix-based American Islamic Forum for Democracy. "They only represent their membership and donors," whose interests often diverge from the greater Muslim community.[17]

Even former CAIR officials, such as ex-chairman Ahmed, agree that CAIR too often neglects Muslim constituents' needs to focus on political and foreign policy matters.

They say the perception of CAIR among the general Muslim public is that it concentrates too much on the Palestinian issue, as well as other foreign matters such as the alleged abuse of terrorist detainees at Gitmo.

Also, former CAIR civil rights manager Salaam says that Muslim constituents complain that CAIR "does not return phone calls" from them when they seek CAIR's help. Headquarters has also improperly handled cases, he says, while showing reluctance to refer cases to other organizations with more expertise or better resources.

"CAIR is very concerned about its reputation in the community," Salaam cautioned CAIR executives in one internal report. "Without the community (and Allah's help), CAIR would fail."[18]

Of course, its reputation hit a new low last year with the Jamil Morris Days fraud case. The scandal and coverup culminated in a lawsuit filed by Muslim constituents against CAIR, as discussed at length in an earlier chapter.

All of this is converging to depress CAIR's membership numbers.

MYTH: CAIR is financially sound.

FACT: CAIR's national headquarters is operating in the red, with losses mounting each year, and it's struggling to keep its doors open.

Income from membership dues slowed to a trickle in 2006, the latest available IRS tax filing, and CAIR operated at a loss of more than $160,000 in that calendar year, following a deficit of nearly $50,000 in 2005. In 2004, in contrast, CAIR reported a surplus of more than $338,000.[19]

During the hemorrhaging, though, its top executives still raked in six-figure incomes, including $121,760 in total compensation for CAIR chief Awad. In fact, headquarters still supports an eye-popping $1 million payroll.[20]

Dues plummeted from more than $700,000 in 2000, when CAIR charged $25 per member, to slightly more than $40,000 in 2006, when dues cost $35, according to IRS statements.[21]

"Membership dues measures the organization's success and base of support," CAIR states in the section of its report to the IRS explaining why it collects dues. Well, CAIR fails to measure up in both areas.

Revenues from CAIR's annual fundraising dinner are also drying up. Tax records show CAIR hauled in just under $90,000 in 2006, compared with a little more than $170,000 in 2004—a drop of nearly 50 percent.[22]

Again, CAIR blames the government for the shortfall, arguing it has scared off donors by linking CAIR to terrorist fundraising.

"The public naming of CAIR as an unindicted co-conspirator has impeded its ability to collect donations, as possible donors either do not want to give to them because they think they are a 'terrorist' organization or are too scared to give to them because of the possible legal ramifications of donating money to a 'terrorist' organization," CAIR lawyers complained in the court brief cited earlier.

But CAIR has only itself to blame. In 2002, as CAIR was complaining about a "lack of funds" and launching a campaign to solicit Muslims for more dues, Awad privately assured CAIR staffers and the Muslim community at large that "all allegations against CAIR are baseless."[23] That turned out to be false, based on reams of government evidence, and now he and CAIR have lost credibility in the community.

A DESPERATE REORGANIZATION

By 2007, CAIR realized it had to do something drastic to stay in business. So it huddled with its auditor Joey Musmar and counsel Joe Sandler and together they hammered out a reorganization plan.

Most key, CAIR changed its IRS tax-exempt status from a 501(c)(4) nonprofit organization to a 501(c)(3) organization in order to attract more donations. Donations to 501(c)(4) organizations are not tax-deductible, while donations to 501(c)(3) organizations are deductible to the full extent of the law.

CAIR also created a holding company to shield its real estate investments. Though cash-poor, CAIR is relatively asset-rich and controls an estimated $3 million worth of real estate in the Washington area, excluding its national headquarters.[24]

But that could soon change. Things are so bad at CAIR that:

• It has considered liquidating some of its investment property to raise cash.

• It's having to rent out the entire first floor of its national headquarters, which is operating with a skeletal staff of ten full-time employees.

• It's begging mosques, including the ADAMS Center in Virginia, for emergency funding.[25]

What's more, CAIR has had to:

• Send interns to classes on writing effective grant proposals so they can research and apply for government and other grants on behalf of CAIR—some of which have been made under false pretenses.[26]

• Deal with liens filed against its Capitol Hill property by unpaid contractors.[27]

• Put on hold its "Hate Hurts America" advertising boycott of the Michael Savage radio show for lack of funds.

With growing cashflow problems and its grassroots support all but gone, CAIR is relying more and more on foreign cash from big Arab donors to survive, raising new questions about CAIR's independence and tax-exempt qualifications.

CHAPTER TEN

CAIR'S ARAB PAYMASTERS

"UAE, sovereign wealth funds, Qatar, Saudi, you name it. Pick anywhere in the Gulf. This is [CAIR's] donor network now."

—*FBI special agent in Washington investigating CAIR and its leaders*[1]

I F THE COUNCIL on American-Islamic Relations doesn't get its money from grassroots members, where does it get its money?

That's a question even members of Congress are beginning to ask, including GOP Representative Frank Wolf of Virginia, co-chair of the Congressional Human Rights Caucus, who recently queried federal agencies: "Does CAIR receive financial contributions from foreign sources?"

Only he and other lawmakers aren't getting clear answers. By IRS law, the identities and addresses of CAIR's major donors—like those of other tax-exempt nonprofit groups—are kept secret. So the bulk of the Hamas front group's financing remains shrouded in mystery.

"CAIR does not publicize the names of individual donors," asserts CAIR spokesman Ahmed Rehab.

But there is no doubt that CAIR receives direct funding from foreign sources—including Arab nations tied to the 9/11 plot and other anti-Western terrorism. It's actively getting major infusions of overseas cash to fund its campaign of deceit.

Of course this is a closely guarded secret at CAIR. Publicly acknowledging it is bankrolled by Arab paymasters would risk raising alarms in Washington that it is controlled by foreign interests in the Middle East, further limiting its access to the political establishment.

CAIR still insists—despite mounting evidence to the contrary—that it is a "grass-roots organization" supported by dues-paying members, while strenuously denying it receives foreign cash.

In fact, in press releases CAIR has stated unequivocally that it receives no "support from any overseas group or government."[2]

Once again, CAIR is dissembling. While there was a time when CAIR got most of its revenues from small American donors and dues-paying members, it's now bankrolled by a handful of fat-cat donors and *sheiks* from the Persian Gulf—raising serious questions about its independence and tax-exempt status.

CAIR has an annual operating budget of more than $2.7 million, and hopes to double it to $5 million by the end of 2010.[3] Records show the group is relying on some two dozen deep-pocketed donors for support, including one generous benefactor who contributes a lump sum payment of $600,000 to CAIR each year.[4]

Together they account for some 60 percent of CAIR's total budget. Who are they? Many of them are Arab donors flush with petrodollars and closely identified with wealthy Gulf governments, according to informed federal law enforcement sources.

"The executive director [Nihad Awad] has gone from just a small pool of [domestic] contributors that were really loyal to that Palestinian cause, and now he's Gulf-coast-wide," says a senior FBI special agent in Washington who's been investigating CAIR and who asked that his name be withheld.

"I mean, UAE [United Arab Emirates], sovereign wealth funds, Qatar, Saudi [Arabia], you name it. Pick anywhere in the Gulf coast," the agent added in an exclusive interview. "This is the executive director's donor network now."[5]

Qatar is where the spiritual leader of the Muslim Brotherhood—Sheik Yusuf al-Qaradawi—is based. Championed by CAIR as a "prominent scholar," Qaradawi has been banned from entering the U.S. due to his *fatwahs* calling for the killing of American troops and his leadership in a charity blacklisted by the U.S. Treasury as a terrorist organization. Doha-based Qaradawi has referred to CAIR as "our brothers there" in America.

WIRE TRANSFERS FROM SAUDI BANKS

Next door in Saudi Arabia, members of the ruling family have transferred hundreds of thousands of dollars in funds directly from their accounts held at the Saudi National Commercial Bank to CAIR's Citibank account in the U.S., records show.

For instance, Saudi Prince Abdullah bin Mosa'ad in 2007 wired $112,000 to CAIR, according to internal bank records kept by CAIR. "CAIR thanks you and HRH Prince Abdullah bin Mosa'ad for this generous contribution to CAIR," the national office wrote in an email to the prince's Saudi-based lawyer after verifying the funds were deposited into CAIR's account.[6]

As CAIR's domestic grass-roots support has dried up, it has stepped up its overseas fundraising efforts. Tax records show its travel budget for fundraising purposes has nearly doubled since 2004.[7]

Awad makes frequent pilgrimages to the Gulf to personally solicit funds. And he's often joined by Hooper, who over the years has obtained several passports and is described by government officials as a "heavy traveler."[8] CAIR's communications honcho boasted at last year's ISNA convention that he and Awad have the ability to bring in substantial amounts of "overseas money," according to video logs.[9]

CAIR's board recently proposed hiring an "international events manager" to help coordinate all the fundraising and other foreign activities. It has even created a special committee on "international affairs" headed by Awad to help tailor its pro-Arab message to American policymakers.

To that end, Awad not long ago took a trip to Saudi to meet with the secretary general of the Organization of the Islamic Conference to "discuss future CAIR-OIC projects." The OIC, a Muslim Brotherhood stronghold which promotes the interests of fifty-seven Muslim nations, has defended Hamas terrorists as "freedom fighters," and rationalized the 9/11 attacks as an act of Muslim "frustration" built up over years of "aggressions committed by the West."

Awad also hosted the secretary general at CAIR's headquarters in Washington, while lobbying to be named the first U.S. special envoy to the OIC (President Bush passed him over, appointing instead a Muslim entrepreneur from Texas with a relatively pro-Western bias). Tax records show CAIR has received at least $300,000 in grant money from OIC to, among other things, help fight "Islamophobia," which the OIC calls the "worst form of terrorism."[10]

To forge stronger ties in the Middle East and attract more financial support among wealthy Arab nationals, CAIR has also approved the development of an Arabic Web site, complete with a link for accepting donations online. (Fittingly, almost 99 percent of the coding and development work for CAIR's existing Web site is performed offshore— by a computer contractor in Karachi, Pakistan, a copy of their confidential contract reveals.)

THE UAE ENDOWMENT

Shortly after a company owned by the United Arab Emirates lost a controversial bid to take over control of several major U.S. ports, Awad and other CAIR officials traveled to the UAE to meet with its rulers. It was agreed that the UAE would set up an endowment in the U.S. run by CAIR to fund an "education" program to change negative perceptions about Islam that the UAE believes contributed to the public outcry that derailed its multi-billion-dollar ports deal.

The endowment caught the attention of the U.S. government, which issued a sensitive State Department cable regarding the unusual deal.[11]

It noted that the UAE Minister of Finance Sheik Hamdan bin Rashid al-Maktoum endorsed a proposal to build a $24 million property in the U.S. to serve as an endowment for CAIR to launch a $50 million image-building campaign through 2011.

"The endowment will serve as a source of income," Awad told the Arab press at the time, "and will further allow us to reinvigorate our media campaign projecting Islam and its principles of tolerance."[12]

Islam's image wasn't the problem with the UAE ports deal, however. It was scuttled as a result of security concerns over UAE's ties to al-Qaida and the 9/11 plot. Dubai served as an operational and financial base for the hijackers. Eleven of the hijackers, including two Emirates, were deployed to the U.S. from Dubai. The alleged twentieth hijacker, Mohamed al-Qahtani, also spent time in the UAE—where he had contacts with high-level UAE officials and received money for trips to al-Qaida's base in Kandahar, Afghanistan, according to Gitmo interrogation logs.

Before 9/11, moreover, the UAE supported and formally recognized the Taliban as the legitimate government of Afghanistan. The Muslim nation still boycotts products (and even professional tennis players) from Israel.

CAIR is working out details of its endowment with the Dubai-based Al-Maktoum Foundation. The anti-Israeli charity has held telethons to support families of Palestinian suicide bombers and other so-called "martyrs." Not surprisingly, the Arab press reported that CAIR "values highly the stances of Al-Maktoum Charity Foundation."[13]

Awad's ties to the UAE over the Palestinian cause run deep. His name appears alongside several contacts from Dubai and the UAE capital of Abu Dhabi on a phone tree for the Muslim Brotherhood's Palestine

Committee, court documents reveal. Most of these UAE contacts are connected to charitable fronts for Hamas.[14]

The Al-Maktoum Foundation is controlled by the ruler of Dubai—Sheik Mohammed bin Rashid al-Maktoum. While the billionaire puts on a good Western front, he has been known to support Islamic extremists. And after 9/11, he came to CAIR's rescue. In 2002, then-CAIR Chairman Omar Ahmad signed a DC land document deeding over controlling interest in CAIR's headquarters property to the *sheik's* foundation in exchange for nearly $1 million, as first reported in the 2005 book *Infiltration: How Muslim Spies and Subversives Have Penetrated Washington.*

Who is Sheik Mohammed? Before 9/11, he requisitioned C-130 military cargo planes to supply Osama bin Laden's camps in Kandahar with jeeps, trucks, generators, weapons, cash, and other material support. He and other members of the Emirates royal family are said to have joined bin Laden on hunting parties in Afghanistan.

In fact, U.S. intelligence officials had to call off a missile strike on bin Laden because they spotted a C-130 airplane with tail numbers identified as belonging to the UAE. They soon realized, to their dismay, that Emirates ministers and princes were members of bin Laden's hunting party, and if they went ahead with the bombing, they "might have wiped out half the royal family in the UAE," as the former CIA director put it.

These camps acted as al-Qaida's boardroom, a place where bin Laden and his henchmen schemed and plotted terrorist strikes. Sheik Mohammed and other UAE officials knew bin Laden is a wanted terrorist, yet they had tea with him and hunted with him for months at a time at his desert camps.

Bin Laden's old hunting partners are now among CAIR's silent foreign partners.

The amount of the UAE's pledge toward the $50 million CAIR endowment is undisclosed. But it is not the only Arab government funding it.

According to CAIR board meeting notes, a Washington PR firm used by the Emirates—Hill and Knowlton—has put together a "business plan" to help CAIR raise money from other Gulf states.

"The UAE ambassador is willing to gather all ambassadors of the Gulf Cooperating Council to listen to a presentation," Awad reported to the board. "In return, hopefully they will write to their respective people to ask for support."[15]

The six-member Gulf Cooperating Council was set up by the Saudis as a regional common market that includes Bahrain, Kuwait, Oman, Qatar, and the UAE.

THE SAUDI PIPELINE

Following its meeting with government officials in Dubai, CAIR traveled to the Saudi capital of Riyadh to solicit additional funds for the endowment, prompting another sensitive State Department cable.[16]

At a press conference held at the headquarters of the Saudi-controlled World Assembly of Muslim Youth, CAIR announced the launch of its massive PR campaign and warned potential donors that the U.S. was trying to curtail the political activity of Muslims.

Awad, with Hooper at his side, said CAIR needed a well-funded endowment to change American opinion. He proposed spending $10 million annually for five years on the media campaign.

"We are planning to meet Prince al-Waleed bin Talal for his financial support to our project," Awad said. "He has been generous in the past."[17]

Indeed, the Saudi prince donated $500,000 to CAIR after 9/11. He also presented a $10 million relief check to then-New York City Mayor Rudy Giuliani—or at least he tried. Giuliani, to his credit, rejected the gift after bin Talal blamed U.S. policy toward Israel for the attacks.

WAMY, the Saudi group that sponsored CAIR's press conference, has also provided substantial financial support to CAIR, notably during the construction of its multi-million-dollar headquarters. WAMY's U.S. branch—located in a Washington suburb and formerly headed by bin Laden's nephew, Abdullah bin Laden—was raided after 9/11 by federal authorities who suspected the group was funding terrorism and radicalizing Muslim youth.

WAMY is listed as a charity, but according to court documents, its real agenda is promoting religious hatred and violent jihad against infidels. Published materials seized by the feds reveal that its goal is to "arm the Muslim youth with full confidence in the supremacy of the Islamic system over other systems." It teaches teenaged Muslims to sacrifice their lives in jihad. "Are you miserly with your blood?!" it asks them in one booklet. WAMY also teaches them to "love taking revenge on the Jews," who it calls "humanity's enemies."

One of its sister organizations, the Saudi-based International Islamic Relief Organization, is also a CAIR booster. Its American branch has contributed at least $17,000 to CAIR.[18]

IIRO's northern Virginia office was twice raided by the FBI as part of a money laundering and terrorism investigation. Before 9/11, IIRO had helped fund six militant training camps in Afghanistan. And its branch in the Philippines was founded by bin Laden's brother-in-law, Mohamed Jamal Khalifah, a senior al-Qaida member.[19]

Despite Khalifah's deep involvement in terrorism, tellingly, CAIR founder and chairman Ahmad testified on his behalf after his arrest on terrorism charges, imploring that the al-Qaida leader had a "good reputation." Asked about IIRO, Ahmad said, "I'm very familiar with their work. I work very closely with their office in Washington DC."[20]

IIRO operates a dozen branch offices inside Saudi Arabia, each overseen by a member of the Saudi royal family. According to court records, the so-called charity is used by the Saudi government as an instrument to spread militant Islam.[21]

The Saudi pipeline to CAIR doesn't end there.

CAIR also has received at least $250,000 from a Saudi-based bank headed by the former director of the Muslim World League, a charity founded by the Saudi royal family and overseen in part by the kingdom's chief Islamic cleric, himself a government official. Osama bin Laden has identified the Muslim World League as a primary source of al-Qaida funds. Its U.S. offices also were raided after 9/11.

'MULTIPLE INVESTORS AS CO-OWNERS'

Ahmad Mohamed Ali, the Muslim World League's former secretary general, has served as president of the Saudi-based Islamic Development Bank for more than twenty years. IDB originally donated a quarter of a million dollars to help CAIR purchase land in Washington to build its headquarters. The grant was announced at the time by the Saudi embassy.

The IDB is not like any bank. It has distributed more than $250 million to the families of Palestinian "martyrs" from two large *intifada* funds it manages—the Al-Quds Fund and the Al-Aqsa Fund, which get most of their contributions from the Saudi kingdom. It also has a special projects branch that funds projects in non-Muslim countries to propagate militant Islam.

Recent board meeting notes show that CAIR and IDB have discussed the creation of a "building endowment," bringing in "multiple investors as co-owners" of CAIR's portfolio of properties.

"Nihad (Awad) reported that IDB is evaluating the building proposal," a copy of the minutes states, "and considering how the entity will be structured financially."[22]

After the book *Infiltration* exposed its silent Dubai partner, CAIR created a limited-liability holding company to shield its real estate investors. The Greater Washington LLC was formed in Delaware, which allows the owners, managers, and directors of the LLC to remain anonymous.

However, CAIR doesn't think the holding company goes far enough to protect its real estate assets from lawsuits. Its lawyers and accountants have warned of "liability concerns in case of lawsuit," explaining that CAIR's assets could be attached to a judgment for damages.

"Our accountant Joey Musmar has serious concerns if CAIR does not create a totally separate entity with (a) different board of directors for the holding company," Awad wrote in a report to the board. "He strongly feels that the current proposed structure will not protect the properties unless there is a clear separation."[23]

Before the recent real estate crash, CAIR estimated the combined value of its real estate assets—including its Capitol Hill headquarters—at almost $10 million.[24] Most of its investment properties are DC townhouses, and include the following addresses (along with purchase price and date of purchase):

- *917 2nd Street, NE* ... $660,000 ... January 21, 2005

- *203 K Street* ... $600,000 ... February 15, 2005

- *205 K Street* ... $600,000 ... February 15, 2005

- *923 2nd Street, NE* ... $1.2 million ... January 6, 2006

- *929 2nd Street, NE* ... $1.2 million ... January 6, 2006

- *210 Parker Street, NE* ... $419,000 ... April 12, 2006

- *919 2nd Street, NE* ... $500,000 ... July 18, 2006

- *208 Parker Street, NE* ... $410,000 ... September 11, 2006

CAIR has also tried to acquire two additional properties on K Street, as well as one on Second Street, an internal spreadsheet listing its assets indicates. (See Appendix.)

QUID PRO QUO?

The large donations from individuals, foundations, and sovereign wealth funds closely identified with Arab governments have raised suspicions within the Justice and Treasury Departments that CAIR may be controlled by foreign states hostile to the U.S. and its interests.

Is CAIR doing their official bidding? Has it been wrongfully acting as a lobbyist or agent for foreign governments?

There's no doubt the group has been acting as their mouthpiece in America. But there are signs it has engaged in political activities on their behalf that are in violation of its charter.

Consider its coordination with the OIC for starters. After receiving $300,000 from the fifty-seven-member Arab alliance, CAIR organized a workshop for its leaders on "Islamophobia" held at the Prince al-Waleed bin Talal Center for Christian-Muslim Understanding at Georgetown University in Washington. During their 2007 symposium, OIC Secretary General Ekmeleddin Ihsanoglu and other participants made several recommendations, including:

• "To work toward having a strong and effective professional lobby in the U.S. to project and protect Muslim interests."

• "To have a broader definition of hate crimes" and "to train law enforcement officials" to identify and crack down on anti-Islamic groups.

- "To consider establishing an international legal instrument to criminalize acts of Islamophobia," including adopting "legal measures against the defamation of religious icons," including publication of cartoons of the Muslim prophet Muhammad.[25]

During his visit to Washington, Ihsanoglu met with Awad at CAIR's headquarters, where Awad briefed him about CAIR "providing training to the U.S. government's agencies and departments including the State Department and Department of Homeland Security," an OIC report says.[26]

While briefing the general secretary, Awad "emphasized the need for partnership with the OIC to counter the phenomenon of Islamophobia," the report adds. "He stated the readiness of CAIR to extend all possible assistance to the OIC."

Internal documents show Awad routinely receives Arab delegations in his office and has hosted dinners for the UAE and Pakistani ambassadors as well as the former president of Iran. CAIR's office calendars also show high-level meetings at the UAE embassy and other Arab consulates.

In addition to the OIC, CAIR has brokered a "strategic plan on correcting the image of Islam and Muslims among the American public" with its paymasters in the UAE, who have a vested interest in changing perceptions in the wake of its failed bid to operate U.S. ports.

The Emirates fear that if that image is not repaired, their business interests will continue on a downward slide in America. CAIR's leaders have promised to act as a bulwark against any further backlash, and described the planned $50 million endowment as more of a business contract than charity.

RETURN ON INVESTMENT

"Do not think about your contributions as donations. Think about it from the perspective of rate of return," former CAIR chairman Parvez Ahmed told finance ministers in Dubai, according to the Arab press. "The investment of $50 million will give you billions of dollars in return for fifty years," if a sufficiently Arab-friendly environment can be created in America to allow *sheiks* to buy up key U.S. assets.[27]

In other words, investing in CAIR means having a reliable lobby for UAE business interests in Washington. CAIR's leaders have clearly stated their intention to use UAE funds to promote UAE interests in America, even though CAIR is not a registered foreign agent or even lobbyist.

Likewise, CAIR receives generous Saudi funding, and turns around and defends and promotes the interests of the Wahhabi lobby.

For example, CAIR has attacked Freedom House reports exposing the Saudi government's dissemination of hate literature in the U.S. The reports have documented clear examples of Saudi materials in mosques and Islamic schools advocating jihad against Jews and Christians and condemning Western societies.

Yet CAIR has pooh-poohed the findings. "The Freedom House report fails to rise to the level of an objective, unbiased, and academically worthy study," sniffed CAIR board member Nabil Sadoun.[28]

Similarly, CAIR has downplayed revelations that textbooks used at the Islamic Saudi Academy in northern Virginia teach Muslim children that Judaism and Christianity are false religions. The *madrassa*, which has graduated terrorists, is run by the Saudi embassy.

CAIR actually helps the Saudi embassy spread its hateful ideology. According to correspondence obtained from CAIR's executive files, CAIR routinely orders religious materials from the embassy to distribute to members and to use in converting Americans to Islam. Here's one request made by a top CAIR official in a letter to the embassy:

"On behalf of CAIR, I would like to request the following:

- Understanding Islam and Muslims ... 2,000 copies

- Islamic Library ... 3 sets

- Riyad us Salehin ... 10 sets

- Sahi Al-Bukhari ... 3 sets

- Tafseer Ibn Kathir ... 3 sets

The request includes volumes of militant Sunni interpretations of the *hadith*, or reports of the sayings and actions of Muhammad. All three texts are violent and call for the killing of Jews, Christians, and Muslims who do not adhere to *Shariah*.

"Brother Nihad Awad, Brother Omar Ahmad, and all the brothers and sisters from CAIR send their *Salaam* and regards to everyone at the embassy," wrote then-CAIR Operations Director Khalid Iqbal in closing out his order to the Saudis.[29]

Despite enjoying major support from such Arab governments and launching a major propaganda offensive in the U.S. on their behalf, CAIR has managed to avoid registering as a lobbyist or foreign agent and all the scrutiny and transparency that goes along with it.

The Foreign Agents Registration Act limits the influence of foreign agents and propaganda on U.S. public policy. The law states that organizations are required to register with the Justice Department when they act on "the order, request, or under the direction or control of a foreign principal." They must submit detailed disclosure reports if they engage in "political activities for, or in the interests of," a foreign principal, or if they "act in a public relations capacity" for one.

Foreign agents, moreover, must file and regularly update complete lists of employees and funds received and disclose copies of any written agreements and the terms and conditions of each oral agreement with a foreign principal. They also are required by law to provide detailed information about any distribution of propaganda and all lobbying contacts they make with any U.S. government agency or official.

If its activities were not hidden under the false claim of civil rights advocacy and protected under the *aegis* of tax-exempt status, CAIR no doubt would have to register as a foreign agent and reveal more than it is willing to reveal about its financing and political activities.

Far from representing grassroots American interests, CAIR acts as an organ for Arab regimes that have facilitated terrorist attacks on America and are fanning a subversive Islamist movement here. Members of Congress who cozy up to CAIR should take heed when its unregistered lobbyists darken their doorways.

As the next chapter uncovers, CAIR is plotting to run a major influence operation against Capitol Hill, and is specifically targeting sensitive committees dealing with homeland security.

CHAPTER ELEVEN

CO-OPTING CONGRESS

"We will focus on influencing congressmen responsible for policy that directly impacts the American Muslim community—for example, congressmen on the judiciary, intelligence, and homeland security committees."

—**Council on American-Islamic Relations 2007-2008 Strategic Plan**[1]

Last year's Democratic landslide was a watershed moment for CAIR and other Muslim Brotherhood front groups. They now have loyal boosters and cheerleaders at both ends of Pennsylvania Avenue.

During the election, CAIR's leaders gave money to Barack Obama and met privately with his campaign officials.[2] And in the final weeks before the election, some CAIR officials left the group's national office to campaign for the Democratic candidate in hotly contested states.

After Obama was sworn in as president, they swooned every time he made an overture to Muslims or sang a paean to Islam, such as the time at the White House National Prayer Breakfast when he read from one of Islam's sacred texts. "Did you see the clip of him quoting *hadith*?!" gushed one CAIR alumna in an email to colleagues.

"We look forward to partnering with the Obama administration," cooed recently seated CAIR Chairman Larry Shaw, a black convert to Islam.

At the other end of Pennsylvania Avenue, CAIR's "fortunes look to be on the rise" as well, worries one senior Republican congressional aide.

Already sympathetic to CAIR's agenda, Democrats have padded their majority in the House, and now enjoy filibuster-proof control of the Senate. They also command key committees dealing with law enforcement, intelligence, and homeland security, providing even softer targets for CAIR.

In a strategy paper marked "Company Proprietary" and written before the election, CAIR outlined a plan to launch an influence operation against members of these committees, while planting CAIR staffers and interns inside congressional offices.

"We will focus on influencing congressmen responsible for policy that directly impacts the American Muslim community. (For example, congressmen on the judiciary, intelligence, and homeland security committees.)," states the document listing CAIR's top long-term goals. "We will develop national initiatives such as a lobby day and placing Muslim interns in congressional offices."[3]

Its influence operation is well under way and already proving effective. Recently, seven House Democrats – including Mary Jo Kilroy of the homeland security committee and Adam Schiff of the judiciary and intelligence committees – delivered a letter to Attorney General Eric Holder demanding he meet with CAIR and ISNA and other Muslim Brotherhood front groups and address their grievances, including the FBI's use of informants in mosques and religious profiling of terrorist suspects.[4]

CAIR's tentacles already reach deep inside the warrens of Congress. Its officials meet regularly with Democratic Representative Keith Ellison, the nation's first Muslim congressman, along with Muslim staffers from both the House and Senate. They hold forums and panel discussions in Capitol Building conference rooms that even members of Congress have a hard time reserving. On Fridays, they gather with other Muslims in a basement room of the Capitol to pray toward Mecca.

That's not all. CAIR leaders have closely collaborated with the head of the powerful House Judiciary Committee on legislation denying law enforcement critical anti-terrorism tools.[5] And they've met privately with the assistant to the Speaker of the House to help hammer out a hate crimes bill and other legislation on their wish list.[6]

CAIR also has forged close alliances with three lawmakers recently appointed to serve on a key House Foreign Affairs subcommittee that has oversight of Mideast military basing rights and all foreign aid sent to the region, including Israel.

CAIR'S SPIES IN CONGRESS

Worse, CAIR has its own people working on the inside of Congress. Internal CAIR communications and other documents reveal that CAIR has strategically placed operatives inside the federal offices of Representative Sheila Jackson-Lee (D-TX), Representative Gregory Meeks (D-NY), and Representative Joe Sestak (D-PA) among others.

And now these CAIR agents are using their positions of power to legitimize a front group for Hamas and the Muslim Brotherhood and advance its subversive agenda.

Sestak aide Adeeba al-Zaman, for one, booked the congressman to speak at a $50-a-plate CAIR fundraiser in Philadelphia where he praised CAIR and Islam's supposedly "peaceful" tenets.

Sestak, a retired vice admiral, shared the spotlight with another special guest that night in April 2007 at the posh Hilton Philadelphia. As he and his congressional staff looked on, CAIR's national chairman presented an award to the founder of Bridges TV—Muzzammil Hassan—who recently confessed to murdering his wife by decapitation.[7]

Before serving as Sestak's outreach coordinator, al-Zaman was communications director of CAIR's Philadelphia chapter. Her stepfather serves on the organization's board and also heads a local mosque controlled by the radical Muslim Brotherhood.[8]

Over at the Senate, CAIR has cultivated Muslim moles inside the offices of key Democrat leaders—including Senator Dick Durbin of

Illinois, chairman of the Senate Judiciary Committee's subcommittee on human rights. His aide Reema Dodin—who's in regular contact with CAIR—is a Palestinian rights activist who organized anti-Israel rallies as a campus radical at UC Berkeley.[9]

Commenting on the 9/11 attacks as a leader of the radical Muslim Students Association—which was founded by Muslim Brotherhood members—Dodin explained away the suicide attacks as a tragic but inevitable response to U.S. support for Israel, which she says is "angering" Muslims the world over.

"No one wants to stop and think that these young men, in the prime of their lives, choose to do this to themselves. Why?" she said in an interview with a campus magazine. "Because now you have three generations of Palestinians born under occupation.[10]

"Maybe if you start to look at Palestinians as human beings," she added, "you will stop the suicide bombers."

Dodin went on to justify violent jihad. "Islam does teach that you must defend yourself," she said. "You cannot lie down and allow yourself, your home, your property, your family, and your people to be consistently oppressed."

At the same time, she condemned U.S. strikes against the Taliban and al-Qaida in Afghanistan, complaining that the military was "just going to hit innocent civilians."

PENETRATING 'THE SYSTEM'

Today, Durbin's legislative aide points to the election of two Muslim congressmen—Democrats Ellison of Minnesota and Andre Carson of Indiana—as proof Muslims can penetrate "the system" and bring about change from within.

All told, there are now upwards of fifty Muslim activists working on Capitol Hill today. Their growing presence raises alarms, counterintelligence officials say, because a stated goal of the U.S. Muslim Brotherhood is the infiltration of key government agencies and institutions like Congress.

During a secret Muslim Brotherhood meeting he organized last decade, CAIR founder and former chair Omar Ahmad expressed the need to strengthen "the influence with Congress." He argued for using Muslims as an "entry point" to "pressure Congress and the decision makers in America" to change U.S. foreign policy in the Middle East and other policies.[11]

The same FBI wiretaps reveal that CAIR's other founder and current leader, Nihad Awad, early on proposed sponsoring internships and fellowships as a vehicle for infiltrating government "institutions."[12]

Until it recently ran out of money, CAIR had been doing exactly that—sponsoring congressional fellowships. In 2007, CAIR budgeted $50,000 for two fellows, according to an internal spreadsheet. It filled at least one of those fellowship positions that year.[13]

In a 2007 report to Awad, a copy of which was obtained during 2008's undercover operation, CAIR Legislative Director Corey Saylor reported that he "placed Samia Elshafie in the office of Representative Jackson-Lee."[14] Elshafie has acted as the congresswoman's office contact for human rights issues.

Since the election, Saylor, a white convert who looks like an accountant, has worked with Jihad F. Saleh, a top Meeks aide and program coordinator for the Congressional Muslim Staffers Association,[15] to promote more Muslims into positions of power. They think the Muslim-friendly 111th Congress and the Obama administration offer fertile ground for planting agents for the cause.

"The past election was a watershed for the Muslim community," says Saleh, a black Muslim convert previously known as Benny "B.J." Williams.

SOLICITING RESUMÉS FROM THE MUSLIM MAFIA

The forty-five-member Muslim staffers association —the only one in Congress centered on religion—is now headed by Pakistani-American Assad R. Akhter, the legislative director for Democratic Representative Bill Pascrell of New Jersey. Pascrell has taken heat for reserving hard-to-get meeting rooms for CAIR in the Capitol.

The Congressional Muslim Staffers Association also includes members of the U.S. Capitol Police Department, responsible for protecting Congress from terrorism and other threats.

"We have a good representation of Arabs, Afro-Americans, South Asians, Reverts, and Latinos," Saleh says, adding that members "discuss Islam when the need arises." During 2008's Ramadan, the group served eight hundred DC Muslims at the annual congressional *Iftar*, which it co-hosts with CAIR. The dinner typically draws several members of Congress and dozens of congressional staffers.

Saleh, 34, has been busy conducting workshops for "Muslim professionals" to "capitalize" on the change in power and "ensure that Muslim Americans are prominent in the Obama administration."

"Muslims would greatly benefit by participating in the new government," he says.

To that end, he has gathered more than three hundred resumés for various positions on Capitol Hill—from chief of staff to committee counsel to press secretary. He also sent his "resumé book" to the Obama administration, where he hopes Muslim applicants will be considered for several thousand jobs in the new government.

Unbeknownst to many in Washington, Saleh has solicited resumés from Muslim Brotherhood front groups including ISNA and CAIR.[16] Last year, in fact, Saleh conducted a workshop at CAIR's offices on Muslim activism in government.[17]

The recruitment from the ranks of ISNA and CAIR is a major red flag, the senior congressional aide warns. He says the resumé book could present a security threat if not properly vetted. "If one person in there has ties to radicals," he says, "then the whole booklet is tarnished."[18]

The White House has confirmed it received the resumé book and has already hired a woman endorsed by Saleh and his group as an advisor on Islamic affairs. Egyptian-born Dalia Mogahed—the first veiled Muslim woman to be appointed to a position in the White House—will brief President Obama on what Muslims want from the U.S. She joins two full-time Muslim hires in the White House.

"He's done a lot" already for the Muslim community, Ellison says of Obama, "and I believe he will do more."

Saleh also is confident Obama—who wants to convene a "Muslim summit" to show his respect for their religion—will consider more Muslims for posts in the administration. "I trust that Americans will accept the principled leadership of Muslims who aspire to establish the Beloved Community, *insha'Allah*," Saleh says without elaborating on what he means by establishing "the Beloved Community."[19]

But Saleh, whose policy portfolio under Meeks includes homeland security, is a fan of the pan-Islamist, pro-jihadist *imam* Zaid Shakir, according to Saleh's posts on Twitter.com, where he tweets under the name "blackjihad." Shakir has declared the 82nd Airborne and other U.S. military fair game in jihad, and has urged followers to transform the U.S. into "a Muslim country" ruled by Islamic law.

'SEEDS FOR 9/11 PLANTED IN 1948'

Saleh also advises Meeks on foreign policy, and has taken "fact-finding" trips to the Middle East, according to congressional travel records.

CAIR boasts internally that it has "many potential allies in Congress," and that its foreign- and domestic-policy agendas dovetail with theirs. Topping their international agenda:

- Cutting aid to Israel.

- Creating a Palestinian state.

- Pulling U.S. troops out of Iraq and Afghanistan.

- Closing the military's terrorist prison camp in Guantanamo Bay, Cuba.

And bringing even Gitmo's most dangerous detainees, such as 9/11 mastermind Khalid Sheik Mohammed, to America (preferably Muslim-dominated Alexandria, Virginia, a move touted by CAIR supporter Representative Jim Moran, who represents the DC suburb), whereupon they can ditch their leg irons and manacles and stand trial in open court.

CAIR hopes more politicians will make a connection between 9/11 and the Israeli "occupation" of Palestinians.

"The seeds for 9/11 were planted in 1948," according to a draft of a "Proposed Muslim Platform" found at CAIR headquarters. "A resolution of the Israeli-Palestinian conflict needs to be based on recognizing and correcting the harm that was done to the Palestinians since 1948."[20]

The memo goes on to suggest that adopting a pro-Muslim foreign policy will buy protection for America.

"Good foreign policy means less worry about homeland security," it continues, "and better environment for a strong economy. Does anyone know what is the financial impact of 9/11 on the country?"

The domestic policy agenda of CAIR and its Democrat boosters is no less disturbing. Among other things, it includes:

• Repealing the USA Patriot Act;

• Weakening the Foreign Intelligence Surveillance Act;

• Outlawing anti-terrorist profiling by police;

• Abolishing quotas and post-9/11 restrictions on immigration from high-risk Muslim countries;

• Expediting security background checks on Arab and Muslim applicants for citizenship; and

• Purging the FBI terrorist watchlist, as well as airline no-fly lists.

CAIR notes in its internal papers that the power to influence such national policy "requires sophisticated lobby" and "access to positions of power." It also requires "engaging in a process where our people are involved (in) money contributions, votes (and) volunteering in campaigns."

VIOLATING IRS RULES AGAINST LOBBYING?

While the poli-sci merits of that formula may be sound, there's just one problem: CAIR is not a registered lobbyist and cannot engage in such activities. In fact, as a tax-exempt 501(c)(3) organization, it is severely restricted from lobbying and expressly prohibited from political campaigning.

The IRS puts strict limits on the amount of time or money such organizations can spend on both direct lobbying—such as meeting face-to-face with a legislator—and grassroots lobbying—such as media campaigns to influence the public on an issue.

By law, CAIR must notify the IRS of any intent to lobby by filing a special form. A 501(c)(3) organization "will lose its tax-exempt status and its qualification to receive deductible charitable contributions if a substantial part of its activities are carried on to influence legislation," the IRS states in Form 5768.

CAIR is flirting with, if not crossing, that line. Internal documentation generated by the group suggests a substantial part of its operations involve lobbying activities.

Take its efforts to repeal the Patriot Act. CAIR's traffic on the Hill on that issue has rivaled the activity of a K Street lobbying firm. In 2005 alone, CAIR officials made a whopping seventy-two separate trips to Congress to protest the anti-terror law, according to internal records.[21] Considering Congress met fewer than 150 days that year, this is an extraordinary lobbying pace indeed.

CAIR also spends $25,000 a year to organize a national "lobby day on the Hill" during which its members across the country come to Washington to meet with their representatives and senators to talk about a single issue—using the same talking points furnished by CAIR.

CAIR also created databases to streamline its lobbying efforts, including one "to track our relationships with congressional offices," and another to automatically alert Hill staffers about policy issues important to CAIR, according to internal CAIR documents. The Hill e-list, or electronic mailing list, is known internally as "Policy-net."[22]

Again, CAIR is not a registered lobbyist. Yet it calls its governmental affairs department a "lobbying office."

"The Governmental Affairs Department better understands the workings and personalities of Capitol Hill," reported Jason C. Erb, Saylor's predecessor, in a post-9/11 memo marked "Not for Distribution—For Board Members Only." "There is much to be learned and many wrinkles to be ironed out before we are a truly efficient and effective lobbying office."[23]

BUSSING MUSLIMS TO THE POLLS

According to IRS statutes, additionally, CAIR cannot in any way support or oppose anyone running for public office. Nor can it engage in partisan political activities. That means absolutely no campaigning.

And no political fundraising may occur at an event hosted by a 501(c)(3) organization. For that matter, such tax-exempt groups cannot endorse or even voice support for political candidates, according to IRS rules.

Yet CAIR has held political fundraisers benefiting Ellison and other Democrats. It has also used its resources to turn Muslim voters out for Ellison and other Democrat candidates in tight races.

CAIR shared its "phone sheets of Muslim voters from the research department's database of Muslim voters to help in get[ting] out the vote effort," Awad reported to CAIR's board just days before the 2006 mid-term congressional elections. "The following requests have been fulfilled:

The 5th district of Minnesota, where Keith Ellison is running for Congress.

The state of Connecticut.

Pennsylvania's 17th and 19th congressional districts.

San Francisco Bay area, California."[24]

During the 2004 election, CAIR bussed Muslim voters from mosques to polls to try to swing elections to Democrats in key Florida counties.

One of CAIR's strategic goals for 2010 is to create a database of registered Muslim voters segmented by congressional district to "quickly" mobilize them and "target" candidates in key races. It also plans to register thirty thousand new Muslim voters by next year's congressional elections.

Meanwhile, it's coaching all Muslims—including noncitizen immigrants who cannot vote—to phone elected officials in Washington to pressure them to adopt CAIR's agenda. Here illegally? No problem. "They cannot ask your citizenship status," CAIR advises.[25]

To make such contacts easier, CAIR has published and mailed its members more than forty-five hundred copies of its *Congressional Guide*, complete with photos and bios of lawmakers, along with their contact information.

ISNA'S NON-ENDORSEMENT ENDORSEMENT

Also according to IRS law, CAIR cannot invite Democrats to speak at its forums and fundraising dinners without also extending formal invitations to Republicans.[26] With the exception of GOP gadfly Ron Paul, an outspoken anti-war critic, however, CAIR generally has not reached out to Republicans. Rather, it's mostly vilified them.

In fact, CAIR is extremely monopartisan, acting almost as an auxiliary of the Democratic National Committee. "We continued to communicate with the Democratic National Committee about ways to get Muslims involved in the political system through participation in election campaigns and other party activities, like training," Erb said in his five-page report, which makes no mention of outreach to Republicans.

CAIR Chairman Larry Shaw insists "nothing we do is illegal." Still, absent an IRS audit, questions loom large—including reports that CAIR uses its DC townhomes and other offsite investment properties to host fundraisers for political candidates.

CAIR's sister organization ISNA is a nonprofit 501(c)(3) organization as well. And like CAIR, it knows it can't endorse political candidates.

But at last year's ISNA convention, the group violated at least the spirit of the law when one of its moderators—a member of ISNA's *shura* council—cleverly endorsed Obama without technically endorsing him.

"Before we get to the next question, I think I have a responsibility to remind everybody that ISNA, as a tax-exempt organization, does not support any particular political candidate for office," said ISNA moderator Asad M. Ba-Yunus. "That being said, you all know who we really support."

With that wink and nod, the ballroom erupted into laughter and applause. Congressmen Ellison and Carson, also in attendance, were seen smiling and clapping approvingly.

CONGRESSIONAL CO-CONSPIRATORS

CAIR's boosters on the Hill, where it's headquartered just three blocks from the Capitol, are not limited to Muslims. In fact, most of them are non-Muslims—and almost all of them Democrats.

And they have known for some time that several people in positions of power within the group have been directly connected to terrorism and have either been prosecuted or thrown out of the country. They also know by now from court evidence that CAIR's founders are part of a secret Hamas support network in the U.S. and are acting as its lobbying arm.

Yet these forty-strong lawmakers, who include members of both the House and Senate, have gone right on singing CAIR's praises and carrying its water—which means that they're carrying out, wittingly or not, the agenda of the Muslim mafia. That agenda includes apologizing for Palestinian terrorism, censoring critics of militant Islam, dismantling U.S. border security, and denying the FBI domestic terror-fighting tools, among other things.

These cheerleaders, who include a couple of Republicans, make up a *de facto* caucus for the dangerous Muslim Brotherhood (see box).

CAIR'S APPEASERS [27]

*The list of compromised politicians who still support CAIR
in spite of its proven ties to terrorism is long:*

Sen. Barbara A. Mikulski (D-MD)	Rep. Gregory Meeks (D-NY)	Rep. Zoe Lofgren (D-CA)
Sen. Paul Sarbanes (D-MD)	Rep. Albert L. Wynn (D-MD)	Rep. John Dingell (D-MI)
Sen. Debbie Stabenow (D-MI)	Rep. Betty McCollum (D-MN)	Rep. James P. Moran (D-VA)
Sen. Dick Durbin (D-IL)	Rep. Lois Capps (D-CA)	Rep. Nick J. Rahall, II (D-WV)
Sen. Kent Conrad (D-ND)	Rep. Bill Pascrell (D-NJ)	Rep. Charles B. Rangel (D-NY)
Rep. Joe Sestak (D-PA)	Rep. Benjamin L. Cardin (D-MD)	Rep. C.A. Dutch Ruppersberger (D-MD)
Rep. John Conyers, Jr. (D-MI)	Rep. Elijah Cummings (D-MD)	Rep. Pete Stark (D-CA)
Rep. Keith Ellison (D-MN)	Rep. Gerry Connolly (D-VA)	Rep. Chris Van Hollen (D-MD)
Rep. Jesse L. Jackson Jr. (D-IL)	Rep. Anna G. Eshoo (D-CA)	Rep. Andre Carson, (D-IN)
Rep. Danny K. Davis (D-IL)	Rep. Bob Filner (D-CA)	Rep. Sheila Jackson-Lee (D-TX)
Rep. Gary Miller (R-CA)	Rep. Wayne T. Gilchrest (R-MD)	Rep. Adam Schiff (D-CA)
Rep. Loretta Sanchez (D-CA)	Rep. Mike Honda (D-CA)	Rep. Mary Jo Kilroy (D-OH)
Rep. Linda T. Sanchez (D-CA)	Rep. Dennis J. Kucinich (D-OH)	
Rep. Jan Schakowsky (D-IL)	Rep. Barbara Lee (D-CA)	

Perhaps some members of Congress had been fooled by CAIR's deception. But now they have no excuse. Now Democratic senator Barbara Mikulski, who saluted CAIR's "important work," and Democratic senator Paul Sarbanes, who applauded "CAIR's mission," know better.

Now Democratic representative Chris Van Hollen of Maryland, who serves as assistant to Speaker of the House Nancy Pelosi, may think twice before meeting with CAIR officials and promising support for their agenda—including, according to CAIR's internal notes from their meetings, laws to broaden hate crimes prosecution, accommodate Islamic holidays, and allow Islamic curriculum in public schools. (Unfortunately, Van Hollen works closely with Muslim activist Arshi Siddiqui—chief policy advisor to Pelosi—and Siddiqui remains high on CAIR's contact list. So Van Hollen is likely to continue his outreach.)

The criminal evidence should also disabuse Democratic Representative John Conyers of Michigan, who's trumpeted CAIR's "long and distinguished history," along with Democratic representative John Dingell—another top recipient of donations from Michigan's Arab and Muslim community—who said "my office door is always open" to CAIR. He now has an obligation to slam it shut whenever CAIR officials darken his doorway.

'YOU HAVE A FRIEND IN THE CONGRESS'

No red-blooded American lawmaker wants to do anything that would facilitate the support of terrorists—not even liberal Democratic presidential hopeful Representative Dennis Kucinich, who's a major recipient of Arab-Muslim cash and whose staff counsel is a Palestinian-rights activist. Perhaps in the future he'll pause before gushing that "CAIR has much to be proud of," or pledging that "you have a friend in the United States Congress."

That includes even Representative Jim McDermott of Washington, who thusly expressed his wholehearted support for CAIR at a CAIR-Seattle banquet:

> I always enjoy being with people like CAIR because you inspire me really to keep fighting...and I think that's why this kind of an organization is so important for people to understand that you have a right to say whatever you believe. And I think you ought to exercise that. That's being a real American.[28]

With overwhelming evidence that CAIR actually speaks against America and for the enemy, maybe McDermott will now think twice before accepting another invitation to speak at a CAIR event.

Then there's Democratic Representative Jackson-Lee of Texas, who last year presented a Certificate of Congressional Recognition to CAIR at its Houston banquet, reading:

> You are soundly recognized by the 18th Congressional District for dedication and commitment of the United States that is truly worthy of respect, admiration, and accommodation of the U.S. Congress.[29]

Jackson-Lee blew more kisses at CAIR while speaking at its 2007 CAIR banquet in Dallas. "How proud I am to have been associated with CAIR's legislative work in the United States," she said. "We need CAIR and we need all of you supporting CAIR."[30]

Such endorsements are promptly posted on CAIR's Web site in an attempt to legitimize itself in the media. It also uses outreach events with the government as a kind of insurance policy against investigation.

Of course many of these politicians represent states or districts with large populations or concentrations of Arab and Muslim immigrants. And they may feel pressure to appease CAIR, which claims to advocate on behalf of their constituents.

Many of these politicians also have been on the receiving end of generous campaign donations from Arab and Muslim political action committees, which have been funded in part by Muslim Brotherhood leaders, as you can see from this table.

TOP 10 RECIPIENTS OF ARAB-MUSLIM CASH*

1. Rep. Nick Rahall (D-WV) ... $16,970

2. Rep. Jim Moran (D-VA) ... $15,000

3. Rep. Darrell Issa (R-CA) ... $14,000

4. Rep. John Conyers (D-MI)... $12,500

5. Rep. Dennis Kucinich (D-OH) ... $12,000

6. Rep. Jesse Jackson Jr. (D-IL) ... $8,500

7. Rep. Barbara Lee (D-CA) ... $8,000

(tie) Rep. John Dingell (D-MI) ... $8,000

8. Rep. Carolyn Cheeks Kilpatrick (D-MI) ... $7,000

9. Rep. Sheila Jackson-Lee (D-TX) ... $6,000

10. Rep. Jim McDermott (D-WA) ... $5,000

* Contributions from Arab American Leadership PAC, National Association of Arab-Americans PAC, and National Muslims for a Better America PAC; 2000 - 2008 elections cycles.

Sources: FEC, Center for Responsive Politics

Still, there's no excuse for any elected U.S. official to kowtow or sell out to subversive anti-American elements—cash or no cash, votes or no votes. It's not just shameless pandering. It's borderline treason. Of CAIR's biggest boosters—or panderers—Representatives Ellison, Conyers, and Gerry Connolly of Virginia deserve special mention.

REPRESENTATIVE KEITH ELLISON: The Minnesota Democrat is a faithful supporter of CAIR and has secretly collaborated with the group on a number of issues. In fact, he spends so much time huddling with CAIR's leaders they might as well make him an honorary board member.

They hold regular power breakfasts on the Hill, where they discuss political strategy and policy. And CAIR can rely on Ellison to make speeches or cameos at its functions, including:

• CAIR's 2008 national fundraising banquet in Washington, where he delivered the keynote address;

• CAIR-Minnesota's 2008 Ramadan dinner, where he was a prominent guest;

• The 2008 annual conference of the Congressional Black Caucus Foundation in Washington, where Ellison joined an official from CAIR's Michigan chapter on a panel; and

• CAIR's 2007 national fundraising dinner where he delivered a speech and singled out Awad for praise.[31]

An FBI investigator in Washington says Ellison and Awad are "tight." Their relationship goes back to the 1980s when they attended the University of Minnesota together.

FEC records show Awad is normally stingy with his money when it comes to donating to elected officials. But he shelled out $2,000 for Ellison's historic 2006 campaign.

(Curiously, he made the donation under the alias "Nehad Hammad." He made another donation under that name, one he no doubt regrets making now. In 2000, when George W. Bush was courting the pre-9/11 Muslim vote, Awad gave the future president $1,000.)

Saylor kicked in another $1,000 for Ellison in 2006, records show, and former CAIR chairman Parvez Ahmed has given a total of $1,250 to his campaigns.

Ellison in recent years converted to orthodox Sunni Islam after following Louis Farrakhan's Nation of Islam. He is serious about his newfound faith. The nation's first Muslim congressman insisted on taking the oath on the Quran. And last year he made the pilgrimage to Mecca with the sponsorship of the Muslim American Society, another Muslim Brotherhood front.

He and CAIR have worked together to protect terrorists. After winning reelection on the strength of the Somali vote in Minneapolis, Ellison defended a local pro-jihad mosque where more than twenty Somali men have been radicalized. One young worshipper became the first U.S. citizen to blow himself up in a suicide strike. At a recent gathering at the Minneapolis Convention Center, Ellison urged Somalis to organize themselves into a powerful political and economic coalition to help fend off FBI investigations.[32]

(The local Somali community has also been the subject of federal investigations into terrorist money laundering. Agents suspect Somali refugees have funneled millions of dollars from food stamp fraud and drug sales through Somali grocery stores into overseas bank accounts used by al-Qaida. CAIR has defended the Somali store owners against the allegations, even meeting with the head of the civil rights unit of the USDA to complain about the agency's food stamp investigations, which it argues are "causing enormous harm to the owners and the Somali community," a confidential CAIR memo reveals.[33] CAIR's Minnesota chapter, meanwhile, has launched a campaign against the FBI, accusing it of operating a witch hunt for young Muslim jihadists there and advising local Muslims not to speak to agents.)

Ellison is also very useful to CAIR and the Muslim mafia in their goal to Islamize America.

"Muslims in elected and appointed government positions have little value for the rest of the community if their presence does not translate into Muslim-friendly public policies," CAIR asserts in internal papers. "On the other hand, Muslim personalities in power can provide access for the community to institutions of power and make their voices heard."

Ellison certainly fits that bill. Not only is he pushing for Muslim-friendly policies, he's trying to clone himself. He helped get Carson elected, and is working closely with his pal Akhter of the Congressional Muslim Staffers Association to get other Muslims elected. Akhter himself wishes to run for office one day.

(It's worth noting that members of Congress are not required to undergo FBI background checks before gaining access to classified information.)

At a 2008 Capitol *juma*, or Friday prayer, Ellison prophesied that

Muslims will soon see many more Muslims in Congress. "*Insha'Allah*," he said, "we will have fifteen next election." Ellison envisions a Congressional Muslim Caucus to rival the Black Caucus.[34]

Ellison and Akhter, along with other young Muslim activists, hope to see in their lifetimes fellow Muslims as U.S. senators and U.S. Supreme Court justices. They sense that with the footholds they have gained already in Washington there is no American institution they cannot penetrate— including one day the Oval Office.

REPRESENTATIVE JOHN CONYERS: CAIR and the terrorists it supports would be hard-pressed to find a better friend in Washington. The House Judiciary Committee chairman wants to kill the Patriot Act, prevent the FBI from profiling Muslim suspects in terror probes, and even criminalize the "disrespect" of Islam.

For that matter, CAIR has worked with Conyers on legislation to ban all private—not just government—entities from profiling Muslims based on security threats and suspicious activity.

Conyers has reintroduced his End Racial Profiling Act, which he co-sponsored in 2005. In 2006, after the "Flying Imams" controversy involving U.S. Airways, CAIR had several meetings with Conyers to push the measure.

"We are arranging meetings in DC and Michigan with Representative John Conyers, incoming chair of the House Judiciary Committee, and his appropriate staff to discuss the incident and the need for hearings on the broader issue of racial and religious profiling," Saylor reported to CAIR's board, according to minutes of one national meeting held at the time.

He added that CAIR's lawyers were trying to help Conyers "find a legislative fix" to prevent airlines from profiling potential Islamic hijackers.

"We are researching an appropriate legislative fix for non-government entities, such as airlines," Saylor said.[35]

Conyers represents the largest Arab population in the U.S. His district includes Dearborn, Michigan—nicknamed "Dearbornistan" because of its large influx of Middle Eastern immigrants and its constant focus of counterterror investigations.

Last decade, Conyers fought FBI outreach efforts in the Arab and Muslim community there, even though they were designed to gather intelligence on potential terror cells and protect homeland security.

Conyers and other Detroit-area Democrats threatened to hold hearings unless the FBI stopped counterterror interviews. Bureau officials tried to explain the national security benefits of the program, but Conyers would have none of it. In the end, they backed off. Today Hamas, Hezbollah, and the Muslim Brotherhood are all active in the area.

As one of the top recipients of donations from the Arab-American Leadership PAC, Conyers not surprisingly has a long history of pandering to Arab and Muslim voters. According to FEC records, Conyers has raked in at least $13,500 from the Arab-American Leadership PAC since 2000.

Little wonder that CAIR turned to the lawmaker for help in pressuring the Justice Department to change the group's status as a co-conspirator in the Hamas terror-funding case. CAIR officials met with Conyers and wrote a letter asking him to lobby the attorney general on behalf of the group.[36]

REPRESENTATIVE GERRY CONNOLLY: The freshman Democratic congressman from Virginia first began nurturing an alliance with CAIR when he was chairman of the Fairfax County Board of Supervisors.

Among other things, Connolly worked with CAIR officials to draft a county resolution condemning the Patriot Act as unconstitutional. The resolution set up a mechanism to monitor all actions taken by federal authorities in the county under the Patriot Act and at the same time directed county employees not to "assist or voluntarily cooperate with investigations."

Furthermore, it directed Fairfax County police to "refrain from racial profiling (or) engaging in the surveillance of individuals or groups (and) from collecting or maintaining information about the political, religious or social views, associations or activities of any individual or group," unless it "directly relates" to an active terrorism investigation.

Finally, the 2003 draft resolution directed county libraries to post notices to Muslim and other patrons that the feds could be monitoring the books they check out. The notice reads:

WARNING: Under the federal Patriot Act, records of the books and other materials you borrow may be obtained by federal agents. That federal law prohibits librarians from informing you if records about you have been requested or obtained by federal agents.[37]

Librarians were directed to ensure that "there is regular and immediate destruction of records that identify a book borrower after the book has been returned or that identify the name of an Internet user after use."

Connolly also organized and attended a 2005 "community forum" in response to CAIR's complaints regarding Fairfax County police enforcement of immigration laws. According to a CAIR press release at the time, Connolly assured local Muslims attending the forum that "Fairfax County police officers are not an arm of federal immigration enforcement agencies." The Fairfax County police chief also attended the forum. Stressing the department's dedication to diversity, he assured them that his department would do more to reach out to the Muslim community. Two months later, CAIR conducted "diversity and sensitivity" training at the Fairfax County courthouse.

Connolly and CAIR have also colluded on a project to save the Islamic Saudi Academy in Alexandria, Virginia, from a growing grassroots movement to permanently shut its doors.

When the Saudi embassy last year asked officials to renew the lease for its radical school, local residents strenuously objected. They argued the school teaches hatred toward Jews and Christians and has become a breeding ground for terrorists.

Connolly, who at the time was head of the county government controlling the Alexandria lease, gave a full-throated defense of the Islamic Saudi Academy, even smearing protesters as anti-Islamic "bigots."

All the while, Connolly was running for U.S. Congress and, according to FEC records, accepting thousands of dollars in donations from Saudi bagmen—including some whose homes and offices were raided after 9/11 on suspicion of terror financing (and whose donations to other Democrats have been quietly returned in shame).

Their investment appears to have paid off. The Saudi *madrassa* got its lease and is still in operation (and now even planning to expand), and Connolly is in a more powerful position on the Hill.

Critics would be forgiven for questioning Connolly's motives for defending the Saudi *madrassa* in light of what appears to be an orchestrated outpouring of donations from CAIR and other radical Muslim Brotherhood leaders with Saudi connections.

FEC records show that on January 12, 2008, Yaqub Mirza gave Connolly $1,000, followed twelve days later by CAIR chief Nihad Awad, who chipped in $500. That same day—January 24—Hisham al-Talib donated $1,000 to Connolly's campaign, along with Omar Ashraf, who gave $500.

Then in May, Esam Omeish donated $250 to the Fairfax County Democratic Committee, which held receptions for Connolly and helped him raise money. And in June, Mirza gave another $1,000 to the Democratic Congressional Campaign Committee, which also helped get Connolly elected.

In addition, the Arab-American Leadership PAC, which is funded in part by Muslim Brotherhood leaders, donated $2,000 to Connolly in 2008, records show.[38]

Investigators say Mirza is a Saudi bagman, acting on behalf of Saudi millionaire and al-Qaida financier Yassin al-Qadi. He, along with al-Talib and Ashraf, runs a Virginia-based network of Saudi-funded fronts called the Safa group, which is still the subject of an active federal investigation into terror financing—in fact, a federal grand jury in northern Virginia has been hearing evidence in the case. All three Connolly donors' homes and-or offices were raided by federal agents after the 9/11 attacks. Mirza, one of the ringleaders of the network, is so dirty that even Muslim Representative Carson returned his terror-tainted cash.

Omeish is an advocate of violent jihad who helps run a Saudi-backed, Muslim Brotherhood-controlled mosque in Falls Church, Virginia, that ministered to some of the Saudi hijackers before 9/11.

As first reported in the book *Infiltration*, Omeish in 2004 used his home to bond out a terrorist suspect jailed for allegedly casing the Chesapeake Bay Bridge. The suspect, Ismail Elbarasse, is also an accused Hamas money man employed by the Islamic Saudi Academy as comptroller. His college roommate, Hamas leader and fugitive Mousa Abu Marzook, sent his kids to ISA. (More on Elbarasse in a later chapter.)

Awad, meanwhile, has personally accepted large checks from Saudis on behalf of CAIR.

Point is, these Brotherhood donors and their families support the Islamic Saudi Academy, an arm of the Saudi government and a patron of Representative Connolly. This spring, ISA's lease came up for renewal, and the Saudis knew they'd face resistance in the local community. The school had made national headlines since their last request for renewal after a former school valedictorian Ahmed Omar Abu Ali was convicted of joining al-Qaida and plotting to assassinate President Bush. His ISA classmates voted him "Most Likely to Be a Martyr." His father works for the Saudi embassy.

Also, reports had detailed numerous hateful passages from academy textbooks, including a twelfth-grade text teaching students that it is permissible for Muslims to kill adulterers and apostates who leave Islam. Other passages in the school's texts state that Muslims are permitted to take the lives and property of Jews and those deemed "polytheists," or Christians.

Connolly shrugged off the complaints and accused critics of "slander" before rubberstamping the school's lease and accepting a rent check from the Saudi embassy for $2.2 million.

"I find no evidence, no grounds, to do anything but renew the lease of an institution that has been a good neighbor," Connolly declared at the board's meeting on the issue last year.

Thanks to Connolly, the Saudis have been allowed to maintain an incubator for jihadists in the shadow of the nation's capital.

But wait. There's more to the story.

A SUDDEN WINDFALL FROM A SAUDI FLACK

The Saudi government's paid mouthpiece in Washington—Qorvis Communications—launched a PR offensive to protect the Islamic Saudi Academy as Connolly and his board were voting on the lease. Qorvis's managing partner Michael Petruzzello personally appeared at a press conference held at the school to defend its textbooks.

Qorvis, whose retainer with the Saudi government is worth tens of millions of dollars, never contributed a dime to Connolly during his dozen years in local office. But then beginning in 2006, when the Saudi academy came under major fire, the money suddenly started rolling into his campaign coffers and continued through the end of his run for Congress last year.

Qorvis, the Saudi's top PR agent in America, pumped at least $10,000 into Connolly's local campaigns—$5,000 in 2006 and $5,000 in 2007—and another $2,300 into his recent federal campaign. Last year,

Qorvis officers opened up their wallets for another $6,458 in individual donations to Connolly's congressional race, including at least $2,300 from Petruzzello himself.

To be clear, the money from Qorvis started appearing when the Saudi *madrassa* started attracting national headlines and continued to flow through the end of Connolly's run for Congress.

QORVIS' DONATIONS TO CONNOLLY
1995-2005 $0
2006 $5,000
2007 $5,000
2008 $8,758
TOTAL: $18,758
Sources: FEC, Center for Responsive Politics, Virginia Public Access Project

"The $10,000 appears to have been a downpayment for the upcoming renewal of the lease," a senior congressional investigator says. Connolly "did not disclose at the meeting where he voted to renew the lease that he had taken Qorvis money."[39]

Curiously, Qorvis has not reported any of the total of $18,758 in donations to Connolly to the Justice Department as required under the Foreign Agents Registration Act. No record of disbursement of these political contributions appears in its latest financial disclosure statements.[40]

"Qorvis may be in violation of the Foreign Agents Registration Act," the congressional investigator says.[41]

Willful violations of the registration law are punishable by up to five years in prison, a fine of up to $10,000, or both.

It wouldn't be the first time Qorvis, which declined comment, has run afoul of the law. After 9/11, the Justice Department conducted a criminal investigation of the firm for failing to disclose required information. Qorvis distributed Saudi propaganda under a different name, in violation of the foreign agents act. FBI agents raided Qorvis's Washington and Northern Virginia offices while Qorvis was in the middle of a $15 million-plus campaign to help the kingdom repair its image in the wake of the Saudi-led attacks.

Upon his election to Congress, Connolly asked the Democratic leadership for a seat on the House Foreign Affairs subcommittee on the Middle East and South Asia, and he got it as his first committee assignment. The panel has oversight of all military basing rights and foreign assistance in the region, which covers Saudi Arabia, the Palestinian territories, Israel, Iraq and Iran, as well as Afghanistan and Pakistan.

Ellison and Jackson-Lee happen to sit on the panel with him. Connolly is also a member of the House Foreign Affairs subcommittee on terrorism, nonproliferation and trade, which has oversight of international finance and customs.

These plum assignments are sure to please his Saudi and Muslim Brotherhood patrons, especially campaign contributor and Hamas supporter Awad of CAIR.

'BEWARE OF CAIR'

While some members of Congress see no problem giving CAIR a political platform, others are warning colleagues of the dangers of continuing to associate with the group.

"Members should think twice before meeting with representatives of

CAIR," a letter signed by five U.S. House members says. "The FBI has cut ties with them. There are indications that this group has connections to Hamas."[42]

The three-page "Dear Colleague" letter, sent earlier this year to every U.S. House member, points out that prosecutors allege CAIR conspired with a charity recently convicted of funding terrorism. It was written under the title, "BEWARE OF CAIR," and signed by Representatives Sue Myrick (R-NC), co-chair of the Congressional Anti-Terrorism/Jihad Caucus; Pete Hoekstra (R-MI); Trent Franks (R-AZ); Paul Broun (R-GA); and John Shadegg (R-AZ).

GOP representative Frank Wolf of Virginia followed up with a letter of his own to the FBI requesting it formally brief all members of Congress about CAIR's terror connections.

"I've talked to CAIR people in the past on a very casual basis," he told Fox News. "They're very active up here on Capitol Hill. I think it's something that we really have to look into."

He added, "Whatever information there is available, we ought to know," so that lawmakers do not risk giving the group undue access or legitimacy.[43]

Republicans aren't the only ones concerned that the political lobbying arm for Hamas is actively lobbying Congress.

Democratic senator Charles Schumer of New York recently joined senators Jon Kyl of Arizona and Tom Coburn of Oklahoma in formally supporting the FBI's divorce with CAIR.

In fact, "We believe this should be government-wide policy," the senators wrote the FBI director not long after the House's "Dear Colleague" letter was distributed.[44]

In a sign even some supporters may be starting to distance themselves from CAIR, outspoken war critic and presidential candidate Ron Paul turned down CAIR's invitation to speak at its annual banquet last year.

And now a Muslim member of Congress apparently is having second thoughts about cozying up to CAIR. Andre Carson, the second Muslim sworn in as a member of Congress, had participated in a townhall meeting in 2008 sponsored by CAIR-California.

But CAIR spokesman Hooper privately worries Carson is leery about being seen with CAIR. According to undercover video captured by researcher Chris Gaubatz, Hooper advised CAIR chapters not to publicly invite Carson to future events, because he may turn them down. And if he declines a public invitation, Hooper warned colleagues, critics will say, "Oh, a Muslim member of Congress won't be seen with CAIR."

No doubt CAIR wants to avoid repeating the humiliating slap it suffered in 2007 when Democratic senator Barbara Boxer of California withdrew an award that she offered the head of CAIR's Sacramento chapter. Boxer later cited "concerns" about CAIR's associations and explained that her office hadn't thoroughly researched the organization before extending the honor.

Internal emails show CAIR debated going "all out against" the senator in a smear campaign but decided against it because she's a popular Democrat and it didn't think it could make an attack on her "hurt enough."[45] Others haven't been so lucky.

CHAPTER TWELVE

BLACKMAILING CORPORATE AMERICA

*"Now when Muslims are targeted, there is a unified and powerful voice that responds.
Never before have corporate America, small business, and large media organizations
alike had to contend with the Muslim community on an activist and legal level."*

—CAIR newsletter, March/April 2007

C AIR SPOKESMAN IBRAHIM HOOPER likes to crow that Nike,
Inc. put CAIR "on the map." He's right, but gaining notoriety
through extortion is nothing to be proud of.

Ten years ago CAIR made national headlines when it led a protest
that forced the athletic footwear giant to remake a line of shoes that CAIR
claimed had "Allah" displayed prominently in Arabic script on the heel.

It was just a stylized font for the word "Air," but CAIR declared
it blasphemous to Islam. Nike clearly meant no offense. But facing
bad publicity and a threatened boycott of its products throughout the
Muslim world, it nonetheless apologized, recalled its entire production
run of some forty thousand pairs of sneakers, and removed the allegedly
offending word.

And as a gesture of goodwill, it financed the construction of playgrounds
at several Muslim schools and mosques selected by CAIR while making
donations to a number of Islamic charities—also at CAIR's choosing.

The mosques on the receiving end of Nike's benevolence included
mosques funded by the Saudis and run by the radical Muslim Brotherhood—
including Dar al-Hijrah Islamic Center, the 9/11 mosque just outside

Washington. In fact, CAIR insisted Dar al-Hijrah be the first recipient of a playground. Nike agreed and shelled out $50,000 for that facility alone. Unwittingly, America's favorite sneaker company helped a mosque that would later help the al-Qaida hijackers—all in the name of tolerance.

As added protection against future CAIR extortion, Nike agreed to adopt Islamic-sensitivity training for its workers. After CAIR's triumph, a CAIR official gloated that the group "forced Nike to submit to the will of Allah and then to the will of the Muslim community."

Since then CAIR has recorded more than six thousand cases of other so-called offenses against Islam or alleged discrimination against Muslims. And it has successfully intervened to win concessions from businesses and employers in many of the higher-profile cases—even though they've often mimicked the Nike case in baseless grievance-mongering.

But CAIR wields two powerful cudgels to beat concessions out of corporate America.

First, it lets them know about all the other Fortune 500 companies that have backed down in addition to Nike—including Office Max, Office Depot, Delta Air Lines, Best Buy, Microsoft, JC Penney, Sears, and Burger King—without mentioning any of the cases it has lost (and there have been plenty as we'll show further on).

At the same time, CAIR reminds its corporate targets that "the population of Muslims in the United States is around seven to ten million people," and that they buy lots of products and services. Even though CAIR's numbers and leverage are illusory—as we pointed out in an earlier chapter—the threat of boycott too often causes Fortune 500 CEOs who don't know better to go wobbly and capitulate to its demands.

Compounding the threat, CAIR often teams up with the progressive left to intimidate the corporate world. CAIR and the ACLU, for one, have formed a strategic partnership to attack board rooms for alleged anti-Muslim discrimination. ACLU has agreed to notify CAIR of any

Muslim cases it receives so they can consolidate their resources, according to internal documents.[1]

As a result, CAIR each year succeeds in bullying corporate America into accepting Islamic law and practices—from letting employees wear beards and head scarves (in spite of time-tested health, safety, and security policies) to allowing breaks for daily Islamic prayer and time off for Islamic holidays. The pressure group has also discouraged John Doe passengers from reporting suspicious activities on airlines and censored media critics from speaking the truth about Islamofascism.

CAIR chief Nihad Awad claims that forcing religious accommodations through legal jihad is a "win-win" for America. He fancies CAIR a kind of ambassador of good will, spreading religious harmony in workplaces across the country.

CAIR VERUS BANK OF AMERICA

"CAIR has a successful track record of negotiating amicably," he claims, "enjoying huge community support, and taking conflicts to a win-win resolution."

Amicably? Tell that to Bank of America. It's one company that knows better, and would no doubt laugh at such a description.

After 9/11, the financial giant found itself on the other side of the negotiating table with CAIR's goons in a trumped-up employee discrimination case. It quickly discovered that CAIR negotiates such disputes with all the tact of a Jersey mobster. CAIR's gambit is simple: Deal, or we'll boycott you and brand you a racist.

A series of "confidential" memos generated by CAIR during its clash with Bank of America provide unreported details and a valuable window into the group's shakedown strategy.

It was 2003, and CAIR thought it had found its "big case"—one that would bring America's biggest bank to its knees genuflecting before Allah.

A part-time Muslim bank teller working at one of Bank of America's branches in Maryland complained to CAIR that she faced a hostile work environment after receiving an offensive anti-Muslim email circulated among bank employees. The message said that "Muslim terrorists" are quick to commit suicide because, among other reasons, "your bride is picked by someone else. She smells like your donkey, but your donkey has a better disposition."

The email was not directed at the Muslim teller, nor was it generated or approved by bank management. It had nothing to do with bank policy, and was simply one of a garden variety of humorous, albeit often tasteless, anonymous chain emails that get passed around the office every day.

But teller Gul Naz Anwar insisted she had been "subjected to humiliation as a result of discrimination," and she teamed up with CAIR to attack the bank.

Awad immediately tasked subordinates to conduct "research on the global Muslim involvement with BoA," even before sending a formal complaint to Bank of America.

Then on July 30, CAIR fired off a letter to Bank of America CEO Ken Lewis listing its demands and implying it would hurt the bank economically if it did not meet them.

"Muslims have long been important investors in Bank of America, not only domestically but internationally," CAIR asserted in its letter, a copy of which we obtained. "The population of Muslims in the United States is around seven to ten million people. Surely, Muslims would not feel comfortable investing in an institution that allows such unbridled prejudice to flourish behind its doors."[2]

With that, CAIR demanded the "following actions be taken immediately:

1. Initiate a formal investigation of this incident;

2. Issue a formal written apology to Ms. Anwar and the American Muslim community;

3. Compensate Ms. Anwar for any damages as well as emotional distress she suffered as a result of this discrimination; and

4. Institute CAIR's Diversity/Sensitivity Training to all employees," including top management.[3]

It closed by noting that "CAIR has resolved a number of acts of discrimination and defamation involving some of America's top corporations, such as Nike, Solectron, the *Los Angeles Times*, JC Penny [*sic*], Sears, Burger King, Office Max, Office Depot, Delta Air Lines, Best Buy, Microsoft, and many others."

In response, the bank conducted a full investigation of CAIR's allegations of "blatant discrimination," and found no substance to them.

"Our investigation did not reveal any evidence of discrimination," Bank of America spokesman Scott Scredon said.[4]

CAIR rejected the findings and mobilized its attack machine against the bank. Awad huddled with Hooper to draft a "BoA Action Alert" sent to members asking them to protest the bank's "bigoted" affront to Muslims. The alert included Lewis's phone and fax numbers, along with his email address.

"Please continue to keep the pressure on Bank of America," CAIR advised members.

CAIR officials also attached CAIR's name to an EEOC complaint filed on behalf of Anwar. They got pledges of support from the NAACP and ACLU and sent letters to Maryland senators Mikulski and Sarbanes and Maryland representative Van Hollen urging them to contact Bank of America. They even sent "letters to ambassadors of all Muslim countries, keeping them informed"—including the ambassador of Anwar's ancestral home of Pakistan—CAIR's internal communications reveal.[5]

When Bank of America continued to balk at their demands, CAIR threatened an international boycott, suggesting it had the power to deny the bank millions of dollars in deposits and transactions worldwide.

"Bank of America enjoys the patronage of Muslim-owned business accounts throughout the United States," it warned in a press statement. "And they also enjoy the benefits of large transactions from the Middle East, Malaysia, and other parts of the Muslim world."

Raising the specter of possible violence against its "branches in the Muslim world," CAIR also warned that Bank of America's "belligerence towards our beliefs" had "angered the Muslims worldwide."

CAIR set more deadlines for "positive action"—including "punitive damages"—from the bank. But the bank ignored them, too, and repeatedly refused to meet with representatives from CAIR.

With its anti-bank jihad now several months old, an increasingly frustrated CAIR promised its members it would hold a "big" press conference announcing a boycott if Bank of America remained silent. It gave the bank a final deadline for resolving the issue.

"If we do not hear from them within the next two weeks, we will then proceed with a big press conference calling on Muslims and concerned Americans to boycott Bank of America," CAIR huffed, railing on about the bank's "insensitivity" toward the Muslim community.

"YOU HAVE JUST SHOT YOURSELVES IN THE FOOT"

Around that time, the bank's legal team bypassed CAIR and reached out to Anwar's personal attorney, cracking the door to a possible settlement, even though she had no case. It requested CAIR not be party to negotiations, however.

When Anwar's lawyer insisted CAIR had to be part of any deal, Bank of America's assistant general counsel allegedly retorted, "You have just shot yourselves in the foot."[6]

CAIR complained it was "utterly disgusted" with the Bank of America counsel, Mary Ulmer-Jones, and her "arrogant comments."[7]

In a last-ditch attempt to ratchet up the pressure, CAIR sent one more threatening letter to CEO Lewis that warned: "We are in talks with your competitors to make arrangements to pick up the slack" from Muslims and mosques canceling accounts in a massive boycott.[8] But it too had little impact.

The promised boycott fizzled and CAIR's aggrieved client eventually left the bank. It turns out she had a reputation as an agitator. Anwar, who is of Pakistani descent, had vocally protested the War on Terror and insisted on wearing a *hijab*, or Islamic head scarf, at the teller window. She'd also demanded time off for Islamic holidays.

And from the start, money, not justice, appeared to be the controlling motive in the case. According to a copy of the agreement Anwar signed with CAIR, she agreed to split 50 percent of "any monetary sum recovered" from Bank of America with CAIR, a nonprofit group.[9]

Publicity also appeared to be an overriding interest. "Nihad [Awad] suggested we move fwd [forward] with this and this may be the big case," CAIR officials in Maryland said in notes recorded in CAIR's confidential case files.[10]

In the end Bank of America called CAIR's bluff after the group got greedy and overplayed its hand. After a relentless months-long assault on the bank, CAIR could only rouse about four hundred Muslims to express a willingness to close their personal or business accounts with Bank of America, according to internal documents. And most of them said the exact same thing in their emails to the bank, repeating the talking points provided by CAIR in an obvious cut-and-paste letter-writing campaign.

That doesn't mean the bank wasn't stung by the charges. It later made some minor changes to internal policies to look more Muslim-friendly in an effort to appease groups like CAIR who flex their legal muscle.

For instance, Bank of America has blocked employee access to Web sites like Jihad Watch, while allowing employees to visit CAIR and Arab news sites. It also now provides space at its offices for Muslim employees who want to pray during work hours.[11]

ANOTHER PAKISTANI TARGETS BANK OF AMERICA

There's an intriguing side note to the clash between CAIR and Charlotte-based Bank of America.

Just a few months after the dust had settled on the case, federal authorities arrested a Pakistani man videotaping buildings in downtown Charlotte where Bank of America has its tower. The suspect, Kamran Akhtar, who was in the U.S. illegally, had also filmed the bank's building in Dallas.

Guess who rushed to his defense, accusing police of harassing him and his family? That's right, CAIR.[12]

CAIR VERSUS MICHAEL SAVAGE

While CAIR touts its victories in an effort to intimidate its prey, it has suffered just as many defeats. And not all its victories are slam dunks. Some have been costly and caused the group unexpected headaches.

CAIR's campaign to run popular conservative radio host Michael Savage off the air, for example, cost the group $160,000. Though it didn't work, Awad says it was "worth every penny," because he says it cost Savage at least $1 million in advertising revenue.[13] CAIR highlighted some "bigoted on-air comments," and pressured corporate sponsors to stop airing commercials on his top-rated *Savage Nation* show.

Still, internal memos reveal CAIR ran into a number of roadblocks in its battle to intimidate Savage's advertisers. CAIR's power-and-coercion game wasn't as effective as it let on.

It launched its campaign in 2007, after Savage called the Quran "a throwback document" and "a book of hate" and demanded CAIR be thrown out of the country for promulgating it. In a series of press releases running into 2008, CAIR trumpeted its success in convincing some twenty companies to drop ad spots on Savage's show. (Those who caved into its demands include previous targets Office Max, JC Penney, and Sears, as well as: Wal-Mart, Sprint, Nextel, US Cellular, GEICO, Union Bank of California, ITT Technical Institute, AT&T, and Intuit.)

However, CAIR and its leftwing allies had hoped to knock off more of Savage's advertisers, reveal internal reports, which document their difficulties and frustration.

"Getting advertisers to withdraw from the *Savage Nation* has its challenges," one report written early last year says. "Some companies are quick to respond and look into the matter, while others are slow or don't even return phone calls."[14]

CAIR and its confederates complained that it's much easier to get the attention of big, national corporations than small local firms, especially franchisees.

"Going after franchises [like Jiffy Lube or Burger King] is hard," the report notes, because "for the most part the parent company cannot tell them not to advertise on a specific show."

Large corporations, on the other hand, are worried about their reputations and easier marks.

"Companies that should be the primary focus are big national companies like AT&T," the report advises. "They are the ones who's [*sic*] reputation is at stake the most, and don't want to associate with anything that might seem controversial."

However, it cautions that some large advertisers have been known to "slip through the cracks and start airing ads again."

"If this happens, which it has, you have to start from square one."

"THEY ARE LOYAL TO SAVAGE"

CAIR and its partners at Hate Hurts America, a nonprofit it helped form to attack Savage, complained that they got nowhere with companies whose products and services Savage personally endorses on the air. These firms refused to succumb to their boycott threats and pull their ad campaigns.

"Companies and products endorsed and/or promoted by Savage are an absolute no (Direct Buy, Life Lock, Swiss America)," the report conveys. "They are loyal to Savage and there is a chance they might sue."[15]

As a result, Savage is still on the air and still railing against CAIR and its efforts to deny critics freedom of speech. (In fact, CAIR is not happy that he still has a microphone to "badmouth" the group.)

CAIR has had more success censoring other radio personalities.

After publishing a list of ABC Radio's advertisers on its Web site, along with their contact information, CAIR forced the media giant to sack popular Washington DC radio personality Michael Graham for arguing that Islam promotes terrorism. Graham, to his credit, refused to bow to "CAIR's wishes and apologize or retract the truth."

Similarly, when syndicated radio legend Paul Harvey asserted that Islam "encourages killing," CAIR instructed its members to blast both Harvey and his corporate sponsors like General Electric with angry calls and emails. GE caved and agreed to pull its sponsorship, prompting Harvey to issue a revised on-air statement saying Islam is a "religion of peace." GE then restored its advertising.

CAIR also took a swipe at Dr. Laura Schlessinger, but she in contrast didn't flinch. The self-help guru held her ground when CAIR demanded she apologize for what it called an "anti-Muslim tirade" on her national radio show.

CAIR and Hate Hurts America had planned to broaden its attacks on right-wing radio hosts before running out of money. "The campaign needs to expand beyond Michael Savage to other bigoted talk show hosts," their report recommends.[16]

CAIR has turned its guns on other media personalities, including:

• Mideast expert and columnist Daniel Pipes, who earlier this year was trashed by CAIR as "the nation's leading Islamophobe";

• Terror expert Steve Emerson, who CAIR recently bashed as "a notorious Islamophobe" who's "staunchly pro-Zionist and anti-Muslim" and creates along with Pipes and a few others "the bulk of the anti-CAIR literature, which is consumed and circulated by others," the group grumbled internally;[17]

• David Horowitz and Joe Kaufman of FrontPageMagazine.com, who also top CAIR's hit list—literally ("Prepare hit sheets on Horowitz, Kaufman, Frontpage mag," CAIR official Corey Saylor recently ordered in a memo);[18]

• Glenn Beck, formerly of CNN and now with Fox News, who gave CAIR such fits that it monitored his "bigoted" show every night for four months and prepared a PowerPoint presentation for his bosses at CNN in Atlanta as part of a campaign—the "Glenn Beck Campaign," as it was known inside CAIR—to oust him from the network over his "inflammatory" coverage of Islam and Muslims;[19]

• Fox News's Bill O'Reilly—along with nationally syndicated radio hosts Michael Medved and Dennis Prager—all of whom CAIR gripes broadcast "lies and conspiracy theories" about CAIR and Islam on their "right-wing" shows; [20] and

• Anti-CAIR.com founder Andrew Whitehead, whom CAIR sued for libel and defamation, budgeting $50,000 to fight him in court and put his Web site out of business. Whitehead countersued and filed an extensive discovery request for internal documents. CAIR never provided the documents, and Whitehead never removed any of the anti-CAIR charges he posted on his Web site. [21]

NO OPPOSITION TO CAIR ALLOWED

CAIR considers all these critics "threats," according to internal memos, and it has assembled an "oppositional research" team to monitor "blogs and anti-CAIR sites" and "put them on the defensive." The memo suggests "framing" critics as "voices of hate" and showcasing them in a "hall of shame."

CAIR has used even heavier-handed tactics to silence the media.

After accusing *National Review* of selling books defaming Muhammad, CAIR pressured the magazine into withdrawing the titles from its online bookstore by essentially blackmailing one of its biggest advertisers. CAIR's Awad sent a letter to the head of Boeing complaining about the books and demanding Boeing stop running full-page ads in *National Review* until the magazine stopped selling the offending books. Awad noted that Boeing enjoyed a multi-million-dollar contract with the UAE—which happens to be one of CAIR's top foreign backers—and he threatened to copy his letter to the UAE.

The dirty trick worked: *National Review* pulled the books from its Web site.

'WE WILL HAVE A DIRECT INFLUENCE ON HOLLYWOOD'

CAIR has also trained its sights on Hollywood, and plans to have a major influence on how Muslims and Islam are portrayed in films in the future.

In the 1990s, CAIR led a nationwide protest against the movie *The Siege* which it complained stereotyped Muslims as terrorists. Awad credited CAIR's campaign with causing the film to show a $20 million loss. "Maybe the film industry learned a $20 million lesson," he sneered.

Then in 2002, with Islamic terrorism more realistic than ever, CAIR pressured writers and directors of a soon-to-be released movie about terrorism—*The Sum of All Fears*—to change the villains from Muslims to neo-Nazis. CAIR had launched a successful preemptive campaign to rid the film of "negative images of Muslims or Arabs." As one columnist opined, the developers should have also changed the title of the film, calling it instead *The Sum of All PC.*

By 2005, CAIR was on a roll, meeting with developers of Fox TV's hit drama *24* and warning them that the show was "going in a dangerous direction" by casting terrorists as Muslim. Fox honchos agreed to air CAIR public service announcements around *24*, along with a disclaimer read by star Kiefer Sutherland stating that American Muslims reject terrorism. CAIR kept the pressure on Fox executives, and the show gradually phased out Islamic terrorists for Russian separatists and other less-plausible national threats.

According to internal strategy papers, CAIR is grooming its own stable of film makers and hopes to soon have "a direct influence on Hollywood."[22]

CAIR VERSUS US AIRWAYS

By now the notorious "Flying Imams" are well known to Americans, along with their CAIR-led war against US Airways. CAIR sued the airline on behalf of six Muslim clerics who in 2006 were bounced off a flight after engaging in behavior that alarmed passengers and crew. Some feared they were testing security procedures in a dry run for a future hijacking. The *imams* insist they were acting innocently.

What has not been widely reported, however, is that the ringleader of the group has a connection to an eerily similar disturbance aboard another airline several years earlier. So does CAIR. And the parallels raise fresh questions about their motives.

Rewind to 1999. That year, two Muslim college students were removed from an America West flight to Washington from Phoenix after twice attempting to open the cockpit. The FBI later suspected it was a "dry run" for the 9/11 hijackings, according the 9/11 Commission Report.

At the time, however, authorities didn't have enough suspicion to hold the students. And as soon as Hamdan al-Shalawi and Muhammed al-Qudhaieen were released, they filed racial profiling suits against America West, now part of US Airways.[23]

Representing them was none other than CAIR, which held a news conference to condemn "this ugly case of racial profiling" and urge Muslims to boycott America West.

"Muhammed and Hamdan had done absolutely nothing wrong," Awad insisted. "Their crime was being Arab, speaking Arabic."

The pair, who spoke loudly in Arabic despite being fluent in English, also switched their seats and roamed the plane from the tail section to the cockpit, while asking suspicious questions about the plane and its routes.

"Flying Imams" ringleader Omar Shahin is familiar with such shenanigans. Witnesses say he prayed loudly in Arabic before boarding his US Airways flight—which also originated from Phoenix. And once on board, he asked for a seatbelt extender even though he didn't need one and never used the one provided him. (He and another *imam* left the extenders on the floor of the plane.) And he roamed the cabin and tried to switch seats with another *imam*.

Shahin also happens to be familiar with both of the students who were kicked off the America West flight. In fact, he ministered to them at his former mosque in Tucson, Arizona, where they attended college on visas from Saudi Arabia. When they were arrested, he rushed to their defense along with CAIR.

Shahin has admitted to being a former supporter of Osama bin Laden while running the Saudi-backed Islamic Center of Tucson, which functioned as one of al-Qaida's main hubs in North America.[24]

FBI investigators believe bin Laden operated a cell at that same mosque. Hani Hanjour, the Saudi hijacker who piloted the plane that hit the Pentagon, worshipped there along with bin Laden's one-time personal secretary, according to the 9/11 report. Bin Laden's former chief of logistics was president of the mosque before Shahin took over.

"These people don't continue to come back to Arizona because they like the sunshine or they like the state," said FBI agent Kenneth Williams. "Something was established there, and it's been there for a long time."

And the America West pair and their *imam* were right in the middle of it.

Al-Qudhaieen's name turned up in Williams's investigation of Islamic flight school students in the Phoenix area and he later became a material witness in the 9/11 investigation. And as it turns out, his partner Al-Shalawi -- far from being an innocent random passenger -- had contacts with al-Qaida operatives, according to the 9/11 report, and trained for attacks in Afghanistan. Both were deported back to Saudi.

Shahin, a native of Jordan, now heads the North American Imams Federation, or NAIF, a sister organization to CAIR also controlled by the Muslim Brotherhood. In fact, he was returning from a private NAIF conference in Minneapolis when he was removed from the flight. During the conference he'd met with newly elected Representative Keith Ellison who had just spoken the previous night at a CAIR event (see timeline below).

ORCHESTRATED STUNT?

Timeline of events surrounding removal of six imams from US Airways Flight 300:

Sat., Nov. 18	Rep.-elect Keith Ellison (D-MN) speaks via video at annual CAIR fundraising banquet in Washington.
Sat., Nov. 18	North American Imams Federation (NAIF) holds private conference in Minneapolis organized by imam and NAIF President Omar Shahin, who holds workshop on "Imams and the Media."
Sun., Nov. 19, 10 am	Ellison speaks to NAIF in Minneapolis about "Imams and Politics."
Sun., Nov. 19, 7 pm	Ellison meets with Imam Shahin.
Mon., Nov. 20	Shahin and five other imams from NAIF conference are bounced from US Airways flight for "odd" and "suspicious" behavior and are detained by police at Minneapolis airport.
Tues., Nov. 21	Shahin returns to US Airways ticket counter with media to claim discrimination.
Tues., Nov. 21	CAIR, a sister organization to NAIF, calls for federal investigation into incident and other alleged Muslim profiling.
Wed., Nov. 22	Ellison sends letter to US Airways CEO and Minneapolis airports commission director demanding a meeting to discuss possible "discrimination" and airline and airport policy for removing passengers from flights.
Mon., Nov. 27	Shahin travels to Washington and organizes with CAIR and congressional officials a protest of US Airways at Reagan Washington National Airport. CAIR attorneys prepare discrimination lawsuit for Shahin against US Airways.

Sources: Police and wire reports; CAIR press releases; NAIF brochure.

Shahin, who has raised funds for the Holy Land Foundation and other charitable fronts for Hamas, was the public face of the Slighted Six *imams* who returned to the US Airways ticket counter at the Minneapolis airport to scold agents before the cameras, and then staged a protest at Reagan International Airport in Washington.

CAIR quickly signed legal retainer agreements with Shahin and the other *imams*, while promising them "large compensation," according to notes taken during one of CAIR's conference calls.[25] "CAIR is taking care of our case," Shahin told the press.

But it hasn't gone as smoothly as CAIR would like. Viewed internally as a "big case," the suit has raised tensions at CAIR headquarters. For instance, Awad scolded CAIR's former legal director Arsalan Iftikhar for initially dragging his feet. "You are not doing your job on this matter," he told the attorney in an email complaining about delays.[26]

NATIONAL SECURITY IMPLICATIONS

The suspicious confluence of events—combined with the *imams'* deliberate attempts to raise suspicions on the plane—has led some law enforcement officials to conclude that CAIR and NAIF staged the controversy to create public sympathy for Muslims and an outcry against airline profiling and counterterror measures in general. CAIR and Congressman Ellison, a former civil rights attorney, immediately used the incident as a platform to call for the criminalization of such profiling.

In addition, "Acts of staged controversy could also be used to desensitize security personnel by making activity that common sense would deem suspicious instead seem routine and not worth any special effort," says New York Police Department detective Edward Sloan.[27]

By suing John Doe passengers, moreover, CAIR intimidated crew and passengers alike, possibly making them more reluctant to report suspicious behavior. Though CAIR later dropped the claims against the tipsters, there may be a residual "chilling effect," Sloan says.

Engaging in deliberately suspicious behavior in order to distract federal air marshals or other security and law enforcement authorities—a tactic that has been discussed on Islamist message boards—is against the law, the detective points out.

The mainstream media, who regularly book CAIR spokesmen to claim to argue the point of view of Muslims, and weak-kneed CEOs and politicians, who let CAIR mau-mau them into changing workplace policies or reserving rooms in the Capitol to hold court, have been used by the enemy.

The days of legitimizing and mainstreaming CAIR—now an officially designated terrorist co-conspirator —must end before it can lobby against one more anti-terror measure, boycott one more airline for protecting passengers from suspicious Muslim men, or sue one more John Doe tipster who could save hundreds of lives.

PART II
MUSLIM MAFIA IN AMERICA

The first section of this book reveals how the Council on American-Islamic Relations functions as a dangerous front organization. More alarming, however, is that CAIR is part of an organized crime network in America made up of more than one hundred other Muslim front groups. Collectively, they are the U.S. Muslim Brotherhood. The following section exposes the inner workings of the mob-like Brotherhood, and outlines its broader conspiracy of infiltrating the American government and "destroying Western civilization from within." For the first time, the constellation of dots in this sinister conspiracy are connected, and connected convincingly.

CHAPTER THIRTEEN

THE MUSLIM BROTHERHOOD: TERRORISTS IN SUITS

"Allah is our goal; the Prophet is our guide; the Quran is our constitution; Jihad is our way; and death for the glory of Allah is our greatest ambition."

—*Muslim Brotherhood credo*

FORTY YEARS AGO, radical Muslim immigrants began organizing in America and developing a criminal underworld that largely escaped federal law enforcement scrutiny. They incorporated nonprofit organizations with benign-sounding names and told anybody who asked they were simply forming a social network or "cultural society" for Muslims.

But in the wake of 9/11, Washington allowed skeptical case agents to start connecting the dots, and they began to see a lot of overlap in the operations of the Muslim groups and their leaders, and a lot of suspicious activity, confirming the hunches of veteran counterterrorism investigators.

Although the groups appear independent of one another, many of them co-mingle funds and even share the same staff and office space. For example, some forty active Muslim charities and businesses have operated at one time or another out of the same office building in Herndon, Virginia. And several others have been headquartered in the same non-descript office park in Alexandria, Virginia, in the shadow of the nation's capital.

Both nexuses are located within Fairfax County. "There's only three degrees of separation between international terrorism and what happens in Fairfax County," observes a senior Fairfax County Police Department detective. "Our society here is totally infiltrated by the bad guys."[1]

Investigators also discovered the groups have interlocking boards of directors. One leader, Abdurahman Alamoudi, sat on the boards of no fewer than sixteen Islamic organizations, including CAIR. Many of the leaders live next door to each other on private, secluded streets.

"When we started to really look at this thing, we found it's all the same people. It's all the same guys," says an FBI official in Washington.[2]

Investigators also confirmed that many of the groups were laundering terrorist-bound funds through a maze of shell companies and fronts. They even used religious charities and think tanks as cover to carry out their illicit activities.

Soon federal prosecutors realized they were dealing with a vast criminal conspiracy and began to look for ways to roll up the entire network of bad guys.

Their first big break came a few years ago with the search of one of the leaders' homes in Annandale, Virginia, following his arrest on suspicions he had cased the Chesapeake Bay Bridge and other bridges for possible terrorist attack. There, in a sub-basement of suspect Ismail Elbarasse's basement, agents uncovered a stash of secret manifestos, charters, and other documents revealing the depth of the conspiracy.[3]

After translating the Arabic-written papers into English, investigators realized they had seized the archives of the U.S. branch of the militant Muslim Brotherhood.

GERM OF JIHAD

Established eighty years ago in Cairo, Egypt, where the "mother group" is based (think Sicily), the Muslim Brotherhood is a secretive society that gave birth to the Egyptian Islamic Jihad, Palestinian Islamic Jihad, and Hamas. It's also the parent organization of al-Qaida. In fact, it is the germ of the entire global jihadist movement now threatening the West.

Before joining al-Qaida, Osama bin Laden, Dr. Ayman al-Zawahiri, Khalid Sheik Mohammed, Blind Sheik Omar Abdul-Rahman, and other notorious terrorists were all adherents of the trans-national Muslim Brotherhood—or *al-Ikhwan al-Muslimun*, as it is known in Arabic. All remain members in good standing—including bin Laden.

The Supreme Guide of the Egypt-based Muslim Brotherhood, Mohammed Akef, recently was asked: "Regarding resistance and jihad, do you consider Osama bin Laden a terrorist or an Islamic *mujahid* (freedom fighter)?"

Akef's answer: "In all certainty, a *mujahid*, and I have no doubt in his sincerity in resisting the occupation, close to Allah on high."

While the Brotherhood now claims to eschew violence against the government, it changed its tune only after Cairo jailed its leaders and banned the group as a terrorist front. The movement still operates semi-openly in Egypt, with some members serving in parliament. And it still supports violent jihad, if clandestinely, while reportedly maintaining a well-armed wing of thousands of trained fighters.

Even in America, it has set up a network of front groups to underwrite suicide bombings carried out by Hamas and other terrorists—mass murders that Brotherhood leaders here have described as "beautiful," according to covert FBI recordings.

"The Muslim Brotherhood has figured that they can be successful promoting radical change from within the U.S. while supporting the armed struggle outside the U.S., primarily through fundraising and closely associated Palestinian terrorist organizations," says former FBI Special Agent George Sadler, who after 9/11 investigated the Brotherhood from the bureau's Washington field office.[4]

While its secret writings call for conquering this nation through political infiltration and mass conversion, it does not rule out violent jihad when the time is right and all its "infrastructure" is in place and strong. To that end, the Brotherhood has set up jihad training camps inside America where its foot soldiers conduct paramilitary exercises, including firearms and other weapons training.

In other words, despite recent attempts to slap a happy face on its movement, the Brotherhood is still an extremely dangerous and subversive organization, investigators and prosecutors agree. It has stated clearly in its recently declassified U.S. charter that it considers the United States to be its enemy.

And the Islamist cult has spent the last four decades infiltrating America. Like a colony of termites, it has become deeply entrenched in our society, undermining it from within.

THE SMOKING GUN

One secret document found during the raid of Elbarasse's home lays bare the Brotherhood's ambitious plans for a U.S. takeover, replacing the Constitution with *Shariah*, or Islamic law.

Written by a U.S. Brotherhood boss, Mohammed Akram Adlouni, the strategy paper describes the group's long-term goal of destroying the U.S. system "from within" by using its freedoms and political processes against it. It is a blueprint for stealth jihad. Under the heading: "The role of the Muslim Brother in North America," it states:

> The Ikhwan must understand that their work in America is a kind of grand jihad in eliminating and destroying the Western civilization from within, and "sabotaging" its miserable house by the hands of the believers, so that it is eliminated and Allah's religion is made victorious over all other religions.[5]

Jihad. Sabotage. Eliminate. Destroy. The miserable West. Sounds like the latest screed from Osama bin laden. But it's from the Muslim establishment in America.

The same eighteen-page document lists as confederates some thirty major Muslim organizations in America—all of which are considered "mainstream" and "moderate" by the media and many politicians, but are in fact U.S. franchises of the radical Muslim Brotherhood.

Many more Brotherhood front groups have been incorporated since the manifesto was written in 1991. (See list, end of chapter.) It and other seized Brotherhood documents are smoking-gun proof that CAIR and the Islamic Society of North America—along with the Muslim Students Association, North American Islamic Trust, Islamic Circle of North America, Muslim American Society, and the rest of institutional Islam in America—were established with a markedly different purpose from what they publicly claim. And they've gone through decades of deceit to conceal their true identities and purposes.

Their secret manifesto is "a clear threat statement of hostile intent," says Pentagon terror expert Major Stephen Coughlin, "with stated objectives that overlap with al-Qaida's."[6]

U.S. prosecutors entered the documents as evidence in the recent Holy Land Foundation terror trial. The chilling courtroom exhibits were unopposed by the defense, further attesting to their authenticity.

Prosecutors outlined the broader conspiracy by listing the entities and individuals named in the Brotherhood documents as unindicted co-conspirators in the case. The government list totals more than three hundred.

As it turns out, "every major Muslim group in the United States is controlled by the Muslim Brotherhood," veteran FBI agent John Guandolo says, who has spent years investigating the subversive group. It's not just a loose network of people sharing a common ideology, he says, but a centrally controlled and directed insurgency.

"It is a genuine conspiracy to overthrow the government, and they have organizations to do it, and they have written doctrines outlining their plan," Guandolo adds.

"And they've got our number."[7]

ORGANIZATIONAL JIHAD

By that, the investigator means the bad guys have closely studied how America works and how it's structured and have determined that it is built on institutions and organizations. America respects formal structure. So the Brotherhood constructed an elaborate covert as well as public organizational structure—a dual internal and external infrastructure that with few exceptions continues to function today.

As CAIR boss Omar Ahmad bragged: "We can have as many organizations as we want," no questions asked, thanks to America's tolerant and pluralistic culture.[8] The only thing the Brothers have to worry about, he advised, is covering up "orders" from abroad, as well as the "financial connections," so that their organizations appear independent.

"If you cover these two bases, you will find that you, as an American organization, can do whatever you want," the FBI recorded Ahmad saying during his secret jihad summit in Philadelphia.[9]

The more organizations, the more legitimacy, the Brothers agreed. And the more legitimacy, the more political cover to infiltrate the government and the more legal cover to protect the group from prosecution.[10]

America's democratic freedoms have allowed the Brotherhood to put up a tremendous front, behind which it hides its subversive and criminal activities. In fact, the Brotherhood privately refers to its own organizations as "fronts."

"The Brothers in Egypt don't have fronts in the same broad way we have in America," Zeid al-Noman, leader of the organization office of the U.S. Muslim Brotherhood, confides in one document seized by authorities. Though the organization is banned over there, it still operates relatively openly—something the Brotherhood is loath to do here, especially after 9/11.

RELIGIOUS CRIME SYNDICATE

The U.S. Brotherhood even set up a committee to study the legal aspects of establishing charities in America. The charities are critical because the Brothers have used them as a "side" or "facade," as they put it in their writings, to launder illegal payments to terrorists.[11] Most of their charitable fronts have been shut down, their leaders convicted. However, they continue to search for clever new ways of funneling cash to jihadists.

The Justice Department earlier this year put away several Brotherhood leaders on conspiracy charges in the case against the Holy Land Foundation charity. Shukri Abu Baker, Mohammad El-Mezain, and CAIR founding director Ghassan Elashi were sentenced to, in effect, life terms for funneling millions to Hamas. Three other Brothers caught up in the investigation have also been imprisoned.[12]

The government viewed the charity and its subsidiaries as a "criminal enterprise" as much as a terrorist front. Such federal racketeering and conspiracy laws are more commonly applied to mafia figures.

A federal grand jury in Northern Virginia has been hearing evidence in another possible Brotherhood conspiracy involving the network of business and charitable fronts in Herndon known collectively as the Safa group.

Brotherhood underboss Taha al-Alwani of Safa said he was bound by the "Brotherhood of faith" when he funneled money, wittingly or not, to Palestinian terrorists through fronts in Florida controlled by another

Brotherhood underboss, according to court documents.

"The matter of the financial support was never the basis of our relationship, for our relationship added to the Brotherhood of faith," Al-Alwani wrote Sami al-Arian in a letter, referring to at least $50,000 Safa transferred to the now-convicted terrorist.

He reiterated that they shared "the same objectives," and that "all of your institutions are considered by us as ours." Al-Alwani is an unindicted co-conspirator in the al-Arian terrorism case.[13]

With each new indictment, the Muslim establishment in America looks more and more like a religious crime syndicate.

KEY U.S. MUSLIM BROTHERHOOD FRONT ORGANIZATIONS[14]

Council On American-Islamic Relations (CAIR)	Taibah International Aid Association
Islamic Society of North America (ISNA)	International Relief Organization (IRO)
Muslim Students Association (MSA)	African Muslim Agency
Fiqh Council of North America (FCNA)	Safa Trust
North American Islamic Trust (NAIT)	SAAR Foundation
Muslim Arab Youth Association (MAYA)	Makkah Mukarramah Charity Trust
Al-Aqsa Educational Fund	Dar El-Eiman USA Inc.
United Association for Studies and Research (UASR)	All Dulles Area Muslim Society (ADAMS)
Islamic Association for Palestine in North America (IAP)	Islamic Assembly of North America (IANA)
Holy Land Foundation for Relief and Development (HLF)	Global Relief Foundation
Baitul Mal Inc. (BMI)	Muslim World League (MWL)
International Institute for Islamic Thought (IIIT)	World Assembly of Muslim Youth (WAMY)
Islamic Medical Association of North America (IMANA)	Muslim Youth of North America (MYNA)
Association of Muslim Scientists and Engineers (AMSE)	Happy Hearts Trust
Islamic Circle of North America (ICNA)	Islamic Academy of Florida
Islamic Free Market Institute (Islamic Institute)	Fairfax Institute
American Muslim Council (AMC)	American Muslim Task Force on Civil Rights and Elections (AMT)
American Muslim Foundation (AMC Foundation)	
Success Foundation	International Islamic Federation of Student Organizations (IIFSO)
Muslim American Society (MAS)	American Muslims for Constructive Engagement (AMCE)
Graduate School of Islamic & Social Sciences (GSISS, aka Cordoba University)	American Muslim Armed Forces & Veterans Affairs Council (AMAFVAC)
North American Imams Federation (NAIF)	Council of Islamic Schools of North America (CISNA)
International Islamic Forum for Science, Technology & Human Resources Development Inc. (IIFTIKHAR)	Islamic Media Foundation
Association of Muslim Social Scientists of North America (AMSS)	

CHAPTER FOURTEEN

THE 'IKHWAN MAFIA'

"These guys talk about murdering Jews like the mob talked about killing—totally casual, like they were ordering pizza."

—*FBI official in Washington*[1]

INVESTIGATORS ROUTINELY COMPARE the Muslim Brotherhood to the mafia, the secret Sicilian terrorist society. Like mobsters, the Muslim Brothers operate an underworld of illegal activities conducted under the cover of fronts with legitimate-sounding names.

They launder money through construction companies such as BMI, Inc., and tax-exempt charities such as Happy Hearts Trust.

"They're all part of the same organized crime family, like the Mob," says FBI agent Guandolo, who worked several years in the Washington field office's counterterrorism division and is familiar with the the bureau's ongoing investigation of the Brotherhood.

"If you're a capo, I know you've killed somebody. I know you're involved in racketeering and crime. And I know you're a member of a major crime family," he says. "If you're a board member of one of these Brotherhood groups, I know you're an enemy of the United States."

For that matter, the Brotherhood is known within Islamist circles as the "Ikhwan mafia," because of its highly organized structure, centralized control, and covert operations. Like the mob, it has its own internal bylaws, security, and military infrastructure. A network of front groups, cutouts, and shell companies shield its criminal activities from the authorities.

A *shura* council controls the U.S. movement. It's made up of the heads of the various crime centers—the godfathers—and is led by a supreme don called a general *masul*. The council directs regional underbosses, or *masuls*, who in turn give orders to capo-like figures known as *naquibs*. The *naquibs* control the front groups, and train the field commanders, or *ikhwans*, who are sworn members, according to Brotherhood documents declassified by the government.

The *ikhwans*, in turn, recruit associates—the foot soldiers—at mosques, Islamic conferences, and college campuses to provide the next generation of leadership and keep the organization growing.

They also provide the muscle for the group. At "*Ikhwan* camps," young soldiers conduct jihadist training activities. Mohammed, the mastermind of the 9/11 attacks, was drawn to violent jihad in Kuwait after joining the Brotherhood at age sixteen and attending its desert youth camps. Convicted CAIR official Royer, who led a group of young Virginia men in jihadist training, is an example of Brotherhood muscle in America.

The religious crime syndicate basically consists of four power centers, or families:

1. THE PALESTINE COMMITTEE is the Hamas wing that operates chiefly out of California, Texas, Illinois, and Washington DC. Prosecutors believe CAIR is its mouthpiece and its lobbying arm in North America. With the federal bust of the Holy Land Foundation, which served as Hamas's fundraising arm in America, CAIR is now the *marque* front group within this family, and investigators believe CAIR founding chairman Omar Ahmad of Santa Clara, California, is its *masul*. He's a Palestinian refugee like many CAIR operatives, whom investigators consider his *naquibs*.[2]

2. THE SAFA GROUP is the Saudi wing made up of more than one hundred business and charitable front groups operating mainly out of Northern Virginia (along the so-called Wahhabi Corridor, just outside DC), as well as Georgia. Before he was sent to prison, Alamoudi controlled the group, along with Jamal Barzinji, who remains at its helm. Safa provides financial and intellectual capital for the cause, while also controlling a vast real estate portfolio. (See timeline, end of chapter, chronicling Saudi money flows to Safa.)

3. ISLAMIC CIRCLE OF NORTH AMERICA is the Pakistani wing based out of New York. ICNA recently merged with the Alexandria, Virginia-based Muslim American Society, setting up shop in a neighboring suburb. MAS organizes prayer and youth camps at Brotherhood mosques across the country. It also conducts ideological training and indoctrination of new recruits, urging jihad, martyrdom, and the creation of Islamic states in the "evil" West. In addition, MAS works with two political fronts based in California to register Muslim voters and groom Muslim candidates for public office.

4. ISLAMIC SOCIETY OF NORTH AMERICA is the founding "nucleus" for the movement in North America, declassified Brotherhood documents confirm. Operating out of both Indiana and Washington DC, it controls campus recruitment, evangelism, banking and investments, and the dispensing of *fatwahs* for the Brotherhood. Through a subsidiary trust, it also owns and controls the lion's share of the major mosques in America. Sayyid Syeed, Muzzamil Siddiqi, Jamal Badawi, and Bassem Osman are said to act as the main bosses of this family.[3]

The heads of the various families galvanize around five fundamental goals:

1. Supporting Palestinian terrorists and seeking Israel's destruction;

2. Gutting U.S. anti-terrorism laws;

3. Loosening Muslim immigration;

4. Converting Americans to Islam, with a special focus on Hispanic immigrants and black inmates and soldiers (attractive white Christian women are another prize conversion); and

5. Infiltrating the government and institutionalizing *Shariah* law in America.

It is no coincidence, investigators say, that Brotherhood leaders have avoided identifying their institutions with the governmental system of the United States, opting instead for territorial recognition. This speaks volumes about not only the respect they hold for their adopted country, but also their broader ambitions.

THE SIGNIFICANCE OF 'NORTH AMERICA'

You'd be hard-pressed to find the words "United States" or "USA" or even "U.S." in the names of their organizations. You commonly find, instead, the geographic term "North America," as in: the Islamic Society of North America, Islamic Circle of North America, Islamic Assembly of North America, Fiqh Council of North America, Islamic Medical Association of North America, and so on. Other Brotherhood groups contain the phrase "North American," as in: the North American Islamic Trust and North American Imams Federation.

That's because the Muslim Brotherhood's ultimate goal is to conquer the entire continent of North America for Allah, and fold its nations into a global Islamic nation, or *caliphate*.

The Brothers believe Islam is a territorial religion. According to their creed, the whole earth belongs to Allah and he has given it to Muslims. As their writings indicate, they believe this land is theirs, and does not belong to you or the United States government. And as slaves of Allah, they are conscripted to conquer it in his name—by hook or by crook.

CLOAKED IN SECRECY

Like the *Cosa Nostra*, members have been sworn to secrecy and speak in code, referring to the Brotherhood generically as the "Group" or the "Movement." Also, "special work" is code for "military work," or jihad, which the West knows as terrorism.

"We resort to secrecy," al-Noman stresses, but only among *kaffirs*, not internally. Sworn members know the identities of the General *Masul* and the *masuls*.

They follow a similar *omerta* as the Sicilians when it comes to law enforcement: keep silent about subversive activities and crimes, and never cooperate with the police. Many wives are left in the dark. Those who know things are ordered to keep quiet about them.

New members take an oath of loyalty to the Brotherhood, reciting its *credo*: "Allah is our goal; the Prophet is our guide; the Quran is our constitution; jihad is our way; and death for the glory of Allah is our greatest ambition." They also swear to "sacrifice all that one has for the sake of raising the banner of Islam."[4]

Members are required to pay 3 percent of their income per year, with the money going to travel, propaganda materials, conferences, and of course, the jihad.

ALL IN THE FAMILY

To ensure secrecy and compartmentalization, the Brotherhood uses family members to hold important, interlocking positions within different fronts. These family members, in turn, often are related to Hamas or Brotherhood figures overseas.

Take the leadership of the now-defunct Holy Land Foundation.

Founder Mousa Abu Marzook is related by marriage to convicted Holy Land officer Elashi and is a cousin of convicted Holy Land co-founder el-Mezain. Marzook is deputy political chief for Hamas and wanted by U.S. authorities. Before leaving the country, he was a *masul* in the U.S. Brotherhood and sat on its *shura* council.

The incestuousness runs deeper. Holy Land officer Akram Mishal, also a fugitive, is a cousin of Hamas leader Khalid Mishal. And Mufid Abdulgader, a top Holy Land fundraiser now serving twenty years in prison, is Khalid Mishal's half-brother.[5]

The children and other close relatives of Brotherhood leaders also serve in leadership roles at ISNA, the Muslim Students Association, and the Fiqh Council, among other front groups. Some leaders' children intermarry. For example, the oldest daughter of Sayyid Syeed, an ISNA founder and its current DC chief, is married to a relative of Brotherhood boss Jamal Barzinji.[6]

Barzinji's brother, meanwhile, heads Amana Publishing, which prints copies of the Quran and other texts the Brotherhood uses for evangelizing. Another Barzinji family member runs a charitable front in Herndon whose bank accounts recently were closed by Wachovia due to suspicious activity.

The firstborn of founding Muslim Brotherhood members are typically groomed to replace them. "Like father, like son," Sadler says.

The pioneer of the U.S. movement is sixty-nine-year-old Ahmed Elkadi. Both his father and father-in-law were early Brotherhood leaders in Egypt.

The firstborn son of the late Mahboob Khan, another founding father of the Brotherhood movement in America, has been a consultant to CAIR and served on committees at ISNA.[7] Suhail Khan infiltrated the U.S. government as a White House staffer, and most recently, the Transportation Department as a senior official.

It's worth noting that CAIR founder and key Brotherhood boss Ahmad has three sons.

'SECURING THE GROUP'

The Brotherhood has devised strict security measures to keep its illicit activities outside the scrutiny of law enforcement, while at the same time monitoring what it calls "outside dangers" such as "the CIA, FBI, etc., so that we find out if they are monitoring us [and] how can we get rid of them," according to Brotherhood boss Zeid al-Noman. [8]

As documented in earlier chapters, CAIR as well as ISNA have accomplished this through their outreach meetings with law enforcement.

"This is what is meant by securing the group," al-Noman is recorded as saying.

Investigators say Brotherhood bosses have hired security firms to sweep their offices for bugs, and have ordered foot soldiers to take advanced training in wiretap detection. They also are known to shred documents after board meetings and maintain incriminating documents in off-site locations.

They've also targeted critics for countersurveillance.

A Brotherhood charter seized from al-Arian's home calls for establishing a unit "to watch the individuals who oppose the Movement and the Islamic actions—to watch them, monitor them, and make files on them."[9]

As detailed earlier, making files on enemies and critics is something CAIR does all too well.

CUL-DE-SACS AND PIPE STEMS

Investigators have taken note that, like mob bosses, suspected Muslim Brotherhood leaders go to great lengths to thwart law enforcement surveillance.

For example, most of them live or have lived on *cul-de-sacs*, including Ahmad, Nihad Awad, Alamoudi, Irfan Totonji, Abdullah bin Laden (Osama's nephew), Hamza Yusuf, Ihsan Bagby, Mohamed Nimer, Mousa Abu Marzook, Esam Omeish, Abbas Ebrahim (bookkeeper of felonious Brotherhood investor Soliman Biheiri), as well as Elbarasse, whose home eventually was searched by FBI agents, yielding the trove of Muslim Brotherhood documents.

Many have built their homes on pipe stems spoking off from *cul-de-sacs*. Pipe stems are narrow, secluded roads that often slope down away from *cul-de-sacs*, making it difficult for law enforcement to conduct stakeouts since homes typically cannot be seen from the street.

Brotherhood leaders al-Alwani, Jamal Barzinji, Yaqub Mirza, Fakhri Barzinji, and Hisham Altalib have all listed addresses on or near the same pipe stem off of Safa Court in Herndon, Virginia.

"They make it harder for us to do trash covers," a method of surveillance where investigators search garbage for evidence, veteran FBI agent Guandolo says. "They don't put cans on the street, but on the long driveway back off the street."

He says many Brotherhood leaders have installed motion-detector security lights—and "this was before 9/11, so they've been protecting themselves from surveillance for a long time."

Their mosques also put up defenses against surveillance.

After Dar al-Hijrah Islamic Center became the focus of federal investigations after the first World Trade Center bombing, mosque leaders planted a tall, thick row of evergreens along the street. After 9/11, when it was learned that some of the hijackers prayed at the so-called "Row Street mosque," FBI agents secretly cut the hedge back so they could spy on activities there. (The mosque reported the tree damage as a case of anti-Islamic vandalism.)

The mosque, whose deed is held by a Muslim Brotherhood bank, has its own phalanx of armed guards patrolling the perimeter of the grounds.

THE MILITARY BRANCH

A Brotherhood charter seized in the raid on al-Arian's flat and translated from Arabic provides for the establishment of a supersecret "Security and Military" branch to, among other things, purchase "arms" for export and for use at training "camps" inside the U.S. Another function: developing "tools" for "spying operations."[10]

Other documents reveal paramilitary camps have been set up in Oklahoma, Missouri, and other states, where the Brothers conduct firearms and other weapons training. They've also frequented shooting ranges in Georgia, Virginia, New York, and other states, while setting up clubs to learn "self-defense techniques" like the hijackers learned.[11]

'OUR DAR AL-ARQAM (SAFEHOUSE)'

Like mob bosses, Brotherhood leaders conduct much of their business behind closed doors. Only the Muslim mafia's hideouts are religious sanctuaries, not topless bars or butcher shops. Mosques serve as "fronts for Brotherhood work," leaders reveal in their writings.[12]

They also serve as recruiting centers. The Brothers invite prospects to come to the mosque and join a small prayer group—or *usra*, Arabic for "family"—where they evaluate their loyalty and commitment to the cause.

These Islamic centers are key nodes in the network. They also serve as "beehives," planting the "seed for a small Islamic society" in every city, according to Brotherhood strategy papers. The mosques will "prepare us and supply our battalions in addition to being the 'niche' of our prayers."[13]

Dar al-Hijrah, the 9/11 mosque in the Washington suburbs, is the spiritual headquarters for the Muslim mafia in America.[14]

Other key hubs: the Bridgeview Mosque in Chicago; MCA Islamic Center and Masjid an-Noor in Santa Clara, California; Orange County Islamic Society in Garden Grove, California; Al-Farooq Mosque in Brooklyn, New York; the Islamic Center of Tucson, Arizona; and ADAMS Center in Sterling, Virginia, where former General *Masul* Ahmed Elkadi lives.

The *imams* of these centers play a vital role not just as spiritual leaders in the movement, but also as recruiters and organizers.

In their internal documents, the Brothers refer to the United States as "our *Dar al-Arqam*"—or safehouse—because of the protections it affords them to freely practice their faith. (Interestingly, influential Brotherhood *imam* Ali al-Timimi ran a radical storefront mosque in Northern Virginia by that name before he was sent to the slammer for soliciting treason against the United States.)

It's also clear from FBI wiretaps of secret meetings that the Brotherhood views America as a pushover. As Shukri Abu Baker put it, America represents "a safe place for the Movement." Another major Brotherhood figure, Abdelhaleem Ashqar, adds that "in America, we have a legal slack, or an atmosphere of freedom."

Unlike the Sicilian mafia, the Muslim mafia is harder to penetrate, investigators say, because it is shrouded by a major religion. Fearing accusations of religious bigotry, Washington is still reluctant to aggressively prosecute it.

RATS AND SNITCHES

What's more, it's harder to infiltrate the group with informants or undercover agents due to its cryptic language, religious rituals, and initiations.

The Brothers also are very careful about whom they recruit. Even immigrants from Muslim nations have to be nominated by the *usra*, and then only a *naquib* can submit a name to the *masul*, who then does a thorough background check. Members swear allegiance to the Brotherhood, and are conditioned to sacrifice everything to protect it. And only trusted members can get into the group's inner circle.

One memo cautions leaders to be careful about "moles" and leaks and other internal security problems. It counsels them to take care in screening potential recruits to avoid revealing too much information. If the recruit asks whether the leader is a Brotherhood member, the leader should respond, "You may deduce the answer to that with your own intelligence."[15]

Additionally, it advises using dead drops when dealing with associates, in case they are arrested and confess to what they know. Dead drops use a hidden location such as a tree or a bridge inside a park for secretly passing cash, weapons, or information between members without requiring a meeting.

Few leaders have been ratted out. "Unlike the mob, you can't flip these guys," says an FBI special agent who investigated the Alexandria, Virginia-based World Assembly of Muslim Youth and other Brotherhood fronts. "They don't care if they go to jail."[16]

He explains they're viewed as "martyrs" for the cause if they're locked up, attaining a higher status within the Brotherhood.

It took the FBI decades to infiltrate the mafia. "It's ten times harder to infiltrate [Brotherhood] groups than the mob," says veteran FBI agent John Vincent, who investigated major Brotherhood figures in Chicago.[17]

PH.D. MOBSTERS

Veteran investigators say they have never faced a more disciplined adversary. They are a lot smarter than mobsters. They are well-educated professionals, including clerics, scholars, doctors, and engineers. In fact, many of the top Brotherhood leaders in America have Ph.D.s or M.D.s.

The crime bosses of the *ummah* underworld are not the suburban goombas depicted on HBO, hanging out at the Bada Bing. While they also launder money, extort, threaten, lie without shame, and conspire to do murder, the members of this mafia, this brotherhood of faith, are not rough around the edges or right off the boat. Many are American citizens fluent in English and highly articulate. They appear sophisticated, even genteel, giving them a veneer of legitimacy that makes them more dangerous.

But make no mistake: These are thugs who, at their core, are really no different than mobsters. They, too, beat their women and pay to have people killed. These same mild-mannered religious leaders have been arrested for domestic violence and bankrolling terrorism.

And some have long rap sheets. Take Mahdi Bray, the head of the Muslim American Society's political arm in Washington. He's a three-time felon and an ex-con who's done serious time, according to police and court records unveiled by Washington-based IPT News.[18] Prior to joining MAS, founded by Muslim Brotherhood leaders, Bray was the political director of the Los Angeles-based Muslim Public Affairs Council, or MPAC. He recently led a Brotherhood campaign to raise $30,000 to help pay for lawyers to free al-Qaida agent and would-be presidential assassin Ahmed Abu Ali, who is serving a life sentence.

FBI agents who have listened in on the private conversations of Brotherhood bosses say they talk about murder as if they were ordering pizza.

"These guys talk about jihad and murdering Jews like the mob talked about killing—totally casual, like they were ordering pizza," an FBI official in Washington says.[19]

He recalls one prominent American Muslim leader expressing his approval of synagogue bombings in a room with other Brotherhood leaders. "And this is a skinny guy with coke-bottle glasses," the official says. "He's a scholar."

He says the Brotherhood and al-Qaida share the same goals but use different methods to achieve them.

"The only difference between the guys in the suits and the guys with the AK-47s is timing and tactics," he says.

TIMELINE OF U.S. MUSLIM BROTHERHOOD MILESTONES

1960s   New wave of Arab immigrants floods America's campuses, particularly at large Midwestern universities in Illinois, Indiana, and Michigan. Some students belonged to the Brotherhood in their homelands and want to spread its ideology here.

1962   "Mother group" in Egypt agrees to start movement in America with financial help of Saudi-based Muslim World League.

1963   Muslim Students Association (MSA) founded in U.S.

1973   World Assembly of Muslim Youth (WAMY) founded.

1973   With massive funding from Saudis, North American Islamic Trust (NAIT) formed as investment vehicle for Brotherhood, acquiring title to more than three hundred mosques and schools in the U.S.

1981   Islamic Association for Palestine (IAP) founded.

1981   Islamic Society of North America (ISNA) founded.

1983   SAAR Foundation, part of the Safa group, incorporated with massive funding from Saudis, including $3.4 million in start-up cash.

1984   Ahmed Elkadi made General Masul, or godfather, of Brotherhood in America.

1985   International Institute of Islamic Thought (IIIT) incorporated (part of Safa group), developed with $25 million from Saudi Islamic Development Bank.

1985   Graduate School of Islamic and Social Sciences (GSISS) founded with Saudi money, but does not enroll students for another decade.

1987	Hamas formed as the Palestinian wing of the Muslim Brotherhood—with stated goal of destroying Israel. Effort led by Sheikh Ahmad Yassin, head of Muslim Brotherhood in the Gaza Strip.
1988	Mousa Abu Marzook, member of the U.S. Brotherhood's shura council, helps organize Hamas, goes on to become its deputy political chief.
1988	Some two hundred Brotherhood leaders trained in U.S.
1989	Holy Land Foundation for Relief and Development (HLF) founded.
1990	American Muslim Council (AMC) formed.
1991	Network of more than thirty Brotherhood front organizations now established to spread Allah's law and raise money for terrorists. Secret strategy paper produced and circulated among leadership.
1991	Brotherhood boss Abdurahman Alamoudi creates the American Muslim Armed Forces and Veterans Affairs Council (AMAFVAC) to promote Muslim chaplains into the U.S. military.
1991	Dar al-Hijrah Islamic Center established in Washington suburbs with Saudi embassy backing.
1992	Muslim American Society (MAS) co-founded in Washington suburbs by Elkadi and two other top Brotherhood leaders, Jamal Badawi and Omar Soubani.
1993	Defense Department certifies AMAFVAC as one of two organizations to vet and endorse Muslim chaplains.
1993	Top U.S. Brotherhood leaders meet with Hamas leaders in secret Philadelphia summit, hatch plot to funnel millions to Hamas suicide bombers, families through charity.
1994	Brotherhood leaders also meet with Hamas operatives in Oxford, Mississippi.
1994	Fiqh Council of North America (FCNA) incorporated.
1994	CAIR incorporated.
1995	Elkadi replaced as General Masul, or godfather, of the Brotherhood.
1997	GSISS opens, trains most of Muslim chaplains in U.S. military (now also known as Cordoba University).

2000   Second (al-Aqsa) Intifada begins, resulting in series of horrific Hamas suicide bombings of Israeli civilians and seventy-seven deaths, including three Americans.

2000   SAAR Foundation dissolved, renamed Safa Trust.

2001   Al-Qaida attacks America, triggering terror financing probes of U.S. Muslim charities and nonprofits.

2002   Federal agents raid dozens of Brotherhood fronts tied to Safa group.

2004   Brotherhood godfather Alamoudi sentenced to twenty-three years in prison for plotting terrorism.

2005   Omar Ahmad steps down as CAIR's chairman of the board.

2005   Federal agents discover Brotherhood manifesto, trove of secret strategy papers during search of DC-area home of terror suspect and Brotherhood leader Ismail Elbarasse.

2006   Brotherhood boss Sami al-Arian pleads guilty to terror conspiracy charges.

2007   CAIR and dozens of other Muslim groups named as unindicted co-conspirators in HLF terror trial.

2008   Several Brotherhood leaders convicted of conspiring to provide material support to terrorists in Holy Land Foundation trial.

2009   Ahmad, named as an individual co-conspirator, leaves CAIR.

CHAPTER FIFTEEN

FAKING OUT THE INFIDEL

"I swear by Allah that war is deception. We are fighting our enemy with a kind heart. Deceive, camouflage, pretend that you're leaving while you're walking that way. Deceive your enemy."

—U.S. Brotherhood leader Shukri Abu Baker, recently sentenced to sixty-five years in federal prison for supporting terrorism[1]

THE TERRORISTS IN SUITS are adroit at manipulating politicians and the media through skillfully parsed propaganda. Bluntly, they're good liars. As their manifesto says, mastery of deception is key to the success of their conspiracy to support terrorism and infiltrate and destroy the American system from within.

Of course, they couldn't do this out in the open. So they set up benign-sounding nonprofits and charities to "camouflage" their traitorous activities.

During their secret meeting at a Philadelphia hotel, the Brotherhood leaders were recorded plotting ways to disguise payments to Hamas terrorists as charity. During their talks, they used the code word *Samah*— Hamas spelled backward—to mislead authorities.

"I swear by Allah that war is deception," Shukri Abu Baker was recorded as saying. "We are fighting our enemy with a kind heart.... Deceive, camouflage, pretend that you're leaving while you're walking that way. Deceive your enemy."[2]

The organizer of the secret Hamas summit was Omar Ahmad, CAIR's founding chairman. Adding to Abu Baker's point, he compared the deception needed to fool the infidels with the basketball move known as the "head fake," whereby a player fools the opponent guarding him into going a different direction in order to clear a path to the goal.

"He makes a player believe that he is doing this while he does something else," Ahmad said. "I agree with you.... Politics is a completion of war."[3]

Ahmad counseled using obfuscatory language when, for instance, talking about Israel "to the Americans" in order to couch the group's extremist views.

"There is a difference between you saying, 'I want to restore the '48 land,' and when you say, 'I want to destroy Israel,'" he remarked.

Ahmad also suggested recruiting more skilled propagandists "whom we could dedicate for the work we want to hide."[4]

The Islamist head fake has worked all too well over the past few decades. Blind acceptance and validation of Muslim leaders with questionable sympathies and loyalties hardly missed a beat in Washington, even after 9/11.

Many were invited to the White House and Congress. The head of the FBI spoke at their conferences, calling them "mainstream" and "moderate." Many gullible officials still confer legitimacy on them.

But what these Brotherhood leaders tell official Washington and what they tell Muslim audiences are often two entirely different things. The degree of deception is breathtaking. Among the standouts:

SAMI AL-ARIAN

A White House guest of both Presidents Clinton and Bush, he assured his hosts he was both peace-loving and patriotic. "I am a very moderate Muslim person," he said. "I also condemn violence in all its forms."[5]

All the while, al-Arian was secretly running a U.S. beachhead for Palestinian terrorists. In a speech at a Cleveland mosque, he once thundered: "Let's damn America, let's damn Israel, let's damn their allies until death."[6]

He's now a convicted terrorist. At his sentencing, the U.S. District Court judge slammed al-Arian as a "master manipulator," adding: "You looked your neighbors in the eyes and said you had nothing to do with the Palestinian Islamic Jihad. This trial exposed that as a lie."

ABDURAHMAN ALAMOUDI

This supposed pillar of the Muslim community also went from the White House to the Big House. But not before developing the Pentagon's Muslim chaplain corps and acting as a goodwill ambassador for the State Department.

He, too, strongly denounced terror. "We are against all forms of terrorism," he claimed. "Our religion is against terrorism."

Privately, however, he raised major funds for the terrorist group al-Qaida and was caught on tape grumbling that Osama bin Laden hadn't killed enough Americans in the U.S. embassy bombings. Like al-Arian, he proved to be an expert in the art of deception, known in Arabic as *taqiya* or *kitman*.

ALI AL-TIMIMI

A noted *imam* and native Washingtonian, he also put on a moderate face in public while secretly plotting against the U.S. The internationally known scholar had government clearance—and even worked for former White House Chief of Staff Andrew Card when he was at the Transportation Department—and was invited to speak on Islam to the U.S. military.

Publicly, the *imam* denounced Islamic violence. "My position against terrorism and Muslim-inspired violence against innocent people is well known by Muslims," he said.[7]

But privately, a darker picture emerged. Five days after the 9/11 terrorist attacks, he called them "legitimate" and rallied young Muslim men at his DC-area mosque to carry out more "holy war" and "violent jihad."[8]

Al-Timimi even cheered the *Columbia* space shuttle disaster, calling it a "good omen" for Muslims because it was a blow to their "greatest enemy." He also said the U.S. "should be destroyed."

This high-profile "moderate" is also now behind bars for soliciting terror and treason.

LIE AND DENY

When confronted with tough questions, the Brothers are trained to lie and deny. Case in point: the Muslim American Society, or MAS, a key Brotherhood front based just outside Washington.

After the *Chicago Tribune* ran an *exposé* linking MAS to the Muslim Brotherhood, MAS spokesman Mahdi Bray issued a denial: "MAS is not the Muslim Brotherhood."[9]

Never mind that the *Tribune* got an exclusive interview with Ahmed Elkadi, who confirmed that he is not only the founding godfather of the U.S. Brotherhood but one of the founding incorporators of MAS.

Bray suggested Elkadi had lost his marbles. "In addition to the reporter's inaccuracies, the primary source used for the article was Dr. Ahmed Elkadi," he said in a column. "Dr. Elkadi suffers from dementia and his cognitive faculties were seriously impaired when the *Chicago Tribune* interviewed him."[10]

Nice try. A magazine published by MAS has praised Elkadi as a great Muslim in the ranks of the Muslim Brotherhood's founding fathers in Egypt.

And one of the secret Brotherhood documents the FBI recently declassified confirms that MAS is controlled by the Brotherhood. It tasks MAS, as well as CAIR (which has also denied Brotherhood links), with defeating "Zionist infiltration" and raising the banner of Palestinian jihad.

"Confrontation work plan: The activation of the role of (MAS) to educate the Brothers in all work centers, mosques, and organizations on the necessity of stopping any contacts with the Zionist organizations and the rejection of any future contacts," says the five-page memo issued by the Palestine Committee of the U.S. Muslim Brotherhood.[11]

The second-in-command of the Cairo-based Muslim Brotherhood hesitated when asked by the media about the mother group's ties to MAS. "I don't want to say MAS is an Ikhwan [Brotherhood] entity," Mohammed Habib says. "This causes some security inconveniences for them in a post-September 11 world."[12]

Why? What does it have to hide? Could it be that, despite claiming to be moderate and patriotic, MAS is preaching anti-American insurrection?

Look no further than its training materials, which assert Muslims have a duty to help form Islamic governments worldwide and should be prepared to take up arms to carry that out.

'INVADE WESTERN HEARTLAND'

Investigators say this "revolution ideology" is taught to Muslim teens by MAS's *tarbiya* department. *Tarbiya* is the process of indoctrinating young or new Muslims.

One passage in its *tarbiya* guide states that Western materialism and secularism are evil and that Muslims should "pursue this evil force to its own lands" and "invade its Western heartland," until all the infidels shout "*Allahu Akbar!*"—Allah is great.[13]

It exhorts the faithful to "wage war," investigators say, so that the

United States is "wiped out" and only the law of Allah—*Shariah*—operates in the land.

The syllabus for the MAS training course, which runs nine months, includes works by radical founding fathers of the Brotherhood movement such as the late Egyptian "martyrs" Hassan al-Banna and Sayyid Qutb, both of whom preached violent jihad, martyrdom, and world Islamic domination. (See quote box, end of chapter.) On its Web site, MAS describes al-Banna as "the founder and leader of a great Islamic movement, the Muslim Brotherhood."[14]

MAS, which has fifty chapters across the country, also runs a Detroit-based correspondence college called Islamic American University, whose former chairman is Sheik Yusuf al-Qaradawi, the Egypt-born spiritual leader of the international Muslim Brotherhood.

Qatar-based al-Qaradawi is barred from entering the U.S. due to his praise for suicide bombers, *fatwahs* authorizing attacks on U.S. soldiers, and ties to charitable fronts for terrorism. He vows that the Brotherhood will "conquer America," and he says his dream is to die a martyr killing Jews.

No wonder MAS has decided to conceal its Muslim Brotherhood affiliation.

An undated internal memo instructs MAS leaders to be evasive when asked about the Brotherhood by outsiders. And if the topic of terrorism is raised, they're told to say that while they're against "terrorism," they believe jihad is among a Muslim's "divine legal rights" to be used to defend himself and his brothers and to spread Islam.[15]

WHO IS ESAM OMEISH?

MAS had been run by Esam Omeish before he stepped down as president this year to run for the Virginia state assembly. Just two years earlier, Omeish was forced to resign from a state immigration commission after a video surfaced showing him championing violent jihad and martyrdom before a crowd of Washington-area Muslims.[16]

Omeish officed right next door to convicted al-Qaida financier Alamoudi in a nondescript professional building in Alexandria, Virginia. His brother Mohamed Omeish and Alamoudi were partners; the two shared the *same* office.[17]

As a board member of 9/11 mosque Dar al-Hijrah, Esam Omeish personally hired the *imam*—Anwar Aulaqi—who helped some of the Saudi hijackers prepare for their "martyrdom" attack on the Pentagon.[18]

The $5 million mosque was built with financial help from the Islamic Affairs Department of the Saudi embassy in Washington.[19] It opened its doors one year before MAS opened its doors just a few miles away.

According to court records first revealed in the 2005 book *Infiltration*, Omeish put up his home as bond collateral to help spring from jail terrorist suspect Elbarasse after he was arrested allegedly casing the Chesapeake Bridge for attack.[20] It was Elbarasse's home that FBI agents raided, uncovering the secret Brotherhood archives.

Elbarasse, a founding member of Dar al-Hijrah, also attended the infamous secret Hamas meeting with Brotherhood bosses in Philadelphia. He had opened a joint bank account with Hamas leader Abu Marzook around that time.

Both Elbarasse and Omeish, a surgeon, show up on CAIR's internal list of financial "supporters." In another document, CAIR lists Omeish among its "Recommended Community Leaders."

Omeish, who lives in a home not far from MAS, has counted as a neighbor the former bookkeeper for Brotherhood banker and terror financier Soliman Biheiri.

But "MAS has no ties to the Muslim Brotherhood," Omeish insists. "The Brotherhood does not exist as far as we know in the United States."[21] Uh-huh. And Omeish is, as he calls himself on his campaign Web site, just a "community organizer" like Obama.

MUSLIM MAFIA HALL OF SHAME

"The Noble Quran appoints the Muslims as guardians over humanity and grants them the right of dominion over the world in order to carry out this sublime commission. It is their duty to establish sovereignty over the world."

—late Muslim Brotherhood founder Hassan al-Banna, heralded by Ikhwans as an "Islamic martyr" after his assassination in Egypt

"Islam wishes to do away with all states and governments anywhere which are opposed to this ideology and program of Islam. Islam requires the earth—not just a portion, but the entire planet."

—Maulana Abul Ala Maududi, late Pakistani disciple of al-Banna

"No political system or material power should put hindrances in the way of preaching Islam. If someone does this, then it is the duty of Islam to fight him until either he is killed or until he declares his submission.... Bringing about the enforcement of the Divine Law (Shariah) and the abolition of man-made laws cannot be achieved only through preaching. When the above-mentioned obstacles and practical difficulties are put in its way, it has no recourse but to remove them by force.... Islam has the right to take the initiative. It has the right to destroy all obstacles in the form of institutions and traditions. It is the duty of Islam to annihilate all such systems.... Jihad in Islam is simply a name for striving to make this system of life dominant in the world. Wherever an Islamic community exists which is a concrete example of the Divinely ordained system of life, it has a God-given right to step forward and take control of the political authority so that it may establish the Divine system on earth."

—late Muslim Brotherhood leader Sayyid Qutb of Egypt, bin Laden's spiritual father *(Milestones)*

"We will conquer Europe, we will conquer America, not through the sword but through dawah [Islamic proselytizing]."

—current Muslim Brotherhood spiritual leader Yusuf al-Qaradawi, an Egyptian-born, Qatar-based cleric, 1995.

CHAPTER SIXTEEN
THE PLAN

"If we put a nationwide infrastructure in place and marshaled our resources, we'd take over this country in a very short time."

—American Muslim cleric Zaid Shakir[1]

MUSLIM BROTHERHOOD PROPAGANDISTS like *imam* Zaid Shakir preach to the Muslim community in America about waging a cultural jihad now, and a violent jihad later—once the proper "infrastructure" is in place.

"The work we should be doing is laying the infrastructure—the administrative, logistical infrastructure—putting that into place, so that if Allah put us in a situation where we did have to fight, physically, we could translate that fighting into tangible political gains," Shakir advised Muslims during a lecture in the San Francisco Bay area, the contents of which are being revealed publicly here for the first time.[2]

This fits with the strategic plan outlined in the Brotherhood's secret manifesto. It calls for achieving domination in the host country of America in stages, following the strategy of their prophet when he fled to Medina.

In the initial stages, when the Brotherhood is weak, the plan is to accumulate power here through peaceful means. Then in the final stages, when the Brotherhood is strong, the plan is to use coercive power—including violence if necessary—to take over the government and enforce discriminatory *Shariah*. The Brotherhood's plan to Islamize America, investigators say, essentially consists of five phases:

Phase I: Establishment of an elite Muslim leadership, while raising *taqwa*, or Islamic consciousness, in the Muslim community.

Phase II: Creation of Islamic institutions the leadership can control, along with the formation of autonomous Muslim enclaves.

Phase III: Infiltration and Islamization of America's political, social, economic, and educational systems, forming a shadow state within the state. Escalation of religious conversions to Islam. Manipulation of mass media, and sanitization of language offensive to Islam.

Phase IV: Openly hostile public confrontation over U.S. policies, including rioting, and militant demands for special rights and accommodations for Muslims.

Phase V: Final conflict and overthrow (jihad).[3]

The Brotherhood is now in Phase III, but patience is key to their strategy. They are willing to wait "a hundred years" to achieve their subversive goal, as Alamoudi put it.

Shakir, mistakenly considered mainstream and moderate by the media, warns that the faithful should be patient and avoid repeating the mistakes of Muslims in other *kaffir* nations who raised their swords too soon and died in vain.

"In many places where Muslims are doing jihad and killing *kaffirs*, this infrastructural work hasn't been done," he said. "As a result, Muslims are fighting and dying, but there's very little tangible political benefit as a result of that fighting and dying."

Be smarter than that—"think strategically"—he advises Muslim Americans, and hold off on the violent phase until it can "translate into political gains."[4]

For now, he says, wage informational and financial jihad, using words and money to defeat the infidels. When the Muslim community's numbers are large enough and its political "infrastructure" is strong enough, then use bombs.

First infiltrate and convert, then wage jihad, he reiterates. Use deception and propaganda—putting on a friendly face—until the time is right. Then drive the sword into the backs of the enemy.

"We have to start doing the real tough, nitty-gritty, unglamorous, boring work of developing our organizational and institutional strength in this country," Shakir said. "If we put a nationwide infrastructure in place and marshaled our resources, we'd take over this country in a very short time."[5]

'BRICK IN THE WALL'

For now, however, the faithful still "have a lot of foundational work to do," he added.

Shakir used the metaphor of a wall to illustrate his point. Right now, he told Muslims, "you're a brick in the wall of the *kaffir*," or the infidel. But once Muslim numbers and political clout grows, the American *ummah*, or Muslim community, will become its own united wall—a "unified front"—strong enough to strike the *kaffir*, Arabic for heathen.

"Patiently persevere," he advised.

It's plain that the Muslim mafia views America as the big prize. If Muslims can conquer her, Shakir says, they can conquer the world for Allah.

"If the American people accept Islam, the implications for the world are obvious. This is the most powerful and influential nation on earth, without any argument," he said. "So if the people here become Muslim, then the implications of that for the world are quite obvious."

He gleefully remarked that this is only made possible thanks to America's blind religious tolerance: "We're safe and free to practice and advance our religion here."

Like CAIR's leaders, he respects American democracy insofar as it can be exploited to help the Brotherhood one day assume power here. And the only thing that could stop the Islamization of America, he notes, is if its people rose up and denied the movement the unbridled freedom it has heretofore enjoyed. (But if Americans did that, Muslims would then be obligated to exercise their supposedly "divine legal right" to wage jihad.)

"What a great victory it will be for Islam to have this country in the fold and ranks of the Muslims," rejoiced Shakir, who is a regular speaker at CAIR functions. For now, he said, following the Muslim Brotherhood playbook, Muslims must continue to "create a state within a state."[6]

Indeed, theirs is a highly organized and self-contained world, or underworld—a parallel secret society:

The Brothers have their own AFL-CIO; it's called ISNA.

They have their own American Bar Association; it's called the Fiqh Council, which advises members on the application of *Shariah* law. (The Brotherhood charter also calls for the creation one day of a "Central Islamic Court" in America.)[7]

They have their own VFW; it's called the American Muslim Armed Forces and Veterans Affairs Council.

They have their own NAACP; it's called CAIR.

Their FCA, moreover, is the MSA, or Muslim Students Association.

Their United Way is (or was) the Holy Land Foundation.

Their NEA is the Council on Islamic Education, or CIE.

And their YMCA is WAMY—except, instead of holding basketball camps, it holds jihad camps.

They also have their own investment bank in the North American Islamic Trust, which holds the title to hundreds of radical Muslim Brotherhood mosques and manages the bank accounts of the Brotherhood's fronts using Islamic financing principles (more on that in a forthcoming chapter).

They have their own think tank—the International Institute of Islamic Thought—and their own colleges—the Islamic American University and the Graduate School of Islamic and Social Sciences (aka Cordoba University), which has trained most of the U.S. military's Muslim chaplains.

They also operate their own travel agency—Dar el-Eiman USA, Inc.—which enjoys an exclusive deal with the Saudi embassy to arrange travel for Muslim Americans to *hajj*. (Brochures and itinerary show the agency has booked Anwar Aulaqi, the 9/11 *imam*, as a tour guide and lecturer for the holy trips to Saudi Arabia.)[8]

The Brothers even have their own *consigliere* in Washington defense attorney Ashraf Nubani, a militant Palestinian activist who has defended some of the most notorious terrorists in America.

But there's more you should know about their secret society.

The Brothers maintain their own media as well. The following publications are propaganda organs for the Muslim Brotherhood: *Islamic Horizons, The American Muslim, The Muslim Link, Washington Report on Middle East Affairs*, and its sister publication, *The Link*, and Islamonline. net. Brotherhood printer Amana Publishing, meanwhile, churns out copies of the Quran and other Islamic materials used to convert Americans.

They also operate their own broadcasting network—Bridges TV— and Hollywood-style production company—SoundVision.

'PARALLEL SOCIETY'

The Brotherhood's "object is to establish, initially, a separate society for Muslims within that of their host nations in which non-Muslims are the majority," says former Pentagon official Frank Gaffney, now head of the Center for Security Policy in Washington. "This is accomplished by insinuating preferential arrangements for Muslims—religious accommodations, their own legal code and courts (that is, *Shariah*), territorial "no-go" zones, and assorted political benefits.[9]

"Initially," he adds, "these seem modest and unthreatening. Separate rules governing dress codes. Accommodations in public spaces for the practice of a single religion. Latitude to deny service or handling of certain products in deference to religious sensibilities. Organized labor contracts that substitute Muslim holy days for Labor Day, etcetera."

But once the Brotherhood gains such toeholds, Gaffney warns, it will keep the pressure on to secure greater and greater concessions, expanding toeholds into footholds and, eventually, beachheads.

"Inevitably," he says, "over time if not in relatively short order, a parallel society is in place that is utterly at odds with the supremacy of the U.S. Constitution, its precepts, freedoms, and institutions."[10]

CHAPTER SEVENTEEN
THE GODFATHER

"Islam isn't in America to be equal to any other faith, but to become dominant. The Quran should be the highest authority in America."

—**CAIR founding chairman Omar Ahmad**[1]

THE MUSLIM MAFIA'S FIRST GODFATHER was Ahmed Elkadi, who headed its *shura* council for a decade before being ousted in 1994 by the other bosses who thought he wasn't conservative enough.[2] Elkadi had also become something of an embarrassment.

A doctor by trade, he set up a medical clinic in Panama City, Florida, where he was accused of performing unneeded stomach surgeries on at least nine patients. State regulators also found that he had performed a mastectomy and other major operations at his clinic without proper precautions, such as an adequate blood supply, and they took disciplinary action against him.[3]

He eventually lost his medical license and his clinic, and moved to Sterling, Virginia, where he and his wife live in a condo and attend ADAMS Center, a Brotherhood mosque, and still pine for an Islamic America.[4]

Federal Election Commission records show he and his wife are fans of Lyndon Larouche, the Holocaust-denying, Israel-bashing ex-convict, and have given Larouche thousands of dollars in campaign donations during his many fruitless runs for president.[5]

It remains unclear who replaced Elkadi as godfather, but federal investigators suspect Abdurahman Alamoudi took over the reins of the subversive, terror-supporting movement.

As head of the Washington-based American Muslim Council,[6]

Alamoudi rubbed elbows with presidents and their staff in the White House—all the while raising millions of dollars for al-Qaida.

He also infiltrated the State Department, as a goodwill ambassador to Muslim countries, and the Pentagon, where he created the Muslim chaplain corps for the Pentagon.

FBI agents who helped put Alamoudi away say he's a much bigger player than publicly disclosed. At the time he was arrested, U.S. intelligence intercepted al-Qaida chatter out of Saudi Arabia lamenting that "one of our main financiers has been taken out." [7]

"Alamoudi was involved in a lot more than money laundering," says a senior FBI officer who was involved in his investigation out of the Washington field office's counterterrorism unit. "He's a f***ing terrorist." [8]

"U.S. law enforcement was not real proactive. It took years to figure out he was a terrorist," the officer adds. "No Muslim was invited to the White House more than Alamoudi."

Investigators say that although Alamoudi is serving a twenty-three-year prison sentence, some of his wealthy Saudi-based relatives remain under scrutiny.

They say his billionaire cousin Mohammed Hussein Alamoudi—who owns a house in McLean, Virginia, and maintains business connections in the area—has pumped at least $350,000 into Muslim Brotherhood front groups in America. According to investigators, Mohammed Alamoudi owns a major interest in the port authority in Aden, Yemen, where the USS *Cole* was bombed. [9]

ALAMOUDI'S TROJAN HORSE

Abdurahman Alamoudi is now behind bars, but the Trojan Horse he built is still doing damage. Islamists have penetrated the military—including

Gitmo—where Muslim chaplains sponsored by Alamoudi, with help from Arabic linguists, have been accused of spying for the enemy.

"Alamoudi placed chaplains throughout our military," says U.S. Representative Sue Myrick, a Republican member of the House Permanent Select Committee on Intelligence. "He's now in jail [but] the chaplains, to my knowledge, are still in their current positions. Go figure."[10]

She says the politically correct Pentagon has not gone back and investigated the backgrounds of the chaplains in light of Alamoudi's al-Qaida ties.

Two Muslim Defense Department officials—who together coordinate military outreach with CAIR, its internal records show,[11] as well as with ISNA, where Alamoudi once served as president—have infiltrated the upper echelons of the Pentagon. They are Bangladesh-born Muslim chaplain Abuhena Saifulislam, a recently promoted Navy lieutenant commander, and Egypt-born Pentagon special assistant Hesham Islam, who has advised the deputy secretary of defense, who has authorized the release of dozens of Gitmo detainees who have resumed terrorist activities.

Saifulislam (whose name means "sword of Islam" in Arabic) served as the first Muslim chaplain at Gitmo, where he closely ministered to the terrorists and furnished them with copies of the Quran and a full menu of *halal* meals. More recently, he created the first mosque in Marine Corps history at Marine headquarters in Quantico, Virginia.

Saifulislam received his formal Islamic training at the Muslim Brotherhood-controlled Graduate School of Islamic and Social Sciences in Ashburn, Virginia, which was raided after 9/11 on terrorism suspicions and is currently run by an unindicted co-conspirator in the al-Arian terror case. GSISS is one of the fronts in the Safa group formerly controlled by Alamoudi.

Alamoudi once told Muslims that, while their goal is to turn the U.S. into an Islamic state, they must exercise patience—even if they have to wait "a hundred years."

"I think if we are outside this country, we can say, 'Oh, Allah, destroy America,'" he said in one speech at a Muslim conference. "But once we are here, our mission in this country is to change it" from within.[12]

Others have picked up where Alamoudi left off as Muslim mafia godfather. Since landing behind bars, Alamoudi's heir appears to be Omar Ahmad of CAIR, investigators say, who also serves as a leader of a Northern California mosque started by one of the founding fathers of the movement, Mahboob Khan.

U.S. prosecutors recently fingered Ahmad as a key Brotherhood figure and an unindicted terror co-conspirator.[13]

Ahmad insists he's a moderate and patriotic American. But last decade he told a group of Muslims in Northern California they are in America to help assert Islam's rule over the country.

"Islam isn't in America to be equal to any other faith, but to become dominant," a local journalist reported Ahmad saying. "The Quran should be the highest authority in America."[14]

MUSLIMS SHOULD RUN AMERICA

CAIR Executive Director Nihad Awad seems to agree. Speaking at an ISNA conference ten years ago, he said Muslims should be running America:

> "Muslims in America are in the best position to show Islam and to show action and to show vision, not only for a Muslim school how it should be run, but for the entire society—how it should be run. Who better can lead America than Muslims?"[15]

CAIR's top spokesman Ibrahim "Dougie" Hooper has also expressed his wish to overturn the U.S. system of government in favor of an Islamic state.

"I wouldn't want to create the impression that I wouldn't like the government of the United States to be Islamic sometime in the future," Hooper said in a 1993 interview with the *Minneapolis Star Tribune*.

That moment of unguarded candor has come back to haunt him—as it should, Islamic terror expert Robert Spencer says.

"You have to understand, he's not just saying something like 'Well, I really wish there would be more Methodists and fewer Baptists,'" Spencer warns. "He's saying that if the United States government becomes Islamic, then the political elements of Islam—and Islam is a political and societal system, not just a religious faith—should be applied to America, and that means the end of the United States Constitution."[16]

Though conceding he made the remark, Hooper argues that he's not advocating violence. He says he and Muslims like him should work instead through the media and political system, and use "education" to help turn America into an Islamic state.

What a relief.

Even today, Hooper does not disavow his unpatriotic dream.

"I do not get up in the morning and think about this," he recently said on a North Carolina radio show when asked if he still wanted an Islamic America. The host pointed out that his answer wasn't exactly a denial.[17]

These anti-American sentiments expressed by CAIR officials dovetail with those revealed in the Muslim Brotherhood manifesto calling for a "grand jihad" to destroy America and the West, "so that Allah's religion is made victorious over all other religions."

Douglas Farah, a former *Washington Post* foreign correspondent who is now an author and terrorism expert at the NEFA Foundation, says the manifesto reveals the "true agenda" of CAIR and other major Muslim organizations in the U.S.—which is "the abolition of the United States government as we know it."[18]

CHAPTER EIGHTEEN

INFILTRATION

"Members of the Group should be able to infiltrate the sensitive intelligence agencies or the embassies in order to collect information and build close relationships with the people in charge in these establishments."

—**Secret U.S. Brotherhood charter found in possession of Brotherhood underboss and convicted terrorist Sami al-Arian**[1]

ALI "THE AMERICAN" MOHAMED was a loyal member of the Muslim Brotherhood who emigrated from Egypt to spy for the Brotherhood in America. After failing to penetrate CIA operations, he infiltrated the U.S. Army as a sergeant and wound up at Fort Bragg training with U.S. Special Forces, where he obtained secret security clearance.

Although he was not a Green Beret, he worked alongside the elite Berets learning unconventional warfare and counterinsurgency operations. The military trusted him, and before long, he was teaching soldiers about the Middle East at the John F. Kennedy Special Warfare Center and School—commonly referred to as "Swick"—where unbeknown to his superior officers, he was stealing classified military secrets.

During weekends and other leaves from Fort Bragg, Mohamed would travel to New Jersey to train al-Qaida operatives in weapons and warfare tactics, which they would later use against the country Mohamed had sworn to protect. In a search of one terrorist's home, authorities found U.S. Army training manuals, videos of Swick warfare instruction, and other classified materials.

After his honorable discharge from the Army, Mohamed moved to Santa Clara, California, where he set up a communications cell for al-

Qaida while fronting as a computer engineer.

In 1995, he brought Dr. Ayman al-Zawahiri to California for a mosque fundraising tour, reportedly raising half a million dollars for the al-Qaida leader. A large chunk of it was raised at CAIR founder Omar Ahmad's mosque in Santa Clara, a key Brotherhood hub. (Ahmad is employed as a computer engineer in the Silicon Valley.)

Five years later, the feds finally got wise to Mohamed, and after his arrest on terrorism charges, he pleaded guilty to five counts of conspiracy for his role in planning the al-Qaida bombings of the U.S. embassies in Africa.

The Mohamed case marked the first in a series of instances in which dangerous Muslim Brotherhood figures have successfully penetrated key U.S. institutions.

After the FBI was called in to break up a Muslim spy ring at the al-Qaida prison camp in Guantanamo Bay, Cuba, officials from the Justice Department and the Treasury Department's Office of Foreign Assets Control gathered with FBI officials to discuss the infiltration of the U.S. government by Brotherhood agents. The high-level Washington meeting— which took place in October 2004—was the first formal discussion of the espionage threat posed by the Islamist enemy since the 9/11 attacks.[2]

Until then, counterintelligence efforts had been directed chiefly at old Cold War threats, such as Russia and China. But authorities have realized, if belatedly, that the new spy threat is potentially more dangerous— and more insidious. Unlike the Communists, the Muslim Brothers can infiltrate under the cover of a religion protected by the First Amendment. And as spies go, they are extremely slick.

'OUTRAGEOUS PENETRATION'

"These guys are good," says veteran FBI special agent John Guandolo, who was involved in the Gitmo espionage investigation and other counterterrorism and counterintelligence cases after 9/11. "They've achieved outrageous penetration at senior levels of our government."

He says infiltration is the key to the Brotherhood's "massive subversive movement in the U.S.," and they're following a plan established years ago.

In fact, documents show the Brotherhood movement is now decades into a North America-wide espionage operation that includes running infiltration operations against governments to collect classified intelligence.

One document, seized by federal agents in a raid of Brotherhood boss Sami al-Arian's home in Florida, is especially instructive. Translated from Arabic, it reveals a comprehensive plan for "spying" on U.S. agencies.

"Our presence in North America gives us a unique opportunity to monitor, explore and follow up," it states. "Members of the Group should be able to infiltrate the sensitive intelligence agencies or the embassies in order to collect information and build close relationships with the people in charge in these establishments."[3]

They should also use every opportunity to "collect information from those relatives and friends who work in sensitive positions in the government."

Unfortunately, our "sensitive intelligence agencies" have not made it very hard for the bad guys to put Muslim agents in place, hypersensitive as they are to complaints of Islamophobia by CAIR and other fronts that run interference for them.

Another al-Arian document explains that the Brothers are at war with the West, and war requires espionage and sabotage.

"We are in a battle of life and death, in a battle of fate and future against the Western hegemony," it says. "What is needed is the dismantling of the cultural system of the West."[4]

Al-Arian managed to penetrate the White House along with his pal Alamoudi before federal authorities caught up with him. He pleaded guilty to terrorism charges, served time in jail, and is now under house arrest on separate contempt charges for refusing to cooperate in the Safa group investigation, despite a federal grand jury subpoena.

The Brotherhood also has a less covert strategy to infiltrate the political system.

"The Muslim strategy for change from within incorporates the secretion of loyal Brothers into political office," warns former FBI agent Sadler.

Groups like CAIR, MPAC, MAS, along with the Islamic Institute and American Muslim Alliance, have aided in this project. Some of them recently formed an electioneering umbrella group—the American Muslim Task Force on Civil Rights and Elections, or AMT—to promote candidates into public office.

And not just at the federal level, but state and local levels as well.

THE LIBRARY PROJECT

CAIR's Ahmad, for example, landed a position on the Santa Clara City library board. He was a library trustee for ten years while CAIR launched its so-called Library Project, successfully targeting some eight thousand neighborhood libraries across the country with packages of books, videos, and other Brotherhood propaganda sanitizing Islam.

Brotherhood leaders, meanwhile, are actively recruiting engineers and other experts for local planning boards to remove roadblocks to expansion for Brotherhood schools and mosques.

In Fairfax County, Virginia, for example, a Muslim traffic engineer who works for the county recently testified on behalf of the radical Islamic *madrassa* run by the Saudi Embassy during a heated county hearing over the school's planned expansion.

His testimony—along with an outpouring of some six hundred local

Muslim supporters—helped the Islamic Saudi Academy win approval of its plan, even though it has been cited by the U.S. government for promoting violence and intolerance through its textbooks, and has acted as a breeding ground for terrorists, graduating even al-Qaida operatives. (Ismail Elbarasse, the Brotherhood figure and terrorist suspect who hid Brotherhood documents in his basement, served as the school's chief financial officer.)

While the Muslim Brotherhood is outlawed in other countries, the U.S. has not yet designated the group a terrorist entity or foreign threat, even though it has stated clearly that it supports violent jihad and is dedicated to replacing the U.S. with an Islamic theocracy.

The Brotherhood continues to perplex policymakers in Washington.

Some have argued for openly including it in politics to draw it out of the shadows. They say there may be moderate elements that could be co-opted. Others argue that once in power, even a politically accountable Brotherhood would pursue policies counter to U.S. interests.

"The complication is they are a political movement, an economic *cadre*, and in some cases terrorist supporters," says Juan Zarate, former chief of the Treasury Department's terrorist finance unit. "They operate business empires in the Western world, but their philosophy and ultimate objectives are radical Islamist goals that in many ways are antithetical to our interests. They have one foot in our world, and one foot in a world hostile to us. How to decipher what is good, bad, or suspect is a severe complication."[5]

Zarate adds, however, that "the Muslim Brotherhood is a group that worries us because it defends the use of violence against civilians."[6]

After 9/11, federal investigators noticed that most of their leads traced back to the Brotherhood. In fact, almost every terrorism case, active or inactive, ties into the Brotherhood nexus, whether directly or indirectly.

"You can't call the enemy just al-Qaida anymore," says an FBI counterterrorism agent in Washington who's actively investigating

Brotherhood figures and their front groups. "It's something else: it's the Muslim Brotherhood."[7]

ISLAMIC REVOLUTION

Indeed, many of the suspected Brotherhood figures identified here in this chapter (see table) have either been convicted or named as unindicted co-conspirators in terrorism-financing and other cases.

While the FBI has knocked out several leaders on various charges, the investigations have come in fits and starts. The Justice Department, politically risk-adverse as it is and still locked in a pre-9/11 mentality, remains reluctant to roll up the entire syndicate under racketeering and conspiracy statutes known as RICO—a broader and more aggressive approach favored by case agents and some prosecutors.

Congress enacted the RICO law to remove the tentacles of organized crime from legitimate enterprise. Too often the mob was able to infiltrate legitimate operations, giving a veneer of legality while secretly engaging in a pattern of criminal behavior.

Likewise, the Muslim mafia engages in a pattern of criminal conduct, laundering illicit funds through a network of legitimate-sounding front organizations. Even worse, this mafia uses religious sanctuaries to solicit holy war and treason against the U.S. government and military.

"The patterns are quite clear," Sadler says. "Certain members of these organizations are known offenders tied to the Muslim Brotherhood. And birds of a feather flock together."

The FBI has known the Brotherhood was a threat since at least the 1980s, and some of the same leaders under investigation then remain under investigation today. Recently declassified case files marked "SECRET" reveal that the bureau identified Jamal Barzinji, as well as Hisham Altalib, Mohammed

Shamma, and Ahmad Sakr, as "members of the Muslim Brotherhood."

"These individuals are in a position to direct the activities and support of Muslims in the U.S. for the Islamic Revolution," the FBI report warned decades ago.[8]

Some say it may be too late to go after the Brotherhood now as a criminal conspiracy due to its deep entrenchment in U.S. society. Because law enforcement allowed the Brothers to conduct their organizational jihad virtually unchallenged and unexamined for decades, they have had time to build up an impressive institutional bulwark.

In fact, their organizations now represent the entire Muslim establishment in America. And few in Washington have the political will to dismantle it.

The Brotherhood has become so brazen that it recently declared war on the FBI over its cancellation of formal outreach with CAIR. It's also targeted prosecutors such as assistant U.S. Attorney Gordon Kromberg for harassment, personally singling out him and his family. Kromberg's district covers Northern Virginia—the base of operations for the Brotherhood—and he has prosecuted many of its leaders.

Kromberg is a threat to the Brothers because he understands their conspiracy and he knows CAIR is integral to it. In a recent terrorism case, he submitted that "from its founding by Muslim Brotherhood leaders, CAIR conspired with other affiliates of the Muslim Brotherhood to support terrorists." He added that "the conspirators agreed to use deception to conceal from the American public their connections to terrorists."

Many counterterrorism experts warn that dismantling this infrastructure of support for terrorists remains an unfought battle in the war on terror. Reason: the syndicate that erected it is religious in nature and protected by political correctness.

Guandolo says this is the main reason he resigned last year from the bureau. He says he was frustrated by the PC handcuffs headquarters put on him and other agents trying to make solid cases against Brotherhood fronts and leaders. He says he was threatened with his job no less than three times by FBI brass who complained that "we were creating waves in the Muslim community."

Guandolo says the Muslim Brotherhood is like "a cancer," and Washington is just feeding it with its PC outreach. The Justice Department has held some seventy-five meetings with Brotherhood front groups who claim to represent the Muslim community, and officials still hold bimonthly meetings with them.

While the FBI has severed formal ties to CAIR, thanks to pressure from Guandolo and other case agents, the agency is still conducting outreach with another dangerous Brotherhood front considered "a nucleus" of the movement in America.

SUSPECTED U.S. MUSLIM BROTHERHOOD FIGURES[9]

Omar M. Ahmad (aka Omar Yehia aka Omar Yeheya)	Ahmed Osman	Abd el-Hassan)
	Louay Safi	Ghassan Dahduli
Nihad Awad (aka Nehad Hammad)	Sayyid Syeed	Abdelhaleem Ashqar (aka Abdel Hassan)
Mohamed Nimer	Irfan Totonji	Soliman Beheiri
Nabil Sadoun	Ahmad Totonji (father of Omer Totonji)	Ghassan Elashi
Ishsan Bagby	Iqbal Unus	Issam el-Siraj
Rafeeq Jaber	Mahboob Khan (late father of Suhail Khan)	Omar al-Soubani
Mohammed al-Hanooti		Ismail Jabir
Muhammad Salah	Samir Salah	Muhammad Abbas
Jamal Badawi	Abdurahman Alamoudi	Fawaz Mushtaha (aka Abu Mosab)
Ismail Jaber	Sami al-Arian	Izat Mansour
Shaker al-Sayyed	Gaddor Ibrahim Saidi	Hammud Salem
Jamal Barzinji	Nizar Minshar	Nadir Jawad
Mousa Abu Marzook (aka Abu Omar)	Raed Awad	Rashid Qurman
Muhammad Akram	Tareq Suwaidan	Shukri Abu Baker
Mohammad Jaghlit	Ahmad Yousif	Muhammad Abu Amriya
Hamid al-Ghazili	Yasser Bushnaq	Jamal Said
Muzzamil Siddiqi	Mohammed el-Mezain	Anan al-Karmi
Bassam Osman (aka Bassem Othman)	Ismail Elbarasse (aka Abdul Hassan aka	

Ayman Saraj al-Din

Ahmad Agha

Akram al-Kharoubi

Walid Abu Sharakh

Mahdi Bray

Walid Ranu

Ayman Sharawi

Hazim Elashi

Basman Elashi

Haitham Maghawri

Akram Mishal

Mufid Abdulgader

Abdulrahman Odeh

Ayman Ismail

Ayman Siraj Eddin

Bayan Elashi

Dalell Mohamed

Fayez Idlebi

Hassan Sabri

Ibrahim al-Samneh

Islam Siam

Izzat Mansour

Kifah Mustapha

Mohamed Abu Amaria

Mohamed el-Shorbagi

Mohammed Akram Adlouni

Mohamed Qassam Sawallha (aka Abu Obeida)

Munzer Taleb

Muin Shabib

Nader Jawad

Omar el-Sobani

Rashid Qurman

Rasmi Almallah

Walid Abu Sharkh

Walid Ranu

Yousef Saleh (aka Ahmed Yousef)

Zaher Salman (aka Osama Abdullah)

Khalid al-Masri

Kamal al-Tamimi (aka Abu Islam)

Esam Omeish

Mohamed Omeish

Shaker Elsayed

Hamza Yusuf

Zaid Shaker

Siraj Wahhaj

Johari Abdul-Malik

Mohamad Adam el-Sheikh

Samir Abou-Issa

Anwar Auluqi (aka Anwar al-Awlaki)

Abdulhamid Abusulayman

Taha al-Alwani

Hisham Altalib

M. Omar Ashraf

Muhammad Ashraf

Bassam Estwani

Jawad F. George

Yaqub Mirza

Tanveer Mirza

Fawaz Mushtaha

Cherif Sedky

Khaled Saffuri

Mohammed Cheema

Ali al-Timimi

Osama M. Kandil

Ashraf Nubani

Abdulwahab Alkebsi

Rabih Haddad

Omar Abdul Rahman (aka Blind Sheik)

Gaddour Saidi

Ahmed Elkadi

Hamed al-Ghazali

Zeid al-Noman (aka Zaid Naman)

Jihad Fahmy

Khalid Iqbal

Hani Sakr

Ziad Abu-Ghanimeh

Mohammed M. Shamma

Mahdi Bhadori

Ilyas Ba-Yunus

Moinuddin Siddiqui

Mahmoud Rashdan

Talat Sultan

Ibrahim Hassaballa

Syed Imtiaz Ahmad

Haroon Qazi

Anwar Ibrahim

Mohamed Hadid

Bassam Othman

Hammad Zaki

Ahmed Elhatab

Mohammed Elharezi

Abdel Jabbar Hamdan

Ghassan Saleh

Riad Ahmed

Abdul-Rahman Baraksi

Akram Kharroubi

Amin Ezziddine

Souheil Ghannouchi

Dawood Abdulrahman

Oussama Elbaba

Abdulkareem Jama

Ali Mohamed

Abdalla Idris Ali

Abdullah bin Laden

279

CHAPTER NINETEEN

NUCLEUS: ISNA

"A logical investigation will confront why four foreign students from Southern Illinois University came to Plainfield [Indiana] to buy a large land mass and build a multimillion-dollar mosque where there were no Muslims within hundreds of miles."

—**Tim Pitchford, retired FBI agent, Indianapolis field office**[1]

I F THERE ARE ANY DOUBTS about the financial might of the Muslim mafia, stop by the headquarters of the Islamic Society of North America next time you're in the Indianapolis suburbs. It reeks of money.

You can't miss it: There, towering above the prairie, looms a mammoth all-brick structure with two rows of tiny slots for windows. The geometric cluster of cavernous buildings resembles an Islamic fortress, and it's surrounded by a fiefdom of privately held land.

More than thirty years ago, a handful of Muslim college students and engineers from the Middle East acquired 124 acres of farmland near the Indianapolis airport and moved the offices of the Muslim Students Association there, forming the roots of ISNA.[2]

They soon announced plans for a forty-two-acre compound on the Plainfield, Indiana, site to include a $3.5 million mosque, along with classrooms, residences, a gym, and a recreational area. Today, the sprawling ISNA campus also includes an eighty-thousand-volume library and a research facility.

Where did these foreign students get the money to erect such an extravagant religious monument?

"Where they got the money is a key question," says Tim Pitchford, a retired FBI agent who worked terrorism and counterintelligence cases in

Indianapolis. "It came from overseas banks, and the FBI never was able to investigate, as we were talking about a 'religion' and bank records," and religious institutions are generally considered off-limits and bank records the domain of the Treasury Department.[3]

However, such restrictions may be easing, he says, now that ISNA has been named a co-conspirator in the war on terror and now that FBI headquarters is better educated regarding the Muslim Brotherhood threat.

"A logical investigation will confront why four foreign students from Southern Illinois University came to Plainfield to buy a large land mass and build a multi-million-dollar mosque where there were no Muslims within hundreds of miles," Pitchford says.[4]

Like CAIR, ISNA was developed as a front for the radical Muslim Brotherhood and bankrolled by shady, terror-tied partners in the Middle East.

The massive ISNA complex was funded with a whopping $21 million raised in part from radical Brotherhood figures Yusuf al-Qaradawi and Saudi-tied Youssef Nada, as well as the *emir* of Qatar, where Qaradawi is based.[5]

Nada, a Brotherhood bigwig originally from Egypt, founded Bank al-Taqwa ("Fear of Allah"), which funneled money to Hamas and al-Qaida through a close associate of Osama bin Laden. Nada is a specially designated global terrorist.

Saudi money also was funding ISNA from the very beginning of the organization.

Muslim Students Association co-founder Jamal Barzinji was business partners with Nada and was working for one of his companies in Saudi Arabia during the time ISNA's headquarters was being planned, funded, and built. Barzinji also headed the financial arm of ISNA—the North American Islamic Trust, or NAIT.

In 1981, ISNA was founded as "a nucleus for the Islamic Movement in

North America," according to an internal Muslim Brotherhood document.[6]

It's now the umbrella organization for the Brotherhood, controlling several front groups and hundreds of mosques and schools. While CAIR enjoys more notoriety and is more visible in the media, ISNA is more venerable and ingrained in U.S. society.

Its predecessor, the Muslim Students Association, still serves as the main recruiting tool for the Brotherhood in the U.S.

MSA'S CAMPUS JIHAD

With 150 campus chapters, MSA is one of the nation's largest college groups. CAIR chief Nihad Awad, for example, got his start as an MSA activist at the University of Minnesota.

MSA also organizes anti-Israel student rallies and hectors college administrators into Islamizing campus facilities.

MSA chapters from New York to California have extolled suicide bombers and other terrorists as "martyrs" and the "only people who truly fear Allah." And they are a big reason why, according to a recent Pew Research poll, one in four college-age Muslims in America support suicide bombings.

MSA is also the catalyst behind *Shariah* creep on college campuses.

The militant group has set up a national task force to pressure college administrators into accommodating Muslim students with, among other things:

- Islamic prayer rooms;

- Paid campus *imams*;

- Special restroom facilities, such as footbaths, for ritual washing;

- Separate food and housing for Muslim students;

- Campus-wide observance of Islamic holidays; and

- Separate athletic hours for Muslim women.

ISNA'S ILLEGAL IMMIGRANTS

After MSA and ISNA established their beachhead in Indianapolis, Pitchford says he noticed that immigrants from the Middle East began pouring into the state. He and other agents observed a pattern: many of the immigrants were in the country illegally, and they were sponsored by ISNA.

"Six-month visitor visas started coming into Indiana sponsored by ISNA by the thousands over the years," Pitchford says in an exclusive interview.[7]

Unfortunately, "the visa fraud cases we presented were not prosecuted by Washington," he says. "These same visa visitors are still here illegally."

ISNA denies any wrongdoing. And it has fought its recent inclusion on a list of co-conspirators in the terrorism case against the Holy Land Foundation. ISNA argues it was "unjustly branded by the government," a move that has "profoundly harmed" its reputation and "adversely impacted the organization's efforts to advance its mission."[8]

The blacklisting may indeed have hurt ISNA. Attendance at last year's ISNA convention was low, and even ISNA's flagship mosque in Plainfield has been drawing fewer and fewer Muslims. Attendance at Friday services is down sharply, local observers say.

ISNA, which promotes itself as a voice of moderation, insists it "has not now or ever been involved with the Muslim Brotherhood, or supported any covert, illegal, or terrorist activity or organization."[9]

In a separate statement on its Web site, the group goes even further, arguing it has never been "influenced" by the Muslim Brotherhood.[10]

Of course this is a blantant falsehood. The evidence designating ISNA as a leading branch of the U.S. Muslim Brotherhood is overwhelming, and ISNA's links to fundraising on behalf of Hamas are equally strong.

TWO DOZEN COURT EXHIBITS

In 2007, the Justice Department officially labeled ISNA and its financial subsidiary NAIT a U.S. branch of the Muslim Brotherhood and listed both entities as co-conspirators in the Holy Land Foundation terror case. When ISNA protested, federal prosecutors pointed to nearly two dozen court exhibits that establish:

> ...both ISNA's and NAIT's intimate relationship with the Muslim Brotherhood, the Palestine Committee, and the defendants in this case. Accordingly, there is no possible basis for petitioner's "expungement" from the government's list of co-conspirators.[11]

For starters, the U.S. Brotherhood's own internal memos confirm that ISNA and NAIT were among those groups created by the Brotherhood. A 1991 memo identified twenty-nine front groups. Topping the list was the Islamic Society of North America.

Another Brotherhood document confirms the relationship by stating that the secret group exercised leadership and direction over ISNA, including "setting expectations for ISNA for the next decade."[12] Yet another Brotherhood document, in the form of a spreadsheet, lists ISNA under the heading: "The Apparatuses."[13]

BANKROLLING HAMAS

Equally convicting is the evidence that reveals ISNA collaborated in the Holy Land Foundation conspiracy to funnel money to Hamas terrorists.

Prosecutors say Brotherhood leaders sent hundreds of thousands of dollars to Hamas through bank accounts controlled by ISNA and its financial arm NAIT. The proof ranges from wiretapped conversations to bank records and other documents, including:

• ISNA checks deposited into the ISNA/NAIT account for the Holy Land Foundation, which were often made payable to "the Palestinian Mujahadeen," the original name for the Hamas military wing;[14]

• An expense voucher from NAIT made out for $10,000 in the name of Hamas leader Mousa Abu Marzook;[15]

• A $10,000 check drawn on a NAIT account made payable to Abu Marzook;[16]

• Another NAIT check for $10,000 made out to Abu Marzook's wife, Nadia Elashi;[17]

• FBI recordings revealing Hamas leaders discussed ISNA during their secret 1993 Philadelphia meeting to plot ways to launder payments through Brotherhood charities and nonprofit organizations;[18]

• A NAIT check for $30,000 made out to a Hamas school in the Gaza Strip with the name of Shukri Abu Baker—the now-convicted U.S.-based leader of Hamas—written in the memo line;[19]

• A Brotherhood phonebook listing Abu Baker and two Indianapolis phone numbers for him—including an ISNA fax number still in use today—indicating the Hamas leader had worked out of ISNA's headquarters near Indianapolis;[20] and

• A three-page internal Brotherhood memo citing Abu Baker as the point man for "coordinating with ISNA in the accounting" of funds for the Palestinian "Intifada," the bloody anti-Israel uprising led by Hamas.[21]

FBI investigators say they're continuing to collect evidence against ISNA that could sway prosecutors to seek a full criminal indictment. The FBI's Washington and Indianapolis field offices recently put together a fifty-page *dossier* on the Brotherhood front group.

ROGUES' GALLERY

In addition, several ISNA founders and board members have been accused of supporting or having ties to terrorism. They include:

• **Jamal Badawi:** a founding father of the U.S. Brotherhood and a current ISNA board member who was listed among unindicted co-conspirators who raised money for the terrorist front Holy Land Foundation;[22]

• **Siraj Wahhaj:** an unindicted co-conspirator in the 1993 World Trade Center bombing who has urged Muslims to overturn the U.S. system of government and set up an Islamic dictatorship. He has served as an ISNA vice president and board member;

• **Abdurahman Alamoudi:** Former MSA president and ISNA regional representative for Washington now in prison for plotting terrorism and financing al-Qaida;

• **Sami al-Arian:** Confessed Palestinian terrorist who admits he was a member of the Muslim Brotherhood during the time he helped found ISNA;

• **Bassam Osman:** Longtime NAIT director and landlord of al-Arian's Islamic Academy of Florida, a *madrassa* accused of raising funds and providing other support for Palestinian terrorists;

• **Yusuf al-Qaradawi:** U.S.-designated supporter of terrorism barred from entering the country. He co-founded ISNA's office in Boston and helped finance ISNA's national headquarters;

• **Sayyid Syeed:** Former board member of Dar al-Hijrah, the 9/11 mosque, and longtime director of academic outreach at IIIT, the Brotherhood think tank under investigation for bankrolling terrorism. He has served as secretary general of ISNA, and is currently director of ISNA's Office of Interfaith and Community Alliances in Washington;

• **Esam Omeish:** Dar al-Hijrah vice president who personally hired the 9/11 *imam*, and who recently was exposed on video encouraging "the jihad way" and praising Palestinian terrorists as martyrs. He's a former MSA president and ISNA board member; and

• **Jamal Barzinji:** Original trustee holding title to Dar al-Hijrah accused by federal authorities of being "closely associated" with Hamas and other terrorist groups, according to court records. He served as president of MSA, and was a key founder and board member of ISNA. As an MSA leader in the early 1970s, in fact, Barzinji hosted top leaders of the Egyptian Brotherhood, just released from sixteen years in prison, for two weeks of meetings in Indianapolis.[23]

In 2008 ISNA awarded Barzinji for his "pioneering service" with its annual Dr. Mahboob Khan Community Service Award. Khan, one of the early founders of the Brotherhood movement in America, started a mosque in Santa Clara, California, which hosted and raised money for Egyptian Brotherhood leader Dr. Ayman al-Zawahiri, now second in command of al-Qaida. (Khan's son, who claims to be a Republican, infiltrated the White House and U.S. Transportation Department during the previous administration.)

THE ISNA-CAIR NEXUS

ISNA is a sister organization of CAIR. The two Brotherhood fronts coordinate operations, share funding, and maintain interlocking boards of directors.

For example, Ihsan Bagby—the Islamic "scholar" who advises Muslims they can "never be full citizens of this country" until they change it—currently sits on the boards of both CAIR and ISNA.

Safaa Zarzour also has a high-level role in both groups, as chairman of CAIR's Chicago chapter and ISNA's Education Forum. Khalid Iqbal, moreover, served as CAIR's national operations director as well as an ISNA vice president and director, chairing ISNA's annual convention for six years, according to a copy of his resumé.

Despite ISNA's proven ties to terrorism and extremism, politicians in Washington continue to reach out to it, fooled as they are by the front group's carefully manicured facade of moderation.

A PRAYER FOR OBAMA

Most recently, a top aide to President Obama this summer provided a keynote address at ISNA's national convention in Washington. The senior adviser, Valerie Jarrett, had the dubious distinction of being the first White House official to address ISNA.

Earlier in the year, Obama invited ISNA President Ingrid Mattson to deliver a prayer at the inaugural National Prayer Service at the National Cathedral. As a woman, Mattson, an ex-Catholic convert to Islam, cannot be a member of the Muslim Brotherhood. But she has served to soften ISNA's image and put a more benign face on its operations.

Mattson also spoke at a prayer service at the Democratic National

Convention in Denver. James "Yousef" Yee, the Gitmo military chaplain accused of spying for al-Qaida, worked ISNA's table at the convention, while serving as an Obama delegate.

In 2007, the Justice Department's civil rights division actually co-sponsored ISNA's annual convention in Chicago over the objections of career prosecutors who feared the outreach would undermine its case against the Holy Land Foundation and its co-conspirators.

Justice officials even manned an information booth at ISNA, angering Republicans.

"It is disgraceful that our Department of Justice was prosecuting ISNA in Texas while attending an ISNA conference in Illinois," said Representative Sue Myrick (R-NC), who fired off a letter to the attorney general protesting the overture.[24]

The Justice Department wasn't alone. The Departments of State, Homeland Security, and Defense also set up tables at the ISNA event.

Most disturbing, the Pentagon put up a job booth to recruit Muslim chaplains and Arabic linguists. Pentagon officials even met with ISNA leaders. One of the military officials was Hesham Islam, an Egyptian immigrant who rose to the position of special assistant to the deputy secretary of defense.[25] Just months earlier, Islam spoke privately with CAIR Governmental Affairs Director Corey Saylor, notes from a CAIR executive staff meeting reveal.

That same year, Islam invited ISNA officials to lunch with then-Deputy Defense Secretary Gordon England at the Pentagon. England spoke at ISNA's 2006 convention. Islam arranged it.

Raising more suspicion, Islam has run major interference for ISNA. For example, he recently convinced Pentagon brass not to renew the contract of Pentagon analyst Major Stephen Coughlin after Coughlin argued in briefings that the Defense Department should cease outreach programs with ISNA because of its radical Muslim Brotherhood ties.

PLANTING MUSLIM CHAPLAINS

Islam's influence is particularly alarming concerning chaplain recruitment.

ISNA maintains a chaplaincy board to recommend Muslim clerics for the military. One of the board members is Ahmed Alwani, dean of the Graduate School of Islamic and Social Sciences. The GSISS president is Taja Alwani, a key Brotherhood figure and an unindicted co-conspirator in the al-Arian terror case.[26]

SITE Institute executive director Rita Katz told the *St. Petersburg Times* that Taja Alwani is a "person who supports and funnels money to terrorist organizations, and he's training Muslim chaplains for the military." He also co-founded a *fiqh*, or Islamic jurisprudence, organization with Sheik Yusuf al-Qaradawi, the Brotherhood spiritual leader who has issued *fatwahs* calling for suicide attacks against U.S. soldiers.

GSISS, which adopted the alternate name Cordoba University after federal agents raided its offices, has trained and certified an alarming ten of the Pentagon's fourteen Muslims chaplains, as well as some of the Federal Bureau of Prisons' chaplains. It counts among its alumni one Warith Deen Umar, a longtime federal and state prison chaplain in New York who applauded the 9/11 hijackings and promoted black inmates who converted to Islam as ideal candidates for future terrorist attacks.

A few years ago, the Justice Department's inspector general recommended that the Federal Bureau of Prisons suspend ties to ISNA until the FBI could conduct a thorough investigation of the group. The inspector general cited reports that ISNA-sponsored chaplains were helping radicalize inmates.

But after pushback from ISNA, the prison bureau lifted its moratorium the very next year. It's now accepting ISNA's endorsement of Muslim prison chaplains—and by extension, GSISS's.

So is the Pentagon. It rejected a recommendation from its own inspector general to use the FBI to help screen ISNA and other religious organizations that certify military chaplains. The Pentagon said it would be "legally problematic" to do so.[27]

As it stands now, the Pentagon will not remove or reject Muslim chaplains unless they have been charged or convicted of terrorism or if the religious organization endorsing them appears on the State Department's list of foreign terror organizations.[28]

Even at the FBI, the PC outreach continues unabated.

Earlier this year, with the conviction of the Holy Land charity still making headlines, the FBI allowed its general counsel to sit on a Yale University panel on civil rights with ISNA official Louay Safi. During the same month, ISNA boasted that it met with the FBI to voice outrage over undercover agents in mosques.[29]

And more recently, FBI Executive Assistant Director Tom Harrington met at FBI headquarters with a vice president of ISNA, a move that followed the bureau's decision "to use ISNA as their official point of contact with the American Muslim community," according to Guandolo, who has worked at the FBI since 1996, most recently in the Washington field office's counterterrorism division.[30]

Career FBI agents say they were scandalized by news of the high-level contacts, which took place over their objections and in spite of ISNA's recent Justice Department blacklisting. They say FBI assistant directors involved in outreach and civil rights are hesitant to cut off formal ties to the group because they remain impressed with the moderate and patriotic rhetoric of ISNA officials.

The FBI officials "are quite friendly with them and refuse to believe they are nefarious, because they say—and I quote—'I have lunch with Sayyid Syeed every week; he is a nice guy,'" Guandolo says.

"Nice or not, he's Muslim Brotherhood," the veteran agent asserts. "And they're the enemy."

And their next target is the Treasury Department—and Wall Street.

CHAPTER TWENTY

NAIT AND THE ECONOMIC JIHAD

"We can communicate grievances and positions that are relevant to the well-being of the Muslim community to these [non-Shariah-compliant American] corporations through shareholder resolutions, press releases, and divestitures ... We are able to implement an economic boycott that reflects our values and priorities."

-- **Omar Haydar, mutual fund director for the North American Islamic Trust (NAIT), 2001 letter to CAIR**[1]

T HE COUNCIL ON AMERICAN-ISLAMIC RELATIONS invests its employee retirement funds and other accounts with the North American Islamic Trust, another Muslim Brotherhood subsidiary in the center of the conspiracy to conquer North America for Allah.

Adopting a relatively low profile, NAIT fronts as an investment bank, managing the financial accounts of most of the organizations in the Brotherhood network and providing the capital that has helped the Islamofascist movement expand from college campuses to major cities including the nation's capital. It also holds title to most of the radical mosques and Islamic schools in America.

Millions of dollars in Brotherhood and Hamas money has flowed through NAIT since its founding in 1973—with ample seed capital from Saudi and other Mideast sources. In fact, U.S. prosecutors recently named NAIT in the U.S. Brotherhood conspiracy to fund Hamas and other terrorists.[2]

While that's bad enough, the Chicago-based trust is at the center of a broader Brotherhood scheme to create a parallel economic system in

America complying with *Shariah* laws against interest, credit, and other "impure" Western financial practices. The ultimate goal is to Islamize the banking industry and Wall Street in an economic jihad.

It is part of the larger civilization jihad, or "grand jihad," to destroy and overthrow the non-Islamic system of the West revealed in the secret Brotherhood manifesto uncovered by the FBI. Deep inside the eighteen-page document is a section calling for the creation of an "Islamic Central Bank" and "an organization for interest-free loans."[3]

The manifesto does not spell out the Brotherhood's tactics for imposing *Shariah*-compliant finance on corporate America. Nor the tools for enforcing it.

However, a letter intercepted from one of the boxes of files that CAIR had marked for shredding at its Washington headquarters provides clues.

The correspondence reveals a "strategic partnership" between NAIT and CAIR to bully publicly traded American firms to conform to *Shariah* rules or face punishments—including shareholder resolutions, divestments, and boycotts.

FORBIDDEN BUSINESS

What are the *Shariah* rules for finance? Among other things, Islamic law forbids any businesses dealing in:

- conventional Western banking;

- alcoholic beverages;

- pork or pork byproducts;

- tobacco;

- Western aerospace and defense;

- movie production and theaters;

- music;

- hotels and casinos; or

- any other entertainment.

Business with Israel also is forbidden.

Now back to the smoking-gun letter, which was written in 2001 by Omar Haydar, director of fund operations for NAIT subsidiary Allied Asset Advisors, Inc. He was following up on a prior "discussion" with CAIR's then-national operations director, Khalid Iqbal.

In his introduction, Haydar informed Iqbal that NAIT has about $20 million under management in one stock mutual fund and plans to offer other Islamic investment products in the future, which would add to its muscle and help it bend Wall Street and corporate America to the will of Islam.

"Currently, we own nearly four hundred U.S. equities, such as Walgreens, Cisco, and Exxon-Mobil. Thus we have some leverage with the companies whose shares we own," Haydar wrote. "More specifically, we can communicate grievances and positions that are relevant to the well-being of the Muslim community to these corporations through shareholder resolutions, press releases, and divestitures."[4]

If a company does not change its business plan and conform with Islamic principles, he proposed, NAIT could threaten to divest its funds.

"If a corporation does not seem to be receptive to the grievances and concerns," Haydar said, "we have the discretion to divest ourselves of the corporation's assets, and making [sic] it a public matter."[5]

With CAIR's help, NAIT could trigger an "economic boycott" forcing targeted corporations to bow to Islamic demands.

"Thus," Haydar said, "we are able to implement an economic boycott that reflects our values and priorities, putting our money where our mouth is."[6]

'PRESSURE DOW JONES'

He advised CAIR that the financial jihad "process" against Wall Street firms would work as follows:

• Pursue the matter quietly through their public relations/press office.

• Draft shareholder resolution.

• Submit resolution as a shareholder for annual shareholder meeting.

• Issue press release statement on stance and issue.

• Divest holdings and pressure Dow Jones to remove company from index with your assistance.[7]

Patrick Sookhdeo, a London scholar and *Shariah* finance expert, says such pressure tactics have worked frighteningly well for the Brotherhood in Britain, which has become a mecca for *Shariah* finance while suffering rapid Islamization.

"Islamic banking and finance is but one of the multiple tools they use to further their cause," Sookhdeo says. "It is economic jihad, a key and integrated part of the larger civilizational jihad."[8]

He elaborates that *Shariah* finance accords with the Brotherhood's wider "vision of the overthrow of non-Islamic systems and the establishment of a pan-Islamic *caliphate* that will rule the earth."[9]

Meanwhile, NAIT and other Brotherhood front groups are lobbying

Congress and the Treasury Department to change banking rules to accommodate Islamic financing principles in everything from stock investments to mortgages to insurance.

Recently, Treasury has encouraged the groups by taking conciliatory steps in their direction.

ISLAMIC FINANCE 101

For example: After acquiring a majority stake in failed insurance giant AIG—the U.S. market leader in *Shariah*-compliant financial products— Treasury co-sponsored a forum entitled "Islamic Finance 101."

Major Stephen Coughlin, a Pentagon consultant and expert in Islamic doctrine, argues that the government's ownership of AIG may be unconstitutional since it tacitly supports the practice of *Shariah,* and *Shariah* is a separate legal system at odds with the law of the land.

"If politicians and the Treasury make an exception to U.S. law and allow *Shariah*-compliant finance," he says, "they are disobeying their oath to protect and defend the U.S. Constitution."[10]

A public-interest law firm agrees, and is suing the department claiming that government ownership of AIG is an unconstitutional government "establishment" of Islam. The Thomas More Law Center also argues there are a number of links between charities that receive funds as a result of *Shariah*-compliant financing and "terrorist organizations that are hostile to the United States."

Indeed, a share of the proceeds from *Shariah*-compliant investments is automatically transferred to Islamic charities, many of which finance jihad.

An elite group of *Shariah* advisors determines how much of the proceeds will be "purified," and which charities will be the beneficiaries. Who are these gurus? Radical Muslim Brothers who support jihad.

One leading *Shariah* advisor, Muhammad Usmani, advocates aggressive jihad against infidels. Fiercely anti-American, he has urged all Muslims to support the Taliban.[11]

Sheik Yusuf al-Qaradawi, who sits on the international advisory board, is an open supporter of suicide bombings, including those targeting U.S. troops. He thinks Islamic charity should be spent on jihad. In fact, the Brotherhood leader says he prefers to call such donations "jihad with money, because Allah has ordered us to fight enemies with our lives and our money."[12]

CHECKERED BOARD

One of NAIT's founding directors is Jamal Barzinji, a major Brotherhood figure who has a criminal record and has been the subject of post-9/11 terror financing investigations. According to federal court documents cited earlier, Barzinji is "not only closely associated with PIJ (Palestinian Islamic Jihad) but also with Hamas."

The FBI has identified Barzinji as a key Brotherhood radical who is "in a position to direct the activities and support of Muslims in the U.S. for the Islamic revolution."[13]

What's more, current NAIT Chairman Muzammil Siddiqi appears in secret Brotherhood documents as a high-ranking member of its *shura* council.[14] And current NAIT Trustee Gaddoor Saidi shows up on the Justice Department's list of unindicted co-conspirators in the Holy Land Foundation scheme to fund Hamas terrorists.[15]

NAIT has established several Islamic mutual funds, including the Iman (Arabic for faith) Fund and Saturna Capital's Amana (Arabic for trust) Growth Fund and Amana Income Fund, which have combined assets of more than $1 billion. About half of the seventy thousand investors who buy the funds through financial advisors aren't Muslim.

Caveat emptor: Investing in NAIT's financial empire may mean investing in the holy war against the United States.

"Within the organizational structure of NAIT, there have been numerous groups and individuals identified as being part of a covert network of revolutionaries," the FBI warned in a previously classified internal memo about the Muslim Brotherhood.[16]

"This faction of Muslims have declared war on the United States, Israel, and any other country they deem as an enemy of Islam," the memo continues. "The common bond between these various organizations is both religious and political, with the underlying common goal being to further the holy war [Islamic jihad]."

AFTERWORD
BACK TO BASICS

AMERICA'S GREATEST CHALLENGE in this ongoing national security threat is our reluctance to admit that our law enforcement agencies are some fifty years behind the intelligence gathering techniques of Islamic terrorist groups and their agents such as CAIR and ISNA.

Many readers will scoff at this notion. America has spent billions of dollars on electronic surveillance and data collection. Law enforcement has the best gadgets known to mankind. Officers today have better surveillance equipment than any other law enforcement agency in the world. And its sophistication is generations ahead of anything used by al-Qaida.

But our first-line defenders at the local, state, and federal levels have become so technologically advanced that they have lost sight of the common sense, street-wise approaches to law enforcement that work best in disrupting terrorist plots and dismantling terror-support networks. These approaches include basics such as talking to people on the street, and studying habits and customs to gain clues about tactics used by the bad guys. Infiltrating their culture and community is key to getting the jump on them.

For robberies, homicides, narcotics, and white-collar fraud cases, keep the Blackberries, laptops, and night vision goggles. Fighting Islamic jihadists, on the other hand, requires learning their mindset, ideology, and tactics. CAIR and other jihadist front groups block the real training officers need. In fact, their "sensitivity" training is designed to throw sand in their eyes.

For starters, police chiefs, sheriffs, and FBI special agents in charge must refocus their efforts on self-study of the materials used by the enemy. If al-Qaida manuals and jihadi literature detailing how to fight the West are produced in Pakistan or Saudi Arabia, then it's incumbent upon our police forces to get these materials. *Note: They are available in virtually every U.S. mosque or Islamic bookstore. Focus on the Sunni materials first.*

Next, start relying on Human Intelligence (HUMINT). This does not have to be limited to recruiting criminal informants to obtain counterterrorism intelligence. Use your own officers after they've been properly trained. Islamic groups and scholars—and the FBI officials they've brainwashed—will tell you the Islamist ideology is very complicated. And they will tell you that if you're not Muslim, or haven't lived in an Islamic country, or don't speak Arabic, then you or your informants will not understand what to look for if they conduct an undercover operation in the local Islamic center.

This is what CAIR and the rest of the Muslim mafia want officers to believe. But don't buy it. Jihadism is not rocket science. There are telltale signs to watch for when identifying radicalism. And you don't need sophisticated tools to help you detect them, according to veteran federal investigator P. David Gaubatz:

> The first-hand research my team and I conducted within CAIR and in nearly two hundred U.S. mosques across the U.S. is very basic. During the training of my researchers, I provided them the kind of old-school training that veteran law enforcement officers have used going back decades. These time-tested methods rely on common sense, street smarts, and the most basic of equipment (pen and notebook), combined with the ability to handle stress in a hostile environment. We had little funding and basic equipment. But my researchers had the ability to adapt quickly to various situations; they utilized basic skills such as human communication. They were very personable, and did not portray themselves to be above others or to know more than they actually did.

Gaubatz stresses humility:

Oftentimes law enforcement officers who work undercover have a hard time checking their egos. Criminals see through this very quickly. When conducting undercover operations, you must realize you most likely do not know as much about your target as they know about the illegal work they are conducting. Build rapport with them. People love to talk about their jobs and accomplishments. Even Corey Saylor and Ibrahim Hooper, who are trained to say as little as possible to people outside CAIR's inner circle, will talk when they do not feel intimidated or threatened. Abide by their *Shariah* law, and always be professional and respectful.

All the while searching out clues to extremism and radical behavior:

Investigators and the public, just as importantly, should understand that Muslims who follow the most violent aspects of *Shariah* law adhere to very specific rituals, habits, and styles of dress that to the untrained eye appear otherwise harmless. But they are red flags signaling extremism. Within *Shariah* law, Muslims must always do everything opposite their enemies the Christians and the Jews. For instance:

• If a Muslim wears a beard it should be a fistful in length, but the mustache should be trimmed because this would be opposite the style of the Christians and Jews.

• In addition, Muslim men are not allowed to wear gold jewelry, as their prophet Muhammad commanded.

• If a Muslim man desires to wear a ring or watch, they must be silver—and always worn on the right hand. Again, the pious strive to do everything opposite their enemies, and everything like Muhammad.

• Wearing silk neckties or other silk garments is also taboo. Muhammad didn't wear silk, didn't approve of it.

• Muslim clerics can also be identified as *Shariah* compliant by their dress. Their robes, for example, will more than likely be cut above the ankle and contain black stitching.

These are just a few examples of the practical tips law enforcement authorities can arm themselves with before knocking on doors in the Muslim community—as opposed to the politically correct disinformation they've received in "cultural-awareness" classes organized by CAIR and other fronts for the bad guys.

U.S. law enforcement must take a more proactive role investigating organizations and people linked to terrorism. We're still handling terrorism in a traditional law enforcement way that is predicated on the bad guys acting first, which is reactionary—and always tragic.

That's minimizing the casualties after the fact.

That's restoring order.

That's returning the damaged buildings and property to some form of usefulness.

That's preparing after-action reports.

That's holding endless hearings on what went wrong.

In short, that's having a nice funeral.

We can no longer afford to have that kind of mindset. We shouldn't have to bleed more to get leaders to change. We've already bled enough.

We need to give law enforcement—the case agents, the detectives, the beat cops—tools to collect predictive intelligence on the bad guys. And not just when the threat level is high—but all the time—because the bad guys never stop casing, infiltrating, scheming, and plotting. Recall that eight full years elapsed between the botched 1993 World Trade Center bombing and 9/11 when the terrorists returned to finish the job.

They're relentless, and law enforcement must constantly poke and prod them and cause them to daylight; then take them out of the picture with whatever charges stick—tax fraud, visa fraud, money-laundering, perjury, obstruction. Whatever will hold up in court. Lock them up, deport them, put them out of business.

Our children deserve leaders who are proactive, who won't be known for heroic activities performed only after responding to a terrorist event they could have prevented. It's madness to continue to allow known terrorists and their supporters to operate inside America.

Ferreting them out and shutting them down requires going back to the basics. Cut the political red tape. Learn the enemy's playbook. And most important, put the basic investigative work back in the hands of the street agents and detectives.

Maybe then we can honestly hope to stop another child—Muslim, Christian, Jewish, or any other belief—from becoming the victim of another major terrorist attack or possibly even worse, a country controlled more by *Shariah* law than our Constitution.

ACKNOWLEDGMENTS

MOHAMMED ODEH AL-REHAIEF rescued POW Private Jessica Lynch in Iraq in 2003. While serving there at the time, I had the opportunity—and honor—to rescue several members of Mohammed's family, including his sister-in-law, father, brothers, nieces, and nephews. The Rehaief family and I spent several months together in Iraq. This family had suffered tragedy, yet they relied on their Prophet to help them live day by day during the war.

The brothers and I had the opportunity to conduct several missions. Their professionalism saved my life and while in Iraq, they were my family.

The Rehaiefs were the family I had left behind in America—my beautiful wife, son, daughter, brother, and sister. I missed my father more than I can describe. He was my hero. He had always been there for me as a youngster. Though he worked twelve to eighteen hours a day, he always had time to play baseball with me. My dear mother had passed away earlier.

Working counterterrorism in Iraq was dangerous, but the battles I have had since returning in 2003 have been tougher by a factor of ten.

After many years in undercover operations, I trusted few, and our lives were in each other's hands. Members of the Al-Rehaief family are the examples of Islam and the Muslim people. I saw the nieces of Mohammed cry each night for several months. Our team rescued them and got them into a safe zone, but the living conditions were not meant for men or women, and certainly not three- and four-year-old girls.

They were all living in one of Saddam Hussein's bombed-out bunkers. There was filthy trash everywhere, and scorpions and dangerous snakes were often seen crawling under the beds of the children. They cried. I cried.

This was the turning point in my life. I dedicated my life to trying to ensure no child ever has to suffer living under a brutal dictator, or suffer from Islamic terrorist attacks. I promised my daughter this as well. I would no longer have a badge and credentials, or the safety of having political red tape to cover for me if I made mistakes during my private research.

I was now on my own investigating Islamic terror groups and their supporters in America. The more I exposed their criminal activities, the more threats I got. I received some offers of help, but in reality, I knew the people who would be there for me were my family, which included the Al-Rehaief family.

They are Muslim, and my family and I are Christian. But we have worked together for several years to identify Islamic terrorist groups and their supporters in America. We have dedicated our lives to this cause, because we know U.S. law enforcement does not have the required training to protect our country. And politicians, for the most part, care only about their next election.

Readers should keep the name Chris Gaubatz in their memories. My son is as bright as they come, and possesses the most important trait in the intelligence field: commom sense. He is my number one asset.

In addition, I want to recognize other valuable members of my counterterrorism research team, including Charety Zhe and Stefanie Creswell, as well as Daniel, Wendy, Maryann, and Camille. They are among the many professionals who assisted in this research. And of course, special thanks to my outstanding co-author Paul Sperry, as well as WND Books's Ami Naramor and Eric Jackson.

Personally, I owe my investigative skills and training to ret. Brigadier General Francis X. Taylor, former commander of the U.S. Air Force Office of Special Investigations (AFOSI) at Andrews Air Force Base, Maryland.

General Taylor led by example, and taught me that intelligence collected for collection purposes alone is useless. The intelligence obtained serves our country only if it is utilized, shared, and not buried in political red tape.

This is the goal of our book: To share with the American people the intelligence we have gathered. Our enemy has deceit and treachery on its side. We, on our side, have the facts. And the Truth will always win.

—*P. David Gaubatz*

ACKNOWLEDGMENTS

While countless people deserve thanks for bringing this book to fruition, I am most indebted to Chris Gaubatz for the courage and composure he showed while operating undercover in the belly of the beast for as many months as he did. By all accounts, he was the consummate professional.

And the trove of sensitive materials he obtained from inside the dark lair of CAIR constitutes more than a bill of indictment against this terror-supporting Muslim Brotherhood front group. It provides a road map to the entire leftist, anti-American movement and its radical underground agenda.

These documents expose the larger conspiracy's tentacles reaching into not only dozens of Islamic NGOs and hundreds of Islamic centers across the country but also their many allies on the left—from the ACLU to the DNC to the broader anti-Israel lobby to the academic establishment, and on and on. Here, for the first time, we have a clear picture of the internal workings of the America-haters and -bashers who feverishly work to undermine corporate America, the military, law enforcement, and the bedrock Judeo-Christian values upon which Western civilization was founded.

Former federal agent P. David Gaubatz and the rest of his intrepid team of undercover researchers also deserve my thanks and admiration.

Personally, this was an exceptionally difficult book to report and write due to the voluminous information and relatively quick turnaround time from manuscript to launch. The deadlines at times seemed insurmountable. But I thank my editor Ami Naramor for her patience and calm while shepherding through the detailed and fact-packed manuscript. I also thank my family for their loving support and forbearance while I was down in my book "bunker."

Special thanks to Eric Jackson for bringing the Gaubatzes and me together on this ambitious project. I was honored they sought me out, and there was immediate synergy as I already had been investigating CAIR and the Muslim Brotherhood since the publication of my book, *Infiltration: How Muslim Spies And Subversives Have Penetrated Washington*. This was a natural sequel—a reverse infiltration by American patriots turning the tables on the bad guys trying to infiltrate and "destroy" this great country "from within."

My New York agent Andrew Stuart was instrumental in making this book a reality, and was a constant source of encouragement through all the heavy lifting.

I also want to acknowledge U.S. Rep. Sue Myrick, one of the few politicians in Washington who have shown the courage to confront the growing Islamofascist threat inside America. Myrick co-founded the Congressional Anti-Terrorism/Jihad Caucus to educate fellow members of Congress and the public at large about the threat from these stealth jihadists.

I'd also like to extend special thanks to the dozens of former and active law enforcement officers—in the field and on the front lines in the war on terror—who were gracious enough to share their time, experience (including internal documents), and insights with me. These FBI case agents and detectives assigned to the JTTF in Washington— unlike their timid bosses who are still slaves to political correctness and promotions—are the gutsy public servants to whom all Americans owe a debt of gratitude. Trust me when I say they care more about your safety and security than most of the politicians and political appointees in Washington. Some of these agents are mentioned by name in the book, while others spoke to me on the condition of anonymity because they are not authorized to publicly discuss their investigations of CAIR, ISNA, and other Muslim Brotherhood front groups.

These dedicated and no-nonsense field agents give me hope that one day we will finally dismantle the terror-support network in America and reliably protect the public from violent jihadists.

—Paul Sperry

APPENDIX

Fig. 1

Strategy

Over the long term:

By December 31, 2010 we will be supporting a $12,000,000 budget, $5,000,000 at national. We will have a presence covering all states, with at least 28 state chapters, and 35 strategically located offices.

We will have grown to at least 60,000 members, looking to represent over 75,000 people.

We will impact local congressional districts with each chapter influencing at least two legislators through strong grass roots responses. We will focus on influencing congressmen responsible for policy that directly impacts the American Muslim community. (For example congressman on the judiciary, intelligence, and homeland security committees.) We will develop national initiatives such as a lobby day and placing Muslim interns in Congressional offices. We will work to add at least 30,000 new voter registrations.

We will support Muslim activists through education and training with guides/tools and annual national projects/campaigns coordinated with chapters. In concert with local chapters we will sustain an ongoing media campaign to change hearts and minds of Americans. The program(s) would be fine tuned to the sensitivities of each community. We will measure the effect of the media programs, with the goal of significantly shifting public opinions: move favorable opinion from 1.6% to 20%, building on 2006's neutral of 67% and 31.4% unfavorable.

We will continue our advocacy, adding the capacity to handle more civil rights cases with an increase of in-house lawyers and systems to monitor progress. We will have a direct influence on Hollywood.

Collaboration – HR commission boards/state; sister organizations; other Muslim organizations.

We will leverage technology with items such as enhanced web site, intranet, and centralized database. We will develop the ability to quickly target segments within our database. (For example, to quickly access registered Muslim voters in a Congressional district.)

We will establish branding standards and maintain a common look and feel across national and all the chapters. We will continue to invest in building recognition of CAIR.

We will support the organization with 30 employees at national - 75 organization-wide. We will institutionalize systems and processes. We will define an idealized chapter and work to have each chapter meet or exceed that quality model.

Over the mid-term:

We will align the organization with our strategic plan, filling new Director positions, reengineering processes for efficacy, and focusing of our core mission. We support efforts with marketing, including deploying consistent branding.

We will hire a dedicated Development Director, develop a development plan, and launch a fund raising program that has at least paid for itself. The development plan will have creative elements such as $6,000 donors. We will develop a grant writing capability.

We will hire a dedicated Chapter Development Director. We will enhance national's value to chapters with specific training and materials, coordinated action, membership drives, etc. We will affect a cultural shift, with more emphasis on local action. We will propagate the chapter handbooks. National will sustain ongoing chapter visits. We will align the organization to more fully support the strategic plan. (Evaluation of the success of the organization will be ongoing.) We will optimize the national office.

We will launch the "hearts and minds" campaign jumpstarting the first production overseas. We will tap into the "new media" with contests for young potential film makers. We will launch an formal educational initiative. (We will look to educate 100 speakers, 50 writers, transform 50 Islamic centers to model outreach cultural centers, establish a scholarship for graduate students, publish points-of-reference material, initiate TV/radio shows, create ideal presentations, a national forum, and Amazon.com like source of all published material on Islam.)

We will complete the installation, training, and deployment of a full range of productivity tools. (Outlook, Sharepoint for document management, eMail, Wiki for management of free form text, CRM, and civil rights database.) We will use an intranet, and Wiki, capturing our best practices. We will centralize our databases to manage contacts, relationships, membership tracking, and civil rights. We will complete the revamping of our website and integration with our systems and processes.

13 Jan 07

Fig. 2

Simple Resolve, Inc.

Report

Prepared by Corey P. Saylor, Founding Partner
Phone: 571.278.4658
E-mail: csaylor@simpleresolve.biz

PERIOD: AUGUST 13-17, 2007
DATE: AUGUST 20, 2007

Thank you for the opportunity to assist with CAIR's mission.

Retainer Agreement Items	August Hours: 56.25

National Government Affairs Coordinator
- Pre-interviewed Faraz Waheed and checked his reputation with CAIR-Ohio. Nihad Awad will interview him on Thursday, August 23rd.

Congressional Fellowships
- Placed Samia Elshafie in the office of Rep. Jackson-Lee (D-TX).

CAIR Government Affairs Report
Submitted to Executive Director and his assistant on Tuesday, August 14th.

Rep. Meeks Press Event
- Statement delivered to Meeks' staff. They requested the additional of one section. No date set for event as yet. Coordinating with CAIR-NY.

2008 Presidential Election
- Drafted questions and place don CAIR shura. CAIR-LA will now distribute to all presidential candidates. Target release is Dec, depending on changes in primaries.
- Building a database of presidential candidate's positions on key issues for release Nov.

Miscellaneous Government Affairs Requests
- Assisted CAIR-NJ with public affairs issues
- Responded to numerous e-mails and phone calls.

Capitol Hill Iftaar (Event to occur Tuesday, September 18)
- All material ready to send. Delaying at request of Communications. Reasonable argument for cancellation can be made, will discuss with CAIR Executives.

August Recess Lobbying
- Minimal response from chapters. CAIR-NJ informs that all their requests received a "schedule full" response.

Special Project Items

Civic Participation Guide (Ready for Distribution Tuesday, November 6)
- Drafting, First Draft Due August 31. Sample pages accompanied last week's report.

Fig. 3

PROPOSED MUSLIM PLATFORM FOR 2004
(MHM TALKING POINTS - ROUGH DRAFT 3/8/04)

During this election year, Muslim Americans believe that all Americans need to think through and debate the following issues away from stereotyping and the 30-second sound bytes. It is the duty of all of us to actively participate in this debate, and to get other social, religious, and political organizations to join in.

ECONOMY

1. Balance the budget and eliminate the deficit.
2. Pay down the national debt.
3. Reduce the size of government.
4. Reduce dependence on Middle East oil.
5. Promote affordable health insurance while maintaining quality of health services.
6. Recognize the impact of domestic and foreign policies on the economy.

LEGAL SYSTEM & HOMELAND SECURITY

1. Identify and debate the costs of the current approach to homeland security.
2. Do not kill the economy in the name of homeland security.
3. Abolish laws that encroach on civil liberties. Long term, these laws will put an end to the American dream as we all knew it. Now it is the Muslims or the Arabs, in the future it will be someone else.
4. Abolish the mentality that came up with the idea that the mailman, or the plumber, or the electrician can be a homeland security asset. This is exactly what the KGB did (and still do) in Russia. Is that what we want long term?
5. Rethink immigration policies, quotas, etc.
6. Hold elected officials accountable for their actions to the same extent that we hold private sector leaders accountable for their actions.
7. Discourage aggressive prosecuting of suspects based on witnesses with faulty backgrounds.
8. Rethink the prison system. It is very expensive, and it ends by generating more criminals.
9. Rethink basic training of police and law enforcement personnel as required to de-emphasize the need for heavy reliance on excessive force. Abolish the go get them mentality that promotes police brutality and misconduct.

SOCIAL & RELIGIOUS ISSUES

1. Religious groups need to become more active in economic, political, and social issues.
2. Allow abortion when the health of the mother is at issue.
3. Outlaw abortion as a method of birth control.
4. Encourage the traditional family.
5. Discourage having children outside of wedlock.
6. Discourage homosexual relationships.
7. Teach children that the only acceptable sex is through marriage.
8. Bring religion to public schools.

AMERICAN – ISLAMIC RELATIONS

1. Abolish the faulty Middle East policy of the past century.
2. Democrats and Republicans need to share the blame for the failure of our Middle East policy, and need to assume responsibility for the damage done to the country as a result of 9/11.
3. Recognize that the seeds for 9/11 were planted in 1948.
4. Don't forget that the thought process that produced 9/11 was created by the inept performance of the corrupt Arab governments of the Middle East.
5. Do not make Fundamental Islam the enemy. It will not work long term, and there is no need for it.

Fig. 4

6. "Fundamental Islam", "Muslim Extremists", and "Islamists" are all homegrown terms that do not serve a useful purpose. Don't get sucked into stereotyping.

7. Stop the support and the use of the corrupt regimes of the Middle East to achieve narrow-minded policy goals. It is time for these people to go. The sooner the better.

8. Attempt to understand Islamic movements in the area, and start supporting Islamic groups including Mr. Ben Laden and his associates.

9. While I am personally very negative with regard to Mr. Busch, I think if he is sincere in his desire to change the Middle East, we can work with him in that regard. It means he will have to make a 180-degree turn, but it can be done.

10. A resolution of the Israeli-Palestinian conflict needs to be based on recognizing and correcting the harm that was done to the Palestinians since 1948.

11. Good foreign policy means less worry about homeland security, and better environment for a strong economy. Does anyone know what is the financial impact of 9/11 on the country?

Fig. 5

KARIMA AL-AMIN
Attorney at Law
392 14th Street, NW
Atlanta, Georgia 30318
(404) 873-1050
Fax (404) 815-4289

April 25, 2007

Mr. Nihad Awad
CAIR
453 New Jersey Avenue, SE
Washington, DC 20003

Re: Justice Fund Contribution

As-salaamu'alaikum:

On behalf of the Justice Fund, we extend appreciation to you and CAIR for the additional contribution of $9,000.00 to be used for legal expenses relative to Imam Jamil Al-Amin's case. The contribution particularly was needed to defray the cost of the recent habeas hearing held in Reidsville, Georgia. We certainly were delighted that you responded to our request in a timely manner.

As always, Imam Jamil sends his greetings and appreciation for the assistance.

Sincerely,

Karima Al-Amin
Attorney at Law

Fig. 6

بسم الله الرحمن الرحيم

مؤسسة النجدة العالمية

Global Relief Foundation

9935 South 76th Avenue, Unit I • Bridgeview, Illinois 60455
Tel: (708) 233-1473 • Fax: (708) 233-1474

July 20, 2000

Br. Mohamed Nimer
Research Director
Council on American-Islamic Relations
453 New Jersey Avenue, S.E
Washington, DC
20003

Aslaamu Alaikum

Dear Br. Nimer

As agreed upon in our conversation earlier, Global Relief Foundation (GRF) will support the North American Islamic Foundation's by donating $18,000. GRF through its *programs in Education and Youth Development* is dedicated to helping the Muslims in North America meet the growing challenges. Please feel free to contact me for any further questions or clarification.

Thanking you for your consideration.

Sincerely yours,

Khaled Diab
Medical Resource Development

Mailing Address: P.O. Box 1406 • Bridgeview, Illinois 60455 • U.S.A.

Fig. 7

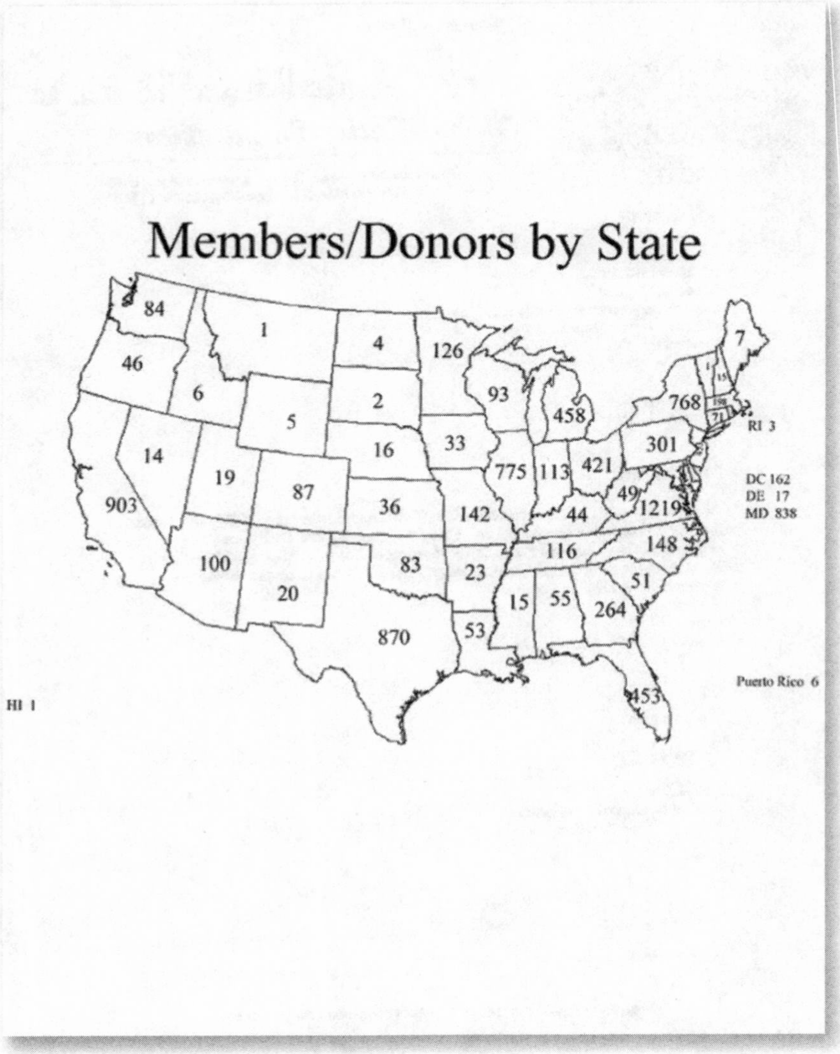
Members/Donors by State
84
1
4
126
7
46
6
2
93
768
5
458
RI 3
14
16
33
301
19
87
775
113
421
DC 162
DE 17
MD 838
903
36
142
49
1219
44
116
148
100
83
23
51
20
15
55
264
53
870
Puerto Rico 6
HI 1
453

Fig. 8

June 2002 Membership Status Report for Board Meeting

Supporter Type	Count	Members	Comments
Husband/Wife	18	36	Represents 36 individuals
Family Membership	1728	3456	
Individual	3451	3451	
Organization	75	75	
Student	411	411	
Gold ($1000/yr)	13	13	
Silver ($35/month)	30	30	
Donors	1432	1432	
Information Request	36		
Unclassified	92		
Monthly Pledges	307	307	177/bank deduction; 130/credit card -- Monthly pledges generate approximately $10,000 per month.
TOTAL	7286	9211	
		+ 500	
		Total 9711	

Total individuals represented: 9349. This number reflects those individuals that we can contact as of June 2002. Approximately 4,600 will be sent renewal notices in July 2002. Close to 3,000 supporters have moved and have not given us their new addresses. Notices should be sent out with Action Alerts for those who move to give us their new addresses.

The above numbers reflect new memberships/donations entered into the system as of June 2002. There are approximately 500 new memberships/donations that need to be entered into the supporters database. These people would primarily represent Individual memberships.

From January to March 2002, 334 new memberships/donations were processed. From April to June 2002, 608 new memberships/donations were processed. These numbers can be attributed to the efforts of the Community Affairs Department and its recruiting efforts. The CAIR website has also been very effective in soliciting donations and new members.

During the beginning of the year, two or three buckets of mail were held by the post office so processing volume was low due to that.

Fig. 9

Year to Date Dollars by Category

Source	Dues	Donations
2001 Fundraising Dinner	$30.00	$9,070.00
2001 ISNA	$0.00	$260.00
2001 Ramadan Solicit	$9,110.00	$250,429.00
CAIR Foundation	$0.00	$1,000.00
Call in	$80.00	$420.00
Chapter/Office	$450.00	$0.00
Citibank	$0.00	$192,942.50
Congressional Guide	$0.00	$300.00
Dawah Program	$0.00	$2,000.00
DC Armory 2002	$10.00	$0.00
E-Mail	$10.00	$415.00
Fundraising Din 2000	$0.00	$250.00
Gov Relations	$0.00	$150.00
Honorary Donation	$0.00	$100.00
Leadership 2002	$63.00	$2,641.00
Letter	$820.00	$1,070.00
Masjid Visit	$10,040.00	$13,464.00
Membership contest	$130.00	$660.00
Newsletter	$50.00	$50.00
None	$8,425.00	$570,627.05
Office Visit	$60.00	$10.00
Pales Rally Apr 02	$80.00	$10.00
PA Quraans and Rugs	$0.00	$8,644.00
Ramadan	$150.00	$0.00
Sensitivity Training	$0.00	$230.00
Telemarketing	$50.00	$350.00
United Way Frederick County	$0.00	$235.00
Voter Registration	$165.00	$115.00
Website	$3,425.00	$14,455.00
WTC Ad Donation	$60.00	$1,200.00
	$33,208.00	$1,071,097.55

From November 2001 to June 27, 2002

Count	Description	Dues Total	Donation Total
313	Masjid Visit	$10,725.00	$16,709.00
401	CAIR Website	$4,585.00	$18,570.00
Totals		$15,310.00	$35,279.00

Fig. 10

TO: CAIR BOARD
From: Khalid Iqbal
Date: September 7, 2004
Subject: Concern about CAIR Staff Turnover

Dear Brothers

Assalaamu Alaykum
I am very concerned about the employee turnover at CAIR National. Last year alone 14 people
left CAIR that is more than 50% of our workforce. I am concerned about:
- Lost productivity
- Low employee moral
- Lack of continuity in work
- Delays in important projects
- Pressure on every department
- Loss of thousands of dollars to CAIR.

Let me share some of the comments that were repeated by many leaving CAIR during the exit
interview.
Negative comments that needs to be improved upon:
- Low wages. Difficult to sustain financially in DC's high cost of living
- Micro management
- Hard to get decisions from the management
- Management quick to point out mistakes
- Employee recognition will help boost the moral
- No feed back from my supervisor
- No clear directions in terms of work or performance
- No career advancement opportunities
- System of promotions not present
- No feedback on good ideas presented to the management. Many seemed to be ignored.
- It is frustrating to hear CAIR projects and decisions from others when things get
  discussed only within a select group of employees and departments
- Better inter-department communications. There is a disconnect between departments.
- Regular performance reviews would be helpful - never got one
- Metro subsidies to ease parking problems
- Open door communication policy between staff and management
- Positive feed back and reinforcement will assist in moral building
- CAIR should have a budget for training staff.

My recommendations:
1. Have a board personnel sub-committee that should oversee employee issues including
   wages, benefits, and other employment issues.
2. Work with National to address the issues
3. Work on a proposal for career advancement and promotion opportunities
4. This committee can also look at employee grievances.

Fig. 11

From: Raabia Wazir <rwazir@cair.com>
Date: Wed, Jul 16, 2008 at 3:27 PM
Subject: Regarding the Online Intern Profiles
To: Raabia Wazir <rwazir@cair.com>, "davidmarshall1215@gmail.com"
<davidmarshall1215@gmail.com>, Asad Uz Zaman <asad.zaman@gmail.com>,
Corina Chang <cc101@duke.edu>, Fariha Quasem <fquasem@gmail.com>,
Farina Zeb <fzeb@gmu.edu>, Ghazal Shaikh <ghazalurooj@gmail.com>,
Jeremy Hunstinger <arsonal3@gmail.com>, Katina Peterson
<pete5547@umn.edu>, "niemaa@email.unc.edu" <niemaa@email.unc.edu>,
Robert McCaw <rmccaw@ufl.edu>, Setphanie Haven <SLH38@georgetown.edu>,
aisha javed <ajaved48@yahoo.com>, "allaha.bahich@ubalt.edu"
<allaha.bahich@ubalt.edu>, "abbeystickney@yahoo.com"
<abbeystickney@yahoo.com>, "abbeystickney@gmail.com"
<abbeystickney@gmail.com>, "ksijuwade@gmail.com" <ksijuwade@gmail.com>
Cc: Yaser Tabbara <ytabbara@cair.com>, Tahra Goraya
<tgoraya@cair.com>, Nihad Awad <nawad@cair.com>

Salaam Interns,

We will not be posting intern profiles on the website as we had
previously planned. A number of individuals voiced concerns regarding
being publically associated with CAIR. While we certainly respect your
right to privacy, we are disappointed that any intern would act out of
fear of prejudice from a few right-wing fringe groups. Activism is
rarely popular and never easy. It is an uphill struggle that we must
face every day with passion and dedication. I thank all of you for
your commitment to CAIR's mission of advocating for justice and mutual
understanding. I pray that you will always have the courage to openly
defend and support our mission and goals.

Warm regards,

Raabia

Raabia Wazir
Outreach Coordinator
rwazir@cair.com
Cel: 304.741.5010

Council on American-Islamic Relations

453 New Jersey Ave SE
Washington, DC 20003
Tel: 202.742.6426 Fax: 202.488.0833   www.cair.com

Fig. 12

In the Name of Allah, The Beneficent, The Merciful

March 19, 2001

To: Mr. Omar Ahmad, Chairman of the Board
CC: Mr. Nihad Awad, Executive Director

Subject: Discrimination at CAIR

Dear Mr. Ahmad,

I am writing this letter to file a formal complaint against the Council on American-Islamic Relations (CAIR). Please also note that I have informed you and the appropriate parties of my decision to resign on Monday March 26, 2001, and that my last day will be Friday March 30, 2001. Since that email was sent to you, Mr. Awad, Mr. Hooper and Mr. Iqbal no one has contacted me regarding this issue except for a brief meeting at 4:00pm EST as requested by Mr. Iqbal. After two years of hard work and dedication I find it appalling and unacceptable.

It should be noted that four hours after receiving my email, Mr. Iqbal called me into his office to "discuss" the issue. He completely denied offering Ms. Serag my position two weeks prior, he accused me of not completing my work while working with Mrs. Qureshi in the Membership Department and continuously rolled his eyes at every comment that I would make. That is not professional or Islamic and I am offended at such behavior.

It should further be noted that both incidents are outlined in my Cited Allegations document that has been included. I would highly encourage that a **thorough** probe into the actions of Mr. Iqbal should take place, and that Mr. Salaam, Ms. Rahman, Ms. Serag and Mrs. Qureshi all be questioned for authenticity of what Mr. Iqbal is claiming. He has had a tendency to "forget" and "miscommunicate," and CAIR can suffer no more.

I am officially requesting a meeting to be set up with the following individuals. Mr. Awad, Mr. Iqbal, Mr. Salaam, Ms. Rahman, Ms. Serag and I. I will be more than willing to come back for this meeting.

I have been a victim of both, gender and religious discrimination. At first glance, it may appear unusual to claim discrimination while working for a civil rights organization. It may seem even more unusual that I am a Muslim claiming religious discrimination while working for a Muslim organization. I urge you to take the time to read through this complaint to find the explanation for both claims. It is due to the fact that I have struggled for two years, along with others, with frustration and acts of discrimination, that these recent incidents made it clear to me that I am working in a hostile environment here at CAIR.

1. **On or about February 7th, 2001**, I worked with Mr. Iqbal to update the Internship Application Form. He informed me that he wanted to ask which sect of Islam the applicants were from. I told him that he would have to do that section because I did

Fig. 13

not feel comfortable putting that on the application. I believe this is where he discovered that my background is Shi'a and from this point his attitude changed towards me.

2. **On February 12, 2001,** Mr. Iqbal called me into his office to inform me that he wanted me to dedicate four hours each day to the membership department to assist Mrs. Qureshi. CAIR has been using Mrs. Qureshi for much of the Website and IT problems that we have had. This has caused Mrs. Qureshi to fall even further behind in her primary workload. Therefore, it was agreed in a staff meeting that CAIR would hire an IT person to take care of our Website and other issues of that nature. I reminded Mr. Iqbal of this and informed him that four hours a day would be detrimental to my own work. He replied by saying that he didn't think I had enough work to do during the day. He stated that the issue was discussed with Mr. Awad, so the decision was final. I later discussed this incident with Mr. Awad. He confirmed that Mr. Iqbal told him that I was one of several employees at CAIR that did not have enough work to do.

Later this same day I met with Mr. Awad to discuss getting a detailed job description. I also mentioned Mr. Iqbal's intentions of ascertaining which sect of Islam an applicant was. He was shocked and said that CAIR has never and will never inquire about such things and that he would clear it up with Mr. Iqbal.

3. **On February 20, 2001,** Mr. Iqbal told me that I was to take the place of Mrs. Robinson as the receptionist while she was trained for the membership department. I was surprised since I was suddenly getting pushed from one position to another. I had helped Mrs. Qureshi in the Membership Department for about a week. I informed Mr. Iqbal that I was dissatisfied with the decision and that four hours of being a receptionist was not in my job description. He replied by saying that it was only for a couple of months until they could find another receptionist.

Later this same day I discovered that Mr. Iqbal did not trust me. Four days prior, I asked for him for clearance to be allowed to attend the Saunders Elementary School symposium that I've attended in the past. It was on this day that he asked another employee if it was indeed true that I had attended this symposium in the past. My honesty has never been questioned at CAIR up until now. I don't know what made Mr. Iqbal feel that he could not believe me.

4. **On February 21, 2001,** I complained to Mr. Awad about my situation. He stated that the final decision for these matters would be up to Mr. Iqbal, but that he would meet with Mr. Iqbal and myself to discuss the controversy. When I informed him about the incident where my honesty was questioned, he was surprised and, once again, said he would clear it up with Mr. Iqbal.

5. **On February 22, 2001,** Mr. Iqbal came into my office to speak to me. He wanted to know what was on my screen and what I was working on. I showed him the Career Services Database that I had been working on since November of 2000. He was

322

Fig. 14

unaware of this project and had never heard of it before. I was extremely shocked and concerned. I did not understand how he could label me as a person who did not have enough to do during the day if he was not aware of the projects I was working on.

Later that morning at 9:00am, Mr. Iqbal reminded me that I was to answer the phones from 9:00am to 12:00pm. I told him that it was my understanding that Mr. Awad was to meet with the both of us to discuss this issue. Mr. Iqbal stated that he met with Mr. Awad yesterday and my concerns were brought up, but the decision was final.

When Mr. Awad arrived at 10:45am I asked him about the meeting that was supposed to take place between him, Mr. Iqbal and I. Mr. Awad seemed confused so I told him that Mr. Iqbal said that they had met yesterday and the decision was final. Mr. Awad said that there must have been a lack of communication and that he would talk to Mr. Iqbal.

At 3:30pm, Mr. Awad requested a meeting in his office with Mr. Iqbal and I. To my surprise, Mr. Awad started the meeting by saying, "I am only here to interfere if there is a personal issue to be discussed. Khalid (Mr. Iqbal) has final authority over this matter." I did not know why, after all of this, Mr. Awad requested a meeting to tell me that he could not do anything. Mr. Awad remained very distant the entire meeting and at times it seemed like he was not listening. I informed them that I was hired as a research assistant and then moved up to the Training and Internship Director. I stated that I had plenty of work to do and I didn't know how they came to the conclusion that I did not without sitting with me and asking what projects I was working on. I told them I would be completely miserable being demoted to answering phones for four hours a day. I even informed them that two other employees were more than willing to split the phone duty with me. This suggested compromise was rejected. At the end of the meeting Mr. Iqbal said he had heard all this before and since his decision was final, there was no use in going back and forth about it. He continued by saying that I didn't have enough to do in the office and that my cell phone was going off too much.

It was at this point that I knew I was being targeted. I believe that Mr. Iqbal retaliated against me as a result of my complaints to Mr. Awad. Not only was it suspicious that out of all the cell phones that go off in the office (Mr. Awad, Mr. Hooper, Mr. Shakir, Ms. Rahman, Ms. Serag, Mrs. Robinson and Mrs. Qureshi) he only noticed mine, but he did not know that a majority of my phone calls are from interns that call me for information. Not only do I receive calls from interns at work; I receive calls from interns at all hours during the night and on weekends. It is unfortunate that no one took the time to find out when, where, and how I do my job before I was demoted to part-time receptionist.

6. **On March 15, 2001,** While having lunch with another employee, I was informed that two days prior (March 13, 2001) Mr. Iqbal approached this particular employee and wanted to meet. In this meeting, Mr. Iqbal offered this employee the opportunity of heading up the Leadership Training Center. This employee was very shocked and

Fig. 15

asked Mr. Iqbal, "Isn't that Tannaz's job?" Mr. Iqbal replied, "Tannaz will not be doing that job. I do not want to give her the position, but I don't mind if she works under you. I don't want her doing it alone." The employee replied, "No…I have no interest in the LTC and plus, I don't want to step on anyones toes." Mr. Iqbal kept on insisting that this employee take the position, while the employee refused.

I would like to make it clear that these recent incidents with Mr. Iqbal were the last straws that broke the camel's back. I have been frustrated with discrimination at CAIR for two years. CAIR has it's own secret history of discrimination before Mr. Iqbal came, that has caused many employees to quit and very few to come back.

I am prepared to file a formal charge of discrimination with the EEOC and to take this matter further. I am not out to get CAIR, nor do I want to make this a public issue to embarrass the Muslims. But CAIR can not continue to overwork and mistreat its employees while telling them not to complain because it's for the sake of Allah (swt).

It saddens me deeply to have to take such steps against CAIR, but alas they have left me with no other options. My job description has completely been taken over. I have no authority in my work. I have been demoted to the position of answering the telephones. My interns are sent to grant writing classes and are given the responsibility of researching and grant writing on behalf of CAIR, while I am not informed of ANY of these things nor have I been asked to participate in such projects. I am completely dishonored and mistreated, and I can not stand for it any longer.

I hope that you will take the time to fully analyze the situation and get back to me as soon as possible.

Sincerely,

Tannaz Haddadi

The following individuals have witnessed some, if not all, of the aforementioned incidents. After reviewing the information in this complaint, it appears that Tannaz Haddadi may have been discriminated against. We are available to discuss the issue further.

_____   _____
Joshua Salaam   Nancy Hanaan Serag
Civil Rights Coordinator   Office Manager

_____
Isra'a Abdul-Rahman
Executive Assistant

Fig. 16

VISITORS REGISTER

Name	Company/Address	To See	Arrive	Depart
Macla Virst	H&K boo Newthampshire	Mihad	12:40	
Brad Bennett	H&K	Mihad	12:40	
James Jwss	self	Khalid	1:05 pm	
Mark Perkins	self	" "	1:07 pm	
Vittorio Felaco	SELF/STATE SELF			
Carlo Bongiovanni	SELF/STATE			
Richard Busai	USCP	Kraus	1:00	
Hisham Seif-Edia	Embassy of Egypt	Mr. Award	12:41 4:	
Milad Besada	ART TV	Mr. N. Award	1:45 p	
Yuni Wilcox	VOA TV	Award	2:45	
Kokab Farshori	VOA TV	Anton Millan	11:56	
Guy Butterworth	VOA TV	"	"	
Luris Foss	AE	Alaa	1:50	
Rasool, Weiss	SELF	Nihad	1616	

325

Fig. 17

VISITORS REGISTER

Date	Name	Company/Address	To See	Time Arrive	Time Depart
3/26	Kamran Baig Vehicle Plate No.	Fmanlinc	Br. Khalid	10:55 Am	
3/26	Islam Abdullah Vehicle Plate No.		Dr. Nimer	1130	
3.27.	Shukri Abu-Baker Vehicle Plate No.	HLF			
	James [illegible] Vehicle Plate No.	PS	Mr. Robinson	8:55	
3/28	Omar Toor Vehicle Plate No. KDB 48A		Khalid Iqbal	9:40	10:10
3/29/01	Vehicle Plate No.		Yassin Akmal		
3/30/01	Javid Sonde Vehicle Plate No.	Globaltechpro	Tena	4:25	4:40
4/3/01	Sharif ElBadawi Vehicle Plate No.	Vertical Blue	Khalid Iqbal	1:00pm	
3/3/01	Abdul Mujeeb Foster Vehicle Plate No.	DC Fire Dept.	Joshua	2:44	
3/3/01	Haskin Hatim Lyons Vehicle Plate No.	DC Fire Dept	Joshua	2:44	
4/9/2001	Vehicle Plate No.	Hali Jilani		4:00	
4-10-01	Ronnie Few Vehicle Plate No.	D.C Fire & EMS		1:30	
4-10-01	Robert Smith Vehicle Plate No.	D.C. Fire & EMS			
	Vincent White Vehicle Plate No.	Child. of Mona. Foun. Dubai UAE	J. Hooper	4:00	

Fig. 18

◀ Back

Recent Account Activity May 01 2007 to May 23 2007		
Debits & Credits for Checking Account: 66731887		
▼Date▲	▼Description▲	▼Amount▲
05/02/07	Transfer to Checking Reference Number: 89194	-150,000.00
05/02/07	Deposited ck ret	-20.00
05/04/07	Deposit TLR Br#: 00904 TID:03 1000 CONN AV NW,WASHNGTN,DC	6.00
05/04/07	Deposit TLR Br#: 00904 TID:03 1000 CONN AV NW,WASHNGTN,DC	50.00
05/04/07	Deposit	2,411.00
05/04/07	Deposit	3,535.00
05/11/07	Deposit TLR Br#: 00904 TID:01 1000 CONN AV NW,WASHNGTN,DC	6.00
05/11/07	Deposit TLR Br#: 00904 TID:01 1000 CONN AV NW,WASHNGTN,DC	5,000.00
05/14/07	Deposit	1,921.00
05/14/07	Deposit	2,887.29
05/15/07	ACH-CAIR PPDOFFSET 051507COUNCIL OFFSET	3,895.00
05/17/07	Transfer to Checking Reference Number: 74482	-100,000.00
05/18/07	ACH-CAIR OFFSET 051807WORK OF =070515	-35.00
05/18/07	Deposit TLR Br#: 00904 TID:06 1000 CONN AV NW,WASHNGTN,DC	20.00
05/18/07	Deposit TLR Br#: 00904 TID:06 1000 CONN AV NW,WASHNGTN,DC	428.00
05/18/07	Deposit TLR Br#: 00904 TID:06 1000 CONN AV NW,WASHNGTN,DC	500.00
05/18/07	Deposit	2,191.00
05/18/07	Deposit TLR Br#: 00904 TID:06 1000 CONN AV NW,WASHNGTN,DC	2,350.00
05/18/07	Deposit	2,801.00
05/21/07	ACH-CAIR OFFSET 052107WORK OF =070515	-130.00
05/21/07	WIRE FROM HRH PRNCE ABDULL052107H BIN MUSAAD	111,982.00

Generated May 24 2007 at 12:47:46

◀ Back

received

Fig. 19

Attachment F, COUNCIL O⬤ERICAN-ISLAMIC RELATIONS, INC., 1511 ⬤treet, N.W., Suite 807
Washington, D.C.

RUN DATE: 05/09/96   COUNCIL ON AMERICAN-   PAGE   1
RUN TIME: 8:35 PM
                        BALANCE SHEET AS OF APRIL 30, 1996
                                AS OF 04/30/96

                              ASSETS

CURRENT ASSETS
105   Cash   46,509.07
135   Investment-Info Com Corp   40,000.00

       TOTAL CURRENT ASSETS   86,509.07

FIXED ASSETS
147   Furniture & Fixtures   1,705.13
150   Office Machinery & Equipt   7,500.22

       TOTAL FIXED ASSETS   9,205.35

OTHER ASSETS
190   Deposit-Rent   1,664.50

       TOTAL OTHER ASSETS   1,664.50

             TOTAL ASSETS   97,378.92
                                                 =============

                        LIABILITIES & FUND

CURRENT LIABILITIES
220   Payroll Taxes Payable   2,534.71

       TOTAL CURRENT LIABILITIES   2,534.71

LONG TERM LIABILITIES

       TOT LONG TERM LIABILITIES   0.00

             TOTAL LIABILITIES   2,534.71

FUND BALANCE
280   Retained Fund   72,837.64
285   Current Year Fund   22,006.57

       TOTAL FUND BALANCE   94,844.21

Fig. 20

Page 4
Schedule L—BALANCE SHEETS COUNCIL ON AMERICAN-ISLAMIC RELATIONS, INC. 52-1887951

		BEGINNING OF TAXABLE YEAR		END OF TAXABLE YEAR	
		(A) AMOUNT	(B) TOTAL	(A) AMOUNT	(B) TOTAL
ASSETS	1 Cash		12448.		24545.
	2 Trade notes and accounts receivable				
	(a) LESS Allowance for bad debts				
	3 Inventories				
	4 Gov't obligations (a) U.S. and instrumentalities				
	(b) State, subdivisions thereof, etc				
	5 Other current assets attach schedule				
	6 Loans to stockholders				
	7 Mortgage and real estate loans				
	8 Other investments attach schedule INFO COMM, TEXAS				40000.
	9 Building and other fixed depreciable assets	5191.		9205.	
	(a) LESS Accumulated depreciation	0.	5191.	0.	9205.
	10 Depletable assets				
	(a) LESS Accumulated depletion				
	11 Land (net of any amortization)				
	12 Intangible assets (amortizable only)				
	(a) LESS Accumulated amortization				
	13 Other assets (attach schedule) RENT DEPOSIT		1664.		1664.
	14 TOTAL ASSETS		19303.		75414.
LIABILITIES AND CAPITAL	15 Accounts payable PAYROLL TAXES PAYABLE		2591.		2577.
	16 Mortgages, notes, bonds payable in less than 1 year				
	17 Other current liabilities (attach schedule)				
	18 Loans from stockholders				
	19 Mortgages, notes, bonds payable in 1 year or more				
	20 Other liabilities (attach schedule)				
	21 Capital stock (a) Preferred stock				
	(b) Common stock				
	22 Paid-in Capital surplus (attach reconciliation)				
	23 Retained earnings Appropriated (attach schedule)				
	24 Retained earnings Unappropriated FUND BALANCE		16712.		72837.
	25 LESS Cost of treasury stock		( )		( )
	26 TOTAL LIABILITIES AND CAPITAL		19303.		75414.

Schedule M—RECONCILIATION OF INCOME AND ANALYSIS OF UNAPPROPRIATED RETAINED EARNINGS PER BOOKS
(Copy from Federal Form 1120)
Itemized entries must below must be identified by account

Schedule M-1—RECONCILIATION OF INCOME PER BOOKS WITH INCOME PER RETURN

1 Net income per books	56125.		7 Income recorded on books this year not included in this return (itemize)		
2 Federal income tax			(a) Tax-exempt interest $		
3 Excess of capital losses over capital gains					
4 Taxable income not recorded on books this year (itemize)			8 Deductions in this tax return not charged against book income this year (itemize)		
5 Expenses recorded on books this year not deducted in this return (itemize)			(a) Depreciation $		
(a) Depreciation $			(b) Depletion $		
(b) Depletion $					
			9 TOTAL of Lines 7 and 8		0.
6 TOTAL of Lines 1 through 5	56125		10 Income (Federal 990) — Line 6 less Line 9		56125

Schedule M-2—ANALYSIS OF UNAPPROPRIATED RETAINED EARNINGS PER BOOKS

1 Balance at beginning of year	16712.		5 Distributions (a) Cash		
2 Net income per books	56125.		(b) Stock		
3 Other increases (itemize)			(c) Property		
			6 Other decreases (itemize)		
			7 TOTAL of Lines 5 and 6		0.
4 TOTAL of Lines 1, 2 and 3	72837.		8 Balance at end of year (Line 4 less Line 7)		72837.

Fig. 21

ASH185

Important phone and fax numbers (Palestine Section/America).

Name/Source	Country/City	Fax	Telephone
1) Musa Abu Marzouk	Ruston	318-255-6102	318-2555534
2) Muhammad Akram	Chicago	312-434-3462	312-563-0937
3) Ahmad Yousif	Chicago	312-434-3462	312-594-3967
4) Yaser Bushnaq	Dallas	214-490-4969	214-490-4969
5) Muhammad Al-Mazin	NWE Jersy	201-279-6362	201-279-3574
6) Isma'il Elbrassei	Washington, DC.	703-922-8730	703-922-7859
7) Ghassan Dahduli	Tuocsan	602-886-8387	602-325-5121
8) Ghassan Elashi	L.A	213-391-0095	213-838-7255
9) 'Isam Al-Saraj	Washington		703-931-0211
10) 'Omar Al-Soubani	East Lansing		517-332-2163
11) Isma'il Jabir	Chicago	315-434-3462	312-423-6089
12) Muhammad 'Abbas			801-583-3325
13) Fawaz Mushtaha	Washington		703-786-7705
14) 'Izat Mansour	Ruston	318-255-6102	318-255-7038
15) Hammud Salem	Stillwater		405-744-1150
16) Nadir Jawad	Washington		703-430-2353
17) Rashid Qurman	Alabama		205-837-0450
18) Shukri Abou Baker	Indpols	317-839-1840	317-243-9520
19) Muhammad Abu 'Amriya'	L.A	213-839-0436	213-839-4851
20) Jamal Sa'id	Chicago	430-5235	312-599-5313
		Fax 430 5235	
21) 'Anan Al-Karmi	Chicago		312-561-2940
22) Muhammad Salah			
23) Ayman Saraj Al-Din	Washington, D.C	765-5569	703-237-9529
24) Ahmad Agha	Oklahoma	765-5569	405-762-7732
25) 'Omar Yeheya	C.A		408-984-1254
26) Akram Al-Kharoubi			
27) Walid Abu Sharakh	Columbia, MO		314-874-5973
28) Walid Ranu			215-977-0689
29) Ayman Sha'rawi	Canada		416-391-0324
30) Hazim Elashi	L.A		213-202-1198
31) Basman Elashi	L.A		213-838-7255
32) Nihad 'Awad	Minapolis		612-378-3086
33) Muhammad Al-Jaghlit	Wisconsin		715-835-0513
34) Nabil Al-Sa'doun	Tulsa	813-836---911	918-836-7404
35) Muhammad Al-Hanooti	New Jersy		201-392-0573

Page 2 of 3

Fig. 22

ATTACHMENT A

26. Majdi Aqel
27. Mohamed Siam, aka Abu Mahmud
28. Mohamed Anati
29. Mohamed Shbeir
30. Mohammed Faraj Al Ghul
31. Muharram Al Arifi
32. Mustafa Mahsur
33. Omar Sobeihi
34. Omar Al Ashqar
35. Qadi Hassan
36. Raed Saleh
37. Rashed Ghanoushi
38. Yussef Al Qaradawi

III. **The following are individuals/entities who are and/or were members of the US Muslim Brotherhood's Palestine Committee and/or its organizations**

1. Abdel Haleem Ashqar, aka Abdel Hassan
2. Ahmed Agha
3. Akram Kharoubi
4. Al Aqsa Educational Fund
5. American Middle Eastern League, aka AMEL
6. Ayman Ismail
7. Ayman Sharawi
8. Ayman Siraj Eddin
9. Basman Elashi
10. Bayan Elashi
11. Council on American Islamic Relations, aka CAIR
12. Dalell Mohamed
13. Fawaz Mushtaha, aka Abu Mosab
14. Fayez Idlebi
15. Ghassan Dahduli
16. Hamoud Salem
17. Hassan Sabri
18. Hazim Elashi
19. IAP Information Office
20. Ibrahim Al Samneh

List of Unindicted Co-conspirators - Page 5

331

Fig. 23

ATTACHMENT A

21. INFOCOM
22. International Computers and Communications, aka ICC
23. Islam Siam
24. Islamic Association for Palestine in North America, aka IAP
25. Islamic Association for Palestine, aka IAP
26. Ismail Elbarasse, aka Abdul Hassan, aka Abd el Hassan
27. Ismail Jaber
28. Issam El Siraj
29. Izzat Mansour
30. Jamal Said
31. Kifah Mustapha
32. Mohamed Abbas
33. Mohamed Abu Amaria
34. Mohamed El Shorbagi
35. Mohamed Akram Adlouni
36. Mohamed Al Hanooti
37. Mohamed Jaghlit
38. Mohamed Qassam Sawallha, aka Abu Obeida
39. Mohamed Salah
40. Munzer Taleb
41. Muin Shabib
42. Nader Jawad
43. Omar Ahmad, aka Omar Yehia
44. Omar El Sobani
45. Palestine Committee
46. Rashid Qurman
47. Rasmi Almallah
48. United Association for Studies and Research, aka UASR
49. Walid Abu Sharkh
50. Walid Ranu
51. Yasser Saleh Bushnaq
52. Yousef Saleh, aka Ahmed Yousef
53. Zaher Salman, aka Osama Abdullah

Fig. 24

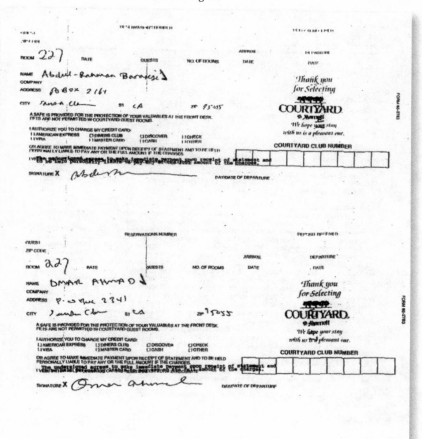

Fig. 25

Allied Asset Advisors, Inc.

January 19, 2009

<u>VIA Electronic Mail</u>

Khalid Iqbal
Council on American Islamic Relations

Dear Br. Khalid Iqbal,

On behalf of Allied Asset Advisors, a subsidiary of the North American Islamic Trust(NAIT), I firstly want to wish you a Ramadan and Eid Mubarak. As per our discussion previously, this letter is to express interest in a strategic partnership with the Council on American Islamic Relations (CAIR). We see the Council of American Islamic-Relations as one of the primary organizations in helping to establish a relationship of mutual respect between the American Community and the Muslim Community. We feel there is an opportunity to further the good work that CAIR does through initiatives that we can take.

Allied Asset Advisors, Inc. was formed in 2000 as an SEC registered investment advisor. We rolled out our first offering in June of last year, the Dow Jones Islamic Index Fund. This fund seeks to track the Dow Jones Islamic Market USA Index, which includes US equities screened according to Islamic principles. Our Board of Directors includes respected scholars and community leaders such as Dr. Muzammil Siddiqi and Abdalla Idris Ali. We have approximately $20 million under management in the fund, and plan to offer other Islamic investment products in the future. Currently, we own nearly 400 US equities, such as Walgreens, Cisco, and Exxon-Mobil. Thus we have some leverage with the companies whose shares we own. More specifically, we can communicate grievances and positions that are relevant to the well-being of the Muslim community to these corporations through shareholder resolutions, press releases, and divestitures. Moreover, if a corporation does not seem to be receptive to the grievances and concerns, we have the discretion to divest ourselves of the corporation's assets, and making it a public matter. Thus, we are able to implement an economic boycott that reflects our values and priorities, putting our money where our mouth is. You can recall this year the strong impact a major religious fund had on Walmart when it publicly divested itself of its holdings in the company due to its practices. The process is as follows:

1) Pursue the matter quietly through their public relations/press office as a result of matter.
2) Draft Shareholder Resolution
3) Submit resolution as a shareholder for annual shareholder meeting
4) Issue press release statement on stance and issue
5) Divest holdings and pressure Dow Jones to remove company from index with your assistance

We thus feel that CAIR and Allied Asset Advisors have much to offer one another in serving the needs of the Muslim community in America. We would like to develop and sustain a relationship with CAIR where we can work together in order to advocate our common core Islamic beliefs and values in our practices.

We look forward to hearing from you and welcome your ideas and future dialogue. May Allah bless you for your efforts.

Your truly,

Omar Haydar
Director of Fund Operations

Fig. 26

MAC

These are only guidelines, please formulate an energetic, passionate and convincing talk that will induce people to support this cause. Give this talk as if it were your last before meeting Allah.

Talking Points

1. Discuss the concept of Justice in Islam

2. Discuss the Sanctity of a Muslim in Islam (Sanctity more important than Khaba)

3. Discuss verses from Quran and ahadith regarding the degree previous Muslim leaders went through to release fellow Muslims prisoners.

4. Discuss the importance of providing our brothers and sisters with a fair trial.

5. Discuss the concept of Innocent until proven guilty.

6. Discuss the importance of working together to protect our community from injustice.

7. Relate Masauds case to a father or a mother in the audience. (This could be your child)

8. Point out again the importance of releasing our brothers over building a structure.

9. Relate the difference between the brothers that have turned on their brothers by pleading guilty and why we should come to the aid of those who are standing firm because of their conviction and Iman.

10. Give the trial date and the urgency of the matter (February 2nd 2004)

11. Relate the fact that this is a local case and the local community must stand up for justice.

12. Zakat money can be used for this purpose.

Jazakum Allah Khairan

Fig. 27

For Khateeb Information

Muslim Affairs Council and CAIR-MD are working to build a legal fund for the purpose of providing high quality legal representation for current and future litigation against our brothers and sisters.

Our community is under direct attack and we must join hands to defend ourselves in this time of uncertainty.

1st Case Masaud Khan –

Case: US vs Randall Royer
Trial Date: February 2nd 2004
Name: Masaud Ahmad Khan
Born: July 3, 1971 – Washington DC
Citizenship: USA
Resident: Gaithersburg, MD
Marital Status: Married, One Son (Ali)
Occupation: Designer-Student
Counsel: Mr. Bernard Grimm, Esq.
Judge: Brinkema
District: Alexandria

Innocent Until Proven Guilty Under US Law

Address: CAIR-MAC PO Box 970, Germantown, MD 20875

Fig. 28

------[Space Above This Line For Recording Data]------

PURCHASE MONEY TO THE EXTENT OF
$978,031.34

DEED OF TRUST

THIS DEED OF TRUST ("Security Instrument") is made on September 12 2002. The grantor is COUNCIL ON AMERICAN-ISLAMIC RELATIONS, a District of Columbia corp whose address is 453 New Jersey Avenue, S.E., Washington, D.C. 20001 ("Donee"). The trustee is David P. Nelson, a resident of the District of Columbia, having a business address of c/o Commercial Settlements, Inc., 1015 15th Street, N.W., Suite 300, Washington, D.C. 20005 ("Trustee"). The beneficiary is AL MAKTOUM FOUNDATION, whose address is P.O. Box 2781, Dubai, United Arab Emirates (the "Beneficiary"). This Security Instrument secures to Beneficiary: (a) the performance by Donee of all of its obligations pursuant to a letter agreement (the "Agreement") of even date herewith between Donee and Beneficiary; (b) the payment of all other sums advanced under paragraph 4 to protect the security of this Security Instrument; and (c) the performance of Donee's covenants and agreements. For this purpose, Donee irrevocably grants and conveys to Trustee, in trust, with power of sale, the following described property located in the District of Columbia:

SEE EXHIBIT A ATTACHED HERETO

which has the address of 453 New Jersey Avenue, S.E., Washington, D.C. 20001 (the "Property Address");

TOGETHER WITH all the improvements now or hereafter erected on the property, and all easements, rights, appurtenances, rents, royalties, mineral, oil and gas rights and profits, water rights and stock and all fixtures now or hereafter a part of the property. All replacements and additions shall also be covered by this Security Instrument. All of the foregoing is referred to in this Security Instrument as the "Property."

DONEE's COVENANTS that Donee is lawfully seized of the estate hereby conveyed and has the right to grant and convey the Property, and that the Property is unencumbered, except for encumbrances of record. Donee warrants and will defend generally the title to the Property against all claims and demands, subject to any encumbrances of record.

THIS SECURITY INSTRUMENT combines uniform covenants for national use and non-uniform covenants with limited variations by jurisdiction to constitute a uniform security instrument covering real property.

UNIFORM COVENANTS. Donee and Beneficiary covenant and agree as follows:

1.   **Charges; Liens.** Donee shall pay all taxes, assessments, charges, fines and impositions attributable to the Property which may attain priority over this Security Instrument, on time directly to the person owed payment. Donee shall promptly furnish to Beneficiary all notices of amounts to be paid under this paragraph. If Donee makes these payments directly, Donee shall promptly furnish to Beneficiary receipts evidencing the payments.

Donee shall promptly discharge any lien which has priority over this Security Instrument unless Donee: (a) agrees in writing to the payment of the obligation secured by the lien in a manner acceptable to Beneficiary; (b) contests in good faith the lien by, or defends against enforcement of the lien in, legal proceedings which in the Beneficiary's opinion operate to prevent the enforcement of the lien or forfeiture of any part of the Property; or (c) secures from the holder of the lien an agreement satisfactory to Beneficiary subordinating the lien to this Security Instrument. If Beneficiary determines that any part of the Property is subject to a lien which may attain priority over this Security Instrument, Beneficiary may give Donee a notice identifying the lien. Donee shall satisfy the lien or take one or more of the actions set forth above within 10 days of the giving of notice.

2.   **Hazard Insurance.** Donee shall keep the improvements now existing or hereafter erected on the Property insured against loss by fire, hazards included within the term "extended coverage" and any other hazards for which Beneficiary requires insurance. This insurance shall be maintained in the amounts and for the periods that Beneficiary requires. The insurance carrier providing the insurance shall be chosen by Donee subject to Beneficiary's approval which shall not be unreasonably withheld.

All insurance policies and renewals shall be acceptable to Beneficiary and shall include a standard mortgage clause. Beneficiary shall have the right to hold the policies and renewals. If Beneficiary requires, Donee shall promptly give to Beneficiary all receipts of paid premiums and renewal notices. In the event of loss, Donee shall give prompt notice to the insurance carrier and Beneficiary. Beneficiary may make proof of loss if not made promptly by Donee.

Unless Beneficiary and Donee otherwise agree in writing, insurance proceeds shall be applied to restoration or repair of the Property damaged, if the restoration or repair is economically feasible and Beneficiary's security is not lessened. If the restoration or repair is not economically feasible or Beneficiary's security would be lessened, the insurance

$1,000,000.00

Page 1 of 5

Commercial Settlements, Inc.
1015 15th Street, NW
Suite 300
Washington, DC 20005

GOAM 721526.1
August 2, 2002

337

Fig. 29

instrument is recorded. Without conveyance of the Property, the successor trustee shall succeed to all the title, power and duties conferred upon Trustee herein and by applicable law.

19. Riders to this Security Instrument. If one or more riders are executed by Donee and recorded together with this Security Instrument, the covenants and agreements of each such rider shall be incorporated into and shall amend and supplement the covenants and agreements of this Security Instrument as if the rider(s) were a part of this Security Instrument. [Check applicable box(es)]

☐ Adjustable Rate Rider   ☐ Condominium Rider   ☐ 2-4 Family Rider

☐ Graduated Payment Rider   ☐ Planned Unit Development Rider

☐ Other(s) [specify]

BY SIGNING BELOW, Donee accepts and agrees to the terms and covenants contained in this Security Instrument and in any rider(s) executed by Donee and recorded with it.

Donee:

COUNCIL ON AMERICAN-ISLAMIC RELATIONS

a _Omar Ahmad_

By:_____ [SEAL]

State of California
DISTRICT OF ~~COLUMBIA~~) SS: Santa Clara

I, _Paresh Afriwawala_, a Notary Public in and for the above jurisdiction, do hereby certify that _Omar M. Ahmad_, who is personally well known to me as the _Chairman_ of COUNCIL ON AMERICAN-ISLAMIC RELATIONS, a _District of Columbia_ corp., the party named as the Grantor and Donee, executed the foregoing instrument, bearing the date of August ____, 2002, for the purposes contained therein in the capacity therein described, and on behalf of the Donee/Grantor named therein, given under my hand and seal this ____ day of August, 2002.

My commission expires: _Feb 15th 2005_

_____
Notary Public

PARESH AFRICAWALA
Commission # 1291088
Notary Public - California
Santa Clara County
My Comm. Expires Feb 18, 2005

GOAN721834.5
August 5, 2002

Fig. 30

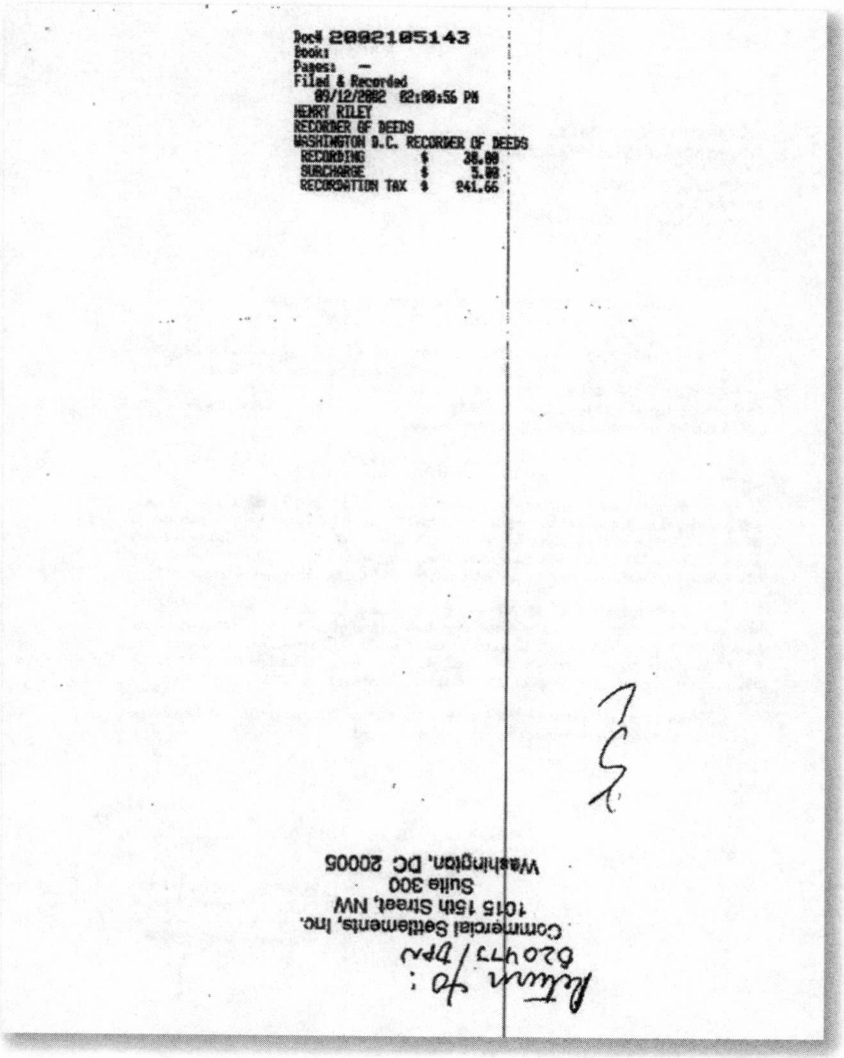

Doc# 2002105143
Book:
Pages: —
Filed & Recorded
09/12/2002 02:00:56 PM
HENRY RILEY
RECORDER OF DEEDS
WASHINGTON D.C. RECORDER OF DEEDS
RECORDING $ 30.00
SURCHARGE $ 5.00
RECORDATION TAX $ 241.66

Return to:
020473/DPM
Commercial Settlements, Inc.
1015 15th Street, NW
Suite 300
Washington, DC 20005

Fig. 31

Doc# 2002105141

RECORDING REQUESTED BY
AND WHEN RECORDED MAIL TO:

WINSTON & STRAWN
200 Park Avenue
New York, New York 10166-4193
Attn: Jean M. Migdal, Esq.

TERMINATION OF MEMORANDUM OF LEASE
AND AGREEMENT TO PURCHASE

THIS TERMINATION OF MEMORANDUM OF LEASE AND AGREEMENT TO PURCHASE (the "Agreement") is made as of the 12th day of August, 2002, by and between THE UNITED BANK OF KUWAIT PLC, with an address at 7 Baker Street, London, W1U 8EG (hereinafter referred to as "Seller/Lessor"), and COUNCIL ON AMERICAN-ISLAMIC RELATIONS (hereinafter referred to as "Buyer/Lessee").

WITNESSETH:

Seller/Lessor and Buyer/Lessee have previously entered into a certain Lease ("Lease") and Agreement to Purchase ("Agreement to Purchase") each dated June 24, 1999, pursuant to which Seller/Lessor leased to Buyer/Lessee, and agreed to sell to Buyer/Lessee, that certain real property commonly known as 453 New Jersey Ave., S.E., Washington, D.C. located in the City of Washington, District of Columbia and more particularly described therein (the "Property").

Pursuant to the Lease and Agreement to Purchase, Seller/Lessor and Buyer/Lessee executed a (i) Memorandum of Lease and an Agreement to Purchase, which was recorded on June 25, 1999, in the office of the Recorder of Deeds by the D.C. Treasurer as Instrument No. 9900057664; and (ii) a Special Warranty Deed, which was recorded on June 25, 1999, in the office of the Recorder of Deeds by the D.C. Treasurer as Instrument No. 9900057663.

Seller/Lessor and Buyer/Lessee hereby agree that such Memorandum of Lease and Agreement to Purchase be terminated and discharged of record.

SIGNATURE PAGE FOLLOWS

Return to:

Commercial Settlements, Inc.
1015 15th Street, NW
Suite 300
Washington, DC 20005

NY:743996.1

340

Fig. 32

APPENDIX I

TRANSACTION COST FOR CAIR REAL ESTATE RESTRUCTURING
Currently owned properties

Property	Sale Price/ Current market Value	Transfer Tax Rate	Total
205 K Street			
203 K Street			
929 2nd Street			
923 2nd Street	1,825,000		
919 2nd Street	$500K		
917 2nd Street	$660K		
208 Parker St.	$410K		
210 Parker St.	$419K		
453 New Jersey Ave S.E.	$7,400,000		
TOTAL	$9,895,320	2.6%	$257,278.32

PROPERTIES IN PROCESS OF AQUIRING IN NEAR FUTURE

Property	Offered or asking price	Transfer Tax Rate	Total
209 K Street	- $500 K		
207 K Street	~$ 500 K		
921 2nd Street	$650K (Owner is now asking for $850K)		
	$1,850,000	2.6%	$48,100

Other Cost:

No	Other Items	Details	Cost
1	Forming Holding Company LLC	Filing Articles	$150
		Annual CT fee	$250
2	Form 453 N.J. Ave LLC	Filing Articles	$150
		Annual CT fee	$250
3.	Legal Fees - Sandler Reiff & Young		$4,500
4.	Bank fees?		$?
5.	Bank legal fees?		$?
6.	Other Office charges		$500
	TOTAL		$5,800

Fig. 33

Schedule B (Form 990, 990-EZ, or 990-PF) (2008)

Page **1** of **7** of Part I

Name of organization
COUNCIL ON AMERICAN-ISLAMIC RELATIONS, INC

Employer identification number
52-1887951

(c) Aggregate contributions	(d) Type of contribution
$ 600,000.	Person [X] Payroll [ ] Noncash [ ] (Complete Part II if there is a noncash contribution.)

(c) Aggregate contributions	(d) Type of contribution
$ 219,563.	Person [X] Payroll [ ] Noncash [ ] (Complete Part II if there is a noncash contribution.)

(c) Aggregate contributions	(d) Type of contribution
$ 199,980.	Person [X] Payroll [ ] Noncash [ ] (Complete Part II if there is a noncash contribution.)

(c) Aggregate contributions	(d) Type of contribution
$ 100,000.	Person [X] Payroll [ ] Noncash [ ] (Complete Part II if there is a noncash contribution.)

(c) Aggregate contributions	(d) Type of contribution
$ 99,985.	Person [X] Payroll [ ] Noncash [ ] (Complete Part II if there is a noncash contribution.)

(c) Aggregate contributions	(d) Type of contribution
$ 99,000.	Person [X] Payroll [ ] Noncash [ ] (Complete Part II if there is a noncash contribution.)

Schedule B (Form 990, 990-EZ, or 990-PF) (2008)

Fig. 34

THIS IS A COPY OF A LIVE RETURN FROM SMIPS. OFFICIAL USE ONLY.

Form 990

Return of Organization Exempt From Income Tax

Under section 501(c), 527, or 4947(a)(1) of the Internal Revenue Code (except black lung benefit trust or private foundation)

▶ The organization may have to use a copy of this return to satisfy state reporting requirements.

OMB No. 1545-0047

2006

Open to Public Inspection

Department of the Treasury
Internal Revenue Service

A For the 2006 calendar year, or tax year beginning _____ and ending _____

B Check if applicable:

C Name of organization: COUNCIL ON AMERICAN-ISLAMIC RELATIONS, INC

Number and street (or P.O. box if mail is not delivered to street address): 453 NEW JERSEY AVENUE SE   Room/suite: 04

City or town, state or country, and ZIP + 4: WASHINGTON, DC 20003

D Employer Identification number: 52-1887951

E Telephone number: 202-488-8787

F Accounting method: ☐ Cash ☒ Accrual ☐ Other

● Section 501(c)(3) organizations and 4947(a)(1) nonexempt charitable trusts must attach a completed Schedule A (Form 990 or 990-EZ).

G Website: ▶ WWW.CAIR.COM

J Organization type (check only one) ▶ ☒ 501(c) (4) ◀ (insert no.) ☐ 4947(a)(1) or ☐ 527

K Check here ▶ ☐ if the organization is not a 509(a)(3) supporting organization and its gross receipts are normally not more than $25,000. A return is not required, but if the organization chooses to file a return, be sure to file a complete return.

H and I are not applicable to section 527 organizations

H(a) Is this a group return for affiliates? ☐ Yes ☒ No

H(b) If "Yes," enter number of affiliates ▶ N/A

H(c) Are all affiliates included? N/A ☐ Yes ☐ No (If "No," attach a list.)

H(d) Is this a separate return filed by an organization covered by a group ruling? ☐ Yes ☒ No

I Group Exemption Number ▶ N/A

M Check ▶ ☐ if the organization is not required to attach Sch. B (Form 990, 990-EZ, or 990-PF).

L Gross receipts: Add lines 6b, 8b, 9b, and 10b to line 12 ▶ 3,086,514.

Part I Revenue, Expenses, and Changes in Net Assets or Fund Balances

1	Contributions, gifts, grants, and similar amounts received:			
a	Contributions to donor advised funds	1a		
b	Direct public support (not included on line 1a)	1b	2,179,394.	
c	Indirect public support (not included on line 1a)	1c		
d	Government contributions (grants) (not included on line 1a)	1d	300,000.	
	Total (add lines 1a through 1d) (cash $ 2,479,394. noncash $)		1e	2,479,394.
2	Program service revenue including government fees and contracts (from Part VII, line 93)		2	334,739.
3	Membership dues and assessments		3	
4	Interest on savings and temporary cash investments		4	41,383.
5	Dividends and interest from securities		5	
6 a	Gross rents SEE STATEMENT 1	6a	198,766.	
b	Less: rental expenses SEE STATEMENT 2	6b	325,762.	
c	Net rental income or (loss). Subtract line 6b from line 6a		6c	-126,996.
7	Other investment income (describe ▶)		7	
8 a	Gross amount from sales of assets other than inventory (A) Securities / (B) Other	8a		
b	Less: cost or other basis and sales expenses	8b		
c	Gain or (loss) (attach schedule)	8c		
d	Net gain or (loss). Combine line 8c, columns (A) and (B)		8d	
9	Special events and activities (attach schedule). If any amount is from gaming, check here ▶ ☐			
a	Gross revenue (not including $ 89,775. of contributions reported on line 1b)	9a		
b	Less: direct expenses other than fundraising expenses	9b		
c	Net income or (loss) from special events. Subtract line 9b from line 9a SEE STATEMENT 3		9c	
10 a	Gross sales of inventory, less returns and allowances	10a		
b	Less: cost of goods sold	10b		
c	Gross profit or (loss) from sales of inventory (attach schedule). Subtract line 10b from line 10a		10c	
11	Other revenue (from Part VII, line 103)		11	32,232.
12	Total revenue. Add lines 1e, 2, 3, 4, 5, 6c, 7, 8d, 9c, 10c, and 11		12	2,760,752.
13	Program services (from line 44, column (B))		13	1,798,268.
14	Management and general (from line 44, column (C))		14	445,198.
15	Fundraising (from line 44, column (D))		15	678,223.
16	Payments to affiliates (attach schedule)		16	
17	Total expenses. Add lines 16 and 44, column (A)		17	2,921,689.
18	Excess or (deficit) for the year. Subtract line 17 from line 12		18	-160,937.
19	Net assets or fund balances at beginning of year (from line 73, column (A))		19	4,916,881.
20	Other changes in net assets or fund balances (attach explanation)		20	0.
21	Net assets or fund balances at end of year. Combine lines 18, 19, and 20		21	4,755,944.

LHA For Privacy Act and Paperwork Reduction Act Notice, see the separate instructions.

Form 990 (2006)

THIS IS A COPY OF A LIVE RETURN FROM SMIPS. OFFICIAL USE ONLY.

343

Fig. 35

Meeting Notes for
Robert S. Mueller, III
Director, Federal Bureau of Investigation
Meeting with Arab/Muslim American, Sikh, and South Asian Leaders
February 26, 2007 at 11:00 a.m.

Attendees

- Nidal Ibrahim, Executive Director of Arab-American Institute (AAI)
- Rebecca Abou-Chedid, Director of Government Relations of Arab-American Institute (AAI)
- Kareem Shora, National Executive Director of the American-Arab Anti Discrimination Committee (ADC)
- Laila Bashir, Legal Advisor and Internship Coordinator of the American-Arab Anti Discrimination Committee (ADC)
- Imam Magid, Vice President of the Islamic Society of North America (ISNA)
- Sayyid M. Syeed, National Director of the Islamic Society of North America (ISNA) Office of Interfaith & Communities Alliances
- Salam Al-Marayati, Executive Director of the Muslim Public Affairs Council (MPAC)
- Haris Tarin, Muslim Public Affairs Council (MPAC)
- Farhana Khera, Executive Director of Muslim Advocates
- Umbreen Bhatti, member of National Association of Muslim Lawyers sister entity of Muslim Advocates
- Rajbir S. Datta, Associate Director of the Sikh American Legal Defense and Education Fund (SALDEF)
- Manjit Singh, Co-Founder and Chairman of the Board of Directors of the Sikh American Legal Defense and Education Fund (SALDEF)
- Chip Poncy, Director for Strategic Policy, U.S. Department of the Treasury

- John Pistole, Deputy Director
- Lee Rawls, Chief of Staff
- John Miller, Assistant Director Office of Public Affairs (OPA)
- A. Brett Hovington, Chief of OPA Community Relations Unit
- Eric Velez-Villar, Section Chief, Terrorist Screening Center

Fig. 36

FBI Responses to Issues Raised at the November 1, 2006

- Initiate a program where New Agent Trainees visit a local Mosque, similar to New Agent Trainees currently visiting the Holocaust Museum.

  OPA toured the All Dulles Area Muslim Society (ADAMS) Center located in Sterling VA and the Islamic Center of Washington to discuss with the Director's of both facilities the possibility of developing a block of instructions for new agents. This would also include touring their facilities to learn about the mosque and Muslim culture.

- Conduct frequent Town Hall meetings within the Muslim community and include presentations on topics other than terrorism, such as identity theft, gangs, and civil rights. Include Arab-American, Muslim, Sikh, and South Asian citizens as participants in Citizens' Academies-

  Since the last meeting there have been 12 town hall meetings in FBI field offices such as St. Louis, Springfield, Cincinnati, New York, Los Angeles, Sacramento, San Diego, Tampa, and New Haven.

  The national leaders will be advised of upcoming Citizen's Academies in their local regions.

- Develop an FBI Camp for high school age Muslim youth

  OPA is in discussion with the Boys and Girls Club of America about developing a camp for children from various ethnic groups.

- Create a video about the FBI for distribution to the Muslim Community

  OPA will discuss with the Department of Justice Civil Rights Division the idea of creating a DVD about the FBI and the laws governing civil rights issues. The DVD would provide a brief overview of the FBI and how the FBI educates their employees on the Arab-American/Muslim culture.

Fig. 37

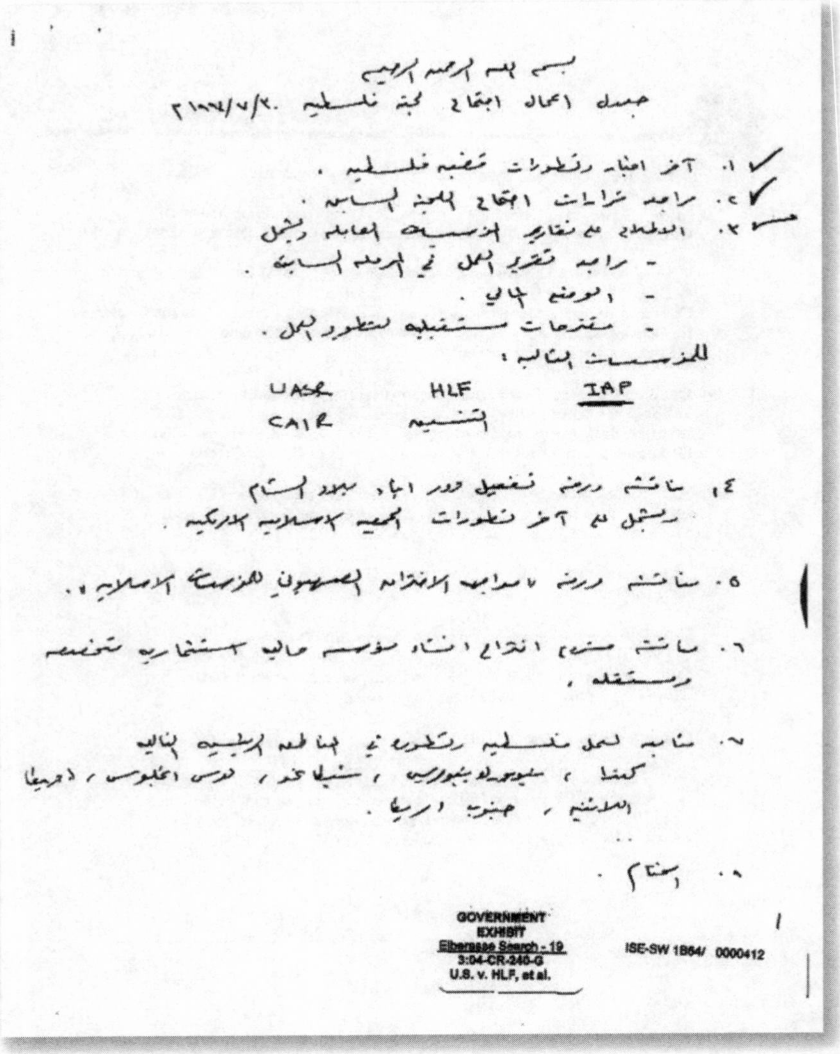

بسم الله الرحمن الرحيم

جدول اعمال اجتماع لجنة فلسطين ٢/٧/١٩٩٢

١. آخر اخبار وتطورات قضية فلسطين .

٢. متابعة قرارات اجتماع اللجنة السابقة .

٣. الاطلاع مع تقارير المؤسسة العامة وتقييم
   - متابعة تقدير العمل في المرحلة السابقة .
   - الوضع حالي .
   - مقترحات مستقبلية لتطوير العمل .

المؤسسات وممثلوها :

UASR   HLF   IAP

CAIR   تنسيق

٤. مناقشة وضع تفعيل دور ابار بعد ان تم
   التسجيل مع آخر تطورات الجمعية الاسلامية الامريكية .

٥. مناقشة وضع واسلوب الاعلام المصمون للمؤسسة الاسلامية .

٦. مناقشة منهج انتزاع انشاء مؤسسة مالية استثمارية تنفيذية
   ومستقلة .

٧. متابعة عمل فلسطين وتطويره في اماكن اخرى اساسية مثل ،
   كندا ، سلوفاكيا بلغاريا ، شيلي ، قبرص ، اليمن ، افريقيا ،
   بلجيكا ، حبشة ، اوروبا .

٨. متنوعات .

Fig. 38

Bate #ISE-SW 1B64/ 0000412

In the name of God, the Beneficent, the Merciful

Meeting Agenda for the Palestine Committee 7/30/1994

1- √ Latest news and developments of the Cause of Palestine.
2- √ Reviewing resolutions of previous Committee meeting.
3- √ Reviewing reports of the working organizations and it includes:
    - Reviewing work report of the previous stage.
    -Financial situation.
    - Future suggestions to develop work of the following organizations:
        IAP   HLF   UASR
        Coordination CAIR

4- Discussing the paper of activation of the role of the sons of the Levant which includes the latest developments of the American Islamic Society.

5- Discussing the paper of the Zionist infiltration of Islamic organizations.

6- Discussing the suggestion to establish a financial investment company that is specialized and independent.

7- A follow-up of the Palestine activism and its development in the following main regions:
  Canada, New York-New Jersey, Chicago, Los Angeles, Latin America, South America

8- Conclusion.

6

Fig. 39

U.S. Department of Justice

Federal Bureau of Investigation

In Reply, Please Refer to
File No. N/A

P.O. Box 568801
Oklahoma City, OK 73156

October 8, 2008

Dear MCOP Invitee:

On behalf of the Oklahoma City Field Office and the
Federal Bureau of Investigation, I thank you for your desire to
participate in the quarterly meeting of the Muslim Community
Outreach Program (MCOP) to have been held on October 16th, 2008.
Regrettably, due to circumstances beyond my control, the meeting
will be postponed until further notice as a result of the planned
participation by the Oklahoma chapter of the Council on American-
Islamic Relations' (CAIR).

This event was to have been hosted by Saleem Quraishi
and the Islamic Center of Oklahoma City at their new mosque
located at 3201 NW 48th Street, Oklahoma City, Oklahoma. The FBI
deeply appreciates their gracious offer to host the event. We
apologize for any inconvenience caused to the hosts or any of the
attendees by the short notice of this cancellation.

The Federal Bureau of Investigation sincerely
appreciates the importance of this event in that it brings
together the Muslim community and Law Enforcement, allowing both
groups a better understanding of the other. This meeting also
empowers American Muslims by ensuring they understand their civil
rights as guaranteed by our Constitution.

As you know, members of the United States Government,
especially those serving in a law enforcement capacity, have a
duty to be judicious in our activities as representatives of the
Federal Government. As a result, if CAIR wishes to pursue an
outreach relationship with the FBI, certain issues must be
addressed to the satisfaction of the FBI. Unfortunately, these
issues can not be addressed at the local level and must be
addressed by the CAIR-National Office in Washington, D.C.

Fig. 40

The FBI continues to be an ardent supporter of maintaining valuable dialogue with American Muslim communities and its leaders to forge new and enhanced relationships at both the local and the national level. The goal of the FBI's outreach efforts is to eliminate retaliatory, hate-motivated crimes against Arab/Muslim-American individuals and to enlist the American Muslim communities' cooperation in the global war on terrorism.

It is hoped the issues with CAIR can be resolved in a expeditious manner. In the near future the FBI will be contacting you to reschedule this important event.

Sincerely,

James E. Finch
Special Agent in Charge
Oklahoma City Field Office

2

Fig. 41

S E C R E T

NORTH AMERICAN ISLAMIC TRUST (NAIT)

Some of the current leaders of the MSA were members of the "Muslim Brotherhood" in their respective home countries in the Middle East and Egypt prior to establishing a residence in the U.S. and their subsequent assimilation into the Muslim community in the U.S. was through ISNA, the MSA, Organization of Arab Students, MAYA and NAIT. These individuals have moved to leadership roles within NAIT and its related Muslim organizations which means they are in a position to direct the activities and support of Muslims in the U.S. for the Islamic Revolution.

The following list identifies NAIT leaders from public records since its incorporation in 1973:

(1) HISHAM ALTALIB, 3702 West 11th Avenue, Gary, Indiana 46404 (headquarters of the MSA of U.S. and Canada in 1973). ALTALIB was an incorporator for NAIT, date of birth [   ] current address 1514 Farsta Court, Reston, Virginia 22090, previous address 6156 Greenfield Court, Lanham, Maryland, employment

b6
b7C

(2) MOHAMMED M. SHAMMA: 3572 Grandin Road, Cincinnati, Ohio 45226 (address in 1973 as an incorporator of NAIT).

(3) AHMAD SAKR: 1205 Chetenham Drive, Apartment 2B, Glen Ellyn, Illinois 60137, address provided in 1973 when SAKR was an officer of NAIT and also on the Board of Directors.

(4) JAMAL AL-BARZINJI: Male, Date of Birth [   ] Height 5' 10", weight 180 Pounds, hair black, eyes brown, [   ] vehicle registered 1986 Subaru station wagon, Virginia License [   ] current address 12710 Longleaf Lane, Herndon, Virginia 22070 (in 1973 and officer of NAIT address utilized Post Office Box 19832, Louisiana State University, Baton Rouge, Louisiana 70803. Prior address used is 1518 Park Grand Court, Reston, Virginia and also listed a prior residence, street unknown, in Atlanta, Georgia. (An officer in NAIT).

S E C R E T

43

Fig. 42

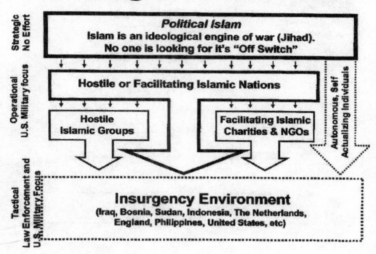

Fig. 43

Counterintelligence Field Activity
251 18th Street
Suite 700
Arlington, VA 22202

TO: PAUL SPERRY   FROM: BILL GAWTHROP

FAX #: 70▓▓▓▓▓▓▓   PAGES: 3 (inc. cover sheet)

RE: DATE:

PHONE: FAX #: 703.699.7498

☐ Urgent ☒ For Review ☐ Please Comment ☐ Please Reply ☐ For Signature

NGO   is   NON GOVERNMENT ORG.

Classification

Fig. 44

Congress of the United States
Washington, DC 20515
January 30, 2009

BEWARE of CAIR

Dear Colleague:

Members should think twice before meeting with representatives of CAIR (Council on American-Islamic Relations). The FBI has cut ties with them. There are indications that this group has connections to HAMAS.

We encourage you and your staff to read the article below regarding this matter.

Sincerely,

Sue Myrick   Pete Hoekstra   John Shadegg

Paul Broun   Trent Franks

FBI Cuts Off CAIR Over Hamas Questions

by Mary Jacoby (*IPT News*)
January 29, 2009

http://www.investigativeproject.org/article/985

The Federal Bureau of Investigation (FBI) has cut off contacts with the Council on American-Islamic Relations (CAIR) amid mounting concern about the Muslim advocacy group's roots in a Hamas-support network, the Investigative Project on Terrorism has learned.

The decision to end contacts with CAIR was made quietly last summer as federal prosecutors prepared for a second trial of the Holy Land Foundation for Relief and Development (HLF), an Islamic charity accused of providing money and political support to the terrorist group Hamas, according to people with knowledge of the matter.

CAIR and its chairman emeritus, Omar Ahmad, were named un-indicted co-conspirators in the HLF case. Both Ahmad and CAIR's current national executive director, Nihad Awad, were revealed on government wiretaps as having been active participants in early Hamas-related organizational meetings in the United States. During testimony, FBI agent Lara Burns described CAIR as a front organization.

Hamas is a US-designated foreign terrorist organization, and it's been illegal since 1995 to provide support to it within the United States.

The decision to end contacts with CAIR is a significant policy change for the FBI. For years, the FBI worked with the national organization and its state chapters to address Muslim community concerns about the potential for hate crimes and other civil liberty violations in the wake of the September 11, 2001 terrorist attacks.

Fig. 45

(7)

Work to be Implemented during the year (91-1992)	Allotted Time	Implementation	Follow-up
Eleventh: The Dawa' Committee:			
152 - Writing the constitution of "The Dawa' Center" and registering it.	6/91	M. Committee	Office
153 - Preparing an informational brochure about the center and distributing it.	6/91	M. Committee	Office
154 - Installing a telephone computer line and another regular one.	5/91	M. Committee	Office
155 - Purchasing a computer specialized for sending and receiving.	5/91	M. Committee	Office
156 - Establishing an audio-visual library and making it available for the Dawa'.	12/91	Committee	M. Committee
157 - Making written material on Dawa' available for whoever needs it.	3/92	Committee	M. Committee
158 - Preparing a list of speakers and making it available to the centers.	8/91	Committee	M. Committee
Twelfth: South America Committee:			
159 - Tallying the studies about South [America] and the Caribbean.	Within a month	Committee	M. Committee
160 - Preparing the studies about the remaining cities.	Within the year	M. Cities	M. Committee
161 - Completing the identification of the levels of the Brazilian and Gayana brothers.	3/92	M. Brazil	M. Committee
162 - Following-up on the cities by mail, phone and fax.	Periodically / Periodically	M. Committee / M. Group	Office / M. Committee
163 - Sending the bulletins, books and tapes to whoever needs them.	Periodically	Committee	M. Committee
164 - Sending financial and in-kind assistance to Gayana.	9/91	Q. Financial	M. Committee
165 - Securing support for an imam of a mosque and a teacher at the institute in Gayana.	Within the year	Q. Financial	M. Committee
166 - Securing a computer and tape-dubbing machine for Brazil.	Within the year	Committee	M. Committee
167 - Attending the major activities South America.	End of '92	M. Brazil	M. Committee
168 - Opening open Usras in Brazil	Within the year	Committee	M. Committee
169 - Organizing the Caribbean group in cooperation with Sh. New York.			

Fig. 46

VISITORS REGISTER

Date	Name	Company/Address	To See	Arrive	Depart
4/12	April Fattinner	PAYCITY	Isra + Khalis	1245	
4/13	Abdelmonem Said	AC-AHRAM	Ghada Awad	3:30	
4/15	April Fattinner	Paychey	Isra	1215	
4/12	Galen Mohammad	Re-Paid Legal Svcs	...dijad...	11:50	12:10
	Akil Verun	...	Khalil / Jabal	2:05	
	Tom Khardous	Blue Wire media	...	3:35	
	Guy Wilhelm	Cushman Jair			
4/21	Hosein Nehistan	Prince William Muslim PAC PO Box 3337 Manassas VA	Hassun Mansur	1:50	
	Muneer Bajp	Prince William Muslim Pac	Hassar Mansur	2:05	
4/21	Amina Goneer	813 Flannery Cn.St, MD	Rabiah Ahmed	4:10	
	Sebastiana Gianci	1324 Vermont	Hassam/Ali	11	
4/22	Waser Elya Sebbiri	13619 Dauphin Way	Ninah Anno	12:00	
4/22	Omar Abu-Ali	Saudi Embassy	Dr. Nihad	12:00	
4/23	Shahar Ali	MCB (VA)	Dr. Nihad		

355

Fig. 47

Nihad Awad

From:	Corey Saylor
Sent:	Wednesday, January 03, 2007 8:32 AM
To:	Ibrahim Hooper; Hamza El-Nakhal; Hussam Ayloush; rashid01@comcast.net; SacVal; dhnakhal@hotmail.com; Omar Ahmad; fouad@khatib.us; North California; Nihad Awad; Parvez Ahmed; Affad Shaikh; Munira Syeda; Edgar Hopida; arsalan@cair-net.org; arehab@yahoo.com; florida@cair-florida.org; dawud07@yahoo.com
Subject:	RE: What now

I'd argue for right-wingers.

We need to become more methodical in responding to this, right now it appears, in my humble opinion, rather ad hoc:

We need to define clear objectives: meet with Boxer, hit Kaufman and Horowitz. Are we deciding to burn this bridge completely and go all out against her or are we going to take the hit and seek to repair things over time? The answer to the question dictates alot of our public statements.

We need people who are specialized, assign a core team comprising people assigned to take the lead
a) politically (meet with Boxer, generate support from friendly elected officials, damage control with other elected officials)
b) media (the key person or persons who do interviews, maybe generate stories that we can have a little more message control in)
c) community (generate letters of support from friendly community leaders, identifying and contacting donors in the lists I sent last week)
d) opposition (prepare hit sheets on Horowitz, Kaufman, Frontpage mag)

I beleive the CA response is key to this, so these people in a, b, and c should be CA based, with outsiders as advisors

This core team should teleconference daily. No more than ½ hour to update from their area of responsibility and then decide next 24-hour action plan.

Sen. Boxer is going to dig in her heels, to reverse herself now publicly would be bad and I'm not sure if our political ground strength in CA is strong enough to make it hurt enough. She won her last election with a low percentage, 58%, and I believe she is up for re-election in 08.

Corey P. Saylor
National Legislative Director
Council on American-Islamic Relations
Cell: (571) 278-4658
E-Mail: csaylor@cair.com
****
What They Say About CAIR:
http://www.cair.com/whattheysayaboutcair.asp

Blog:
http://coreysaylor.blogspot.com/

-----Original Message-----
From: Ibrahim Hooper
Sent: Wed 1/3/2007 6:59 AM
To: Hamza El-Nakhal; Hussam Ayloush; rashid01@comcast.net; SacVal; dhnakhal@hotmail.com; Omar Ahmad; fouad@khatib.us; North California; Nihad Awad; Parvez Ahmed; Affad Shaikh; Munira Syeda; Edgar Hopida; Corey Saylor; arsalan@cair-net.org; arehab@yahoo.com; florida@cair-florida.org; dawud07@yahoo.com
Subject: Re: What now

1

Fig. 48

CAIR Staff Meeting
First Tuesday of the Month
5-01-07
Meeting stated at 11:10 a.m.   Ending at 12:10 pm

Nihad opened the meeting by thanking Nailiah Abdul Qayyum, and other volunteers from PGMA, for coming out volunteering their time on Sunday, April 28, 2007, and spending three to four hours helping to update the names and addresses, by inputting data for the membership Department.

The following departments were asked to speak on their progress for this years first Quarter.

Membership/Fundraising: Tena Qureshi
4 Volunteers from PGMA came in on Sunday, with Najlaa and Nailah for three to four hours to help processes mail for the Membership Department. Letters of appreciation to be sent out to them.
CAIR has a total of 5, 133 members.

Khalid will take forty tubs of return turn mail will be going to CAIR MD/VA to be processed.

Cleaning up mailing list, have 8,500 pieces of mail that, have not been processed .

COVIA setting up new vendor accounts.

Civil Rights Khadija Athman
  Cases completed 2,400 .
  - How many cases documented
  - How many resolved
  - How many worked on cases
  - How many cases pending or closed.
  - How many referred out
  - How many pending: positive or negative.

Br. Riazi working on database with Chapters, he will check to see if it is possible to upload the database, so chapters can respond.

Airport profiling:
  - **Resolved**
  - 116 in April
  - 42 referred – out
  - 37 documented
  - 15 pending
  - 22 resolved

1

Fig. 49

\
Civil Rights: Arsalan Iftikhar
  Civil Rights Manual
  Other issues
  Arsalan's contact at FBI would like to visit the office to investigate threats

Government Affairs: Corey Saylor

Civic Guide needs to be published before September 2007
June 26 – Hill Advocacy Day on the Hill
Join in with Torture Awareness Month ACLU, Amnesty International:

Appointments with:
  - Father Francis Tiso, Associate Director, Secretariat for Ecumenical and Inter-religious Affairs, US Conference of Catholic Bishops

  - Rabbi Arthur A. Waskow :Founder: The Shalom Center and Director Progressive Faith Media:

  - Joe Leonard, Executive Director of Black Caucus

  - Wade Henderson: President and CEO of the Leadership Conference on Civil Rights (LCCR) and Counselor to the Leadership Conference on Civil Rights Education Fund (LCCREF)

Communications: Ibrahim Hooper/ Rabiah Ahmed/Amina Rubin

Preparing new guidelines for external communications. New website to be launched July 1st.
Action Alerts overlapping:

Muslim CAIR Campaign:
To join in with other Muslims for *Susan G. Komen Race for the Cure* -- On Saturday, June 2, 2007.
  - CAIR Hunger Awareness
  - PSA
  - Media Guide

Research: Dr. Mohamed Nimer
`Final touch ups for *Islamophobia and Anti Americanism* Book
Panel discussion with Fr. Tiso
Waiting for Board to OK Two Survives.

Events:
  Amr Khaled: May 20, 2007 9:30 -10 p.m. with ISNA

2

Fig. 50

OIC Meeting update
Banquet updates

Internship:
June 4 – August 10th 2007: Need 6 interns

Adminstration: Najila
Guest book sign in sheet.
Taking empowerment courses
Seminars offered by CAIR for employees

Security Update: Khalid Iqbal
Security update for the office.
Khalid to work on: 1) new doors on E Street and in reception area 2) buzz-in
system 3) magnetic card reader system

3

Fig. 51

A Media Analysis on Glenn Beck's Statements on Islam and Muslims aired on CNN between
September 1, 2006 and December 31, 2006

Produced by the CAIR National Communication Department
January 7, 2007

I. **Introduction:**

The Council on American-Islamic Relations, CAIR, is America's leading Islamic
advocacy group whose mission it is to enhance understanding of Islam, encourage
dialogue, protect civil liberties, empower American Muslims, and build coalitions that
promote justice and mutual understanding.

Over the past 12 years, CAIR has successfully worked with several media outlets in to
avoid misrepresentation of our community.

Recently, CAIR has received numerous complains from its members regarding CNN's
Glenn Beck Show. Many in our community have written to CAIR, expressing concern
over the regular anti-Muslim guests that frequent the show and the inflammatory language
used to discuss issues relating to Islam and the Muslim community.

In this report, CAIR's communication department analyzes the treatment of Islam and
Muslims in Glenn Beck's show over the last 4 months. Our conclusion is that the Glenn
Beck's coverage of Islam and Muslims has displayed a marked imbalance and bias in the
topics that are chosen, the tone in which they are discussed, and who are called on to speak
on them.

We have no desire to censor products or to deprive you of the right to distribute any
product you wish, no matter how bigoted and inflammatory; however, it is our duty as
America's leading Islamic civil rights group to defend both the image of Islam and the
safety of the American Muslim community.

Our aim in conducting this survey is also to raise CNN's awareness of its own coverage.
As a news company that prides itself as the "most trusted name in news," it is CNN's
corporate social responsibility to take into account the potential social impact its television
personalities have on public perception and understanding of Islam and Muslims.

For all of these reasons, balanced conversations are necessary to help Americans reach fair
conclusions about issues relating to Islam and Muslims.

II. **Methodology**

CAIR collected transcripts of Glenn Beck's Show from September 1, 2006 until December
31, 2006 via Nexis and Factiva. The transcripts were reviewed for coverage of Islam and
Muslims and relevant passages from the transcript were excerpted.

Fig. 52

Opposition

Action	Lead	Due
Prepare and distribute "Who is" sheet on Horowitz.	Recommended: Corey Saylor. Ibrahim Hooper	
Prepare and distribute "Who is" sheet on Kaufman	Recommended: Corey Saylor. Ibrahim Hooper	
Prepare and distribute "Who is" sheet Front Page Magazine.	Recommended: Corey Saylor. Ibrahim Hooper	

TALKING POINTS

Senator Boxer is citing non-credible sources and anti-CAIR conspiracy theories; the credibility of the message depends on the credibility of the messenger.

1. Attacks on CAIR are the work of a very finite and interrelated band of career Islamophobes, whose own credibility is in doubt, who profit economically and politically by bashing Muslims and smearing their leaders and organizations.
2. This band includes Daniel Pipes, Steven Emerson, Joe Kaufman and David Horowitz together with affiliates like Stephen Schwartz and Andrew Whitehead. These individuals who are all staunchly pro-Zionist and anti-Muslim and create the bulk of the anti-CAIR literature, which is consumed and circulated by others.
3. All of them spew their bigoted conspiracy theories primarily through the internet which is an un-relegated medium with no professional standards as far as content or fact-checking.
4. They promulgate their content through thousands of affiliated blogs operated by amateurs who are powered by little more than their own Islamophobic sentiment.
5. Some of their lies and conspiracy theories seep through right wing AM and Cable TV radio talk shows that lean towards accepting their conspiracy theories about Muslim Americans and their organizations (Savage, Medved, Prager, O'Reilly, Carlson, Beck, etc).

Senator Boxer cruised anti-Muslim hate sites on the Internet and consulted with anti-Muslim bigots. You do the math.

1) Front Page Magazine, the online hate site where Senator Boxer is reported to have obtained her information about CAIR, also smears her:
   a. David Horowitz, "whose Web site first got Boxer's attention", asserts that she is "unpopular even with Democrats" and used "a phony but effective attack" to beat then opponent Matt Fong.[2]
   b. Articles on FrontPageMagazine.com call Senator Boxer "rude," and unable to "fathom that a black American could embrace conservatism;"[3] assert that she and other Senators would "prefer a bloody failure" in Iraq,[4] and term her "the nation's dumbest Democrat."[5]

---

[1] Newsweek, 12/29/2006, web exclusive
[2] FrontPageMagazine.com, 8/11/2003. http://www.frontpagemag.com/Articles/ReadArticle.asp?ID-9320
[3] FrontPageMagazine.com, 6/19/2006, http://www.frontpagemag.com/Articles/ReadArticle.asp?ID-27960
[4] FrontPageMagazine.com, 1/31/2005. http://www.frontpagemag.com/Articles/ReadArticle.asp?ID-16828
[5] FrontPage Magazine.com, 11/06/2006. http://www.frontpagemag.com/Articles/Printable.asp?ID-25322

NOTES

A word about primary sourcing: The dates and modes of first-hand interviews with unnamed FBI agents and local JTTF detectives are documented extensively below. These sources requested anonymity due to the sensitivity of the active investigations or open cases they are either working on or familiar with, and because they fear reprisals from management if they speak to the press.

Intermixed with these quotes are dozens of interviews on the record with former FBI agents and other key law enforcement officers. Several veteran FBI investigators and officials are quoted on the record, including: Tim Pitchford, John Guandolo, Lara Burns, John Vincent, Ben Furman, Robert Wright, and George Sadler, among others. Federal prosecutors are quoted as well, including assistant U.S. Attorneys Gordon Kromberg and Jim Jacks.

In addition to more than twelve thousand pages of exclusive documents and other material, the conclusions and allegations in this book are based on more than one hundred interviews, spanning several years, conducted with more than a dozen FBI agents and officials; half a dozen police detectives working with the JTTFs in New York, Los Angeles, Miami, Washington, and other major cities; as well as Pentagon officials and consultants, Homeland Security officials, congressional investigators and members of Congress, and professional counterterrorism analysts and other experts.

Though numerous quotes from a particular interview may be used throughout a chapter, the interview will be cited in the notes only once to avoid repetitious citations.

PREFACE

1   Sarwat Husain, who in 2005 chaired CAIR's San Antonio chapter, worked with Gaubatz Arabic and Counterterrorism Lecture Services training Texas Department of Public Safety troopers. Also, Saffia Meek of CAIR's Dallas-Fort Worth chapter often lectured for Gaubatz's company.

2   "Talking Points" memo, 2006; CAIR internal email, from Corey Saylor to Nihad Awad, 3 January 2007; "CAIR Executive Staff Meeting" memo, 3 January 2007. Also see Appendix. Beck now hosts a hit program on Fox News.

3   CAIR "Talking Points" memo, 2006.

4   CAIR email, Saylor to Awad, 3 January 2007.

INTRODUCTION

1   CAIR board meeting minutes, 5-6 January 2002, CAIR headquarters, Washington DC, 1.

2   http://umarlee.com/2009/01/22/clarification-on-the-controversy-of-my-statements-regarding-sahabah-and-jihad/

3   Ibid.

CHAPTER ONE: MUSLIMS VICTIMIZING MUSLIMS

1   CAIR Civil Rights Department, "Status Report," Joshua Salaam, 27 June 2002, 1.

2   Email from Iqbal to Awad, et al., 11 February 2008. Also, hand-written phone message to Iqbal, 15 February 2008.

3   Undated internal CAIR ledger (computer-generated spreadsheet) listing 28 complainants and their individual claims of the "amount taken" from them by CAIR , totaling "$23,235 "so far," 1.

4   Hand-written phone message (undated) to Iqbal describing Muslim woman's demand that CAIR pay back "all the money" taken from her.

5   "What course of action to take – Issue with Br. Jamil and Ahmad Obaid family," email from Iqbal to Awad, et al., 8 February 2008.

6   "Request permission to work from CAIR MD VA for the next few weeks," email from Iqbal to Tahra Goraya, Parvez Ahmed, and Awad, et al., 11 February 2008.

7 "What course of action to take – Issue with Br. Jamil and Ahmad Obaid family."

8 Days, who recently died of an illness, last decade served time as an inmate in Philadelphia jails. In 2001 and 2002, he pleaded guilty to DWI and other criminal offenses in Virginia. See: "CAIR 'Lawyer' Has Own Legal History," IPT News, 3 December 2008. Moreover, Days signed an internal CAIR statement in March 2008 confessing: "I misrepresented to the public that I was an attorney licensed to practice law." See also: Rene Arturo Lopez, et al., v. Council on American-Islamic Relations Action Network Inc., et al., U.S. District Court for the District of Columbia, October 2008, 17. To wit: "Days was not and is not a lawyer. He never attended law school nor was he licensed as an attorney to practice law in any jurisdiction in the United States." CAIR's lawyers did not refute this statement when they filed a "motion to dismiss" the class-action lawsuit on Jan. 15, 2009.

9 CAIR ledger, 1.

10 "What course of action to take – Issue with Br. Jamil and Ahmad Obaid family." Also, "Request permission to work from CAIR MD VA for the next few weeks."

11 "Closing of CAIR MD VA Checklist," undated CAIR spreadsheet, 1, 2.

12 Email from Iqbal to Awad, et al., 11 February 2008.

13 CAIR ledger, 1. Plus attached page of handwritten notes.

14 "Voluntary Agreement and Release of Claims," 2.

15 "Anti-Hate: CAIR Refutes Racist Group's 'Smears,'" CAIR press release, 9 September 2008.

16 "Subject: Termination Notification," CAIR letter to Days signed by Iqbal, 10 February 2008, 1.

17 "Plaintiffs' Opposition to Motion to Dismiss," Rene Arturo Lopez, et al., v. Council on American-Islamic Relations Action Network Inc., et al., U.S. District Court for the District of Columbia, January 2009, 11.

18 Council on American-Islamic Relations MD/VA Chapter newsletter, March/April 2007, Volume 1, Issue 1, 1.

19 "Subject: Termination Notification," 1. CAIR finally terminated Days on Feb. 10, 2008, following a written warning on Feb. 6, 2008. However, Days was also "informed" he was violating official policy way back on Oct. 1, 2007. He joined CAIR in June 2006. It's not clear how many Muslim immigrants Days and CAIR helped shepherd through to citizenship over the course of his employment, or whether the Department of Homeland Security has reviewed any of those cases for possible application fraud.

20   Email from Iqbal to Awad, et al., 11 February 2008.

21   "Anti-Hate: CAIR Refutes Racist Group's 'Smears.'"

CHAPTER TWO: TERRORIST TURNSTILE

1   Author (Sperry) interview by phone, 1 May 2008.

2   "'Virginia Jihad' Member Convicted of Perjury, Obstruction," press release regarding Sabri Benkahla, U.S. Attorney's Office, Eastern District of Virginia, 2.

3   U.S. v. Masoud Khan, U.S. District Court for the Eastern District of Virginia, 4 March 2004. Also, "Two Defendants in Virginia Jihad Case Plead Guilty to Weapons Charges, Will Cooperate with Ongoing Investigation," press release, Department of Justice, 16 January 2004, 2. CAIR's employment records for Royer, details of which are revealed here for the first time, indicate he was first hired in July 1997 before resigning April 9, 1999, to join the jihad overseas. Then, within two months of firing live rounds at Indian targets with al-Qaida-tied terrorists in Pakistan, he was rehired by CAIR on July 10, 2000. CAIR's national operations director Khalid Iqbal accepted his resignation letter on Oct. 1, 2001, whereby he joined the jihad against his own country. Prosecutors say Royer called LeT officials on or just before Aug. 21, 2000, to help another local Virginia terrorist join a training camp in Pakistan. They also say Royer helped other terrorists gain entry to the LeT terror-training camp following a meeting in Virginia on Sept. 16, 2001. In both instances, Royer was gainfully employed by CAIR. According to prosecutors: "Royer said that anyone who wanted to fight [with the Taliban and al-Qaida against Americans] in Afghanistan would first need to participate in military training, that the LeT camps in Pakistan were a good place to receive that training, and that Royer could facilitate their entry to the LeT camps." Despite CAIR's repeated denials, its former senior staffer was in fact aiding the enemy and engaging in jihadist activities while on the payroll at CAIR's national headquarters.

4   "CAIR Executive Staff Meeting," tasks memo, 15 May 2007, 1. CAIR executive Ibrahim Hooper was the point of contact for the lawyer and family of Royer, his longtime protégé.

5   Videotaped conversation between Chris Gaubatz (posing as David Marshall) and Quasem, 5 August 2008 (Part 3 of video, starting at 54:42).

6   CAIR National visitors register, 22 April 2004. Entry reads as follows: "Name: Omar Abu Ali. Company: SAUDI EMBASSY. To See: Br. Nihad. Time Arrive: 12:00." See Appendix.

7   Author (Sperry) interview by email, 11 February 2009.

8   Author (Sperry) interview by phone, 1 May 2008.

9   Steve Emerson, "Paper of CAIR," *National Review Online*, 8 February 2008.

10   Farah Stockman, "Iraqi Sunnis plan lobbying operation in Washington," *Boston Globe*, 18 March 2007. Also, "Another Ex-CAIR Official in Legal Trouble," *IPT News*, 27 March 2008.

11   Federal Election Commission records, 2000.

12   "List of Unindicted Co-conspirators and/or Joint Venturers," Attachment A, U.S. vs. Holy Land Foundation, et. al., 6. See Appendix.

13   FEC records, 2002.

14   Affidavit in Support of Application for Search Warrant, "In the Matter of Searches Involving 555 Grove Street, Herndon, Virginia, and Related Locations," U.S. District Court for the Eastern District of Virginia, unsealed October 2003, 39.

15   "List of Unindicted Co-conspirators," 6.

16   FEC records, 2002.

17   "List of Unindicted Co-conspirators," 5.

18   Government Exhibit 004-0001, U.S. v. Holy Land Foundation, et al., 4. See Appendix.

19   Author (Paul Sperry) interview in person, 12 February 2009. The special agent noted that politics had previously throttled the investigation of Awad thanks to an official photo he managed to have taken with President Bush at the National Cathedral after 9/11.

20   "List of Unindicted Co-conspirators," 6.

21   Government Exhibit, Ashqar Wiretap-1, 3:04-CR-240-G, U.S. v. HLF, et al., 2, 6 (recorded 13 September 1993). Also, Government Exhibit, 016-0047, 3:04-CR-240-G, U.S. v. HLF, et al., 11.

22   Joel Mowbray, "Boxer's stand; Why she repudiated a Muslim group," the *Washington Times*, 11 January 2007, A21. Addressing a youth session at the 1999 IAP annual convention in Chicago, Ahmad also said, "Fighting for freedom, fighting for Islam, that is not suicide. They kill themselves for Islam," according to a transcript provided by the Investigative Project on Terrorism.

23   Author (Sperry) interview by phone, 6 March 2009. Ahmad's address was 215 Monroe St., Santa Clara, Calif. 95050, Apt. 11. The Blind Sheik reception took place in 1990. Hyslop recalls Ahmad taking the *New York Times*. He also recalls Ahmad's then-

infant son, Osama, wearing a green T-shirt with the word "Intifada" emblazoned across the front. Ahmad left the apartment with no forwarding address. Public records show he has maintained four P.O. boxes in Santa Clara since then.

24   Paul Sperry, *Infiltration: How Muslim Spies and Subversives Have Penetrated Washington*, (Nashville, Tenn.: Nelson Current, 2005), xi.

25   Government Exhibit, 016-0069, 3:04-CR-240-G, U.S. v. HLF, et al., 13.

26   "List of Unindicted Co-conspirators," 6.

27   *Infiltration: How Muslim Spies and Subversives Have Penetrated Washington*, 249.

28   Letter from Global Relief Foundation officer Khaled Diab to CAIR Research Director Mohamed Nimer, 20 July 2000, 1. The two discussed an $18,000 donation.

29   *"Grand Deception,"* trailer to documentary film, Steve Emerson, Investigative Project on Terrorism, Summer 2009.

30   Siraj Wahhaj, "Stand Up for Justice," videotaped sermon, Masjid At-Taqwa, Brooklyn, N.Y., 8 May 1992.

31   *Infiltration: How Muslim Spies and Subversives Have Penetrated Washington*, xi.

32   Al-Hajj Idris A. Muhammad, *What Should You Do If You Are Arrested or Framed by the Racist, Fascist, Criminal Police? Or the Racist, Fascist, Criminal FBI?* (New York: El-Amin Publishers, 2002, Third Edition), 65, 66.

33   "CAIR Fund Raising Plan 2006," 1.

34   "Ellison at CAIR: 'Obama Not Our Salvation. God Is,'" The Muslim Link, 28 November 2008, 2.

35   "Depreciation and Amortization Report," IRS Form 990, CAIR, 2004, 13.

36   Transcript of Hooper interview with Fox New's Rita Cosby, 29 October 2001.

37   "Raid on Texas Business is 'Anti-Muslim Witch Hunt' Say Muslim Leaders," PR Newswire, 6 September 2001.

CHAPTER THREE: FRONTING FOR HAMAS

1   Assistant U.S. Attorney Gordon D. Kromberg, U.S. Justice Department, "Brief for the United States," USA v. Sabri Benkahla, U.S. Court of Appeals for the Fourth Circuit, December 2007, 58. CAIR defended Benkahla, convicted of a obstructing a terrorism probe, and even filed a friend-of-the-court brief in his appeal. But that only backfired when prosecutors slapped CAIR down as a terror-supporting Brotherhood front.

2   Jason Trahan, "FBI: CAIR is a front group, and Holy Land Foundation tapped Hamas clerics for fundraisers," *Dallas Morning News*, 7 October 2008. Agent Burns testified Oct. 7, 2008, during her redirect examination in federal court in Dallas.

3   Government Exhibit 003-0065, 3:04-CR-240-G, U.S. v HLF, et al., 12, 13. Hand-written letter (in Arabic) from Hamas charitable front Islamic Relief Committee faxed to U.S. Muslim Brotherhood underboss Ismail Elbarasse, 12 August 1992.

4   Government Exhibit 003-0078, 3:04-CR-240-G, U.S. v. HLF, et al., 6, 7. This smoking-gun document, which can be viewed in the Appendix, was found during FBI search of Elbarasse's home in the D.C. suburbs.

5   CAIR's "advocacy model -- work closely with media and provide direct services to local Muslim communities -- was developed when Nihad Awad and Ibrahim Hooper worked as community activists" in the early '90s, CAIR acknowledges on page one of a recent 10-page statement posted on its website under the heading, "Top Internet Disinformation About CAIR."

6   Steven Emerson, "One Muslim Advocacy Group's Not-So-Secret Terrorist Ties," *The New Republic Online*, 28 March 2007.

7   In its brief filed in the summer of 2007 with the U.S. District Court for the Northern District of Texas, CAIR accused the government of "demonization of all things Muslim." The co-conspirator designation, the brief argues, is "particularly insidious and ironic as CAIR is an organization dedicated to fostering acceptance of Muslims in American society and protecting the civil liberties of all Muslim Americans."

8   "Government's Memorandum in Opposition to Council on American-Islamic Relations' Motion for Leave to File Amicus Curiae Instanter and Amicus Brief in Support of the Unindicted Co-Conspirators' First and Fifth Amendment Rights," USA v. Holy Land Foundation, U.S. District Court for the Northern District of Texas, 3:04cr240, 4 September 2007.

9   U.S. v. Sabri Benkahla, 58.

10   "CAIR is not a 'front group for Hamas' (or) 'part of a wider conspiracy overseen by the Muslim Brotherhood,' " the group insists ("Top Internet Disinformation About CAIR," 1).

11   Canceled check No. 1881, paid to the order of CAIR by Holy Land Foundation for Relief and Development, amount of $5,000, Bank One Texas, 5 October 1994.

12   "There is probable cause to believe that those contributors to HLF who knew the leaders of Hamas or HLF, contributed their money to support suicide bombings and terrorism conducted by Hamas," said federal agent David Kane in 2002 affidavit for search warrant, U.S. District Court for the Eastern District of Virginia, unsealed

October 2003, 34.

13   D-20 Corporation Franchise Tax Return, District of Columbia, CAIR-DC, 1995, 4 (obtained by author Sperry); Supplemental Schedule, CAIR-DC, Balance Sheet as of 30 April 1996, 2 (Sperry). See Appendix.

14   "Senior leader of Hamas and Texas computer company indicted for conspiracy to violate U.S. ban on financial dealings with terrorists," press release, Justice Department, 18 December 2002, 1.

15   Indictment, U.S. v. Holy Land Foundation, et. al., U.S. Disctrict Court for the Northern District of Texas, 26 July 2004, 22. The $40,000 wire transfer was issued on Feb. 15, 1996.

16   Government Exhibit 003-0065, 12, 13.

17   D-20 Corporation Franchise Tax Return, 4.

CHAPTER FOUR: TERROR SUPPORT GROUP

1   "Proposed Muslim Platform for 2004," 8 March 2004, 2. The two-page document, marked "draft," was found inside one of CAIR chief Nihad Awad's files labeled "AMT," which stands for the American Muslim Taskforce on Civil Rights and Elections. The file included notes from an "AMT Teleconference" held the same month the platform memo was drafted. See Appendix.

2   Al-Amin faced the death penalty but was sentenced to life without parole. A close ally of CAIR adviser and fundraiser Siraj Wahhaj believes Al-Amin was "framed and railroaded" by a "racist" judge. "The incompetent racist, fascist, Zionist Jew lowlife pervert, so-called judge (Stephanie B.) Manis is an open enemy to the Muslim community," snarls Al-Haff Idris A. Muhammad in a publication sold at a bookstore associated with Wahhaj's mosque in Brooklyn. He also calls Al-Amin's victims "bootlicking" and "corrupt" cops.

3   Letter from Al-Amin to Awad, 25 April 2007, 1. ("Re: Justice Fund Contribution.") See Appendix. It's worth noting that the lawyer described CAIR's gift as an "additional" contribution, suggesting this was not the first time CAIR has financially supported the cop killer.

4   Interoffice email from Iftikhar to Awad and Hooper, 3 January 2007, 1.

5   Cindy George, "Pakistani found guilty of gun charge," Houston Chronicle, 31 January 2007, B1. Ali Khalili was the CAIR cheerleader in the Taliban wannabe's corner.

6   CAIR National visitors register.

7   "Case Summary," Omar Abu Ali, et al. v. John Ashcroft, et al., U.S. District Court for the District of Columbia, 16 December 2004.

8   Ibid.

9   "CAIR backs film praising convicted terror supporter," *WorldNetDaily*, 4 December 2007.

10   "American Brotherhood: Sami's Our Man," *IPT News*, 5 September 2008.

11   Affidavit in Support of Application for Search Warrant, 37-39.

12   "Semiannual Report," CAIR Governmental Affairs Department, Not for Distribution – for Board Members Only, 1, 2.

13   Affidavit in Support of Application for Search Warrant, 37-39.

14   "Closing of CAIR MD VA Checklist," 1. The internal spreadsheet document lists under checklist item No. D-3: "Give notice to Sterling Management, only if national decide [sic] not to continue in this office. We might have to pay an extra month rent."

15   "CAIR MD-VA Opens New Office in Virginia," CAIR interoffice memo, December 2004, 1. "Local Community Leader Yaqub Mirza, PhD (gave some encouraging words of support)."

16   Laurie Goodstein, "U.S. Muslim Clerics Seek a Modern Middle Ground," *New York Times*, 18 June 2006. Shakir's treasonous statement is buried in the last paragraph of long story designed to rehabilitate his image to appear moderate.

17   Zaytuna Speech Request Form, 11 September 2003, 1.

18   "U.S. Muslim Clerics Seek a Modern Middle Ground."

19   Nihad Awad, "Report from CAIR National," CAIR National Board Meeting, 29 October 2006, 2.

20   "American Muslims: A Journalist's Guide to Understanding Islam and Muslims," CAIR, 21.

21   "Obama's Gitmo Delegation," editorial, *Investor's Business Daily*, 5 June 2008.

22   Author (Sperry) interview via teleconference; senior Gitmo security official, U.S. military intelligence analyst; 28 March 2009.

23   "Radical Islamic/Anti-Western Threat Within Government Intelligence Bodies," JTF-Guantanamo, U.S. Southern Command, May 2009, 2. (High-level briefing obtained by author Sperry.)

24   Ibid, 3.

25   Ibid, 2.

26   Ibid, 5.

27   Jake Tapper, "Islam's flawed spokesman," *Salon.com*, 26 September 2001.

28   Paul Vitello, "The War on Terror: Attack consensus is elusive," *Newsday* (New York), 14 October 2001, A08. Khankan also claimed that "Atta is living in the United Arab Emirates. His passport was stolen ... Yet the FBI insists he was one of the hijackers." On Oct. 7, 2001, speaking at CAIR's 7th Annual Fundraising Dinner in Vienna, Virginia, Khankan asked: "Who is impersonating these Muslim names? Who benefits?" He implied the U.S. was trying to "cover up" the real identity of the hijackers. Also, on Oct. 5, 2001, CAIR's New York office encouraged Muslims to write letters to the *New York Times* questioning the identity of the 9/11 hijackers, because Muslims "could NOT be the culprits," it insisted in one letter it posted on the CAIR website (emphasis in original). "Who could 'benefit' from" the attacks? it pondered, echoing Arab conspiracy theories that Mossad orchestrated the attacks with the CIA and FBI to spark a war on Islam.

29   Letter from Global Relief Foundation officer Khaled Diab to CAIR Research Director Mohamed Nimer.

30   Sperry, *Infiltration: How Muslim Spies and Subversives Have Penetrated Washington*, 258.

31   "Proposed Muslim Platform for 2004," 1, 2. This is a rough draft of talking points found in Awad's executive files, along with minutes of conference calls regarding the AMT Presidential Outreach Committee, which took place March 31, 2004, and April 25, 2004. The date 1948 cited in talking point No. 3 refers to the year the Israeli state was created.

32   Joe Kaufman, "CAIR Assassination Plot?" FrontPageMagazine, 7 August 2008.

33   Anwar Aulaqi, "44 Ways of Supporting Jihad," January 2009.

34   Sperry, *Infiltration*, 119-132. Anwar Aulaqi, aka Al-Awlaki, aka Abu Atiq, was born in Las Cruces, N.M., in 1971 to Yemeni parents. He grew up in Yemen and returned in 1991 to study engineering at Colorado State University. On October 10, 2002, Aulaqi was detained at JFK International Airport after arriving on Saudi Arabian Airlines Flight 35. He gave an address of 3159 Row Street, Falls Church, Virginia -- the Dar al-Hijrah mosque, which has been the subject of several terrorism investigations over the past 16 years. (The mosque uses the Falls Church Church of Christ parking lot across the highway for extra parking during Friday prayer and Muslim holidays. The traffic is so bad on Fridays that the Church of Christ minister has to take off work to avoid it.) At JFK, Aulaqi was referred to secondary inspection as an "anti-terrorist passenger." Phone records suggest Aulaqi also spoke by phone several times to the hijackers, along with a

Saudi intelligence agent who helped them. Aulaqi has denied knowing the hijackers.

35   Author (Sperry) interview by phone, 3 May 2005.

36   Ibid. Authorities also considered bringing a prostitution case against Aulaqi while he was in Virginia under the Mann Act, a federal statute. They had a photo of him at an ATM with a hooker he allegedly picked up in Washington, D.C. Aulaqi previously had been arrested twice for soliciting prostitutes in San Diego. Apparently the young cleric had worked himself into such a lather preaching about the carnal delights of the Islamic Hereafter that he couldn't wait to redeem his own earthbound "dark-eyed damsels with swelling breasts."

37   Charles E. Allen, undersecretary of Homeland Security for intelligence and analysis, keynote address, GEOINT conference, Nashville, Tennessee, 28 October 2008.

38   Susan Schmidt, "Imam from Va. Mosque Now Thought to Have Aided Al-Qaida," *Washington Post*, 27 February 2008, A03.

39   Paul Sperry, "Al-Qaida angle emerges in CAIR-tied terror case," *FrontPageMagazine*, 22 June 2007.

40   It's also noteworthy that Aulaqi, like CAIR founder Awad, was chummy with the Blind Sheik and his entourage. More, Aulaqi has spoken at Islamic conferences with longtime CAIR director and fundraiser Siraj Wahhaj.

41   Letter from CAIR's national legislative director, Corey P. Saylor, to U.S. Rep. Sue Myrick, co-founder of the Congressional Anti-Terrorism/Jihad Caucus, 2 February 2009, 1.

42   "MAC: Talking Points," memo, 2004, 1. Page 2 of the memo, put out jointly by the Muslim Affairs Council and CAIR, cites the Royer and Khan cases.

43   Ibid.

44   Ibid.

45   Memorandum, "Re: Proposal for Lebanon Lawsuit," Omar T. Mohammedi, Esq., to Br. Parvez Ahmed and Br. Nihad Awad, 7 August 2006, 3.

46   Ibid.

CHAPTER FIVE: CAIR'S BAD COP

1   William Gawthrop, "Islamic Investigations Issues," Counterintelligence Field Activity, Department of Defense, unclassified briefing paper, 2.

2   "Statement of Facts," USA v. Weiss Rasool, U.S. District Court for the Eastern District of Virginia, 31 January 2008, 2.

3   "Position of the United States with Respect to Sentencing Factors," USA v. Weiss Rasool, U.S. District Court for the Eastern District of Virginia, 6 April 2008, 3. Prosecutors said Weiss's NCIC security breaches undermined the Violent Crime and Terrorist Offender File, a system put in place to assist in the investigation of terrorist suspects after 9/11.

4   "Plea Agreement," USA v. Weiss Rasool, U.S. District Court for the Eastern District of Virginia, 31 January 2008, 1.

5   Author (Sperry) interview by phone, 1 May 2008. Rasool also claimed not to remember tapping in to the federal database. And according to court records, "on April 14, 2008, the defendant appeared for a polygraph examination conducted by an FBI examiner but was not fully compliant with the test procedures despite warnings from the examiner to cease in his behavior. Because of the countermeasures deliberately used by the defendant during the test, the FBI examiner was unable to conduct a true polygraph examination."

6   Rasool resigned effective Aug. 1, 2008, according to FCPD spokeswoman Mary Ann Jennings. Insiders say the internal affairs division gave him the option of resigning or being terminated.

7   Author (Sperry) interview by phone, 16 January 2009.

8   Letter from Saylor to U.S. Magistrate Judge Barry R. Poretz, 20 February 2008.

9   Author (Sperry) interview by phone, 1 May 2008.

10   One entry in the CAIR National visitors register, 7 November 2005, reads as follows: Name: RASOOL, WEISS. Company: SELF. To See: NIHAD. Time Arrive: 16:16 [4:16 p.m.]." See Appendix. Rasool also appears on CAIR's guest register for the days Dec. 8, 2007, and Jan. 4, 2008.

11   Email from Rasool to Saylor, Awad, and other CAIR officials, 27 July 2006.

12   Author (Sperry) interview by phone, 16 January 2009. The high-level FCPD official first raised concerns about Rasool and his cozy dealings with CAIR during a 2006 phone interview.

13   Author (Sperry) interview by email, 9 July 2008.

CHAPTER SIX: COOPERATION? WHAT COOPERATION?

1   Author (Sperry) interview by phone, 27 November 2006.

2   Letter from Leitner to FCPD Chief David Rohrer, 24 April 2008, 1.

3   Paul Sperry, "CAIR's Traitorous Cop Ally," *FrontPageMagazine*, 25 Jue 2008.

4   Author (Sperry) interview by phone, 16 January 2009. The high-level FCPD official first raised concerns about Rasool and his cozy dealings with CAIR during a 2006 phone interview.

5   Steven Emerson, "Fairfax Cop Who Tipped Terror Suspect Helped Kill Training Program," *IPT News*, 9 May 2008.

6   "Sources of Dawah Training Material," undated document found in CAIR headquarters files. Maududi's book "Towards Undersanding Islam" is one of seven books recommended.

7   Letter of support for defendant Weiss from Sgt. Butt to U.S. Magistrate Judge Barry R. Poretz, 12 February 2008.

8   CAIR's national guest registry shows Butt entered the building with Rasool on Dec. 8, 2007, and Jan. 4, 2008.

9   "Activity Report: Meeting with FF County Police Department at Criminal Justice Academy Re: FFPD Training of Employees on Bias-Related Incidents," CAIR, 15 August 2005, 1, 2.

10   Ibid, 1, 3. FAITH also approached the Justice Department about educating law enforcement regarding Islamic law and domestic violence. Meanwhile, CAIR has conducted "diversity and sensitivity" training for the staff of the Fairfax County Juvenile and Domestic Relations District Court, which has jurisdiction over cases of "spousal abuse family violence/domestic violence."

11   Affidavit in Support of Application for Search Warrant, 99.

12   "Activity Report: Meeting with FF County Police Department at Criminal Justice Academy," 1. Sgt. Butt could not be reached for comment.

13   Council on American-Islamic Relations MD/VA Chapter newsletter," March/ April 2007, Volume 1, Issue 1, 2. Days filed his complaint with the FCPD Internal Affairs Bureau on Jan. 31, 2007.

14   CAIR's national legal director continues to threaten and intimidate the FCPD. "We have noticed what may be a pattern and practice of the Fairfax County Police Department to discriminate against persons of the Islamic faith," wrote CAIR's Nadhira Al-Khalili in an April 2008 letter to FCPD chief Rohrer (in spite of his groveling

speeches and accommodations). "We are bringing this issue to the attention of the United States Department of Justice and are requesting a full investigation of the Fairfax County Police Department's repeated and relentless attacks on American Muslims."

15 The one-page letter to Nimer was dated 12 August 2007.

16 Interoffice memo marked "CONFIDENTIAL: PLEASE DON'T DISCLOSE" from Faiza N. Ali, community affairs director, CAIR-NY, November 2007, 1.

17 "'Mapping' A Danger," editorial, *Investor's Business Daily*, 12 November 2007.

18 Ibid.

19 Ibid.

20 "U.S. Muslim Coalition Considers Suspending Relations With FBI," press release, *American Muslim Taskforce*, 17 March 2009.

21 Author (Sperry) interview by phone, 22 March 2009.

22 Letter from Saylor to Rep. Myrick, 1.

23 Transcript of lecture by Imam Zaid Shakir, "Jihad or Terrorism?" CD recording, *Rumi Productions*, 2001.

24 *Muhammad, What Should You Do If You Are Arrested or Framed by the Racist, Fascist, Criminal Police? Or the Racist, Fascist, Criminal FBI?* 39.

25 http://www.cairchicago.org/knowyourrights.php.

26 Sperry, *Infiltration*, 323.

27 Author (Sperry) interview in person, 19 April 2005.

28 Michael McAuliff, "Rudy Backs King in Mosque Flap," *Daily News* (New York), 21 September 2007, 7.

29 Memo from Shama Farooq to Dr. Sayeed Ahmed, 1 September 2004, 1.

30 Ibid.

31 Shama Farooq, "Report on Meeting Between FBI Agents and Dr. Ahmed," DO NOT RELEASE, 27 September 2004, 1-6.

32 Ibid, 5.

33 "Law Enforcement Official's Guide to the Muslim Community," CAIR, 2003, 6.

34 Author (Sperry) interview by phone, 27 November 2006.

35 David Harrison, "Federal Agents Raid Merrifield Muslim Center," *Fairfax*

Connection, 8-14 July 2004, 3.

36   "CAIR Maryland and Virginia Chapter 1st Leadership and Empowerment Conference," agenda, 29-30 March 2008, 22.

37   Author (Sperry) interview by phone, 27 November 2006.

38   Ibid.

39   Dana Canedy and Eric Lichtblau, "THE MANHUNT: Family Members Defend Man Sought as 'Imminent Threat' by FBI," *New York Times*, 22 March 2003, B12. Also, Deirda Funcheon and Jeane MacIntosh, "Fugitive Eludes His Own Mom," *New York Post*, 5 June 2007, 8.

40   "THE MANHUNT: Family Members Defend Man Sought as 'Imminent Threat' by FBI," B12.

41   Government Exhibit, Elbarasse Search - 9, 3:04-CR-240-G, U.S. v HLF, et al., 34.

42   Handwritten minutes from 2001 staffwide CAIR meeting that included members of CAIR board and heads of all the chapters, 23.

43   Author (Sperry) interview by phone, 22 March 2009.

44   Faxed copy of hand-written note to Awad marked "Urgent," 29 August 2007. Sender's signature at bottom of page is cut off.

45   Government Exhibit 003-0089, 3:04-CR-240-G, U.S. v. HLF, et al., 13.

CHAPTER SEVEN: PC OUTREACH RUN AMOK

1   Jamie Glazov, "Terrorists Among Us," *FrontPageMagazine*, 16 March 2009.

2   Transcript of remarks by Bush, Islamic Center, Washington, D.C., 17 September 2001.

3   http://www.cair.com/AboutUs/WhatTheySayAboutCAIR/ WhatTheySayAboutCAIRBush.aspx

4   Rowan Scarborough, "CAIR trains FBI agents as new report cites links to terror," *Insight*, 18 March 2008.

5   http://www.cair.com/AboutUs/WhatTheySayAboutCAIR.aspx

6   As the book was going to press, neither official had been charged with a crime.

7   Author (Sperry) interview by phone, 22 March 2009.

8   Letter from Miller to U.S. Rep. Frank R. Wolf, 9 March 2009. Without providing details, Miller explained in an March 20, 2009, interview with CNN that "our concerns relate to a number of distinct narrow issues specific to CAIR and its national leadership."

9   "U.S. Muslim Coalition Considers Suspending Relations With FBI," American Muslim Taskforce, *PRNewswire-USNewswire*, 17 March 2009.

10   "We regret the recent FBI decision to sever some of its ties with us," CAIR National Legislative Director Corey P. Saylor, letter to Rep. Sue Myrick, R-N.C., 2 February 2009, 1.

11   Noreen S. Ahmed-Ullah, "Administration is urged to hire Muslims," *Los Angeles Times*, 29 March 2009.

12   Author (Sperry) interview by phone, 30 January 2009; also author (Sperry) interview in person, Tysons Corner, Virginia, 16 January 2009. Case agents investigating the Muslim Brotherhood convinced the Washington SAC who convinced Art Cummings at headquarters to sign off on the policy to cut ties with CAIR. Cummings is executive assistant director for national security covering counterterrorism at the FBI.

13   "Saving Los Angeles: supercop Bill Bratton has conquered crime in Boston, New York and now L.A. His next challenge: rescuing the rest of America," *Playboy*, 1 February 2008, 70. Miller's father was a gossip columnist in New York. Another FBI official who has been effusive in his praise of CAIR is FBI assistant director Steve Tidwell -- a crony of Miller from Los Angeles. He once called CAIR "an important bridge for the FBI" into the Muslim community.

14   Transcript of Miller interview on "Talk of the Nation" with John Ydstie, NPR, 10 September 2007.

15   "Meeting Notes for Robert S. Mueller, III, Director, Federal Bureau of Investigation," FBI community outreach meeting with Arab/Muslim American, Sikh, and South Asian leaders, 26 February 2007, 6. Document obtained from FBI headquarters by author Sperry.

16   Ibid, 6.

17   Anisa Abd el-Fattah, "Knowledge with an Islamic flair," *Islamic Horizons*, May/June 2007, 36.

18   "Meeting Notes for Robert S. Mueller, III, Director, Federal Bureau of Investigation," 6.

19   "CAIR and Law Enforcement," report by CAIR, 24 April 2008, 3.

20   "Demystifying 'Urban Legends' about CAIR," CAIR report, 19 January 2007, 2. (The report has since been scrubbed from CAIR's website.) Former CAIR chairman

Parvez Ahmed himself recently presented classroom "diversity training" to agents at FLETC.

21   Rob Margetta, "Experts Debate Efficacy of FBI Otreach to CAIR," CQ Homeland Security, 10 July 2008.

22   "CAIR-Chicago Conducts Sensitivity Training for ICE Officers," CAIR press release, 2 April 2006.

23   "CAIR-Chicago, Muslims, Meet with U.S. Customs & Border Protection at O'Hare," CAIR press release, 26 June 2006, 1.

24   Author (Sperry) interview by phone, 21 April 2006.

25   Middle Eastern Cultural Sensitivity training video, Department of Homeland Security, 1 January 2006.

26   Author (Sperry) interview by phone, 27 June 2007.

27   Internal department email from DHS Employee Communications to DHS-ALL, Subject: "MESSAGE FROM SECRETARY CHERTOFF," Department of Homeland Security, 10 August 2006, 7:57 a.m.

28   "Words that Work and Words that Don't: A Guide for Counterrorism Communication," 3-page memo, FOR OFFICIAL USE ONLY, National Counterterrorism Center, 14 March 2008, 1, 2.

29   "Terminology to Define the Terrorists: Recommendations from American Muslims," memo, Office for Civil Rights and Civil Liberties, Department of Homeland Security, January 2008, 1, 4.

30   Jamie Glazov, "Terrorists Among Us."

31   Letter from Kevin Favreau, assistant director of intelligence, national security branch of FBI, to U.S. Rep. Sue Myrick, R-N.C., 22 September 2008, 3 (copy obtained by author Sperry). The figure does not include the number of employees who threaten to file lawsuits, as the FBI does not track that data.

32   "ACLU-MD Board Meeting," 1-page document of notes from CAIR's files, undated (circa 2003). Relevant passage: "ACLU-NY asked for FBI ethnicity related cases (CAIR Natl)."

33   Letter from Hoekstra and Myrick to then-Attorney General Alberto Gonzales, 28 August 2007.

34   John Mintz, "Report Cites 'Hate' Writings in U.S. Mosques," *Washington Post*, 6 February 2005, A18. Freedom House also found anti-American literature in the ADAMS mosque, which stands for All Dulles Area Muslim Society. A Saudi pamphlet,

called "Religious Edicts for the Immigrant Muslim," said "it is forbidden for a Muslim to become a citizen of a country (such as the United States) governed by infidels." In a press release, ADAMS denied the claims and suggested "Christian" evangelicals "planted" the offensive materials inside the mosque.

35   Transcript of town hall meeting with FBI officials Timothy Healy, Dave Bennett and two FBI recruiters and Northern Virginia Muslim community at ADAMS Center, Sterling, Virginia, 8 February 2008. Moderator: ADAMS Center president Rizwan Jaka, who's employed by Oracle Corp.

36   Sperry, *Infiltration*, 151-154.

37   Letter from Favreau, 3.

38   Author (Sperry) interview by email with veteran FBI special agent Robert Wright, 28 December 2007. "I am confident he is a MB (Muslim Brotherhood) plant" within the FBI, Wright said of Gamal Abdel-Hafiz, with whom he worked on counterterrorism cases. FBI agent Abdel-Hafiz refused to record two Muslim Brotherhood leaders under investigation, and attended a Muslim Brotherhood mosque. Attempts to reach Abdel-Hafiz for comment were unsuccessful. But in a prior interview with author Sperry, he exalted one of the Brotherhood targets he refused to record, Sami al-Arian, as a "very smart man" (cf. Infiltration, 188). Al-Arian, no thanks to Abdel-Hafiz, was later convicted of terrorism.

39   Fox News Network Inc. and Bill O'Reilly, appellants v. Gamal Abdel-Hafiz, appellee, Court of Appeals of Texas, Second District, Fort Worth, case summary, Lexis 9073, 15 November 2007. On Oct. 20, 2003, Abdel-Hafiz secretly tape-recorded O'Reilly when the Fox News host personally phoned him and invited him to come on his show to tell his side of the story. Abdel-Hafiz at the time was planning to sue O'Reilly over a prior broadcast, and he introduced a transcript of their phone conversation at a deposition in his lawsuit. O'Reilly revealed at the deposition that he was unaware Abdel-Hafiz had tape-recorded him, and remarked, "It is certainly unprofessional to tape somebody without telling them." (Of course, it's entirely another case for law enforcement to tape the target of a terrorism investigation -- something agent Abdel-Hafiz said he couldn't do, because "a Muslim does not record another Muslim.")

40   "FBI sponsors Axis of Evil show in funny attempt to recruit Muslims," *National Post* (Canada), 14 June 2007, A24.

41   Author (Sperry) interview by phone, 5 April 2009.

42   "Law Enforcement & Arab American Community Relations After September 11, 2001: Engagement in a Time of Uncertainty," Vera Institute of Justice, June 2006, 24.

43   Author (Sperry) interview by email, 23 August 2005. Sadler, who has an

undergraduate degree in Middle Eastern Studies and military training as an Arabic linguist and intelligence analyst, returned to corporate America after resigning from the bureau. In his resignation letter, he stated: "I have come to the unquestionable conclusion that the FBI provides neither the cultural fit nor the career potential for which I had hoped. Initially motivated by patriotism and a deep desire to fight back after the events of 9/11, I find myself overcome by a constant struggle between my core values and those of the FBI." He complains the FBI was consumed by political rear-covering: "It's much safer to chase criminals who have already committed a crime than to aggressively and proactively strive to prevent these acts from occurring."

44   http://www.isna.net/Leadership/articles/ILDC-News/Behind-the-Blindfold-of-Justice.aspx

45   http://www.isna.net/articles/news/a-call-for-fbi-accountability.aspx. "We will not allow for the marginalization of mainstream Muslim organizations," ISNA asserted in its March 2009 press release. "We have called on the FBI to re-engage with CAIR, our respected sister organization, and will continue to do so."

46   Sayyid Qutb, *Milestones*, (Cairo, Egypt: Kazi Publications, 1964). Also, Sayyid Qutb, Milestones (Chicago: American Trust Publications/NAIT, 1991, revised), Chapter 10: "Far Reaching Changes." "Building bridges" is a favorite buzz phrase among Muslim Brotherhood figures in America, such as Nihad Awad. The Brotherhood even started a TV network by that name -- Bridges TV.

47   "An Explanatory Memorandum On the General Strategic Goal for the Group In North America," 22 May 1991, 15. (Government Exhibit: 003-0085; 3:04-CR-240-G; U.S. v. HLF, et al.) One such "friendship society" is the Coordinating Council of Muslim Organizations (CCMO), which does a lot of interfaith outreach and works closely with CAIR. CCMO Chair Asma Hanif last year proved just how insincere such interfaith dialogue is when she made the following remark on a Muslim blog: "It is written that the worst of Muslims is better than the best of non-Muslims. And so I want to go on record as saying that pious or not, the only thing that a non-Muslim man can personally do for me is to step out of the way of my Muslim Brothers." (http://www.tariqnelson.com, 28 May 2008.)

CHAPTER EIGHT: CAIR'S TEN BIGGEST WHOPPERS

1   Ibn Taymiyah, *The Sword on the Neck of the Accuser of Muhammad*, 221.

2   "Urgent Fax Letter to CAIR Executive Director and Board Members," Jameila Al-Hashimi, MBA, to Nihad Awad, et al, "Re: Profound Problems at CAIR," 21 August 2000, 2.

3   Internal CAIR records show Hooper rode herd on convicted jihadist Royer's appeal, personally speaking with his attorney, among other things. Hooper hired and rehired Royer around his protege's jihadi tours in Bosnia. The two shared a burning passion over the Bosnian issue. In fact, Hooper early last decade was manager of communications and media relations for Islamic Information of Bosnian Relief Committee. Awad was coordinator of the committee.

4   Nihad Awad, "Muslim-Americans in Mainstream America," *The Link*, February-March 2000, Volume 33, Issue 1.

5   U.S. Government Exhibit 016-0069, 3:04-CR-240-G, U.S. v. HLF, et al., FBI transcript of 2 October 1993 meeting, 15-20.

6   Nihad Awad, "Muslim-Americans in Mainstream America."

7   In 2006, the latest IRS filing, CAIR National spent a whopping $100,000 for "research and information services."

8   http://www.mca-sfba.org/guests/ibrahim_hooper.htm. Hooper also anonymously operates a blog touting the ancient holistic benefits of honey (he claims it can heal wounds better than conventional treatment methods involving modern medicine). The blog is located at http://www.apitherapy.blogspot.com. In Minneapolis, he owned a business dealing in halal foods – Halalco Export Management -- state business records show.

9   Paul Findley, *Silent No More* (Beltsville, Md.: Amana Publications, 2001), 215.

10   Written testimony of Nihad Awad before the Senate Judiciary Committee's Subcommittee on Terrorism, Technology and Homeland Security, "Terrorism: Two Years after 9/11, Connecting Dots, American Muslim Community Under Seige," 10 September 2003. Awad declined an invitation by the Senate Judiciary subcommittee to answer the charges under oath during a Sept. 10, 2003, hearing. He submitted written testimony instead. Later, when presented with evidence of the Holy Land check, Awad changed his story in supplemental testimony, stating: "CAIR is a nonprofit, grassroots organization. Our only source of income is through donations, and the amount in question was a donation like any other. HLF was not indicted for any criminal activities at the time of its donation in 1994, and its assets were frozen by the Justice Department seven years later in December 2001." Why he stenuously denied the existence of the donation in his earlier testimony remains unexplained.

11   Boim v. Quranic Literacy Institute, et al., "Deposition of Omar Ahmad," 133-134. During the 2003 civil deposition, CAIR founder Ahmad was asked, "Did they [HLF] give you any money to help start CAIR?" Ahmad replied unequivocally, "No."

12   David Koenig, "Documents said to provide insight ino Hamas support in U.S.,"

Associated Press, 26 August 2007.

13   Boim v. Quranic Literacy Institute, et al., OOC-2905, "Deposition of Nihad Awad," 195 (E.D. CA October 22, 2003). Boim v. Quranic Literacy Institute, et al., OOC-2905, "Deposition of Omar Ahmad," 221-225 (E.D. CA May 27, 2003). See Appendix for copy of Ahmad's Courtyard Marriott reservation voucher.

14   "Important phone and fax numbers (Palestine Section/America)," U.S. Government exhibit 004-0001, 3:04-CR-240-G, U.S. v. HLF, et al., 2. (See Appendix.)

15   Boim v. Quranic Literacy Institute, et al., "Deposition of Omar Ahmad," 122-123.

16   "Deposition of Omar Ahmad," 196-199.

17   Letter from Powers to Sen. Jon Kyl, Senate Judiciary Committee, 28 April 2009.

18   "Demystifying 'Urban Legends' About CAIR," 4.

19   "CAIR Staff Meeting, First Tuesday of the Month," minutes, 1 May 2007, 1. CAIR Executive Director Nihad Awad opened the meeting. Under the heading, "Membership/Fundraising," the minutes state that "CAIR has a total of 5,133 members." (See Appendix.)

20   "CAIR Accuses Washington Times of 'Agenda-Driven Reporting;' Civil rights group says paper falsely suggested drop in its grassroots support," CAIR, *PRNewswire-USNewswire*, 12 June 207.

21   Amicus Curiae Brief of the Council on American-Islamic Relations, U.S. v. Holy Land Foundation, No. 3:04-CR-240 (TX ND), 14 August 2007. Alexandria, Va.-based lawyer Moffitt, who also defended terrorist Sami al-Arian, recently passed away.

22   "Demystifying 'Urban Legends' About CAIR," 9.

23   Transcript of Hooper interview with radio host Keith Larson, WBT-1110 AM, Charlotte, N.C., 3 October 2006.

24   Sperry, *Infiltration*, 255-257.

25   Transcript of U.S. Rep. Frank Wolf (R-Virginia) speech, "Council on American-Islamic Relations – CAIR," on floor of House of Representatives, 12 June 2009.

26   Transcript of Hooper interview with Tucker Carlson, "Tucker" show, MSNBC, 18 September 2006.

27   *American Muslims: A Journalist's Guide to Understanding Islam and Muslims*, CAIR, 2007, 35.

28   Sperry, Infiltration, 23.

29   Patrick Sookhdeo, *Faith, Power and Territory: A Handbook of British Islam*, (McLean, Va.: Isaac Publishing, 2008), 103.

30   Sperry, *Infiltration*, 21. Also: Transcript of speech by Ahmad Totonji, "The Universality of Islam," Cornell University, 1971, 3. Totonji is chairman of ADAMS Center, the Brotherhood mosque that the FBI has agreed to do formal outreach with outside Washington.

31   Letter from Egyptian Ambassador (to U.S.) Nabil Fahmy to then CAIR Chairman Parvez Ahmed, 29 March 2007, 2.

32   *American Muslims: A Journalist's Guide to Understanding Islam and Muslims*, 37.

33   Emerson, "Grand Deception." Sperry, *Infiltration*, xi.

34   Transcript of sermon by Wahhaj, "Stand Up for Justice," Brooklyn, N.Y., VHS recording, IBTS Distributor, 8 May 1992.

35   Transcript of speech by Totonji, 7. "Do you Muslims marry more than one? Yes."

36   Ann Rodgers and Bill Schackner, "Muslim writer embroiled in dispute at Morgantown mosque," *Pittsburgh Post-Gazette*, 11 May 2004.

37   Shama Farooq, "Report on Meeting Between FBI Agents and Dr. Ahmed," 3.

38   Abdullah Yusuf Ali, *The Meaning of the Holy Quran* (Beltsway, Md.: Amana Publishing, 1989), 195. Yusuf Ali in his commentary confirms that "some slight physical correction may be administered" against disobedient wives.

39   Ibid, 90.

40   Robert Spencer, "Beheading in Buffalo," *FrontPageMagazine*, 18 February 2009.

41   Jamal Badawi, "Wife Beating in Islamic Perspective," *IslamOnline.net*, 21 April 2004.

42   Muzammil Siddiqi, "Wife Beating in Islamic Perspective," *IslamOnline.net*, 21 April 2004.

43   *American Muslims: A Journalist's Guide to Understanding Islam and Muslims*, 20, 48.

44   Imam Zaid Shakir, "Jihad or Terrorism?"

45   Ibid.

46   Wahhaj, "Stand Up for Justice."

47   Sookhdeo, *Faith, Power and Territory: A Handbook of British Islam*, 104.

48   Wahhaj, "Stand Up for Justice."

49   Ibid.

50   Imam Zaid Shakir, "Jihad or Terrorism?"

51   Transcript of speech by Totonji, 6.

52   *American Muslims: A Journalist's Guide to Understanding Islam and Muslims*, 40, 41.

53   Olivier Guitta, "The Cartoon Jihad: The Muslim Brotherhood's project for dominating the West," *The Weekly Standard*, 20 February 2006, Volume 011, Issue 22.

54   "Rejoice! The good news of the establishment of the Khilafa," *Islamic Educational Services*, Mt. Holly, N.J., 3.

55   FBI Hate Crime Statistics, http://www.fbi.gov/ucr/hc2007/table_01.htm. Even in 2001, when anti-Islamic incidents saw a small spike, they still accounted for just 26 percent of total religious hate crimes, with anti-Semitic crimes making up the majority. CAIR acknowledged the most recent drop in anti-Muslim hate crimes with only "cautious optimism," and demanded the FBI continue to vigorously investigate and prosecute anti-Muslim hate crimes.

56   "Hyping Hate Crime Vs. Muslims" (editorial), *Investor's Business Daily*, 3 December 2007.

57   "CAIR's Fuzzy Math" (editorial), *Investor's Business Daily*, 23 May 2007. Also, Sperry, *Infiltration*, 263, 264.

58   "CAIR Maryland and Virginia Chapter 1st Leadership and Empowerment Conference." In his presentation, Hooper described the "characteristics of a journalist" as follows: "They will expect you to do their work." Also, the typical journalist "does little primary research," so they are easy to spoonfeed info. Hooper has equally low regard for police. On Aug. 13, 2007, after an FBI agent visited CAIR's headquarters, he cracked to Awad that the agent was "wet behind the ears" and probably only "a high school graduate."

59   Ibid.

60   *American Muslims: A Journalist's Guide to Understanding Islam and Muslims*, 29.

61   "CAIR Maryland and Virginia Chapter 1st Leadership and Empowerment Conference." (Presentation by Rabiah Ahmed, former CAIR spokeswoman.)

62   Ibid.

63   "Media, PR and Politics," 2nd Annual Caribbean Islamic Conference, 2.

64   Transcript of Hooper interview with Carlson, "Tucker" show, MSNBC, 25 July 2007.

65   Undercover video log (Chris Gaubatz) of Hooper at ISNA convention, 30 August 2008. Hooper's wife, Rhonda Reese, also had been a regular speaker at ISNA conventions, conducting workshops on homeschooling to "help your child develop a stronger Islamic identity and get the information you need on integrating Islamic studies." Hooper declined to be interviewed.

66   "CAIR Elects N.C. State Senator Larry Shaw as Board Chair," CAIR, *PRNewswire-U.S. Newswire*, 3 March 2009. Shaw is listed as vice president of another nonprofit group called the Muslim Peace Foundation, which was started to "build alliances between people of all faiths who are working for the cause of peace and justice in this nation and worldwide." According to its articles of incorporation recently filed with the District of Columbia, the entity lists CAIR's Awad and Hooper as fellow officers. Its registered office is located at 227 Massachusetts Ave., SE, but the IRS says it "has not filed an application and has not been recognized as a tax-exempt organization."

67   Author (Sperry) interview by phone, 22 March 2009.

CHAPTER NINE: PULLING THE CURTAIN BACK ON CAIR

1   Joshua Salaam, "Status Report," CAIR Civil Rights Department, 27 June 2002, 1.

2   Memo from Iqbal to CAIR board, "Subject: Concern about CAIR Staff Turnover," 7 September 2004, 1. (See Appendix.)

3   Salaam, "Status Report," 2.

4   Email from Wazir to staff interns, along with Awad and other executives, "Subject: Regarding the Online Intern Profiles," 16 July 2008.

5   http://themuslimguy.com/about-a.i.html

6   Jeff Brumley, "Chairman of Council on American-Islamic Relations resigns," *Florida Times-Union* (Jacksonville), 8 July 2008.

7   Undercover video of Hooper taken by Chris Gaubatz at ISNA convention, 30 August 2008.

8   Ibid. Hooper declined comment, arguing he doesn't talk to "Islamophobes."

9   Letter from Haddadi to Omar Ahmad and Awad, "Subject: Discrimination at CAIR," 19 March 2001, 1. (See Appendix.)

10   Ibid, 4.

11   "CAIR Staff Meeting," minutes, 1 May 2007, 1. "CAIR has a total of 5,133 members." (See Appendix.)

12   "CAIR Board Meeting," minutes, Washington, D.C., 5-6 January 2002, 3.

13   "Council on American-Islamic Relations 2007-2008 Strategic Plan," memo, *Company Proprietary*, 14 January 2007, 2. ("Long-term" goals.)

14   "The public naming of CAIR as an unindicted co-conspirator has impeded its ability to collect donations as possible donors either do not want to give to them because they think they are a 'terrorist' organization or are too scared to give to them because of the possible legal ramifications of donating money to a 'terrorist' organization," CAIR's lawyers said in an amicus brief filed in the U.S. District Court for the Northern District of Texas. Also, a June 2009 ACLU report, "Blocking Faith, Freezing Charity: Chilling Muslim Charitable Giving in the 'War on Terrorism Financing,'" complains that CAIR's Dallas-Fort Worth chapter has suffered a drop in contributions since the naming of CAIR as an unindicted co-conspirator. The ACLU reports the chapter president, Moufa Nahhas, saying the following: "Contributions to CAIR have gone down, so we can hire fewer people, can run fewer activities. People are afraid to come to events. Mosques are also hesitant to open the doors to us, to the organization. In Richardson (Texas, the headquarters of the Holy Land Foundation), the mosque doesn't even want the administration of CAIR to come and pray there, because of fear. ... People don't want to serve on the board. They say they support us and want to help, but they don't want to be named as a member of the board. People don't want a letter or newsletter from CAIR coming to their house -- they don't want their name on the mailings."

15   "June 2002 Membership Status Report for Board Meeting," 1. The 9,211 total includes 3,000 supporters CAIR could not locate, so the 9,211 total represents a cold, not active, list of members. In addition, CAIR counted family memberships twice, padding the total by 1,728.

16   Ibid. Map of CAIR's "Members/Donors by State." (See Appendix.)

17   Audrey Hudson, "CAIR Membership falls 90% since 9/11," *Washington Times*, 12 June 2007, A01.

18   Salaam, "Status Report."

19   CAIR IRS Form 990, 2006, 1. CAIR IRS Form 990, 2005, 1. CAIR IRS Form 990, 2004, 1.

20   CAIR IRS Form 990, 2006, 4, 31.

21   Ibid, 10.

22   CAIR IRS Form 990, 2006, 25. CAIR IRS Form 990, 2004, 14.

23   "CAIR Board Meeting," minutes, 2.

24   See Appendix for internal CAIR listing of its investment properties (excluding the New Jersey Ave. headquarters property) plus current market value.

25   Letter from CAIR official Rizwan Mowlana to ADAMS Center Board of Trustees, RE: "Emergency Fund for CAIR MD/VA," 11 March 2005. "I urge you to consider allocating us a sizeable donation."

26   Letter from Haddadi to Omar Ahmad and Awad, "Subject: Discrimination at CAIR," 4. "My interns are sent to grant-writing classes," she complained, "and are givin the responsibility of researching and grant-writing on behalf of CAIR." CAIR appears to have provided misleading information while applying for public grants. CAIR's national office often shares its fundraising proceeds with its chapters, but at least one chapter repeatedly denied any such co-mingling of funds while soliciting grant money. "CAIR-MD [Maryland] does not receive any financial assistance from CAIR-National," former CAIR-MD Executive Director Seyed Rizwan Mowlana wrote in a 2003 proposal to the National Conference for Community and Justice for a $100,000 grant to help fight "severe discriminatory backlash" against the local Muslim community. Also, in soliciting Muslim members for donations, Mowlana claimed: "CAIR-MD does not receive funds from CAIR-National, which means your donations keep us alive." Yet that same year, Mowlana confirmed in a letter faxed to then-CAIR National Operations Director Khalid Iqbal terms of an agreement struck between headquarters and the chapter for revenue-sharing. In the letter, dated Nov. 10, 2003, Mowlana wrote that "ALL funds raised by CAIR-National [at Maryland mosques], including monthly pledges, will be split 60/40 (60 percent for CAIR-Maryland and 40% for CAIR-National)."

27   Notice of Mechanic's Lien, Mark Merino Construction vs. Council on American-Islamic Relations (453 New Jersey Ave.), Government of the District of Columbia, $1,918, 14 October 1999.

CHAPTER TEN: CAIR'S ARAB PAYMASTERS

1   Author (Sperry) interview by phone, 22 March 2009.

2   "Islamaphobic Smear Campaign Goes Public," CAIR Press Release, 8 November 2001. More recently, in a statement made on its "Urban Legends" rebuttal now missing from its website, CAIR admits taking gifts from foreign individuals, but still denies they're tied to foreign governments. "There is nothing criminal or immoral about accepting donations from foreign nationals," CAIR maintained. "The U.S. government, corporations, and non-profit organizations routinely receive money from foreign nationals."

3   "Council on American-Islamic Relations 2007-2008 Strategic Plan," 2. In August 2009, CAIR co-hosted with the Hollywood-based Writers Guild of America a seminar to help Muslims write screenplays. CAIR had held a similar seminar with Fox Entertainment.

4   Schedule B (IRS Form 990), CAIR, 2006. Identities of individual donors are redacted by IRS. (See Appendix.)

5   Author (Sperry) interview by phone, 22 March 2009.

6   Email from Saudi lawyer Yusuf Giansiracusa to Awad assistant Tena Qureshi, 20 May 2007. "Please be advised that on Saturday, 19th May 2007, an amount of SAR 420,000 ($112,000) was deducted from the account of HRH Prince Abdullah Bin Mosa'ad at NCB (National Commercial Bank) and transferred to the CAIR account." A Citibank report of CAIR's account activity reveals that on May 21, 2007, the amount of $111,982.00 was wired from "HRH Prince Abdullah" to CAIR's checking account. (See Appendix.) On May 23, 2007, Qureshi emails Giansiracusa: "CAIR thanks you and HRH Prince Abdullah Bin Mosa'ad for this generous contribution to CAIR."

7   CAIR IRS form 990, 2006, 2. Travel expenses related to fundraising that year totaled $93,436, compared with $56,617 in 2004 (and a total travel budget of $8,847 in 1995). Also, "CAIR National Office 2005 Goals and Achievements," CAIR report, 2. "Br Nihad made more than two overseas fundraising trips."

8   Hooper was issued his most recent U.S. passport in February 2006, according to State Department records. Born in Canada, he has obtained six U.S. passports beginning in 1981, an unusually large number considering the time span.

9   Transcript of spycam video of Hooper taken by Chris Gaubatz at ISNA convention, 30 August 2008. Hooper boasts that Awad is good for bringing in, single-handedly, "over a half-million in overseas money" each year.

10   CAIR IRS Form 990, 2006, 1. Also, Siraj Wahhab, "'Islamophobia Worst Form of Terrorism," *Arab News*, 17 May 2007. And, "1st Annual Report on Islamophobia – 2007," (Draft), OIC, November/December 2007, 3.

11   In a June 12, 2009, House floor speech, U.S. Rep. Frank Wolf, R-Va., said the sensitive but unclassified May 2006 State Department cable was brought to his and other members' attention on Capitol Hill. He says U.S. embassy staff in Abu Dhabi cabled that the UAE press was reporting "that Sheikh Hamdan bin Rashid al-Maktoum, deputy ruler of Dubai and UAE minister of finance and industry, has 'endorsed a proposal to build a property in the U.S. to serve as an endowment for CAIR.'"

12   "UAE Hamdan Okays Setting Up Endowment in U.S.," *Financial Times/Global News Wire/The Emirates Source*, 21 May 2006.

13   Ibid.

14   "Important phone and fax numbers (Palestine Section/America)."

15   "CAIR National Board Meeting," Report from CAIR National, Submitted by Nihad Awad, meeting held in Chicago, 28-29 October 2006, 1.

16   According to Wolf, the sensitive but unclassified June 2006 State Department cable was written by U.S. embassy staff in Saudi Arabia, who reported the following after meeting with a CAIR delegation: "One admitted reason for the group's current visit to the KSA (Kingdom of Saudi Arabia) was to solicit $50 million in governmental and non-governmental contributions." The core delegation, according to the cable, consisted of then-CAIR Chairman Parvez Ahmed, Awad, and Hooper. Just three months after the trip, Hooper denied soliciting Saudi government funds. "To my knowledge, we don't take money from the government of Saudi Arabia," he said in a September 2006 MSNBC appearance on the Tucker Carlson Show.

17   Javid Hassan, "Media Campaign in U.S. to Dispel Islamophobia," *Arab News*, 21 June 2006.

18   Sperry, *Infiltration*, 258. Also, Check No. 1958, Account 056001118, First Virginia Bank, Falls Church, Virginia; IRS Form 990, International Relief Organization, 1995; IRS Form 990, IRO, 1997.

19   Chris Mondics, "Follow the Saudi Money," *Hoover Digest*, No. 2, 2009, 91.

20   Testimony of Omar Ahmad, In the matter of Mohammad Jamal Khalifah, File A29 457 661, 20 December 1994.

21   Mondics, "Follow the Saudi Money," 91.

22   "CAIR Board Meeting," minutes, CAIR National, Washington D.C., 5 May 2007, 1.

23   "CAIR National Board Meeting," 28-29 October 2006, 2, 3.

24   In 2006, CAIR secured a $3.5 million line of credit from Virginia Commerce Bank to acquire additional property. Since then, it's watched its portfolio of D.C. townhouse investments lose value in the real estate bust. CAIR receives rental income from some of its properties. Before the crash, it estimated the market value of its main 453 New Jersey Ave, SE, property at $7.4 million, well in excess of the value of the more than $2 million that CAIR claimed in its tax filings.

25   "1st Annual Report on Islamophobia – 2007," (Draft), OIC, November/December 2007, 2. On page 3 of the report, the OIC speculates the CIA may be feeding the media disinformation about Islam to link it to terrorism and put it in a bad light. "The secretary general said that the possibility of involvement of intelligence agencies in

influencing the media could be there."

26   Ibid, 4. The heads of OIC and CAIR met at CAIR's headquarters on Sept. 20, 2007.

27   "UAE Hamdan Okays Setting Up Endowment in U.S."

28   Nabil M. Sadoun, "Visit Dallas Central Mosque, and You'll Find Tolerance and Faith," *Dallas Morning News*, 20 February 2005.

29   Letter from Iqbal to Royal Embassy of Saudi Arabia, Washington D.C., 12 November 2002.

CHAPTER ELEVEN: CO-OPTING CONGRESS

1   "Council on American-Islamic Relations 2007-2008 Strategic Plan," *Company Proprietary*, 14 January 07, 2.

2   CAIR National Board Member Ahmad al-Akhras, for one, contributed $250 to Obama on Nov. 3, 2008, according to FEC records. CAIR's former legal director has also donated to Obama's campaigns. Jamal Barzinji, another Muslim Brotherhood leader, gave Obama $1,000 on Feb. 6, 2008. Since 9/11, Barzinji has been the subject of a federal terror money-laundering investigation. While other Democrats including Democratic Rep. Jim Moran have returned Barzinji's terror-tainted donations, Obama has decided to keep his.

3   "Council on American-Islamic Relations 2007-2008 Strategic Plan." (See Appendix.)

4   Steven Emerson, "House Dems Carry Islamists' Water," *IPT News*, 28 July 2009.

5   Corey P. Saylor, "Conference Call on MN Imams Case," internal memo to CAIR board, 30 November 2006, 2. "We are arranging meetings in DC and Michigan with Rep. John Conyers, incoming chair of the House Judiciary Committee, and his appropriate staff to discuss the need for hearings on the issue of racial and religious profiling."

6   "Meeting with Congressman Van Hollen," CAIR meeting notes, 2003. "Proposed Agenda: Hate Crime Prosecution Bill," Senate. "Congressman Van Hollen assured us that if a bill similar to this one were to be introduced in the House, he will definitely support it."

7   At the April 7, 2007, fundraiser, then-CAIR Chairman Parvez Ahmed presented a plaque to Hassan for his work at Bridges, a Muslim TV network. Hassan had approached Ahmed with "a business plan" to make CAIR a partner in the venture (but Ahmed

claims he had reservations about his character and turned him down). Police earlier this year found his wife Aasiya Hassan's decapitated body lying in a hallway of his studio. Ahmed now insists he didn't know he would be giving out an award to Hassan until the last minute. "I found out about the awardees the same time when the audience did," he claims in a Feb. 21, 2009, message posted on Muslim feminist Zerqa Abid's blog. He also says that CAIR can't be expected to vet those it honors. "No organization or business can pry into the private lives of those they associate with," Ahmed says in his post. "So how can Muslim organizations be held accountable for Mussammil's private failings?"

8   Mohammad Aziz is a CAIR-PA Philadelphia Executive Committee member, and chairman of the board of the Islamic Society of Greater Valley Forge, which is controlled by the Islamic Circle of North America, a Muslim Brotherhood front group, according to federal court documents.

9   Andrea O'Brien, "UC-Berkeley groups rally to end Mideast clashes," *University Wire*, 6 October 2000. Also, Dodin in 2001 was among more than 100 protesters calling for the University of California to divest from Israel, according to the Berkeley Daily Planet. Thirty-two of the demonstrators were arrested when they stormed the largest lecture hall on campus. Dodin caucuses with CAIR when its leaders host breakfasts or attend Friday juma prayers on Capitol Hill. Her name is also prominent in the digital rolodex of CAIR's legislative director, internal records show. She's listed under "Hill Staff."

10   Anmol Chaddha, "Muslims, Sikhs, and South Asians talk about the Backlash," *Hardboiled* (UC Berkeley newsmagazine), October 2001, Issue 5.1.

11   Government Exhibit 016-0075, 3:04-CR-240-G, U.S. v. HLF, et al.

12   Government Exhibit 016-0069, 3:04-CR-240-G, U.S. v. HLF, et al.

13   "CAIR National 2007 Action Plan (DRAFT)," 1.

14   "Report, Prepared by Corey P. Saylor," 20 August 2007. The report was written under the letterhead, Simple Resolve Inc., which is Saylor's consulting firm. He has operated as a contract consultant under "retainer agreement" with CAIR.

15   Congressional Muslim Staffers Association was founded by Jameel-Aalim Johnson to educate Capitol Hill on Islam. Formerly chief of staff to Meeks, Johnson now works as a lobbyist for the NASDAQ stock exchange, and continues to do business with CAIR.

16   http://www.isna.net/Services/pages/CMSA-REQUESTING-RESUMES-FOR-111th-CONGRESS.aspx.

17   "CAIR Maryland and Virginia Chapter 1st Leadership and Empowerment Conference," agenda, 29-30 March 2008, 2. Jihad Saleh was one of the speakers in CAIR's workshop: "How to Start Your Career in Public Affairs," which had "a focus on working on Capitol Hill."

18   Author (Sperry) interview by email, 31 March 2009.

19   "'Muslim Americans: A National Portrait," The Muslim West Facts Project, *Gallup*, 2009, 114. Saleh could not be reached for comment.

20   "Proposed Muslim Platform for 2004," 8 March 2004, 1, 2.

21   "CAIR National Office 2005 Goals and Achievements," CAIR report, 1.

22   Ibid. Also, "CAIR National 2007 Action Plan (DRAFT)," 2.

23   Jason C. Erb, "Semiannual Report – June 2001," Governmental Affairs Department, CAIR, 28 June 2002, 5. Also, Saylor in his 2007 report cited earlier references CAIR's "August Recess Lobbying."

24   Nihad Awad, "Report from CAIR National," CAIR National Board Meeting, 29 October 2006, 2.

25   "CAIR Maryland and Virginia Chapter 1st Leadership and Empowerment Conference."

26   CAIR National is aware of the IRS rules. According to minutes of its May 5-6, 2007, meeting in Washington, its lawyer Joe Sandler informed the board that "C3 is prohibited from engaging in partisan political activities. Invitations should be sent to all parties." He also warned them that they can do only a "limited" amount of lobbying and political work, and to mind IRS guidelines covering such activities.

27   "Devil May CAIR" (editorial), *Investor's Business Daily*, 8 February 2008. Also see CAIR website for list of congressional endorsers.

28   "Congress cozying up to CAIR," *IPT News*, 17 October 2008.

29   Ibid.

30   Ibid.

31   Ellison recently even snapped a photograph with the former roommate of convicted terrorist and CAIR official Randal Ismail Royer. The roommate, Umar Lee, posted the photo on his blog at: http://umarlee.files.wordpress.com/2009/05/page3.jpg?w=450&h=337. Lee has described the Muslim prophet Muhammad as a "warrior" who loves "straight-up killers." He also has written that jihad permits "masculine" Muslim men to take "young girls" as sex slaves from the ranks of vanquished "kaffirs," or infidels.

32   Janet Moore, "At Somali town meeting, a show of solidarity," *Star Tribune* (Minneapolis), 10 May 2009, 7B.

33   "Semiannual Report," Governmental Affairs Department, CAIR, June 2001, 2.

Report is marked "Not for Distribution -- For Board Members Only."

34   "Muslim Americans: A National Portrait," 48. Ellison: "I want to see many more Muslims serving in Congress," including as U.S. senators.

35   Corey P. Saylor, "Conference Call on MN Imams Case," internal memo to CAIR board, 30 November 2006, 2.

36   "CAIR's Savior In The Congress" (editorial), *Investor's Business Daily*, 27 November 2007.

37   "Resolution Addressing the 'USA PATRIOT Act' to Ensure the Constitutional Rights of Citizens and Residents of Fairfax County," (DRAFT THREE), 14 November 2003. The draft was found in CAIR's executive files.

38   Paul Sperry, "The Saudis' New Man in Congress," *FrontPageMagazine*, 5 December 2008.

39   Author (Sperry) interview by email, 9 December 2008.

40   Supplemental Statement, Form CRM-154, Pursuant to Section 2 of the Foreign Agents Registration Act, U.S. Department of Justice, six-month period ending 30 September 2007, Attachment F. Also, Form CRM-154, 31 March 2007; Form CRM-154, 30 September 2006; Form CRM-154, 31 March 2006.

41   Author (Sperry) interview by email. Qorvis' Petruzzello could not be reached for comment. Phone calls to Connolly's office were not returned.

42   See Appendix.

43   Joseph Abrams, "House Leaders Wary of CAIR after FBI Shuns Islamic Advocacy Group," *Fox News.com*, 3 February 2009.

44   Letter to FBI Director Robert Mueller from Schumer, Kyl, and Coburn, 24 February 2009.

45   CAIR email from Saylor to Awad, et al., "Subject: What now," 3 January 2007. "We need to define clear objectives: meet with Boxer ... Are we deciding to burn this bridge completely and go all out against her or are we going to take the hit and seek to repair things over time? ... Sen. Boxer is going to dig in her heels. To reverse herself now publicly would be bad, and I'm not sure if our political ground strength in CA is strong enough to make it hurt enough." The memo considered playing up criticism of Boxer as "the nation's dumbest Democrat."

CHAPTER TWELVE: BLACKMAILING CORPORATE AMERICA

1   "CAIR and the ACLU have had a long and positive relationship as a coalition," read undated notes from a CAIR-ACLU meeting in Washington. They are "best allies for one another in any civil-liberties issues." Also: in a June 2009 ACLU report, "Blocking Faith, Freezing Charity: Chilling Muslim Charitable Giving in the 'War on Terrorism Financing,'" the ACLU rushed to CAIR's defense against government charges it conspired to support terrorists in the Holy Land Foundation case, demanding its name be expunged from the blacklist of co-conspirators along with ISNA's and NAIT's. The government "list smeared these mainstream organizations," the ACLU complained, and has scared off contributors.

2   Letter from Awad to BoA CEO Ken Lewis, 30 July 2003, 2.

3   Ibid.

4   Jamie Smith Hopkins, "Council on American-Islamic Relations Threatens Bank of America Boycott," *Baltimore Sun*, 11 December 2003.

5   Letter from CAIR official Seyed Rizwan Mowlana to Pakistani Ambassador Ashraf Jehangir Qazi, 27 October 2003.

6   "Gul Naz Anwar v Bank of America," CAIR memo, **CONFIDENTIAL**, November 2003, 3. The BoA lawyer allegedly made the remark on Nov. 4, 2003.

7   Letter from CAIR lawyer Hassan M. Ahmad to CEO Lewis, 12 November 2003.

8   Ibid.

9   "Agreement," signed by Anwar and CAIR's Mowlana, Ibrahim Moiz and lawyer Ahmad, 11 June 2004. Anwar eventually hired a private attorney to pursue the case.

10   "Gul Naz Anwar v Bank of America," 1.

11   Tim Funk, "Muslim bank employees look for offices to pray in," *Augusta Chronicle* (Georgia), 22 December 2007, D03.

12   Stacy Hutchins and Michelle Mittelstadt, "Family says man merely a tourist," *Dallas Morning News*, 12 August 2004, A1.

13   "Ellison at CAIR: 'Obama Not Our Salvation. God Is,'" The Muslim Link, 28 November 2008, 2. Also, "See how Savage lost ... ," draft of CAIR flier it planned to distribute before running out of funds. "Savage said he's lost at least $1 million in advertising revenue because of CAIR's efforts," the flier states under a photo of Savage at his microphone.

14   Faxed report from Hate Hurts America Community and Interfaith Coalition (HHA) to CAIR, 29 January 2009, 1-3. CAIR is a member of HHA.

15   Ibid.

16   Ibid.

17   CAIR memo regarding "oppositional research" listing individual targets for "hit sheets" under TALKING POINTS, with recommendations for Saylor and Hooper to take the "lead" in attacking the "Islamophobes" and hurting their "credibility," 3 January 2007.

18   Ibid.

19   "A Media Analysis on Glenn Beck's Statements on Islam and Muslims aired on CNN," CAIR National Communication Department, 7 January 2007, 1. CAIR officials traveled to Atlanta to complain to CNN executives on Jan. 10, 2007.

20   CAIR memo regarding "oppositional research."

21   Ibid.

22   "Council on American-Islamic Relations 2007-2008 Strategic Plan," 2. In August 2009, CAIR co-hosted with the Hollywood-based Writers Guild of America a seminar to assist aspiring Muslim screenwriters. CAIR had held a similar seminar with Fox Entertainment.

23   The lawsuit filed by Al-Qudhaieen and al-Shalawi against America West was dismissed in 2003 by a federal judge, who ruled that even if racial profiling occurred, airline captains have wide latitude to take security precautions to protect passengers.

24   Paul Sperry, "Imams Gone Wild," *FrontPageMagazine*, 30 November 2006.

25   Corey P. Saylor, "Conference Call on MN Imams Case," internal memo to CAIR board, 30 November 2006, 1.

26   Internal CAIR email from Nihad Awad to Arsalan Iftikhar, "Subject: URGENT/ Important Issues on 6 Imams Case," 20 April 2007. "I raised these issues with you today in the meeting and in previous meetings (and) you became upset and made a face," Awad fulminated. "Had you responded to my request this morning, we would not be in this situation. I asked you specifically today, and before, to follow the startegy [sic] outlined and to stay on the case."

27   Madeleine Gruen and Edward Sloan, "Are Acts of Staged Controversy an Islamist Strategic Tactic?" *IPT News*, 27 February 2009.

CHAPTER THIRTEEN: THE MUSLIM BROTHERHOOD:

TERRORISTS IN SUITS

1   Author (Sperry) interview by phone, 16 January 2009.

2   Author (Sperry) interview by phone, 22 March 2009.

3   Elbarassee was a founding member of the Dar al-Hijrah Islamic Center in nearby Falls Church, Va. One of the mosque's imams, Johari Abdul Malik, told attendees at a 2001 Islamic conference in Chicago: "You can blow up bridges," similar to the Chesapeake Bay Bridge, as long as civilian casualties are minimized. Authorities in 2004 caught Elbarassee and his wife videotaping the bridge's stanchions.

4   Author (Sperry) interview by email, 25 August 2005.

5   Mohamed Akram Adlouni, "An Explanatory Memorandum On the General Strategic Goal for the Group in North America," 22 May 1991, 7. Adlouni, a member of the U.S. Brotherhood shura council, attended the secret 1993 Hamas meeting in Philadelphia.

6   "Analysis of Muslim Brotherhood's General Strategic Goals for North America Memorandum," Stephen Coughlin, 7 September 2007, 3.

7   Author (Sperry) interview in person, 2 February 2009.

8   Richard H. Curtiss, "Omar Ahmad: Jordanian-Born Silicon Valley Entrepreneur Is Influential Muslim-American Activist," *Washington Report on Middle East Affairs*, 30 June 2000, 35, Vol. XIX; No. 5.

9   Government Exhibit, 016-0069, 3:04-CR-240-G, U.S. v. HLF, et al., 3, 4.

10   "It was mentioned that the United States provided them with a secure, legal base from which to operate," says former FBI official Dale Watson, describing in a high-level Nov. 5, 2001, memo what Ahmad and other Brotherhood and Hamas leaders discussed during their wiretapped 1993 meeting in Philadelphia.

11   Affidavit in Support of Application for Search Warrant, 31, 36.

12   The FBI believes Shukri Abu Baker "is a U.S.-based leader of Hamas." A Texas resident, he has paid visits to CAIR's headquarters in Washington. His name appears on CAIR's visitors register on March 27, 2001, for example. (See Appendix.)

13   Affidavit in Support of Application for Search Warrant, 36.

14   Department of Justice, Attachment A, List of Unindicted Co-Conspirators, U.S. vs. Holy Land Foundation; "An Explanatory Memorandum On the General Strategic Goal for the Group In North America," 22 May 1991, 18; Attachment C, Safa Group

Businesses and Corporations, Affidavit in The Matter of Searches Involving 555 Grove Street, Herndon, Virginia, and Related Locations, U.S. District Court for the Eastern District of Virginia, unredacted, October 2003.

CHAPTER FOURTEEN: THE 'IKHWAN MAFIA'

1   Author (Sperry) interview in person, 15 April 2005.

2   Government Exhibit, Elbarasse-Search-10, 3:04-CR-240-G, U.S. v. HLF, et al., chart ("Committee Chairman/Palestinian Action Aspects"). "List of Unindicted Co-conspirators," 6. Government Exhibit, Ashqar Wiretap-1, 3:04-CR-240-G, U.S. v. HLF, et al., 2, 6 (recorded 13 September 1993). Also, Government Exhibit, 016-0047, 3:04-CR-240-G, U.S. v. HLF, et al., 11. Also, Author (Sperry) interview by phone, 22 March 2009. The Muslim Brotherhood has not been designated a terrorist organization by the U.S., and it is not a crime to belong to it.

3   Steven Merley, "The Muslim Brotherhood in the United States," Hudson Institute, April 2009. Also, Author (Sperry) interview by phone, 22 March 2009. The Muslim Brotherhood has not been designated a terrorist organization by the U.S., and it is not a crime to belong to it.

4   The Brothers also quote the Quran (Surah 49:10): "The believers are but a single Brotherhood," which revered Quranic scholar Abdullah Yusuf Ali interprets to mean: "The enforcement of the Muslim Brotherhood is the greatest social ideal of Islam. On it was based the Prophet's Sermon at his last pilgrimage, and Islam cannot be completely realized until this ideal is achieved."

5   Indictment, U.S. v HLF, et al., U.S. District Court for the Northern District of Texas, 26 July 2004, 7.

6   Merley, "The Muslim Brotherhood in the United States."

7   "CAIR Maryland and Virginia Chapter 1st Leadership and Empowerment Conference." Also, Khan's name and contact info was found in CAIR National's email directory under the heading "VIP." Khan, moreover, served as an official on ISNA's 2004 convention coordinating committee.

8   Government Exhibit, Elbarasse-Search-2, 3:04-CR-240-G, U.S. v. HLF, et al., 13.

9   Affidavit in Support of Application for Search Warrant, 31.

10   Ibid.

11   "An Explanatory Memorandum On the General Strategic Goal for the Group In North America," 22 May 1991, 17.

12   Government Exhibit 003-0092, 3:04-CR-240-G, U.S. v. HLF, et al., 23.

13   "An Explanatory Memorandum On the General Strategic Goal for the Group In North America," 10, 11.

14   Government Exhibit (Elbarasse Search - 11) 3:04-CR-240-G, U.S. v. HLF, et al., 3.

15   Noreen S. Ahmed-Ullah, Sam Roe and Laurie Cohen, "A rare look at secretive Brotherhood in America: Muslims divided on Brotherhood," *Chicago Tribune*, 19 September 2004, C01.

16   Author (Sperry) interview in person, 19 April 2005.

17   Sperry, *Infiltration*, 314.

18   "Mahdi Bray's Secret, Checkered Past," *IPT News*, 25 March 2009.

19   Author (Sperry) interview in person, 15 April 2005.

CHAPTER FIFTEEN: FAKING OUT THE INFIDEL

1   Government Exhibit 003-0069, 3:04-CR-240-G, U.S. v. HLF, et al.

2   Ibid.

3   Ibid. Abu Baker and Ahmad echo the 9/11 planners, who boasted of blindsiding U.S. intelligence through superior deception. "As the prophet has stated: 'War is to deceive,'" wrote al-Qaida detainees Khalid Sheik Mohammed, Walid bin Attash, Ramzi bin As-shibh, Ali Abd Al-Aziz Ali, and Mustafa Ahmed Al-Hawsawi, in their February statement responding to U.S. military charges.

4   Ibid.

5   "The Islamist Head Fake," editorial, *Investor's Business Daily*, 28 September 2007.

6   Ibid.

7   Ibid.

8   "The Islamist Head Fake," editorial, *Investor's Business Daily*. Al-Timimi is serving a life term in prison.

9   Mahdi Bray, "Counterpoint: We're proud of our Muslim 'face,'" *Dallas Morning News*, 18 December 2005.

10   Ibid.

11   Government Exhibit 003-0078, 3:04-CR-240-G, U.S. v. HLF, et al., 5. Also:

additional declassified Brotherhood documents identify current MAS leaders as Brotherhood members. Finally, the Justice Department in December 2007 concluded in a U.S. court briefing: "MAS was founded as the overt arm of the Muslim Brotherhood in America."

12   Habib also was asked about CAIR in the Egyptian media last year. INTERVIEWER: "The Council for [sic] American-Islamic Relations: Many say that they are your front. Do they really represent you?" HABIB: "Ehh, this is a sensitive subject, and it's kind of problematic, especially after 9/11." INTERVIEWER: "For them to say that there is a relationship between you two?" HABIB: "Yes. You can say that."

13   Noreen S. Ahmed-Ullah, Sam Roe and Laurie Cohen, "A rare look at secretive Brotherhood in America: Muslims divided on Brotherhood."

14   http://www.masnet.org/tarbiyya.asp.

15   Noreen S. Ahmed-Ullah, Sam Roe and Laurie Cohen, "A rare look at secretive Brotherhood in America: Muslims divided on Brotherhood."

16   "IPT Footage Takes Down Omeish," Investigative Project on Terrorism, 27 September 2007.

17   Sperry, *Infiltration*, 115.

18   Ibid.

19   Caryle Murphy, "Facing New Realities as Islamic Americans," *Washington Post*, 12 September 2004, A01.

20   Ibid.

21   "MAS' Esam Omeish Seeks Virginia Office," *IPT News*, 1 May 2009.

CHAPTER SIXTEEN: THE PLAN

1   Transcript of lecture by Imam Zaid Shakir, "Jihad or Terrorism?"

2   Ibid.

3   Also, Sookhdeo, *Faith, Power and Territory*, 75. And author (Sperry) interview in person with Maj. Stephen Coughlin, 12 February 2009.

4   Transcript of lecture by Imam Zaid Shakir, "Jihad or Terrorism?"

5   Ibid.

6   Ibid.

7   Government Exhibit 003-0085, 3:04-CR-240-G, U.S. v. HLF, et al., 31.

8   Dar El-Eiman President Fawaz Mushtaha is an unindicted co-conspirator in the Holy Land Foundation terror case. Investigators found videotapes, cell phones, maps, and other evidence burned or buried in the backyard of his Falls Church, Virginia, home. His travel agency's Washington-area office is located in the same building as the radical Dar Al-Arqam mosque run by convicted terrorist Ali al-Timimi.

9   Frank Gaffney, "Shariah is Anti-Constitutional and Seditious," prepared remarks, *The Harbor League*, Baltimore, Md., 7 October 2008.

10   Ibid.

CHAPTER SEVENTEEN: THE GODFATHER

1   Sperry, *Infiltration*, xi. Though Ahmad now insists he was misquoted, he has not denied the substance of the statement, which has caused him untold grief. Meanwhile, the reporter, Lisa Gardiner, stands by the accuracy of her 1998 story. The newspaper that published the story, "The San Ramon Valley Herald" (and sister publication "The Argus" of Fremont, Calif., where the article also ran) has not retracted any of it. Ironically, Ahmad several years earlier issued a prophetic warning to fellow Brothers at their secret 1993 meeting to support Hamas: "It is possible you could be destroyed by the media without the law touching you. They could hold things against you and destroy you on the media front before you're destroyed by the government and the law." He was referring to the media supposedly trumping up charges against his fellow Muslim Brother, the blind Sheik Omar Abdul-Rahman. "There are no, what you call, crimes against him, you see?" Ahmad contended in the FBI recordings. U.S. courts reached a different conclusion, sending the Brotherhood cleric to prison for life for conspiring to blow up New York City landmarks.

2   Government Exhibit, Elbarasse Search-4, 3:04-CR-240-G, U.S. v. HLF, et al., 5. (In Brotherhood documents, Elkadi is also known as "Al-Qadi.") Also, Noreen S. Ahmed-Ullah, Sam Roe and Laurie Cohen, "A rare look at secretive Brotherhood in America: Muslims divided on Brotherhood."

3   Ibid, "A rare look at secretive Brotherhood in America: Muslims divided on Brotherhood."

4   Ibid. Ahmed Elkadi's wife, Iman A. Elkadi, is a therapist, who heads a clinic in Falls Church, Virginia, for "survivors of torture" called the Center for Multicultural Human Services.

5   FEC records, 1996-2003. Elkadi and his wife, Iman, gave a total of $2,000 to

LaRouche (D).

6   The AMC largely disappeared following the 2004 conviction of Alamoudi on terror charges. Many of the political functions of the AMC are now being performed by MAS and the Muslim Public Affairs Council, or MPAC.

7   Author (Sperry) interview in person, Washington, 15 April 2005. Also, a July 14, 2005, Treasury Department press release stated: "According to information available to the U.S. government, the September 2003 arrest of Alamoudi was a severe blow to al-Qaida, as Alamoudi had a close relationship with al-Qaida and had raised money for al-Qaida in the United States." Full details of Alamoudi's case remain classified.

8   Ibid, Author (Sperry) interview in person, Washington, 15 April 2005.

9   Author (Sperry) interview in person, NCTC officials, Fairfax County, Virginia, 17 June 2005. Also, Glenn R. Simpson, "U.S.-Tracked Account Held By Saudi," Wall Street Journal, 6 October 2004, B3.

10   Paul Sperry, "Congressional Paul Revere Warns Nation About Islamofascist Threat," Investor's Business Daily, 19 November 2007.

11   "CAIR Executive Staff Meeting," task report, 3 January 2007. CAIR official Corey Saylor "to call Saiful Islam, Hisham Islam."

12   United States v. Abdurahman Muhammad Alamoudi, criminal complaint filed in United States District Court for the Eastern District of Virginia, 30 September 2003, 11.

13   Government Exhibit, Elbarasse-Search-10, 3:04-CR-240-G, U.S. v. HLF, et al., chart ("Committee Chairman/Palestinian Action Aspects"). "List of Unindicted Co-conspirators," 6. Government Exhibit, Ashqar Wiretap-1, 3:04-CR-240-G, U.S. v. HLF, et al., 2, 6 (recorded 13 September 1993). Also, Government Exhibit, 016-0047, 3:04-CR-240-G, U.S. v. HLF, et al., 11. Also, Author (Sperry) interview by phone, 22 March 2009. The Muslim Brotherhood has not been designated a terrorist organization by the U.S., and it is not a crime to belong to it. Although Ahmad remains under FBI counterterrorism investigation, he has not been charged with a crime as this book was going to press.

14   Sperry, Infiltration, xi.

15   "CAIR's War on Truth," IPT News, 13 March 2009.

16   Robert Spencer, prepared remarks, Young America's Foundation, annual student conference, Washington DC, 4 August 2007.

17   Transcript of Hooper interview with The Keith Larson Show, WBT-1110 AM Radio, Charlotte, N.C., 3 October 2006. Larson called Hooper's answer "cagey."

18   "Guilty verdicts in terror case deal blow to CAIR," *WorldNetDaily*, 25 November 2008.

CHAPTER EIGHTEEN: INFILTRATION

1   Affidavit in Support of Application for Search Warrant, 30, 31.

2   Author (Sperry) interview by email with FBI official, 6 April 2005, and in person, 15 April 2005.

3   Affidavit in Support of Application for Search Warrant, 30, 31. Federal authorities in a separate court filing described the al-Arian document, entitled the "Charter of the Center of Studies," as setting forth a detailed description of the structure and operation of "a hostile intelligence organization in the United States." They said it included: "the organizational structure, duties, responsibilities, espionage methods and targets, counterintelligence and precautionary measures, methods of reporting, and a cipher system to make the hostile intelligence organization appear to be affiliated with a university."

4   Ibid, 33.

5   John Mintz and Douglas Farah, "In Search of Friends Among the Foes: U.S. Hopes to Work with Diverse Group," *Washington Post*, 11 September 2004, A01.

6   Guitta, "The Cartoon Jihad: The Muslim Brotherhood's project for dominating the West."

7   Author (Sperry) interview by phone, 22 March 2009.

8   "North American Islamic Trust," FBI memo marked "SECRET," 1986, 43. Recently declassified in response to a Freedom of Information Act request by the Washington-based Investigative Project on Terrorism, 1986, 43. Neither Barzinji nor the other Brotherhood members cited in the FBI memo have been charged with a crime. It currently is not a crime to belong to the Muslim Brotherhood in America. Another more recent federal document, an affidavit for a search warrant of Barzinji's home that was unsealed in 2003, connects Barzinji to Hamas and other Palestinian terrorists. Barzinji's lawyer Nancy Luque has denied any linkage between her client and terrorists or the Muslim Brotherhood. Also representing Safa group interests, she told the Washington Post her clients "love this country," and "are absolutely not involved in any way in supporting terrorism," adding that the government's investigation of them is "a smearing." However, Barzinji admitted to the Post that he was a member of the Ikhwan, or Brotherhood, and hosted Brotherhood bigshots from Egypt. Also, he is listed in secret U.S. Brotherhood documents as a leader of the group in America.

9   Attachment A, List of Unindicted Co-Conspirators, U.S. vs. Holy Land Foundation, 2007; "An Explanatory Memorandum On the General Strategic Goal for the Group In North America," 22 May 1991, 18; Government Exhibit 004-0001, 3:04-CR-240-G, U.S. v. HLF, et. al., ; Attachment C, Safa Group Businesses and Corporations, Affidavit in The Matter of Searches Involving 555 Grove Street, Herndon, Virginia, and Related Locations, U.S. District Court for the Eastern District of Virginia, unredacted, October 2003; Link-analysis chart, Abdurahman Alamoudi investigation, JTTF-Washington, 2003; Steven Merley, "The Muslim Brotherhood in the United States," Hudson Institute, April 2009; Guest charges summaries, Courtyard Marriott, Philadelphia, 3 October 1993; Dale L. Watson, Assistant Director, FBI Counterterrorism Division, "Holy Land Foundation for Relief and Development/International Economic Emergency Powers Act," Action Memorandum (To: R. Richard Newcomb, Director, Treasury Department Office of Foreign Assets Control), 5 November 2001.

CHAPTER NINETEEN: NUCLEUS: ISNA

1   Author (Sperry) interview by email, 10 April 2009.

2   Margaret Moore Post, Our Town Yesterday: Plainfield, Indiana: A Pictorial History (Plainfield, IN: Allan Rivers Starken Printing Company, 1986), 102. Also, "Islamic Trust to Build Mosque," *Indianapolis Star,* May 5, 1977.

3   Ibid.

4   Ibid.

5   Mintz and Farah, "In Search of Friends Among the Foes."

6   Government Exhibit, Elbarasse Search - 1, 3:04-CR-240-G, U.S. v. HLF, et al., 4. The three ISNA incorporators were listed as: Iqbal J. Unus, Talat Sultan, and Mahmoud Rashdan. The initial board of directors included: Sultan, Sayyed M. Syeed, M. Naziruddin Ali, Syed Imtiaz Ahmad, and Haroon Qazi.

7   Author (Sperry) interview by email, 10 April 2009.

8   Prosecutors responded to ISNA's request to have its name expunged from the list with this July 2008 statement to the court: "Numerous exhibits were entered into evidence establishing both ISNA's and NAIT's (the North American Islamic Trust, an ISNA subsidiary) intimate relationship with the Muslim Brotherhood, the Palestine Committee, and the defendants in this case" against the Holy Land Foundation.

9   "The Truth About ISNA: Past, Present & Future," ISNA report, 2008, 8.

10   "Islamic Society of North America, HLF Verdict Press Statement," October 2007.

11   "Government's Memorandum in Opposition to Petitioners Islamic Society of North America and North American Islamic Trust's Motion for Equitable Relief," U.S. v. HLF, et al., U.S. District Court for the Notrthern District of Texas, 10 July 2008, 2, 3.

12   "Implementation Manual for the Group's Plan for the Year (1991-1992)," declassified Muslim Brotherhood document, 6.

13   Ibid, 5.

14   "U.S. Brotherhood's Boomerang Effect," *IPT News*, 18 July 2008.

15   Emerson, "ISNA's Lies Unchallenged Again," 27 October 2007.

16   Ibid.

17   Ibid.

18   "U.S. Brotherhood's Boomerang Effect."

19   Emerson, "ISNA's Lies Unchallenged Again."

20   Government Exhibit 004-0001, 3:04-CR-240-G, U.S. v. HLF, et al., 3. "Important phone and fax numbers (Palestine Section/America) ... 18) Shukri Abou Baker ... Indpols [Country/City] ... 317-839-1840 [Fax] ... 317-243-9520 [telephone]."

21   Government Exhibit, Elbarasse Search – 11, 3:04-CR-240-G, U.S. v. HLF, et al., 4.

22   "List of Unindicted Co-conspirators and/or Joint Venturers," 4.

23   Mintz and Farah, "In Search of Friends Among the Foes."

24   Sperry, "Congressional Paul Revere Warns Nation About Islamofascist Threat."

25   Omer bin Abdullah, "A Faith in Service to Humanity," *Islamic Horizons*, November/December 2007, 42, Vol. 36; No. 6. "Government officials met with ISNA," the story said. "Several government agencies put up job booths to recruit chaplains and others who speak Arabic."

26   Indictment, U.S. v. Sami Amin al-Arian, U.S. District Court for the Middle District of Florida, 21 September 2004, 76. Al-Alwani is listed as "Unindicted Co-Conspirator Five."

27   "U.S. Military Chaplain Program," newsletter, Office of Rep. Sue Myrick, 28 July 2008, 1.

28   Ibid.

29   In turn, the Justice Department's civil rights division asked its employees to volunteer at this year's ISNA convention in Washington D.C. by handing out literature and asking questions, according to an internal email obtained and published

by Pajamas Media.

30   FBI Assistant Director John Miller, who coordinates public outreach, denies that the bureau decided to make ISNA its official point of contact with the Muslim community.

CHAPTER TWENTY: NAIT AND THE ECONOMIC JIHAD

1   Letter via electronic mail, Omar Haydar (director of fund operations, Allied Asset Advisors Inc.) to Khalid Iqbal (Council on American-Islamic Relations), 2001, 1. (The date on the letter in the Appendix is an automated transmission date generated from the original Word document during a subsequent electronic transmission.)

2   "List of Unindicted Co-conspirators," 8.

3   "An Explanatory Memorandum On the General Strategic Goal for the Group In North America," 16.

4   Letter from Haydar to Iqbal.

5   Ibid.

6   Ibid.

7   Ibid.

8   Patrick Sookhdeo, *Understanding Sharia Finance: The Muslim Challenge to Western Economics* (McLean, VA: Isaac Publishing, 2008), 56.

9   Ibid, 39.

10   Author (Sperry) interview, in person. 12 February 2009.

11   Sookhdeo, *Understanding Sharia Finance*, 86.

12   Frank Gaffney, "Sell-off or sell-out?" *Washington Times*, 28 October 2008, A16.

13   "North American Islamic Trust," FBI memo marked "SECRET," recently declassified in response to FOIA request by IPT, 1986, 57. (See Appendix.)

14   Government Exhibit, Elbarasse Search – 11, 3:04-CR-240-G, U.S. v. HLF, et al., 6. Also, "Implementation Manual for the Group's Plan for the Year," 5.

15   "List of Unindicted Co-conspirators," 8.

16   "North American Islamic Trust (NAIT)," FBI report, SECRET, 1987, 57.

INDEX